Dylan

Visions, Portraits & Back Pages

Dylan

Visions, Portraits & Back Pages

EDITOR-IN-CHIEF: MARK BLAKE

**LONDON, NEW YORK,
MUNICH, MELBOURNE, DELHI**

DORLING KINDERSLEY
Managing Editor Debra Wolter
Managing Art Editor Louise Dick
Publisher Special Projects Stephanie Jackson
Production Melanie Dowland
DTP Designer John Goldsmid

MOJO
Editor-In-Chief Mark Blake
Art Editor Lora Findlay
Picture Editor Dave Brolan
Production Editor Andy Fyfe
Assistant Editor Ian Gittins
Designers Isabel Cruz,
Nick Edwards, Paul Effeny
Sub-Editor Justin Hood
Mojo Editor Phil Alexander
Publishing Director Stuart Williams
Creative Director Dave Henderson
Managing Director Marcus Rich

First American Edition, 2005. Published in
the United States by DK Publishing Inc, 375
Hudson Street, New York, New York, 10014.
This edition published in 2008.

A Penguin company

09 10 9 8 7 6 5 4 3

A CIP catalog record for this book is
available from the Library of Congress

ISBN 978-0-7566-3725-5

Color reproduction by Rival Colour
Printed and bound in Singapore by Star
Standard

Discover more at **www.dk.com**

For more information about MOJO magazine
go to **www.mojo4music.com**

Mappin House, 4 Winsley Street,
London W1W 8HF

© Jerry Schatzberg/Corbis

Contents

Editor's Letter

TO BORROW THE title of his own Never Ending Tour – the round-the-world junket that's kept our hero busy since the '90s – being a Bob Dylan fan is something of a never-ending journey. Until personal choice or the hand of fate decides that it's time for him to stop making music, his audience can be sure that there will always be another twist or fork in the road to negotiate. Dylan's like that: he keeps you interested, keeps you on your toes...

A songwriter who made his first album in 1962 and challenged all the preconceived notions of what constituted pop music throughout the rest of the '60s, some might have expected him to coast through the next three decades and beyond. Of course, that was never going to happen. Right up until the present day, Dylan has continued to make music that inspires and challenges. It's a trait that has kept MOJO magazine fascinated since it first ran his picture on the cover of their launch issue in 1993.

Visions, Portraits And Back Pages draws together the finest writing on Bob Dylan from the archives of MOJO and its sister publication Q, together with some newly commissioned pieces throwing fresh light on the story. Here, the world's greatest music critics and photographers get to grips with this most enigmatic of subjects. Beginning with the former Robert Zimmerman's first hesitant steps as a would-be protest singer trying his luck in New York's Greenwich Village up to his current incarnation as the Mount Rushmore of rock, immovable and towering over contemporary music's lesser beings, the Dylan story is as enthralling and unpredictable as the man himself. Along the way, he's written some of the most celebrated songs in popular music, made a string of groundbreaking albums, sparred with countless musical collaborators, scored points off The Beatles, kept conspiracy theorists  in business and, more than anything, consistently defied both critics and devotees by making the music he wants when he wants. It's the reason Bob Dylan still matters – and why we still care.

We hope that you enjoy the never-ending journey.

**Mark Blake
Editor-In-Chief**

© David Gahr

Foreword

By Bono

I **WAS THINKING** about Bob Dylan the other day and trying to define what it was about him that I respect so much, and what came to me was a line by the poet Brendan Keneally from the Book Of Judas, a line which I used for guidance on the Zoo TV tour but which I realised applies to Bob Dylan's whole career. The line is: The best way to serve the age is to betray it. That is the essence of Bob Dylan: not just as simple as being on whatever the other side is, because that's just being a crank, and cranks at the end of the day aren't interesting because you always know their position. Dylan was at one point in time the very epitome of what was modern, and yet his was always a unique critique of modernity. Because in fact Dylan comes from an ancient place, almost medieval. It was there at the beginning, when he sang like an old geezer - this ancient voice in a young man's body.

The anachronism, really, is the '60s. For the rest of his life he's been howling from some sort of past that we seem to have forgotten but must not. That's it for me. Bob Dylan keeps undermining our urge to look into the future.

The first time I met him he completely disarmed me by asking to have his picture taken with me; a very Dylan thing to do. But then he started asking me about the McPeak Family. I was wondering whether this was a punk group from Arkansas but it transpired it was Irish folk music I had never heard of. This was 1985. U2 were making *The Unforgettable Fire* and feeling like we were from outer space, with no roots at all. Bob Dylan was playing Slane Castle and in one day made us reassess a lot of things. He was the one that sent us on this journey into the past that ended up with *Rattle & Hum*. He did that to us! Blame him! Anyway, Dylan asked us all these questions about Irish music. He then recited at least 10 out of the 13 verses to the Banks Of The Royal Canal (aka The Auld Triangle) by Brendan Behan and I realised he had total recall for old tunes. He told me ballad singer Liam Clancy was his hero and insisted that what the Irish had that the Americans and other people all over the world were giving up was their past. Van Morrison was sitting with us and he understood completely what Dylan was on about, but I felt uncomfortable. My father used to listen almost exclusively to opera, partly because folk music had Republican/Nationalist connotations that, my father having married a Protestant girl, weren't very auspicious.

So this conversation with Dylan and later, another with Keith Richards about the blues, allowed U2 to rediscover our past.

Looking back, of course, that feel that Bob Dylan has for balladry, and the biblical nature of his imagery, was ingrained in Irish people. It was a language that we shouldn't really be familiar with, but instinctively we were. Maybe it's that little-known Irish/Jewish axis. My mother's family is called Rankin, and some of them contend that we are, in fact, part Jewish.

BOB DYLAN IS there for you at every stage of your life. And there are songs that made no sense when you were 20 that suddenly become clear later on. Visions Of Johanna is one of them. It's extraordinary. He writes this whole song seemingly about this one girl, with these remarkable descriptions of her, but this isn't the girl who's on his mind! It's somebody else! He does it again in Brownsville Girl, one of his most underrated songs and a song, I would suggest, that altered songwriting. It's a completely new kind of song and also has this spectacular line because he can always make you burst out laughing: "If there's an original idea out there/I could really use it now". And Brownsville Girl is a beautiful rhapsody about this Hispanic woman with her teeth like pearls, and then, in the middle of the song he says, "She ain't you, but she's here/And she's got that dark rhythm in her soul". Again, this song is not really about the Brownsville girl, but rather it's addressed to this other woman who seems to be his muse. And his muse, of course, he refers to obliquely in Tangled Up In Blue. He talks about the Italian poet whose every word came off the pages like burning coals. And at some point you realise that - of course! - this Italian poet is Dante. Every word that Dante wrote was for his muse, Beatrice, and there's a Beatrice there in most Bob Dylan songs. If she's real or imagined isn't important to me, but it's extraordinary. In your twenties you're not so much interested in ideas like that. You're more interested in The Times They Are A-Changin'.

But Bob Dylan's got you from the cradle to the grave. For instance, I loved *Slow Train Coming*. I even loved *Saved*. People thought *Saved* was his bumper-sticker Christianity album, but for me it sounds like a real cry for help. I don't know if he was in trouble, but it sounds like it. His journey into nursery rhyme – that God gave names to all the animals stuff – is beautiful, like Picasso

"Bob Dylan's got you from the cradle to the grave."
BONO

drawing with a marker pen. And really Picasso is the only character you can compare Bob Dylan to. So I adore his nursery rhyme digressions, the rhyming of "bowl of soup" with "rolling hoop" on *Under A Red Sky*. I also like the terse verse, the almost Raymond Carver anti-metaphor movement of recent times.

My favourite Bob Dylan album, for its exuberance, is *Bringing It All Back Home*, but the lines that I can't get out of my head are the opening lines of Visions Of Johanna: "Ain't it funny how the night plays tricks on you when you're tryin' to get some quiet / We all sit here stranded, doing our best to deny it.". That's as good as it gets, really, although Death Is Not The End from Down In The Groove comes close. And Every Grain Of Sand (the Biograph version over the one on Shot Of Love) is everything you should aspire to in popular music.

I saw him open a casino in Las Vegas. He was shining in good health. He seemed really happy: you know the way that he flashes that smile occasionally from stage, that seems so

generous? Anyway, I noticed that the place wasn't full, and it had been full earlier for The Blues Brothers, and I wondered how that must feel. And I looked at him and realised that at a very deep level he really, really didn't mind. And I thought, Now that's freedom. Having seen him perform for the Pope and seen him perform in a casino, it struck me that this was again the very medieval idea of the troubadour: you pay, I'll play. It doesn't matter who turns up, or how many. Your music is there for whoever wishes to listen to it, from the saints to the damned.

Bob Dylan: suffice it to say I would carry his luggage. And as anyone in U2 will tell you, I'm not great with the old gear.

BONO

9

POSITIVELY 4th STREET
b/w
From a Buick 6

COLUMBIA
4-43389

Chapter One

MINSTREL BOY

How Robert
Zimmerman
became Bob Dylan,
wowed The Beatles
and helped invent
rock'n'roll…

WHO IS BOB DYLAN?

He's all about love, loss, life, death, war, peace and a thousand things beside. And he's showing little sign of slowing down. John Harris casts his eye over the enigmatic history of Bob Dylan, and wonders exactly what it all means.

Under the spotlight: Dylan on tour in the UK, 1966.

WE COULD BEGIN anywhere, but Manchester on May 17, 1966 seems a better place than most. Countless roads had led there, and countless roads stretched out. This, more than any other place, was where what we know as rock music – more cerebral than mere "pop", more artful than rock'n'roll, laying a greater claim to contemporary relevance than any musical form that had gone before – was born.

It had stirred before, of course, but the run of incidents that broke out that night decisively jumpstarted its heart. Besides, we have it on CD – people can theorise all they like about this unrecorded event or that behind-closed-doors epiphany, but Bob Dylan's concert at the Free Trade Hall can stream out of your home hi-fi any time you choose. Just as we know past civilisations from the stuff they left behind, so we know Bob Dylan's pivotal importance thanks to a recording.

Rock is more than mere music. It is clothes and drugs and generational revolt, and the sense that loads of people will never understand. On all those scores, what happened at the Free Trade Hall is spot on. But music is the core, and the music Bob Dylan and his band created that night was something breathtakingly new.

The sound was molten. Guitar, organ and piano bubbled up and down. The bass and the drums sounded unstoppable – listen to the opening seconds of Baby Let Me Follow You Down and you instantly know why people came away from that year's concerts amazed at the simple loudness of it all.

Then there was Bob Dylan's voice. Here, he seemed to mock and taunt, yelping into his cupped hands like a football fan shouting insults at the opposing team's players. But that was a mere detail: 30 minutes before, he had performed songs as tender and intimate as It's All Over Now, Baby Blue and Visions Of Johanna; on the closing Like A Rolling Stone, spite was supplanted by the joy that comes from creative liberation.

Just as important was the commotion it created. It's all there on the CD: the slow-clapping, the opposing applause, the heckles that reach their apex when a very earnest young man called Keith Butler shouts "Judas" (later on, he told the camera crew filming Eat The Document that Dylan "wanted shooting"). In response, after growling, "I don't believe you – you're a liar", Bob Dylan tells the band to "play fucking loud".

And that, more than anything else on the CD, is rock in excelsis. And there at its centre was an impish Jewish American with bird's nest hair and a Carnaby Street suit, looking like the dictionary definition of cool and yelling about one-eyed midgets and leopard skin pillbox hats. What, people wondered, does he mean?

TO SAY THAT Bob Dylan's music is representative of the last 40 years of history is an understatement. Some of his songs are as much a part of humanity's progress as any politician's speech, epochal novel or era-defining play. Is Shakespeare "representative" of history? Well, yes – but his plays are also part of it all. And so it is with Dylan.

In four action-packed years, between 1962 and 1966, he marked the world's consciousness as much as any musician ever has. That isn't to diminish what he did in the slipstream of all that; simply to marvel at the epic scale of Dylan's initial achievement. Look in even the squarest modern dictionary of quotations, and you'll find all the evidence you need.

"The answer my friend, is blowin' in the wind"; "The times they are a-changin'"; "I was so much older then, I'm younger than that now"; "You don't need a weatherman to know which way the wind blows"; "Something is happening, but you don't know what it is, do you, Mr Jones?"; "Everybody must get stoned". All stitched into our language, doubtless destined to be occasionally echoing around moonbases in 2080.

In the heat of the moment, some people didn't get it. Dylan was prompting putdowns way before he plugged in. "I am still unable to see in him anything other than a youth of mediocre talent," wrote British folk singer Ewan MacColl in September 1965. "Only a non-critical audience, nourished on the watery pap of pop music, could have fallen for such drivel."

Thankfully, others understood. "It's not rock, it's not folk, it's a new thing called Dylan! There's a new swingin' mood, and Bob Dylan is the spearhead of this new mood! It's a new kind of expression, a new kind of telling it like it is." This was American DJ Murray "The K" Kaufman, the self-styled "Fifth Beatle", orating from the stage before Dylan played at Forest Hills, New York in August 1965. "Mr Dylan," he concluded, "is definitely what's happening, baby." Cheers, "The K".

Back then, there was the abiding idea that Dylan's electric music was something entirely novel – the same kind of shock-of-the-new that was spread by punk rock. Yet, even at his most incendiary, Bob Dylan's muse stretched back whole centuries.

The same month that Ewan MacColl wrote his broadside, Dylan was asked what he understood by "folk music". "The main body of it," he said, "is based on myth and the Bible and plague and famine and all kinds of things like that which are nothing but mystery, and you can see it all in the songs. Roses growing right up out of people's hearts and naked cats in bed with spears growing right out of their backs and seven years of this and eight years of that, and it's all really something that nobody can really touch."

The description applies to whole swathes of Dylan's music. And understanding what he does in those terms allows us to grasp why he sounds so significant. Dylan stood at the endpoint of a path that went back into US history: railroad brakemen, freed slaves, harried missionaries, bluesmen pursued by the Devil. Dylan may play rock music, but he also deals in something altogether older; ancient, even.

That is why his music has endured and his best records are held in ever-higher esteem. "Now there's this fame business," he said in 1964. "I know it's going to go away. It has to. This so-called mass fame comes from people who get caught up in a thing for a while and buy the records. Then they stop. And when they stop, I won't be famous any more." Yeah, right...

BACK TO THE question at hand, anyway. What does it all mean? Bob Dylan has never told us. "I'm a song and dance man," remains his favourite gambit – like Albert Einstein saying he writes things on blackboards.

All too often, Dylan's precise intentions are unclear. Take I Want You from *Blonde On Blonde*: "The guilty undertaker sighs/ The lonesome organ grinder cries/ The silver saxophones say I should refuse you." What's all that about? It probably doesn't matter. It sounds beautiful; it's backed by an arrangement that knows that, while it's painful to be smitten by love, that is the essence of being alive. Chiselled into Jack Kerouac's gravestone are the words "He honoured life". Even at his most oblique, that quality drips from Dylan's every word.

In the wake of 1966's bike crash, mind you, he became less of a tease. On 1969's *Nashville Skyline*, there are songs as affectingly see-through as I Threw It All Away; lovelorn tragedy, plain and simple. The title track of the following year's *New Morning* is one of the most euphoric love songs anyone has ever created, with nothing in the way of distracting artifice.

Later on, there is Forever Young, from 1974's *Planet Waves*, an affectingly unadorned expression of every parent's wish for their children. Then comes *Blood On The Tracks*: "coded", as its author put it, but so obviously about Dylan's wracked split from his wife Sara that his obfuscation seems ludicrous. Idiot Wind, for example, deals with spite, confusion, self-loathing and so much more. It's a song for that moment when a relationship slides beyond repair, and the human mind loses the ability to think straight. We've all been there.

Fourteen years later comes Most Of The Time from *Oh Mercy* – the letter that says "I'm doing fine" while making it clear that nothing could be further from the truth. And eight years later comes the terrifyingly bleak *Time Out Of Mind*, whose abiding mood is encapsulated by Love Sick: no chance of redemption, any faith in love seemingly smashed to pieces.

It was succeeded in 2001 by *Love And Theft*, the album on which Dylan carries on bravely staring into the void ("the emptiness is endless") but decides to combine his bleakest insights with a wizened, life-affirming humour. Within some of its best songs, in fact, lurks the possibility that, for all the scars of experience – all over such songs as Mississippi, Sugar Baby and Lonesome Day Blues – renewal might be as easy as getting up in the morning.

One more thing, while we're here. If ever you tire of Dylan's eloquence, or the acres of print devoted to his words, or the suspicion that perhaps Dylan-loving can take you a little too far from the fact that "rock'n'roll" was once a more ornate way of saying "fuck", you can take heart from the fact that no one does lust like Bob Dylan.

On the 1976 live album *Hard Rain*, there is a rewritten version of Lay Lady Lay. The ghosts of Blake, Arthur Rimbaud,

Dylan may play rock music, but he also deals in something altogether older; ancient, even.

© David Gahr

Shakespeare and Walt Whitman have left the building; this is a very simple carnality. "Forget this dance/Let's go upstairs," Dylan bellows. "Let's take a chance/Who really cares?"

Dead man,
dead man:
Dylan, Viking Hotel,
Rhode Island, 1963.

IN BETWEEN ALL the music, there proceeded the life, rocketing its way up to The Bike Crash, moving at a measured pace thereafter but still oozing intrigue and fascination. In an era when people make their first albums when they are 31, marry at 33 and start a family at 35, the velocity and precocity of the first phase is startling: Dylan made his recorded debut at 20, sang alongside Martin Luther King at 22, went electric at 24, and opted for a period of family life at 25. To put that into perspective, when Oasis released their first single, Noel Gallagher was 26. What kept him?

During the '70s, Dylan divorced, took painting classes that revolutionised his art, and – unfathomably – became a born-again Christian. In the '80s, he lost his way, made a run of mediocre albums, starred in a rubbish film and wore terrible clothes while proving ropey attire is no barrier to romantic adventure: Bob Dylan has never lacked female company.

In the '90s, Dylan fell victim to writer's block, suffered a heart complaint called histoplasmosis, and watched his son Jakob become an American rock star. By the mid-point of the next decade, he had published the first instalment of his memoirs and co-operated with Martin Scorsese on a biographical movie, while continuing what has long been known as the Never Ending Tour: a stop-start global walkabout with little to do with release schedules or the promotion of "product".

The voice may be a little shot, the shows sometimes way too perfunctory – but what exactly might appear in the setlist is the subject of fevered anticipation. On the night this article was written, Dylan entertained a crowd in Victoria, British Columbia with a set that included the celebrated outtake Blind Willie McTell, the title track from *New Morning*, Positively 4th Street and God Knows from the not-exactly-revered *Under The Red Sky*. Tomorrow he might do a straight reading of Tombstone Blues, a reggae version of It Ain't Me Babe, the English folk standard Wild Mountain Thyme and Pretty Vacant. You never know.

But whatever Bob Dylan plays, and wherever he goes, it's the same stuff that burns through. Love, hate, lust, loss, light, dark, family, divorce, revenge, cowardice, war, peace – the usual. And he may be dealing in such thrills for a long time to come.

A few years ago, someone posted a message on a Bob Dylan newsgroup. It referred to a 92-year-old Cuban musician called Compay Segundo, who was playing a show in Chicago that night. The posting was titled, "Bob could conceivably tour for another 33 years".

So let's imagine. The bus pulls into a Mancunian car park and Bob Dylan hobbles out and on to the stage. "I think I remember this city," he mutters. "Something happened here, 67 years ago…"

Hibbing heart-throb: high-school yearbook photo of Dylan, mid-1950s, his birth certificate, and '40s Hibbing postcard (note how proud the good burghers are of their strip mine).

BOY WONDER

ROBERT ZIMMERMAN'S CHILDHOOD AND TEENAGE YEARS ARE STEEPED IN HALF-TRUTHS AND OUTRIGHT LIES. SO WHERE DID BOB DYLAN COME FROM? BY PETER KANE

EVERYBODY HAS TO come from somewhere – even Bob Dylan. Given the choice, though, small town Minnesota, up near the Canadian border, probably wouldn't come top of many lists. It's a land of lakes, rivers, millions of trees and once-rich mineral deposits; mining, in fact, was what brought most people there in the first place. During the long winter months temperatures plummet to 20 degrees below freezing and, year round, Mother Nature calls the shots. For any adolescent bristling with plans or ambitions, dreaming of escape someday often provides the only solace. It was ever thus.

One particular teenager growing up in these parts during the '50s found the lack of stimulation and the surfeit of holes in the ground more suffocating than most. Robert Allen Zimmerman came from a good Jewish home, had a heavy James Dean fixation and would occasionally grease his hair into an extravagant Little Richard pompadour.

A devourer of books, he also fancied himself as something of a poet and, thanks to the wonders of the radio, increasingly found that music could take him places far removed from reality. He didn't fit in with his surroundings, nor did he want to. Carefully cultivating an outsider persona – 1955's Rebel Without A Cause was his favourite movie – seemed to be the point.

It was all just an accident of geography. "Like, if I was born and raised in New York or Kansas City," he once said, "I'm sure everything would have turned out different."

A dab hand at blurring the line between fact and fiction, Dylan has always guarded the secrets of his private life. Such subterfuge has, of course, only added to the myth, giving decades of amusement to his disciples. Right from the word go, playful obfuscation has been the game, the rules of which only he has known. So, if he once said he was an orphan who ran away to join a travelling show at the age of 13, who were we to disbelieve him? Somehow it sounded a lot more credible than the truth – that he was the victim of a comfortable middle-class upbringing, some way off the beaten track.

WEIGHING A HEFTY 10lbs and with, it's said, a disproportionately large head, Robert Allen Zimmerman was born on May 24, 1941, making him a Gemini. The firstborn of Abram and Beatrice (a second son, David, would follow five years later), he spent the first few years of his life in Duluth, Minnesota where his father worked as a functionary for Standard Oil.

Both Abe's and Beatty's forebears had – like tens of thousands of other new Americans – fled from Eastern Europe in the hope of finding prosperity and, as Jews, avoiding persecution. They believed in the virtues of hard work and the sanctity of the family. By the standards of the day they were comfortably off: Beatty's grandfather owned a small chain of regional theatres. 1946, though, was not a great year. Abe had lost his job and worse was to follow when he was struck down by polio, an illness that would leave him with a permanent limp.

With Beatty having enough to do nursing newborn David, never mind keeping an eye on little Bobby, shifting the family 75 miles upcountry back to her hometown of Hibbing looked like the best option. Not only could they move straight in with her own parents until things got straightened out, but Abe could join his brothers, Paul and Maurice, in their new business venture, selling furniture and electrical goods. With the war finally over and mass market consumerism about to go through the roof, it would prove a prescient decision.

Scarred by a huge open-pit mine sitting right on its doorstep, Hibbing wasn't much to look at: just an overgrown mining village where the rich iron ore deposits had brought some prosperity, especially during the '20s. Its fortunes would ebb and flow over subsequent decades according to demand. By the '50s, with the best ore already taken, the good days looked to be gone forever. By then work was in short supply and its people were once again having trouble putting food on the table. Hibbing, not for the first time, seemed a town without prospects.

While not subject to much in the way of physical hardship, the fledgling Dylan found himself in a tough, unglamorous environment. It was a place he would tellingly revisit on North Country Blues (The Times They Are A-Changin', 1964) where, with the pits closed down, the children must leave because, "there ain't nothing here now to hold them".

"Hibbing was just not the right place for me to stay and live," he said later. "There really was nothing there. The only thing you could do there was be a miner, and even that kind of thing was getting less and less. The people that lived there, they're nice people; I've been all over the world since I left there and they still stand out as being the least hung-up. The mines were just dying, that's all, but that's not their fault. Everybody my age left there. It was no great romantic thing. It didn't take any great amount of thinking or individual genius, and there certainly wasn't any pride in it. I didn't run away from it; I just turned my back on it."

Employing his customary diversionary tactics, Dylan has revealed very little about his early life. "My childhood is so far away," he once claimed, "it's like I don't even remember being a child. I think it was someone else who was a child. Did you ever think like that? I'm not sure what happened to me yesterday was true."

On another occasion he declared: "I just don't have any family. I'm all alone." Then again: "When I was young, my life was built around the family. We got together all the time. There weren't many Jews around." Confused? Who wouldn't be?

While no child prodigy, the nascent Dylan was nevertheless a capable student – when he could be bothered. According to his mother, he spent hour after hour in his room scribbling poetry and drawing. From there, scratching out his own

> # "I don't even remember being a child. I think it was someone else who was a child."
>
> **BOB DYLAN**

tunes on a cheap guitar was a logical next step; the prematurely deceased King Of Country Music, Hank Williams, was an early inspiration.

Out in the wider world, though, times were already changing, even in a backwater such as Hibbing. For the first time, being a teenager was suddenly not all bad news: authority, not least parental authority, was being challenged and traditional values and mores questioned.

Conveniently, just as the Zimmerman hormones were beginning to buzz, there were James Dean and Marlon Brando up on the big screen. And, seemingly out of the blue, there was rock'n'roll, too: Elvis, Chuck Berry, Little Richard. Abe's hopes that his elder son might fall into line or even eventually join him in the family business probably went belly-up the moment Tutti Frutti's fearsome "Awopbopaloobopawopbamboom" first came howling over the Minnesota airwaves.

Suitably inspired, and with a crew of school buddies under the collective name of The Shadow Blasters, Dylan took his first public steps to stardom sometime in 1956 (hard facts are, as ever, in short supply). Dylan played piano, an instrument he pounded with more gusto than ability.

The Blasters soon auditioned for a talent contest organised by Hibbing Junior College. Sadly, their version of (most likely) Long Tall Sally failed to impress the judges. Barely out of the blocks, The Shadow Blasters had already run straight into history.

Rather more successful were The Golden Chords, for whom Dylan once again bashed the piano; they managed to build a reputation as Hibbing's loudest, rowdiest band, playing small barbecue joints and the like. That, for the moment, was enough – not least as a way of impressing his peers and winding up his teachers and parents.

A cigar-chewing, golf-playing disciplinarian, Abe was having trouble handling his son's new ways and concluded that there were some serious psychological problems that needed rectifying. Briefly, he packed his eldest off to a special school in Pennsylvania for similarly skewed adolescents. Whatever was supposed to be achieved there patently didn't work. Dylan came home the same as before and, worse still, a permanent chasm had opened between father and son.

Following on from The Golden Chords, Elston Gunn & The Rock Boppers – no prizes for guessing who was Gunn – set Hibbing tongues wagging for a while. By 1958, though, with his own motorcycle, the old man's car and a hitchhiker's thumb at his disposal, Dylan began venturing further afield, discovering different kinds of music – black rhythm and blues especially – among the bright lights of Minneapolis and St Paul.

According to biographer Robert Shelton, a taste for plump and large-breasted young women had also entered the frame; another reason for pursuing his creative muse?

Down in Duluth he formed a group with a cousin. Named The Satin Tones, they enjoyed some celebrity by appearing on local TV and radio, but that was as good as it got. But with a final swivel of the hips, there was one more splendidly unlikely rock'n'roll failure still in store.

Nowheresville: Howard Street, Hibbing, 1941 (the newborn Robert Zimmerman not pictured).

IN JUNE 1959, after graduating from high school, Dylan was staying with relations in Fargo, North Dakota, working as a busboy at the Red Apple Café. A local band, The Shadows, were looking for a piano player. Fronted by a fresh-faced Bobby Vee (né Velline), they modelled themselves on Buddy Holly & The Crickets, whose very shoes they had bizarrely stepped into at a local hop just a few days after the bespectacled Texan's fatal plane crash in February 1959.

Having recorded a few tracks for a tiny Minneapolis label, Soma (Suzie Baby was a regional hit of sorts), The Shadows already had stars in their eyes. A huge Holly fan himself – he had seen the great one on stage in Duluth just three days before his death – Dylan convinced them he was just the man for the job.

Vee, a teen idol on both sides of the Atlantic during the early '60s (Rubber Ball, More Than I Can Say, Take Good Care Of My Baby), later recalled: "My brother met with him and they went over to the radio station to use the piano. He sort of plonked around a bit and played Whole Lotta Shakin' in the key of C. He told my brother that he'd played with Conway Twitty.

"He was a scruffy little guy, but he was really into it, loved to rock'n'roll. He was pretty limited by what he could play. He liked to do handclaps, like Gene Vincent & The Bluecaps, who had two guys who were hand-clappers. He would come up *[to my mic]* and do that every now and then and then scurry back to the piano."

After a few dates together, a barely competent, happy-clappy piano player was something Bobby Vee decided he could do without. Dylan returned to Hibbing, telling everybody he was the real star of Suzie Baby, knowing that nobody knew any better. Besides, he was about to flee the nest and head for college in Minneapolis.

It was time to say goodbye to Robert Zimmerman, rock'n'roller, and hello to Bob Dillon *[sic]*, troubadour…

19

Talk About The Passion

Satirist, bluesman, heartsick romantic, avenging angel... Dylan's many sides came together magnificently on _The Freewheelin' Bob Dylan_

AROUND THE COLUMBIA offices at 799 Seventh Avenue in New York City, they'd referred to Bob Dylan as "Hammond's Folly". "Hammond" was John Hammond, the hippest A&R guy of all time (with the possible exception of Ahmet Ertegun), who'd promoted the legendary Spirituals To Swing concerts at Carnegie Hall, supervised Bessie Smith's last session and Billie Holiday's first, hooked Charlie Christian up with Benny Goodman, would later cajole Aretha Franklin away from gospel and sign both Bruce Springsteen and Stevie Ray Vaughan. His colleagues considered his sponsorship of Bob Dylan, a 20-year-old folk singer he'd found in Greenwich Village, inexplicable. Mediocre sales of his debut, _Bob Dylan_, would seem to prove them right. At least the album had been cheap to cut: one guy, singing and playing guitar and harmonica, recorded live in the studio.

Misgivings notwithstanding, the company greenlighted Hammond to produce a second album of Dylan. He was now represented by über-manager Albert Grossman, which couldn't hurt. Unlike the warmed-over traditional songs which made up most of the first album, _The Freewheelin' Bob Dylan_ consisted almost entirely of the original compositions with which Dylan was beginning to attract attention, and which would lead established folkies like Joan Baez and Peter, Paul & Mary to cover him.

A few tracks were recorded with backing musicians, though only one ensemble performance, Corrina Corrina, actually made the final cut. (Nat Hentoff's liner notes, reproduced unchanged on the current CD reissue, still cite a line-up of backing musicians on Don't Think Twice, even though that version was replaced by the familiar Dylan solo performance before release). After this one, the phrase "Hammond's folly" was never heard again.

It wasn't until a couple of albums further down the line that the label dragged out the title _Another Side Of Bob Dylan_, but the _Freewheelin'_... album displayed enough sides of its creator's talent

> ## It was bursting with energy and exuberance and idealism.

and sensibility to qualify as a dodecahedron, at the very least. There was the comedian and satirist showcased on I Shall Be Free, Talkin' World War III Blues and Bob Dylan's Blues; the heartsick romantic picking his way through the mazes of lost love in Don't Think Twice It's All Right and Girl From The North Country; the avenging angel cawing out his apocalyptic denunciation of greed, corruption and militarism on the epic Masters Of War; the master of metaphorical imagery taking his first great symbolist-poet stand on A Hard Rain's A-Gonna Fall; the young white bluesman paying tribute to mentors and masters on Down The Highway and Corrina Corrina; the whoopingly exuberant strummer and honker glorying in the sheer joy of making a noise on Henry Thomas's Honey Just Allow Me One More Chance.

And the album opened with Blowin' In The Wind, the deceptively simple three-chord anthem which defined not only its composer and the folk movement at the head of which he had already placed himself, but the shift of mainstream white American opinion behind the growth of the civil rights movement. The song's lyrics were coded, but it was a code only the most wilfully bigoted or terminally ignorant could fail to break. It was the sweetly anodyne version by Peter Paul & Mary which scored the hit (they would repeat the trick with Don't Think Twice), but it was Dylan's original which everyone rightly remembers. No more significant curtain-raiser could possibly be imagined.

IT WAS AN older sister who first introduced me to _Freewheelin'_... Not mine, unfortunately: every boy should have an older sister, but I was forced to borrow one from a friend. She was hip to the max, the first person I ever met who actually owned records by people like Muddy Waters, Howlin' Wolf and John Lee Hooker, and one day my friend told me that Big Sis had a new musical squeeze. "His name's Bob Dylan," my friend said, "and he sings all weird through his nose."

The needle dropped on Oxford Town (a scarifying civil rights anecdotal song characterised by its composer as "a banjo tune I play on the guitar"), and there was the strangest voice I'd ever heard in my life, completely unlike any of the usual pop, R&B or rock singing. The only point of comparison I had was Lonnie Donegan, but I then had no way of knowing that both Dylan and Donegan were devotees of Woody Guthrie (of whom, needless to say, I had never heard).

THE FREEWHEELIN' BOB DYLAN

Blowin' in the Wind
Girl From the North Country
Masters of War
Down the Highway
Bob Dylan's Blues
A Hard Rain's A-Gonna Fall

Don't Think Twice, It's All Right
Bob Dylan's Dream
Oxford Town
Talkin' World War III Blues
Corrina, Corrina
Honey, Just Allow Me One More Chance
I Shall Be Free

This strange voice soon became a familiar part of the musical furniture. The subtleties of that deceptively rough-hewn guitar and harmonica style gradually revealed themselves. There were a couple of other albums to check out, and then a year or so later, the man Norman Mailer would characterise as "a snotty little son-of-a-bitch" bought a new wardrobe and a couple of Fender guitars and went pop in one of the culture's biggest of Big Bangs, which is not so much another story as an entire anthology of them.

If that original album introduced Dylan as a performer and persona, it was *Freewheelin'...* which provided the first indication of his powers and range as a composer as well as the first hints of how potent a cultural presence he was about to become. If the whole long weird Dylan saga was a movie, that first album would serve as the pre-credits sequence, but *Freewheelin'...* was where the action really began.

The Bob Dylan of those days was a youth puckishly adopting the characteristics of much older men: a lovingly developed simulation of the seamed voice of experience emerging from behind that boyish countenance. Yet *Freewheelin'...* is most assuredly a young man's album. As the title implies, it's bursting with energy and exuberance and idealism and the sheer sensual pleasure of making music, of picking and hammering those strings, honking and squeaking that harp, and exploring and expressing what was on his mind.

Each successive album would be a dispatch from a different way-station along his journey, and each of those '60s albums would have new stories to tell, but he would never be so carefree and freewheelin' ever again. *Charles Shaar Murray*

Folk Hero

Stumbling across folk icon Woody Guthrie would set off a lifetime of hero worship for Bob. By Phil Sutcliffe.

When Robert Zimmerman, aged 18, graduated from Hibbing High School, he wrote under his photograph in the class yearbook that he was off "to follow Little Richard". Not Woody Guthrie, note. He was still more or less the kid who had grown up with greasy rock'n'roll, pounding piano in his own band The Golden Chords. But a new persona was quietly taking shape.

Eric Schaal/Time Life Pictures/Getty Images

THIS MACHINE KILLS FASCISTS

Fighting the right: Woody Guthrie in, New York, 1963.

He had just begun to listen to Depression-era folk singers, Guthrie among them, and that autumn he moved on to the University of Minnesota in Minneapolis and found fertile ground for an adjustment of musical taste. Without it he might not have made his mark. Imagine: what if Bob Dylan had gone straight to Like A Rolling Stone?

Abandoning his official arts studies at once and – telling everyone his name was Bob Dillon (supposedly after an uncle whose surname was Dillion) – he immersed himself in Minneapolis's boho district, Dinkytown, where he played laborious versions of traditional folk songs at a club called The Ten O'Clock Scholar. The catalyst was a radical-about-town called David Whitaker, who drew Dylan into paying serious attention to Guthrie. One day, as they pored over the Dust Bowl Ballads LP, Whitaker told Dylan he must read the singer's autobiography, Bound For Glory.

Dylan scrounged a copy and devoured it in a day, ensconced at The Ten O'Clock Scholar. Guthrie told a wonderful story. His family decimated by fiery tragedy and illness, he hit the road at 16, hoboed across the country in freight cars, busked for a crust until he got on the radio in California and began a larger life as a singing campaigner for the downtrodden. Along the way he wrote a thousand songs: This Land Is Your Land, So Long It's Been Good To Know You, This Train Is Bound For Glory, Reuben James, Tom Joad…

It was an inspirational true romance and Dylan was instantly obsessed. In no time, he had learned more than 200 Guthrie songs and got down a decent imitation of the Oklahoman's nasal drone.

In December 1960, Dylan learned that Guthrie, still only 48, was dying under the slow onset of the hereditary degenerative disease Huntington's chorea. Boldly, he rang Greystone Park Hospital in Morristown, New Jersey, and asked to speak to his hero. He was told that Mr Guthrie couldn't get to the phone but liked to have visitors. Dylan set off immediately.

He took a while to get there, mind, pausing for some weeks in Chicago, then Madison, Wisconsin. While he hesitated, he worked up his own mythic autobiography. Either en route or on arrival in New York, he told various people that he was an Okie, an orphan, that he had met Guthrie in California when he was 10, travelled with a Texan carnival at 13, and learned guitar at the knee of blues veteran Mance Lipscomb.

This was impressively Guthrie-esque and far more intriguing than his real, uneventful childhood as the son of a smalltown Jewish shopkeeper. But it created mystery and probably fed the self-confidence he needed as he winged it day by day.

Eventually, on January 24, 1961, he completed the journey, hitching a ride to New York. That night, quiet but never shy, he played Guthrie covers at the Café Wha? in Greenwich Village. The next day he took a bus to Morristown.

Dylan has never spoken in detail of his meetings with Guthrie, but no sooner had he chalked up the first hospital visit than he was on the Guthrie family's door-step in Queens, New York, befriending his wife and children – including Arlo, later a Dylan-esque singer-songwriter – and turning up in East Orange, New Jersey to ingratiate himself with Bob and Sidsel Gleason, a couple who took Guthrie back to their house every Sunday for musical afternoons.

DYLAN WAS SOON a regular at the living room hootenannies where Guthrie's old friends such as Ramblin' Jack Elliott and Pete Seeger would gather to play for him. With his nervous system wrecked, his limbs jerking uncontrollably and speech a struggle, Guthrie still contrived to express his appreciation. Moreover, his biographer Joe Klein attests that "a real rapport seemed to develop between Woody and Dylan". Guthrie once hollered to his pals, "That boy's got a voice. Maybe he won't make it with his writing, but he can sing it."

There was a sorry moment when Guthrie demanded a guitar to play This Land Is Your Land for his young acolyte and couldn't manage a note. Some time later, Dylan did talk of his

The folk cap fits: Dylan in Columbia Studios, New York, 1962. Inset: The bill for his first professional engagement.

Guthrie sings his songs about the downtrodden and dispossessed to the downtrodden and dispossessed at McSorley's Bar, New York, 1943.

© Don Hunstein for Sony Music; Eric Schaal/Time Life Pictures/Getty Images; Blank Archives

The lyric was an appropriately humble celebration: "Hey, Woody Guthrie, but I know that you know/All the things that I'm a-sayin' an' a-many times more."

It freed Dylan's creative spirit, and for years to come he was a songwriter in flood.

WHEN DYLAN MADE his New York professional debut on April 11 at Gerde's Folk City, Greenwich Village, supporting John Lee Hooker, Sidsel Gleason lent him one of Guthrie's jackets for the night. This must have been some kind of epiphany for Dylan. Yet it was also both a practical conclusion to his period of hero worship and a beginning to life as a man-cum-globe-bestriding icon.

Visiting Guthrie faithfully up to four times a week in 1962, at the Gleasons', Greystone Park and then Brooklyn State Hospital, Dylan came to know the rounder truth of him. He saw his vanity: Guthrie's song requests were always for his own stuff. He came to understand his self-promotional shrewdness: Guthrie "dwelled on simpleness because he was getting attention for it", Dylan noted.

But unlike the archetypal fanatic encountering feet-of-clay revelations, Dylan did not allow his passion to become twisted into scorn. He modified his view and looked to what he might be able to do with his own character and abilities.

Contrary to later enigmatic outpourings, he explained this profound evolution. The sleevenote to his second album *The Freewheelin' Bob Dylan* (1963), quotes him as saying, "The most important thing I know I learned from Woody Guthrie is I'm my own person... I'll never finish saying everything I feel, but I'll be doing my part to make some sense out of the way we're living, and not living, now."

When he headlined a big-league concert for the first time, at New York Town Hall on April 12, 1963, he read out a poem, meaningfully titled Last Thoughts On Woody Guthrie (the performance is on *The Bootleg Series Volume 1-3*). Seven minutes of quickfire questioning about an artist's role, charlatans, the real thing and such, it closes: "You can either go to the church of your choice/Or you can go to Brooklyn State Hospital/You'll find God in the church of your choice/You'll find Woody Guthrie in Brooklyn State Hospital/And though it's only my opinion/I may be right or wrong/You'll find them both/In the Grand Canyon/At sundown."

Guthrie died on October 3, 1967. Dylan, living in Woodstock, heard about it on the TV news and immediately rang Guthrie's manager, Harold Leventhal, offering to sing at any memorial event.

The following January, he emerged from his bike crash-induced 18-month retirement after the to play the tribute concert at Carnegie Hall, New York. With The Band, he blasted huge electric versions of Guthrie's Grand Coulee Dam, Mrs Roosevelt and Roll On Columbia at the assembled folkies.

For all the decibels down the decades, Dylan never forgot. In the booklet for the *Biograph* box set in 1985 he said: "I always thought one man, the lone balladeer with the guitar, could blow an entire army off the stage if he knew what he was doing... To the aspiring songwriter and singer I say, Disregard all the current stuff, forget it, you're better off if you read John Keats, Melville, and listen to Robert Johnson and Woody Guthrie."

"Woody is the greatest holiest godliest one in the world."

BOB DYLAN

horror at the notion of "decaying" with disease "like Woody".

But a mixture of awe and excitement must have given him sufficient empathy to stand by his hero. He wrote ecstatically to Whitaker in Minneapolis: "I know Woody... I know him and met him and saw him and sang to him. Goddam... He's the greatest holiest godliest one in the world."

Seismically, these encounters started Bob Dylan writing songs. On February 14 (at either Mills' Bar in Bleecker Street or the 8th Street drugstore, according to different accounts by Dylan) he jotted down Song To Woody, "the first song I ever wrote that I performed in public" (the melody was cribbed from Guthrie's 1913 Massacre, says Joe Klein – but the old master magpie didn't mind).

EYEWITNESS
JAN 24 – DEC 22, 1961

DYLAN HITS NEW YORK

He arrived a country boy with not enough money to eat. But by Christmas he had a record deal and a burgeoning following.

JANUARY 24, 1961

Bob Dylan and his friend Fred Underhill arrive in a wintry New York, having driven from Madison, Wisconsin, in a four-door Pontiac. That night he performs a couple of songs at Cafe Wha?, Greenwich Village.

BOB DYLAN New York was the centre of activity for folk music, the Mecca. Everything was coming out of New York, but I didn't go there as quickly as I could. I managed to get there in a roundabout way. It was all that I ever thought it was supposed to be.

JAC HOLZMAN (*Elektra Records founder*) The Village scene was a few square blocks of clubs, bars, red-sauce Italian restaurants that had been family run for generations and, of course, the coffee houses.

BD It [*Cafe Wha?*] opened at noon and it closed at six in the morning and it was just a non-stop flow of people. Usually they were tourists who were looking for beatniks in the Village.

JANUARY 28

Dylan visits Izzy Young's Folklore Center on MacDougal Street.

IZZY YOUNG Dylan came in, the way everyone else did, as I was the place to go. He played an autoharp, but I cannot say that I noticed him

especially. He didn't look so interesting and everyone was playing all the time in my place.

JANUARY 29

Dylan visits Woody Guthrie at the home of Sid and Bob Gleason in East Orange, New Jersey.

CAMILLA DAMS HORNE (*friend of the Gleasons*) Bob didn't say a word for a long while. And finally he did sing something, and it was impressive. It was probably one of Woody's. I do remember that night Woody saying, "He's a talented boy. Gonna go far."

FEBRUARY 20

Dylan first performs at the Monday night hootenanny in Gerde's Folk City.

TOM PAXTON (*singer-songwriter*) Dave Van Ronk [*folk singer*] and I were there and this kid got up and sang and we both thought that he was just marvellous—no limit to his potential.

JOAN BAEZ He was singing his Song To Woody, and he knocked me out completely. As I remember him, it seems he was about five feet tall. He seemed tiny, just tiny, with that goofy little hat on, and I just thought about him for days.

MARCH 27

Gerde's owner Mike Porco offers Dylan a two-week John Lee Hooker support slot.

MIKE PORCO I called him into the kitchen, which was my office. I said, "You did a nice set, Bobby. Tell me, would you like to work a couple weeks?" He said, "With who?" I said, "With John Lee Hooker." "Oooh, yeah," he said. "Oooh, Mike. Great."

> **"He seemed tiny, just tiny, with that goofy little hat on."**
>
> JOAN BAEZ

Recording his debut album *Bob Dylan* at Columbia's Studio A, 1961.

©Don Hunstein for Sony Music

APRIL 5

Dylan plays at the Loeb Music Center for the University of New York Folk Society. In the audience is Suze Rotolo.

MP He started to go out with Suze, and she used to come in with him or I would go to their apartment for dinner, so we became a little more friendly.

APRIL 11-25

Dylan plays a five-song set as support to John Lee Hooker at Gerde's Folk City.

MP They didn't break the doors down to come in. John Lee Hooker was the headliner, and Bobby didn't get the applause John Lee Hooker got. But he built up a following from the show.

DAVE VAN RONK He did his Song To Woody, with a long set of harmonica breaks consisting of one note at a time spaced so as to be so totally unpredictable that you could never tell when he was going to hit that one chord on the harmonica.

JOHN LEE HOOKER After work we'd sit there and drink white wine. He was kind of a fun person to be around. His talk was real funny. He said he wanted to become a star — and a good star.

MAY

Dylan begins hawking himself around trying to secure a recording contract.

BD I went up to Folkways *[the Smithsonian Institute's non-profit folk label, which released Woody Guthrie records]*. I says,

"Howdy. I've written some songs." They wouldn't even look at them.

IY I took him to Jac Holzman. When I asked Jac about that years later, he said that he doesn't remember me bringing him. Then I took him to Vanguard Records. Manny Solomon *[Vanguard boss]* later said, "Listen, Izzy, I'm glad I didn't put him out on a record, because I don't want a freak on my label."

SEPTEMBER 26

Dylan's begins a two-week residency at Gerde's Folk City, supporting The Greenbriar Boys.

JOHN HERALD *(Greenbriar Boys)* Dylan took us by storm when he opened for us. He was getting a bigger hand than we were. I was getting a little envious. I didn't really understand what he was doing.

> "I signed Bob Dylan. They all thought I was crazy. Dylan thought I was crazy."
>
> **JOHN HAMMOND, COLUMBIA PRODUCER**

SEPTEMBER 29

New York Times publishes a rave review by critic Robert Shelton of the Gerde's gig.

SUZE ROTOLO Robert Shelton's review, without a doubt, made Dylan's career, because that brought the establishment.

SEPTEMBER 30

Dylan meets Columbia Records producer John Hammond Sr during a Carolyn Hester album session.

JOHN HAMMOND She had him playing harmonica and guitar. It was at a rehearsal on West 10th Street. I was so delighted with what I heard, I suggested he come up to the studio. I asked him if he could sing and he said, "Yeah." I asked him if he could write, and he said, "Yeah." And that's how I signed Bob Dylan.

OCTOBER 26

Dylan signs a five-year contract with Columbia Records.

JH They all thought I was crazy. Dylan thought I was crazy. He had been turned down by Folkways and every other label there was at the time. But I thought he had something.

MARC SILBER (folk musician) The night Dylan signed his Columbia contract I was at the Gaslight Cafe with my friend Perry Lederman, who was one of the outstanding folk pickers of the day. Perry knew everybody and Bob actually asked Perry to be his guitarist! Perry responded with, "I don't think so... see, I am going to go to the top of the music world and be famous!" We often laughed about that in later years.

OCTOBER 29

Dylan appears on Oscar Brand's radio show, Folksong Festival.

IY I took him to Oscar Brand around the corner who recorded him for his radio programme on WNYC and so he could brag forever after that he was the first to have him on the radio. The performance was not so hot. He was mumbling too much.

NOVEMBER 4

Dylan's first concert hall appearance, at New York's Carnegie Chapter Hall.

JEAN RITCHIE (folk musician) About 40 minutes late, Dylan

THE FOLKLORE CENTER

Presents

BOB DYLAN

IN HIS FIRST NEW YORK CONCERT

SAT. NOV. 4, 1961   8:40pm

CARNEGIE CHAPTER HALL

154 WEST 57th STREET • NEW YORK CITY

All seats $2.00

Tickets available at: The Folklore Center
110 MacDougal Street
New York City 12, New York

walks up on stage and talks about what a little country boy he was, and how he got lost on the subway. Then he started tuning his instruments. We thought, "Poor thing." He had a table with about 20 harmonicas on it and he was blowing into each one. After about 15 minutes of experimenting, he said, "I think I won't sing that song." The whole concert was like that.

IY The agreement I had *[as the gig's promoter]* with Bob Dylan was that we would share the profit. Well, 52 people came. I took the loss but, coming from my working class background, I gave him 10 or 20 dollars because I thought that a man should get paid for his work.

GERRY GOFFIN *(songwriting partner of Carole King)* After Carole and I first went to

see Bob Dylan at Carnegie Hall in '61, we took all our old demos and broke them in half. We said, "We have to grow up."

NOVEMBER 20-22

Records debut album, *Bob Dylan*, at Studio A, Columbia Records, Seventh Street.

JH My first album with Dylan cost $402, union scale for him as an artist. Bob was writing three or four songs a day and was unused to mike techniques. His guitar playing, let us say charitably, was rudimentary, and his harmonica was barely passable, but he had a sound and a point of view and an idea. He was very disenchanted with our social system. I encouraged him to put all his hostility on tape because I figured this was the way to get to the true Bob Dylan.

Columbia's John Hammond listens in on his protégé, New York, 1961. Above: Dylan's Gibson and two of his harmonicas take a break.

DECEMBER 22

On his way home for Christmas, Dylan makes a tape in the Minneapolis sorority house room of Bonnie Bleecher—the basis of the Great White Wonder bootleg.

BONNIE BLEECHER I ended up shoplifting for him, stealing food from my sorority house. He sits down to make a tape and he says to me, "I don't want you ever to let anyone copy these tapes, so that when someone from the Library of Congress asks you for them, I want you to sell them for $200." What kind of a remark is that to make to somebody that is shoplifting food for someone so incompetent that he can't even shoplift his own food? But I promised him, and I never did let anybody make copies of those tapes. And then they were stolen.

Cotton-pickin' protest: Dylan and Pete Seeger (left of him) at a voter registration rally, Greenwood, Mississippi, July 1963.

PROTE

IF YOU'RE SEARCHING for a definitive image of the protest singer then look no further than Bob Dylan at the Newport Folk Festival, July, 26, 1963. He was the classic model: tousled, skinny, dressed in hard-times chic, a bit arrogant and handsome in spite of it all. He was singing songs from his recent album, *The Freewheelin' Bob Dylan*. The songs were great. The crowd adored him. He was in prolific form, keeping up with a volatile age.

Near the end of that Friday night set, his friends and mentors joined him on stage to share the occasion. They crossed their arms and reached out for the hands of those nearby. And then they celebrated, like they often did, with their favourite anthem, We Shall Overcome.

To the far right of Dylan were Peter, Paul & Mary, who had just recorded a version of Blowin' In The Wind which would go on to sell 300,000 copies in its first two weeks of release. Joan Baez stood to Dylan's immediate right. Back in 1959 she had upped her own reputation at Newport, and now she was endorsing Dylan, recording his songs and making the requisite introductions. To Bob's left stood The Freedom Singers from Albany, Georgia – as well as veteran folkie Pete Seeger, regarded as the conscience of the folk revival. He was flanked by Theodore Bikel, the actor, singer and festival organiser.

We Shall Overcome was based on an old Afro-American hymn, I Shall Overcome, the revised version putting its faith in collective action instead of personal salvation. With Seeger's encouragement, the song had been taken up by the Student Non-Violent Co-ordinating Committee, one of the organisations stoking up the civil rights movement in the Deep South. Dylan and his friends were singing the gospel of social progress, of an American society that might be a better, fairer place.

People were singing We Shall Overcome throughout that year. It was an anthem for the Battle Of Birmingham, when Dr Martin Luther King addressed thousands in the Alabama town across April and May, appealing for desegregation and voting rights. The protesters had faced down police dogs, water hoses and batons, but they had come away with some gains. Non-violent direct action, based on the Ghandi model, was apparently working. And to many, the righteous songs of the young Bob Dylan provided the perfect soundtrack.

© Danny Lyon/Magnum

Civil rights, imminent apocalypse – there were no shortage of themes for the young protest singer Dylan to complain about, at least until his rock'n'roll instincts got the better of him.
By Stuart Bailie.

SURVIVE

Sing-ins, freedom rides, marches, boycotts and voter registration drives were the order of the day throughout 1963. What remained of the Old Left had made their painful recovery from the Communist witch-hunts and the blacklists that lingered for a long time after World War II. They had sustained themselves with message songs, carried by the likes of Woody Guthrie, now slowly expiring from Huntington's chorea.

DYLAN WAS MAKING a decent living out of presenting this tradition to white liberal audiences, but he had also honed his art in more demanding places. In July 1963 he had visited Greenwood, Mississippi, singing at a voter registration concert by the edge of a cotton patch. Before a mainly black audience, Dylan had performed one of his new topical songs, Only A Pawn In Their Game.

It dealt with the recent killing of Medgar Evers, an official from the National Association for the Advancement of Coloured People (NAACP). In it, Dylan suggested that the assassin, a white man from Greenwood, wasn't entirely to blame, that the system that had warped him was at fault.

But in 1963 there was a great deal of consensus in the folk community. Dylan's encore at Newport suggested that there was a common purpose for blacks and whites, for north and south, between the Old Left and the new anti-authoritarians. The centre was holding. Malcolm X and the Black Muslims were still on the fringes, calling for separatism. Vietnam was not yet a flaming issue. The riots in Harlem and Watts were some way off.

On several levels, in fact, America was loosening up. The US Supreme Court had ordered the desegregation of public schools in 1954. In many states, the colour bar was lifted from

The weakest link? Dylan flanked by folk revivalists Peter Yarrow, Mary Travers, Paul Stookey, Joan Baez, The Freedom Singers, Pete Seeger and Theodore Bikel, Newport Folk Festival, 1963.

lunch counters, public transport and rest rooms. Black voters were registering, often in the face of redneck opposition. Thankfully, the media was more sympathetic to progressive politics than before. Perhaps you really could teach the world to sing in some kind of harmony.

Dylan was the embodiment of such hopes. Few suspected that his name was bogus, that his personal history was cooked up to suit the act, that his voice and manners were borrowed from elsewhere – all that was something to argue about later.

In the wake of a debut album that was way more "folk" than "protest", The Freewheelin' Bob Dylan had been released in May 1963, revealing the weight of his new writing. Masters Of War attacked the armaments industry and the double-speak of their salesmen. In Dylan's view, age and experience were actually a hindrance to clear-sightedness, a theme that would endear him to the baby-boomers. "I'm only 21 years old," he said, "and I know that there's been too many wars."

It was Pete Seeger who had encouraged the new wave of American artists to write about topical issues. He'd visited England and discovered that British folk singers were eager to take on big themes. In the wake of that visit, he began to contribute to new folk journal Broadside.

Dylan often previewed his songs – as sheet music – in Broadside, starting with Talkin' John Birch Paranoid Blues, in Issue 1, published in February 1962. The song, which ridiculed anti-Communist hysteria, was later taken off the Freewheelin'... album and pulled from Ed Sullivan's The Toast Of The Town TV show for fear of legal action.

The community for whom Broadside spoke had bonded further when Seeger had been left off the regular television show Hootenanny. Broadcast on the ABC network, the programme was a contrived but popular response to the era, regularly pulling in over 10 million viewers. The suspicion was that Seeger had been barred because of an old dispute with the House Of Representatives' Un-American Activities Committee. Baez, Dylan, Phil Ochs, Tom Paxton, Judy Collins, Carolyn Hester and others refused to go on the show and were further incensed when the ABC network asked Seeger to sign a loyalty oath. Ultimately, the show was axed, but the artists felt they had gained a moral victory.

On August 28, 1963, Dylan took part in the march on Washington DC, at which Martin Luther King outlined his famous dream to over 200,000 people. As at the aforementioned voter registration rally, he sang Only A Pawn In Their Game. Privately, however, he was starting to pen much less assured songs and to question his place in the protest milieu.

Events only deepened his doubts. John F Kennedy was shot on November 22. The next night Dylan played a show in upstate New York, opening with The Times They Are A-Changin', and was floored by the reaction. "Something had gone haywire in the country," he said. "And I couldn't understand why they were clapping or why I wrote that song, even."

Things were certainly awry when Dylan attended a fund-raising dinner for the Emergency Civil Liberties Committee in December. He was awarded the Tom Paine Award for his work (Bertrand Russell was the previous designate), and made a messy, drunken speech in return. He called politics "trivial". He dismissed some of the aspirational features of the march on Washington, namely that some of the men were wearing their best suits: "I didn't see any negroes that looked like none of my friends."

In January 1964 he delivered a third album, *The Times They Are A-Changin'*. Several songs alluded to his fractured relationship with Suze Rotolo, who had appeared on the cover of *Freewheelin'*… She was a politically sussed New Yorker from a free-thinking family, who had given Dylan an interest in the political theatre of Bertolt Brecht, which he was now putting to use on songs such as The Lonesome Death Of Hattie Carroll, a venomous tale of class and racial iniquities.

On the whole, it was a noticeably schizoid album. On the title track he was supremely stern, declaring a generational divide and warning that the flood tides were imminent. Elsewhere, though, he sang about poverty and cruel times with an almost bemused tone. In retrospect, he was losing interest.

The protest singer had been something of a media invention, according to the supposed kingpin of the genre. "There never was such a thing," he said later. "It was like the term beatnik, or hippy… made up by magazine people who like to put a label on something to cheapen it." Nonetheless, the folk scene had created its own conventions. It put a value on hard-won knowledge ("You can't write a good song about a whorehouse unless you have been in one," Woody Guthrie had insisted).

Money-making was scorned, and the message was more important than the messenger. The young Dylan, like many contenders, overcompensated, with the result that he sometimes came across like a wizened Jeremiah, old before his time.

Soon enough, Dylan started acting like an individual again. He bookended 1964 with *Another Side Of Bob Dylan*, an LP that sounded deliberately provocative. He was determined to be irreverent, have more fun with the music.

By now The Beatles and The Rolling Stones were livening up both sides of the Atlantic. The Animals had done an electric version of The House Of The Rising Sun, partially inspired by the version on Dylan's debut album. By April 1965, Bob was touring the UK oozing a clear rock'n'roll attitude.

IN OCTOBER 1965, Dylan gave a startling interview to the Long Island Press, dismissing his former songs as "ghosts". "I never wanted to write topical songs," he said. "That was my chance. In the Village was a little publication called Broadside, and with a topical song you could get in there. I wasn't getting far with the things I was doing, songs like I'm writing now, but Broadside gave me a start."

Then, of course, there was the famously petulant electric show at Newport in 1965. Pete Seeger wept and threatened to chop through the power lines with an axe. Dylan's manager, Albert Grossman, wrestled in the dirt with folk archivist and festival committee member Alan Lomax.

Of course, no one should ever take all Dylan's cynical explanations at face value. What we do know is that he needed to destroy the image of Bob Dylan at Newport in 1963, a version of the artist that was limiting his artistic space. Besides, while he may have thieved ideas and integrity from the New York set, he also bequeathed them some of the best songs of freedom, ever.

It should also be noted that Dylan revisited those areas on frequent occasions, particularly during the mid-'70s. In May 1974 he appeared with Ochs and Van Ronk at a Friends Of Chile benefit, aimed at helping prisoners of the Pinochet regime. And The Rolling Thunder Revue Tour of 1975 was a conscious throwback to the old scene, taking the likes of Baez and Ramblin' Jack Elliott along for the ride. The *Desire* album came early in 1976, famously containing the Hurricane single, making a case for the imprisoned boxer Rubin Carter.

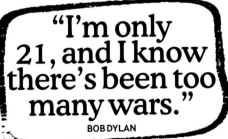

"I'm only 21, and I know there's been too many wars."
BOB DYLAN

In the '80s he made a case for not playing Sun City in South Africa and gave blighted American farmers a plug at Live Aid, which in turn gave rise to the Farm Aid project. But Dylan didn't even pretend to have the fixity of purpose that had made him famous two decades previously. Certainly, Dylan couldn't seem further from his protesting past than right now, with the news that he's signed a deal with Starbucks to exclusively sell his *Live At The Gaslight 1962* album from their coffee shops.

In his typically contrary way, Dylan has even suggested that his move from "folk" and "protest" to "rock" was not nearly the rupture that many have suggested. "I played all the folk songs with a rock'n'roll attitude," he once said. "That's what allowed me to cut through all the mess and be heard."

You can see his point, but there's no doubt that, between 1963 and 1964, Bob Dylan revolutionised himself. In place of the sureties of politics, topical tunes and collective action, Dylan chose a world that the poet Louis MacNeice called "incorrigibly plural". A loss for the protest song, perhaps, but a pretty good bonus for rock'n'roll.

© Jim Marshall

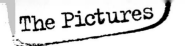
Marshall's Law

Legendary photographer Jim Marshall worked with Dylan in the early years and watched the star become more reclusive as his celebrity grew.

JIM MARSHALL'S FASCINATION with the camera began at an early age. "When I was nine or ten, I won a track race at school and a local photographer took a shot of me crossing the line," he says. "The picture was razor sharp and I thought, 'Wow, that must be a magic box!' I started cutting pictures of cameras out of magazines and sticking them into a scrapbook. I still have the book."

Sharing an apartment in San Francisco, he first dipped a toe into professional photography in the late '50s. "My rent was $37 per month and I sold my first picture for $15," he recalls. "It was a comedian called Lord Buckley playing a coffee house. My first shoot with a major artist was John Coltrane."

Marshall soon began specialising in music photography ("It was fun, and you got into the clubs for free") then moved to New York in 1962 "to make my mark in the world". Within weeks of arriving in Manhattan he watched a nascent Bob Dylan play New York Town Hall, and began shooting him for magazines soon afterwards.

"I thought straight away that Bobby was one of the greatest singer-songwriters I had ever heard. At first, he was good to work with. He was always a little distant and aloof, and I wouldn't say that we ever got close, but I got some fantastic pictures of him. He trusted me, because trust was my strongest suit – he knew I wasn't going to do anything that he didn't like.

"You know that Churchill quote, that Russia is like a riddle wrapped in a mystery inside an enigma? That's how I saw Bobby. He had a real mystique. I never asked him to do things for me, because I'm not interested in directing people and contriving pictures. I just hung around and snapped him with my Leica M2 whenever I could.

"Dylan was great to work with at first, but I saw him change. As his fame grew, so did his paranoia and mistrust of people. He became less generous with his time, and his manager, Albert Grossman, was pretty tough to deal with. One time I was at a party in Waylon Jennings' room at the Hyatt House in LA when Dylan arrived, and his goons came over and said I had to leave. Bobby would never have done that in the early days.

"I understand why Dylan got more remote – to protect the little privacy he had left – but as it got harder to gain access, I just wasn't that interested in trying to work with him any more. I wish Bobby well, but the last time I photographed him was in 1980, and I don't imagine that I will ever do it again."

Interview by Ian Gittins

For more information, see www.jimmarshallvault.com

Wheel Of Fortune

New York, 1963

I had been commissioned to shoot Bobby for the Saturday Evening Post in 1963 and we were walking to breakfast in Manhattan. Dylan saw a tyre by the road, picked it up and kicked it twice, and I shot it. It was a totally spontaneous moment. They became the most iconic photos I ever took of Bobby, because they capture the innocence that he had at that time.

Soul Food

New York, 1963

I took this the same morning as the tyre shots. We were in a diner at about nine in the morning — Bobby, his girlfriend Suze Rotolo, *[New York musician]* Dave Von Ronk and me. Back then Dylan really looked up to Von Ronk, so I just snapped away as they ate breakfast. They weren't posing but they didn't mind.

With God On Your Side

Newport Folk Festival, 1963

I didn't see Bobby go electric at Newport in '65 but I was there in '63 and '64. In those days his live shows were like religious experiences. They had such intensity and people would do anything to be there, and that was how I felt about him as well. Back then you were allowed to photograph the entire set so I would fire off about 200 shots.

Cash On Demand

Nashville, 1969

Bobby loved Johnny, and went to appear on his TV programme, the Johnny Cash Show. While I was photographing them, Dylan's people came up and said I had to stop because their artist didn't want his picture taken. Johnny's wife June Carter heard them, came over and said it was her show, she had asked me to take photos, and she wanted me to carry on. You didn't mess with June.

Alone In A Crowd

Newport Folk Festival, 1963

Bobby was a big deal by now and people had started following him around. Here he was backstage talking to *[folk singer]* Len Chandler. I don't think they were particularly close, but by now I was seeing a real change in Dylan – he valued musicians a lot more than he did anybody else, and he was beginning to be wary around other people.

Alley Cats

San Francisco, 1965

This is Bobby with Robbie Robertson, *[San Francisco poet]* Michael McClure and Allen Ginsberg, leaning against the City Lights bookstore in San Francisco in an alley that's now called Kerouac Strasse. Bobby was playing the tour where he first went electric. He had some pretty hostile reactions on that tour, but the crowd in SF loved it and it was a fantastic show.

She Belongs To Me

Hotel Viking, Newport, 1964

Bobby and Joan Baez were very close when they were an item and I think they had a pretty intense couple of years together. Their relationship was pretty good when I took this. My spare camera is on the table in front of Dylan and Joan is wearing my hat. It looked a lot better on her than it did on me.

Bob Dylan's Blues

Newport Folk Festival, 1963

This was right before Bobby went onstage at the festival and he was walking around backstage thinking about which songs to play. He would get kind of nervous before he went on and go really quiet. He didn't seem to mind me being there, but it was clear that it would be a good idea for me to keep my distance.

The Beatles loved Dylan. Dylan loved The Beatles. Between them, they managed to invent the '60s, but their mutual appreciation society had its drawbacks. By Steve Lowe.

The Fab Five

During the early part of 1964, Bob Dylan was being driven through the all-American wilderness of Colorado when he experienced a revelation. Listening to the local radio station's singles chart, he was stunned to hear that eight songs in their Top 10 were by The Beatles. Such immense popularity would almost be explainable somewhere hip such as New York. But in Colorado? Something had clearly changed forever.

Legend has it that Dylan marked the moment by leaping out of the car and frenziedly banging its bonnet in time to the music.

NEW YORK - THE EMPIRE STATE

BEATLES

"They were doing things nobody was doing," he later remembered. "Their chords were outrageous, just outrageous. You could only do that with other musicians. That was obvious. And it started me thinking about other people. But I just kept it to myself that I really dug them. Everybody else thought they were for the teenyboppers, that they were gonna pass right away. But it was obvious to me that they had staying power. In my head The Beatles were it. It seemed to me a definite line had been drawn."

DYLAN WASN'T ALONE in his thinking. I Want To Hold Your Hand was a hit with the New York Beat elite; Allen Ginsberg surprised his circle by getting up and dancing to the song in a club. But Dylan temporarily hid his fascination with the group, even dismissing them as "bubblegum" to girlfriend Suze Rotolo and journalist friend Al Aronowitz, both of whom had swiftly become Beatles addicts. Even when the two ganged up on him, he publicly refused to budge.

The Beatles were less coy about their Dylan obsession. Fittingly, considering their future friendship, George Harrison was the first to make the discovery. "I think it was his second album we heard first in February or January of '64," he said. "We were in Paris at the Olympia Theatre and we got a copy of *Freewheelin'*... and we just wore it out. The content of the song lyrics and the attitude – it was just incredibly original and wonderful."

John Lennon was quickly smitten. Whenever at home during 1964, he would listen repeatedly to these strange, Spartan songs. He and Dylan were the same age, both turned on to music by Elvis, but they'd since been dragged in wildly different directions. In the classic rock'n'roll dilemma, one had opted for popularity, the other credibility – and neither was satisfied with their choice.

Lennon, from the start, began worrying that he was missing out, that in opting

for clean-cut pop he was acting against his rebellious impulses. In parallel, The Beatles suggested to Dylan that preaching to the converted compared rather feebly with changing the world. The folk singer with the intellectual following would never be quite so keen on trotting out his protest hits again. But, for the moment at least, he would sit on his hands.

The two parties' symbiosis began before they even met. A Melody Maker article in early 1964 claiming that "The Beatles Dig Dylan" substantially aided Dylan's cause in the UK. Talking about Dylan's influence in the same year, Lennon foresaw how their relationship would pan out: "Anyone who is one of the best in his field – as Dylan is – is bound to influence people. I wouldn't be surprised if we influenced him in some way."

Although I'm A Loser on *Beatles For Sale* is usually hailed as his first attempt to fatten The Beatles' sound with some downbeat Dylanisms, Lennon even admitted the influence when writing A Hard Day's Night – although, of course, "we Beatle-fied it before we recorded it".

Despite his obsession, Lennon never quite bought the notion that Dylan's lyrics contained the secrets to the universe. Typically, he preferred to revel in the songs' overall tone of solid self-possession. "Did you listen to the words?" Dylan proudly inquired of Lennon in 1965. "I didn't need to, man," came the shrugging reply. Indeed, Lennon told the British press that "it's not what Dylan sings – it's the way he sings it".

As mutual friends of both, Aronowitz knew he would be the one to arrange an initial meeting. The big day was delayed, though, by Lennon's nerves. "As soon as I got to know John well enough," Aronowitz recalled, "I started telling him that he ought to meet Bob. John kept saying he wanted to wait until he was Dylan's 'ego equal'. 'Yeah, I wanna meet him,' Lennon told me, 'but on my own terms.'"

But by The Beatles' summer '64 US tour, Lennon was snapping to him on the phone: "Where is he?" When Aronowitz replied that "he" was staying in Woodstock, but could probably come down to New York City, Lennon ordered gruffly, "Do it!"

On August 28, 1964, Dylan was brought to The Beatles' suite in the Hotel Delmonico on Park Avenue. Introductions were stiff – akin, Aronowitz remembers, to "Billy The Kid and the Jesse James Gang acting like bashful little girls".

Dylan requested his favourite drink of choice, cheap wine. Brian Epstein apologised that the suite only had champagne. When The Beatles offered pills, Aronowitz instead suggested they smoke some pot. Famously, Dylan was amazed The Beatles had never tried marijuana, having misheard "I can't hide" in I Want To Hold Your Hand as "I get high".

The Beatles were understandably curious about how it would make them feel. After telling them that it would feel very, very good, Dylan began rolling US-style pure weed joints, although far from expertly. To avoid the smell being detected by the 20 or so police stationed in the corridor, the whole party decamped to the bedroom. Dylan handed the first joint to Lennon, who suggested Ringo Starr, his "royal taster", have

"Their chords were outrageous. In my head, The Beatles were it." BOB DYLAN

I want you: Dylan arrives for his Beatles-attended Albert Hall gig, London, 1966.

the first puff. Knowing nothing of smokers' etiquette, Ringo continued smoking the lot himself. More joints were produced for everyone and, amid the ensuing giggles, Paul McCartney began feeling increasingly disembodied.

"Till then, we'd been hard scotch and coke men," McCartney confirmed. "It sort of changed that evening."

OVER THE NEXT 12 months, the extent to which both parties sought to take on the prime attributes of the other was evident in Lennon's adoption of the Dylan peaked cap (which he eventually abandoned after the others' piss-

taking) and in Dylan decking himself out in Carnaby Street finery. Musically, The Beatles' next two albums (*Beatles For Sale* and *Help*) were both suffused with an organic, acoustic feel, partly in emulation of Dylan and partly thanks to the increased aural sensitivity brought on by their new favourite drug.

It took a little longer for Dylan to let new, Beatles-derived influences permeate his work. But by the end of 1964 he'd had it as a lone voice howling away in the darkness. Released in late 1964, *Another Side Of Bob Dylan* temporarily maintained his acoustic sound but suggested a figure in the process of putting his old identity out to pasture.

Crush hour: Beatles fans shortly before the band's first meeting with Dylan at the Delmonica Hotel, New York, August 28, 1964.

Lennon adopts Dylan-esque headwear for the Hard Day's Night film, 1964.

In the next year, Bob Dylan would become a pop star. When he met The Beatles again in London's Mayfair Hotel, the awkwardness still hadn't subsided. In Marianne Faithfull's description of one meeting after Dylan's Royal Albert Hall date in May 1965, they appear less like gods communing on Olympus than cool kids from neighbouring schools nervous of appearing 'square'.

"Dylan went into the room where The Beatles were sitting all scrunched up on the couch, all of them fantastically nervous," she recalls. "Nobody said anything. They were waiting for the oracle to speak. But Dylan just sat down and looked at them as if they were all total strangers at a railway station."

Lennon eventually turned to Dylan and said, "Lovely gig, man."

After a pause, Dylan grumbled, "They didn't dig It's Alright Ma…"

"It's the price of being ahead of your time, you know," Lennon suggested.

"Maybe, but I'm only about 20 minutes ahead as it is," came the response.

"There was a lot of petty role-playing going on," Don't Look Back director DA Pennebaker recalls of the suite's atmosphere.

McCartney proudly put an acetate on the turntable. Dylan walked out.

"A lot of hip one-liners filled with innuendo were fired off every second."

Still, in the wake of the post-Royal Albert Hall rendezvous, Lennon felt sufficiently relaxed in Dylan's company to invite him back to Kenwood, his palatial home in Weybridge. They reputedly worked on an unfinished doodle, sung into a tape recorder and long since lost.

"I dug his situation where he lived," Dylan later told biographer Robert Shelton. "It was a 22-room house. Do you know what I did when I got back from England, man? I bought me a 31-room house – can you imagine that? Mine! I bought one just as soon as I got back. And it turned into a nightmare!"

As is the case with a great deal of the Dylan-Beatles interface, the exact details of the hastily purchased pile have long remained unclear.

IF DYLAN GENUINELY admired Lennon, he treated McCartney coolly, deriding the likes of Yesterday and Michelle as MOR muzak. Faithfull recalls McCartney walking into the Mayfair suite with an acetate of his distorted, electronic, genuinely ground-breaking pre-*Revolver* tape experiments. McCartney proudly put it on and stood back. Dylan simply walked out of the room. "It was unbelievable," she claims. "The expression on Paul's face was priceless."

That meeting came in the wake of Dylan's hysteria-plagued tour of the UK, at which his exit from the folk enclosure was so loudly mourned. Poetically, The Beatles were on hand to support their new campadre, sitting in a box at the Royal Albert Hall, and – according to Melody Maker's Ray Coleman – responding to the endless catcalls and slow hand-claps by shouting, "Leave him alone! Shut up!"

The same British trip gave rise to the best evidence of the two parties interacting: 20-odd minutes of footage featuring Lennon and Dylan on a limousine ride around London on 25 May 1966, a snippet of which was shoe-horned into the unreleased documentary Eat The Document. The car had been lent to Dylan by The Rolling Stones, replete with chauffeur Tom Keylock, occasionally referred to in the dialogue.

What's striking about the scene isn't so much the quick-witted, absurdist babble but the air of intimidating competition. There have always been rumours, fuelled by a Lennon remark about the pair being "on junk", that heroin was involved – but according to insiders, they ingested nothing more potent than beaujolais and marijuana.

Consequently, Lennon is stoned, Dylan far more so – on the edge, in fact, of both sickness and unintelligibility. Lennon gamely bats around Dylan's speed-freak skits, but the banter is far from carefree, predicated rather on each trying to keep up with the other's freeform lunacy.

Made awkward either by Dylan's disrepair or by the cameras, Lennon stone-facedly blanks some garbled conversational overtures, finally gazing away as though embarrassed by his

Rolling stoned: Lennon and Dylan take a trip in Jagger and co's limo, May 1966.

Meanwhile Dylan
gets into some
Fabs gear on
Carnaby Street,
London, 1964.

When I Met Bob...

RECORD PRODUCER JOE BOYD

"I went to Boston in the summer of '64 and ran into a girl that I'd always quite fancied but never got to know particularly well. I didn't really have a place to stay, so she said, Stay with me. Because she had to work as a waitress and then she was going to see the Dylan concert at Symphony Hall, and hoping to get backstage with some friends, she told me to come to her place sometime after 12.

"I was quite pleased by this turn of events, strutting around all evening, knowing that treats were in store, so around 12.30 I roll up at her place. There's a key under the mat and a note with a big sign 'JOE' and the door to her bedroom is closed. And the note says, 'I'm afraid there's been a change of plan. You'll never guess who's here!' So I went to sleep on the couch and in the morning I had breakfast with her and Dylan. She told me later, I was looking forward to it, Joe, but you know, I couldn't turn down that opportunity."

companion's troubles. He does, however, finally offer some sound advice: "Do you suffer from sore eyes, groovy forehead, or curly hair? Take Zimdon!"

As the '60s progressed, the links between the artists weakened. Dylan and The Beatles were equally responsible for the global hegemony of hippyism, but while The Beatles embraced their roles as countercultural icons, Dylan went out of his way to avoid it. Loathing the artificiality of psychedelia, he found little merit in the McCartney-esque soundscapes of *Sgt Pepper*. "Turn that shit off!" was his reported verdict.

Dylan even indirectly aided The Beatles' eventual split by allowing George Harrison to experience a working environment that didn't involve playing second or third fiddle. Harrison returned from a trip to Woodstock to the freezing confines of Twickenham Film Studios, where McCartney was leading The Beatles into the Let It Be debacle; the eventual result was a temporary walk-out that placed yet another crack in their already fragile relations.

"I'd just spent the last six months producing this album by *[solo Apple artist]* Jackie Lomax, and hanging out with Bob Dylan and The Band in Woodstock and having a great time," Harrison recalled. "So for me to come back into the winter of discontent with The Beatles in Twickenham, it was very unhealthy and unhappy." He duly walked out on the sessions – a temporary spat, but a crucial one.

Later that year, once *Abbey Road* had been completed and The Beatles had started to adjust to their demise, Harrison, Lennon and Starr visited the Isle Of Wight festival to catch Dylan's performance. Rumours were inevitably sparked of an all-star jam finale but, as it turned out, all the musical interchange took place in private at Dylan's rented farmhouse. Soon after his performance, Dylan was taken by helicopter to Lennon's Tittenhurst mansion near Ascot. The details of that summit – and whether the pair were any less "uptight" – have been lost to history: Dylan may or

may not have jammed with Lennon on an unreleased take of Cold Turkey.

In 1970, Harrison and Dylan engaged in recording sessions in New York. The music press became sufficiently excited to splurge out headlines like "Dylan And Harrison Make LP Together". Though nothing as earth-shaking emerged, the sessions did result in the co-composition I'd Have You Anytime, the beautiful love song that opens Harrison's *All Things Must Pass*, If Not For You, featured on both that album and Dylan's *New Morning* (their joint version eventually surfaced on *The Bootleg Series*), and one enlightening doodle – widely available on bootleg – entitled Working On A Guru.

Taking its lead from Solomon Burke's Everybody Needs Somebody To Love, it finds Harrison playing lead guitar in a Beatles-circa-'64 style. "Rain all around," Dylan sings, "I need me an umbrella/Water on the ground/I'm the kind of fella/Working on a guru." In truth, it sounds a little like a friendly dig at Harrison.

OVER THE NEXT two decades, the "Quiet Beatle" was responsible for two Dylan comebacks. First, in August 1971, he cajoled Dylan out of exile for the Concert For Bangladesh at Madison Square Garden. Lennon had blown Harrison out because of the latter's refusal to let him appear with Yoko Ono; in terms of 'name' performers, Dylan arguably saved Harrison's bacon.

"Right up to the moment he stepped on stage I wasn't sure if he was going to come on. So it was kind of nerve-racking," Harrison recalled. "I had a little list – after Here Comes The Sun it just said 'Bob' with a question mark."

Against all expectations, Dylan arrived, his copious nerves not halting a triumphant performance. Surprisingly, he even performed Blowin' In The Wind – surprising because when George previously requested the song as a guaranteed crowd-pleaser, Dylan turned and sneered, "Are you gonna sing I Want To Hold Your Hand?"

While Harrison's relationship with Dylan deepened, Lennon's slipped. Irked by Dylan's apparent retreat and seemingly of the opinion that he was part of the '60s 'dream' that had to be jettisoned, on 1970's God Lennon spat, "I don't believe in Zimmerman."

Later, towards the end of Lennon's own withdrawal into domesticity, he was infuriated by Dylan's conversion to Christianity. In October 1979 he stumbled upon Dylan's performance on Saturday Night Live, during which he played three songs from *Slow Train Coming*: I Believe In You, When You Gonna Wake Up and, most crucially, Gotta Serve Somebody.

If not for you: Bob joins George Harrison's Concert For Bangladesh, August 1971.

Lennon was instantly moved to pick up an acoustic guitar and write an acid riposte: the drone-backed rant entitled Serve Yourself, officially released on *The John Lennon Anthology* in 1998. The two ex-campadres had decisively pulled apart, Lennon still sounding the hippy mantra of self-belief and inner development; Dylan advocating the diametrically opposed notions of original sin and redemption through Christ. "He did feel a little let down," McCartney said later. "But John was like that. John liked gurus."

The Saturday Night Live episode contains one flatly creepy element that confirms its importance in Beatles lore. After the show, Dylan was photographed with an autograph hunter named Mark Chapman.

Harrison and Dylan, by contrast, remained close – and their friendship led to more than a few questionable scenarios. Most notably, in 1985, Harrison covered an unreleased Dylan song called I Don't Want To Do It for the soundtrack of the teenage nudge-fest Porky's Revenge (strangely, he was not alone: other

> # "Bob's very funny. If you know him and his songs, he's such a joker."
> ## GEORGE HARRISON

contributors included Robert Plant, Phil Collins, Dave Edmunds and Jeff Beck).

Three years later, Harrison performed a welcome favour indeed, placing Dylan on the track that would lead to an overdue creative renaissance. In urgent need of a B-side, Harrison phoned him requesting the use of his Malibu garage studio to record a hastily written Handle With Care with Roy Orbison. After Tom Petty popped over, a party ambience developed and The Traveling Wilburys were born. Working with the jocular supergroup caused the revival in Dylan's spirits that led to 1989's *Oh Mercy*.

"Bob's very funny," Harrison declared of the sessions. "I mean, a lot of people take him seriously and yet if you know Dylan and his songs, he's such a joker, really. Jeff *[Lynne]* just sat down and said, 'OK, what are we gonna do?' And Bob said, 'Let's do one like Prince!' And he just started going, 'Love your sexy body.'"

A true guru indeed.

The Traveling Wilburys, minus the late Roy Orbison, shoot the video for She's My Baby, 1990.

Graham Keen, Neal Preston/Henry Diltz/Corbis

51

Bob Dylan
Bringing It All Back Home

Reaching out: Dyla[n]
recording *Bringin[g]
It All Back Home*
Columbia Studio[s,]
Hollywood, 196[5]

52

Revolution In His Head

In 1965, Dylan walked into Columbia's Studio A. When he left he had invented rock music and presented the world with the exhilarating *Bringing It All Back Home*. By Ben Edmonds. Photos by Daniel Kramer

AS BOB DYLAN PREPARED to record his fifth album for Columbia during January 1965, he had much to ponder. Only 12 months had elapsed since the release of *The Times They Are A-Changin'* but the landscape was already unrecognisable. Beatlemania had come into full, frenzied bloom in 1964, and what might at first have seemed a mere diversion, a four-man hula-hoop, had become a cultural phenomenon. The Beatles had shaken culture to the core, and remade the world.

Bob Dylan had changed dramatically himself. The 22-year-old Greenwich Village folk singer had cemented his position as the most important figure on America's most vibrant music scene. A songbook that included Blowin' In The Wind, Don't Think Twice, A Hard Rain's A-Gonna Fall and With God On Our Side had brought him an unprecedented notoriety.

"I remember witnessing this one cataclysmic moment," says Lovin' Spoonful leader John Sebastian. "Dylan walked into the Gaslight Café and played Hard Rain and Masters Of War. He was trying out this new material, and it was... jaw-dropping. These songs spread like wildfire through the Village. Suddenly everybody just knew these songs. It was unbelievable. It was still a moment when he could be this endearing, Chaplinesque

character, but that was changing. As much as people invested in his songs emotionally, that's how much they seemed to have invested in him."

In an age when heroes are measured in statistics, it's hard to believe any pop figure could matter that much. But Dylan mattered in a way now nearly impossible to convey in words. "What can I say?" chuckles journalist Al Aronowitz unapologetically. "I thought he was the new Messiah. I thought his lyrics were like the words of a new Bible. I still do, though in retrospect it might have been a mistake to trust him with my wife..."

Yet the expectations accompanying

success were troublesome. "You can't imagine what it was like to be Bob Dylan at this time," his late running buddy David Blue noted. "One day he was a respected young songwriter, the next he was this thing. The Voice Of A Generation. The Man With All The Answers. People were at him all the time. Tell me what to think. Tell me where to stand. Tell me who to be. It was relentless. You or I couldn't have stood that kind of pressure. We'd have been crushed by it. Dylan not only stood up to it, he continued to do great work on his own terms in spite of it. But as his life got more surreal, his writing got more surreal. His songs were always true to the life they were written in."

EVEN AS HE was being anointed Woody Guthrie's successor, master of the topical folk song, Dylan had one eye on the door. The sloganeering of what he would soon refer to as his "finger-pointing songs" came easily (on the evidence of The Times They Are A-Changin's title track maybe a little *too* easily) and no longer satisfied its creator. When his search for a way to make his words express more led to a deeper investigation of poetry – particularly the febrile works of 19th-century French enfant terrible Arthur Rimbaud, the original poetry punk – Dylan's writing suddenly took a giant step.

The origins of this new phase can be traced to a three-week American tour undertaken in

February 1964, in which Dylan and road manager Victor Maymudes, folk singer Paul Clayton and journalist Pete Karman (replaced mid-trip by painter and songwriter Bob Neuwirth) drove coast-to-coast in a blue Ford station wagon. Dylan sat in the back, listening to The Beatles on the radio, pecking incessantly at a portable typewriter, fuelled by Beaujolais, cigarettes, the odd Benzedrine, and parcels of marijuana mailed to themselves at various stops along the way, letting the words spill out and watching them dance in new and unexpected ways.

Chimes Of Freedom captured this dramatic expansion of consciousness. Though suggesting yet more topical protest,

Band apart: the *Bringing It All Back Home* sessions, 1965, with drummer Bobby Gregg (back, centre) and guitarist Bruce Langhorne (back, right).

its stream of images aims higher, an elevation of the despised and dispossessed that would have done François Villon, patron poet of the cursed and criminal, proud. This prayer for "every hung-up person in the whole wide universe" was miles away from the new album he was ostensibly touring to promote. And during a Mardi Gras stopover in New Orleans, he began work on a song that would be as far removed from Chimes Of Freedom as that song was from his earlier work. It was called Mr Tambourine Man.

Eric Andersen, another of the Village's young turks, remembers Dylan's return vividly. "I was at Phil Ochs' apartment," he says, "sitting around with Phil and David Blue. There was a knock on the door, and in rushes Bob with Victor Maymudes. They'd literally rolled into town minutes before. Bob sat down on the couch and spread out all the writing he'd done on the road. Pages and pages and pages. Poems, songs, notes, it went on and on. Everything seemed of epic proportions. This was the raw material, and it was amazing to see it all spread out like that. He sang Chimes Of Freedom and stunned everyone. He had bits of Mr Tambourine Man. Bob was excited about what he'd written and wanted us to hear it immediately. He knew he'd tapped into something significant, and the work was pouring out of him."

Dylan had recorded with a band once already, a reluctant 1962 experience seemingly instigated by John Hammond Sr. The undistinguished single, Mixed Up Confusion (available on *Biograph*), contained only the faintest echoes of his adolescent passions for rockabilly and R&B, but one shudders to think what would have happened if they'd followed manager Albert Grossman's suggestion that his client should be backed by a Dixieland band.

THE ALBUM HE cut in one marathon session on June 9, 1964, *Another Side Of Bob Dylan*, wasn't electric, but came as no less a shock to his folk following.

Conspicuously absent were "finger-pointing" songs, the material alternating between poetic and personal. The latter reinforced what John Sebastian terms "Bob's revolutionary approach to the love song. Don't Think Twice and It Ain't Me Babe had been radical compositions. They're romantic, but with an edge, real bite. He had a different way of seeing almost everything."

The August release of *Another Side...* prompted howls of abandonment and wounded lectures from the protest crowd, but they were scolding a space he'd already vacated. While it wasn't rock'n'roll by any known yardstick, many of its songs – Chimes Of Freedom, It Ain't Me Babe, All I Really Want To Do, My Back Pages – would find their way into the repertoires of the bands he was about to make possible.

Shortly after this recording date, Dylan attended a session for his friend John Hammond Jr that was like a musical premonition. Hammond had recorded with an electrified black blues quartet in 1963, pre-dating even the Paul Butterfield Blues Band. For the mid-'64 sessions released the following year as *So Many Roads*, Hammond assembled the best young white players of his acquaintance.

Hammond: "I played Toronto regularly, where I became friendly with a group called Levon & The Hawks. They'd been the backing band for Ronnie Hawkins, and they sort of inherited his touring circuit. They'd play the wild blood 'n' guts clubs on the Jersey shore and then come to New York and play places like Joey Dee's Starlite Lounge. They were an insanely good live band. So I got Robbie Robertson to play guitar, Levon Helm on drums and Garth Hudson on organ. I'd seen Mike Bloomfield, and thought he'd be great alongside Robertson. But when he heard Robbie, suddenly he didn't want to play guitar!

"Robbie was really intense. He had this Telecaster sustain-note reality that was phenomenal; Hubert Sumlin and Roy Buchanan rolled into one, a real gunslinger. So Bloomfield decided he'd rather play piano. Michael had brought Charlie Musselwhite with him from Chicago to play harp. It was Charlie's first time in a studio. Bob stopped by, which was not unusual. That's when I introduced him to the guys in The Hawks. Dylan was there checking it out, and you could tell he was really digging it."

Dylan wasn't the only one in the Village thinking about plugging in. Fred Neil and Tim Hardin both played with amplified accompaniment on occasion, though unassailably in the jazz/blues tradition. One of their regular accompanists, John Sebastian, was also part of a loose cast of adventurous Village musicians assembled by producer Erik Jacobsen to investigate post-Beatle possibilities; others included Jerry Yester, Jesse Colin Young and Felix Pappalardi. Sebastian was about to meet Zal Yanovsky, a refugee from another folk mutation called The Mugwumps (featuring half the future Mamas And The Papas); together they'd hatch The Lovin' Spoonful.

Then, in summer 1964, came The Animals' worldwide Number 1 hit with a tempestuous arrangement of a folk standard tentatively essayed on Dylan's first album. "House Of The Rising Sun in rock," Dylan would marvel. "Rock! It's fuckin' wild! Blew my mind."

"It wasn't surprising to us that Bob would be fascinated with amplified sound," says Sebastian. "We knew that he'd had teenage rock'n'roll bands back in Minnesota; that was common to those of us of a certain age. Some of my earliest memories of Bob involve the two of us sitting in the basement of Gerdes Folk City playing old rock'n'roll, Johnny Cash, gospel, surf music! Buddy Holly was a big favourite. It wasn't all Woody Guthrie."

> "I THOUGHT HE WAS THE NEW MESSIAH, BUT IT MIGHT HAVE BEEN A MISTAKE TO TRUST HIM WITH MY WIFE." AL ARONOWITZ

Mr piano man: the
*Bringing It All Back
Home* sessions, 1965.

Dylan's youthful parade of heroes had been varied, electric and invariably intense. First it was Hank Williams And The Drifting Cowboys, a song machine and a band that kept it moving. Then it was big-beat blues via Gatemouth Page's No-Name Jive radio show.

"Late at night," Dylan told Rolling Stone, "I used to listen to Muddy Waters, John Lee Hooker, Jimmy Reed and Howlin' Wolf, blastin' in from Shreveport. I used to stay up till two, three o'clock in the morning. Listened to all those songs, then tried to figure them out." The piano pounding of Little Richard and the Sun singles of Elvis Presley sealed the deal. As he recalled in 1987, "When I first heard Elvis's voice I just knew that I wasn't going to work for anybody and nobody was gonna be my boss. Hearing him for the first time was like busting out of jail." This validation of the outsider, always central to rock'n'roll, would lead Robert Zimmerman to Woody Guthrie, and it would lead Bob Dylan back to rock'n'roll.

AS HE WOULD sing in Maggie's Farm, in late '64 Dylan had a head full of ideas, driving him insane. You can sense the turmoil on *The Bootleg Series Vol. 6*, the concert recorded at New York's Philharmonic Hall on October 31, where the tension between the old-school finger-pointing of Hard Rain and the good, randy fun of If You Gotta Go, Go Now (essentially pre-plugged rock'n'roll) is palpable. Then there's It's Alright Ma (I'm Only Bleeding), Gates Of Eden and Mr Tambourine Man: complex, deep and powerful lyrics, operating on a whole new level.

Mr Tambourine Man, begun on the station wagon trip in February, had been finished two months later at the New Jersey home of Al Aronowitz. "He stayed at our house a lot," Aronowitz recalls. "This one night he asked to borrow my portable typewriter, which he set up in the breakfast bar off the family room. He said he had something he needed to write. He sat there typing away in a cloud of smoke, listening to Marvin Gaye sing Can I Get A Witness. Every time it ended, he'd have to get up and walk into the living room to put the needle back at the beginning. He played that record over and over and over again while he wrote. I was still hearing Can I Get A Witness as I drifted off to sleep.

"The next morning he played us what he'd stayed up all night writing: Mr Tambourine Man. Is it any wonder I was convinced he was our Shakespeare? Later, as I was taking out the trash, I saw that he'd thrown away his false starts and rough drafts, all sorts of stuff he hadn't used. So I smoothed out the pages and put them in a file, where they remain."

A publisher's acetate of an early version of Mr Tambourine Man, cut at the *Another Side...* session with Ramblin' Jack Elliott singing harmony, had found its way into the hands of Los Angeles hipster Jim Dickson. He was working with The Jet Set, another group of disaffected folkies who'd got an electric shock from The Beatles. Somehow Dickson envisioned Dylan's long, surreal song-poem as a snappy addition to their repertoire. Dickson contends that Dylan dropped by to watch his charges — who'd soon rechristen themselves The Byrds — rehearse the song, exclaiming, "Wow, you can even dance to it!"

Tom Wilson, Dylan's producer since 1963, was intrigued by similar possibilities. A musical adventurer who'd cut his teeth producing Sun Ra and Cecil Taylor, he'd later shepherd the debut recordings of The Velvet Underground and Mothers Of Invention. In December he took three of Dylan's old tracks into the studio and attempted to modernise them with electric overdubs. (Interestingly, he was assisted in this experiment by doo wop icon Dion, then forsaking pop for the folk scene downtown, tracing Dylan's trajectory in

reverse.) The mediocrity of the one track that has surfaced — a pallid replication of The Animals' House Of The Rising Sun arrangement included on the 1994 *Highway 61* CD-ROM — fully explains the obscurity of the rest. The following year Wilson would apply this overdub strategy more successfully to Simon & Garfunkel's The Sound Of Silence.

All of these currents were swirling around Bob Dylan when he set about recording his fifth album in January 1965, but he had no concrete plans. When it comes to recording, planning is not Dylan's thing. "*[The Beatles]* work much more with the studio equipment,

they take advantage of the new sound inventions," he told a Sing Out! interviewer in 1968. "I don't know anything about it. I just do the songs and sing them and that's all."

On the album he would call *Bringing It All Back Home*, his MO was no less mysterious. Despite the precedents pushing him toward electrification, he was looking for a sound nobody had ever heard, by implication a sound that nobody had ever played.

THE FIRST SESSION, on January 13, found Dylan playing solo, with the unlikely addition of John Sebastian on bass. Sebastian was a harmonica virtuoso who could also handle guitar and autoharp, but was completely unfamiliar with bass.

"I told *[Dylan]* I wasn't a bass player," Sebastian says today. "But he just said, 'Don't worry, it'll be fine.' I showed up, was handed a Fender bass, and did the best I could. I don't want to use the word 'tentative', because if Dylan wasn't committed he didn't perform, but I got the distinct impression that this session was for Bob to hear himself and consider his options. He hinted that something more would probably happen, but he wasn't specific. I don't know that we came away with any keepers that day."

They didn't. Dylan acoustically ran through

 ## "BOB SAT DOWN AND SPREAD OUT PAGES AND PAGES AND PAGES OF POEMS, SONGS, NOTES."
FOLK SINGER ERIC ANDERSON

many of the songs he'd subsequently cut with electric backing, plus two unusually tender ballads not destined to make the final cut. I'll Keep It With Mine (included on *Biograph*) and Farewell Angelina (on *The Bootleg Series*) would've been jewels in any other setting, but there was no room for them on an album already bursting its vinyl seams at 47-plus minutes. Also attempted this first day was an obviously major new piece, It's All Over Now, Baby Blue. In light of all that was about to happen — that had in fact been happening for some time now — this was a farewell song that people would have a field

day interpreting. Was it a kiss-off to older singer Paul Clayton, to Dylan's relationship with Joan Baez, to his existing audience, to his former self, or all of the above?

On January 14 and 15, he nailed the album's 11 keepers in an assortment of configurations from solo to full band, the cast shifting continually as the singer searched for the right combination of musical colours. Each band was an ad hoc jumble of seasoned session pros such as drummer Bobby Gregg, guitarist Al Gorgoni and bassist Will Lee (father of filmmaker Spike), friends such as John Sebastian (who'd step aside for Spoonful bassist Steve Boone the following evening) and John Hammond, plus the occasional wild card. In the latter category was Kenny Rankin, a young pop-jazz singer then signed to Columbia, who was not only not a session man, but had never played rock'n'roll – or even an electric guitar – before being drafted by Tom Wilson to do both in the combo that cut Maggie's Farm and On The Road Again.

"I had just begun to play, really," Rankin recalls. "I didn't know many chords, but I guess Tom liked my sense of rhythm. Columbia owned Fender guitars, so they got

laughter that's preserved on the final record, a revolutionary bit of audio verité.

"Oh yes, the famous false start where the band forgets to come in," Langhorne laughs. "Well, we didn't forget. We had no idea to begin with! The band didn't know anything about the tune. Bob would just step to the microphone and launch into a song. No warning, no explanation, no nothing. We'd just leap in and try to keep up. Somehow everybody found a way to tune in to what Bob was going for. He didn't really know what he wanted, but his absolute certainty about the songs pulled us all behind in its wake. He didn't try to arrange people's performances. It was spontaneous, almost telepathic. We had to catch the moment, because there was no going back and fixing things with overdubs. I thoroughly enjoyed myself."

Dylan appeared to agree. Despite his short musical attention span and the shifting personnel, he attacked each song with relish.

"There's a picture that really captures that moment for me," says Sebastian. "Bob and I are playing guitars to each other, just goofing off and stomping in the studio before tape started rolling. I was singing to him, 'I got a car

sessions show someone who often can't contain his glee. He's transported back to the kid who, friends recall, upon hearing Rock Around The Clock in the 1955 film Blackboard Jungle shouted, "Hey, that's our music! That's written for us." In the aftermath of Buddy Holly's tragic death he'd come to feel that rock-'n'roll no longer spoke for him. Now, a decade later, he was reclaiming its voice for his own.

Nowhere is this illustrated more exhilaratingly than on Subterranean Homesick Blues. This first-take masterpiece swings like crazy (at a tempo that trims the time of the previous day's acoustic version by a full half-minute), bringing out a rhythmic swagger in Dylan's singing that marks it as not simply inspired by Chuck Berry's Too Much Monkey Business but a true inheritor of its tradition, another link in the linguistic chain that would lead to rap. But notwithstanding that obvious debt, this is rock'n'roll that has little to do with Berry's contained duckwalk; it's a rattling noise that these musicians rustled up off the top of their heads. It existed in this moment and then never again. Adding to the record's feel is a somewhat buried but nonetheless historic fuzztone guitar, this being a good five months before The Rolling Stones sparked garageland fuzzmania with Satisfaction.

"THERE WAS NO INSTRUCTION. HE'D JUST START PLAYING, AND YOU BETTER BE READY."

GUITARIST KENNY RANKIN

me a Telecaster and I sat down and played rhythm. I didn't know anybody else who was there. There was minimal soundcheck; they got basic balances and checked the mike. There was no rehearsal to speak of, no charts, and no instructions I can recall. Dylan would just start playing, and you'd better be ready. We did our best to fall into a groove behind him. There might be two takes, if that. It was almost a blur. There wasn't much interaction with anybody. I didn't even shake his hand. I don't think we exchanged a word."

Lead guitarist Bruce Langhorne played the previous day, but the approach was the same. His band was the one that fails to start playing at the beginning of Bob Dylan's 115th Dream, causing the take to break down into the

it's a white convertible/I race down the highway in my white convertible/My white convertible.' It was a song I used to play in teen bands, probably a local record that came out of some New Jersey garage. Nothing profound; just good dumb fun."

THE SESSIONS RECONNECTED Dylan with what it was like to crank it up and play, the exhilarating rush he'd gotten from his high school combos The Shadow Blasters and Elston Gunn & The Rock Boppers.

For a man who prided himself on the infrequency of his smiles – he and Neuwirth reportedly attended the funniest movies they could find for the express purpose of training themselves not to laugh – photos from these

Maggie's Farm, cut the final day with a different band, is almost as good: a song of surreal defiance that musicologists say is derived in part from Pete Seeger's Down On Penny's Farm. (Some of the cadences of Subterranean Homesick Blues can be traced to Taking It Easy, a song Seeger wrote with Woody Guthrie; does this make folk patriarch Pete one of the secret collaborators in Dylan's 'sell-out' to rock'n'roll?) Outlaw Blues and On The Road Again are based on fairly generic blues-rock progressions, but what a joyful, sloppy noise they make. The words of his rockers detail frustration with a world turned inside out, but it's like he's lining up shadows for this amplified racket to blast away.

The album's non-rock material is as big a revelation. Love Minus Zero/No Limit and She

Time out: Dylan with producer Tom Wilson (left) and with John Sebastian at the album's sessions.

Belongs To Me are softer full-band performances that give the electric side its breathing room; the former is tender, the other seductively mean-spirited. Rick Nelson, whose records the teen Zimmerman admired, took a country-inflected She Belongs To Me into the American Top 40 in 1969 (and his version of outtake If You Gotta Go may be definitive). Nelson, who died in 1985, once told this writer, "She Belongs To Me is sung like a love song, but it's not really a love song, is it? It's something different, darker. I was a fan of Dylan's folk songs. Who wasn't? But this was the album that really did it for me, because it seemed to contain everything you'd ever need."

The four acoustic songs that comprise side two were cut on the third and final day of

recording. Dylan is known for trying different arrangements, tempos and doorways into his material. But the three of these songs he'd been playing live – Mr Tambourine Man, It's All Right Ma (I'm Only Bleeding), Gates Of Eden – hadn't changed; their development was about Dylan's command of them, each performance another step toward this moment of committing them to tape. As impressive as these songs had been at the Philharmonic Hall only weeks before, the performances here reduce all previous versions to mere sketches.

In the text accompanying his 1967 book of Dylan photographs, Daniel Kramer recounted how the singer recorded all three in one continuous, uninterrupted take. Talking

today, Kramer says it may have been only two songs. Session logs point toward It's Alright Ma and Gates Of Eden, still a formidable accomplishment.

"My memory is a bit hazy," Kramer admits, "because I was involved in photographing the moment rather than watching it. But I definitely remember Bob announcing to the booth that he was going to do these numbers straight through once and once only, and they better not make any mistakes because he wasn't going to do it again. And that's exactly what he did. No false starts, no stumbles, no mistakes. Magic was being made right in front of our eyes."

It took six takes to get Mr Tambourine Man. But what they got – with only the singer's

acoustic guitar and harmonica, and the firefly electric lines of Langhorne – is not simply the perfect expression of the "new" Dylan he'd discovered on the station wagon odyssey, but a performance for the ages. He admitted years later that he'd once tried to write a follow-up to this song and failed miserably.

THE EXPANDED HEADWORLD of *Bringing It All Back Home* was perfectly captured in Daniel Kramer's cover photograph. Taken in Albert Grossman's Woodstock living room, it features an intense Dylan, in a dark jacket and holding a blue-gray cat, making full eye contact with the camera. Grossman's wife, Sally, in a red dress, lounges on the couch behind him, while various objects are scattered about the room – paintings, a fallout shelter sign, a glass sculpture by the singer, and albums by Lord Buckley, Robert Johnson, Eric von Schmidt, Lotte Lenya, The Impressions. His most recent album *Another Side...* is tucked away in the background, suddenly as antique as the 18th century painting on the mantle behind it. The edges of the square image are blurred in a circular fashion, lending an extra touch of unreality to this portrait of what appears to be the world's first psychedelic classical composer.

"No one had seen Dylan look like that before," says Kramer with justified pride. Indeed, each time you saw a new picture of the singer in this 1964-66 period he looked a little different, like some giant alien flower slowly unfolding.

"This was my first album cover," explains the photographer. "I knew that the music was special and different, so I didn't want the image to have any relationship to anything people would recognise. Until this, Dylan wouldn't pose for me; he preferred that I capture him in motion.

"On the morning of the shoot I made a rough test shot without Bob in it, and he grasped immediately what I was going for. He selected many of the objects. I selected some, and Sally probably put something in. It got too crowded at one point, a little too over-produced, and we had to back off. This was decades before Photoshop, so the blurry effect was something I had to create by hand. I built a rig that

Bob Dylan
Bringing It All Back Home

enabled me to rotate the camera, and the shot combines static and moving exposures. I wanted it to feel like the universe moving around him."

The cover would be almost as revolutionary as its contents, but the record company fought it.

"The Columbia art director didn't like it," Kramer explains. "He hadn't wanted me to do it. He resented being presented with a guy who'd never done an album cover. But Albert Grossman said in no uncertain terms that I was doing it, and that was that. The art director wasn't going to like anything I did; it was a rather uncomfortable political moment. I got to laugh about it later, though. The cover was nominated for a Grammy and the art director was nominated along with me, so our names are linked forever."

Eric Andersen was also around when Dylan heard the first acetate of *Bringing It All Back Home*. "It was at Albert Grossman's townhouse in Gramercy Park," he says. "Me, Bob, Joan Baez, my first wife Debbie Green, Bobby Neuwirth. It was the first time anybody had heard the album. Bob put it on this rickety old record player and turned it up. He was obviously happy. We were dancing around the room for the entire length of the first side, and we were transported by the performances on side two. It was like the old Ezra Pound adage that the further the words are from the music, and the further the music is from the dance, the poetry atrophies. Dylan got them all together. He got people tapping their feet and listening to the lyrics at the same time. I remember Joan dancing around the room with Neuwirth. It was exciting. Bob felt he'd succeeded in pushing himself to someplace new, a place he'd never been before. I flashed back on that time when he'd returned from the road trip and played us Chimes Of Freedom, so excited about the artistic leap he was making. It seemed like a lifetime ago, but it was only a few months."

JOAN BAEZ LATER recanted her Funky Chicken. "I didn't like what he was doing," she said of Dylan's folk rock. "It was haphazard, and it was sloppy and too negative for me. There was hardly anything positive in it. I thought he just went one step too far in a very negative direction."

Bringing It All Back Home begins the trilogy of electric albums – continued with *Highway 61 Revisited* later in '65 and *Blonde On Blonde* the following year – that touched off a firestorm of controversy, flames Dylan did his best to stoke with his blasphemous electric set at the 1965 Newport Folk Festival and the ensuing world tour with The Hawks. Yet from today's standpoint, the wails of abandonment emanating from the folk establishment seem ludicrously overstated. Dylan's ramshackle new music was no commercial sell-out, no emulation of Merseybeat chart rock. In fact, the one song that might have fit that bill, If You're Gonna Go, Go Now, didn't make the album (freeing it to become a hit for Manfred Mann).

Unlike Richard Fariña, who'd used electric instruments as props on a couple of songs, Dylan was engaged in the serious search for a new musical language, one that could keep up with the advances he'd made as a writer. While it is true that side one of this album represents his first steps toward this language, a style he would further explore and refine, no album in the Dylan catalogue contains as much joy, even when he's expressing paranoia or cataloguing madness. There's the joy in his heightened level of word play, and in the elemental act of play that has turned countless garages into the walls of Jericho. Joan Baez thought she knew Bob Dylan, but she'd never met Elston Gunn, the Shadow Blaster.

Decades on we can hear that this supposed sell-out is as dense with social insight as any album he ever recorded, and contains a higher concentration of unforgettable lines: "Money doesn't talk, it swears"; "There's no success like failure, and failure's no success at all"; "You don't need a weatherman to know which way the wind blows"; "He not busy being born is busy dying". Then there's the one so many Americans were hoping to trot out after the last election: "Even the President of the

Hustlin': Dylan takes a break, Kingston, New York, 1965.

United States must sometimes have to stand naked." And, perhaps most pointedly, "Don't follow leaders".

There are those who have interpreted the electric-side/acoustic-side format as timidity on Dylan's part, an unwillingness to fully commit to the new music. But there's a larger picture. What we find here is every song taken on its own terms and getting what it needed.

On the electric side are acoustic songs with a rhythm section; on the acoustic side he is sometimes supported by an electric guitar. No song is denied anything, and what he is saying is that anything is possible. Dylan abhorred the term "folk rock". He preferred to call this "vision music", and it is less about a new style than it is the expression of a new consciousness.

Much was made of the impact on the folk scene of Dylan's departure, but nothing

"YOU'VE GOT TO DO SOMETHING ABOUT THIS BOB DYLAN – HE'S KILLING US!"

FREDDIE GARRITY, FREDDIE & THE DREAMERS

would be the same after this album. Label executive Andy Wickham recalls Freddie Garrity of Freddie And The Dreamers screaming at him, "You've got to do something about this Bob Dylan – he's killing us!" Dylan had slipped the expectations of his folk audience, but in creating a new rock audience he also created a new set of expectations, another trap he'd eventually have to extricate himself from.

For the present, however, while he waited for the album's March release, he was still doing a dance with his past. There was a joint tour with Joan Baez in February, the king and queen of folk music lording over a kingdom that was already a memory. From there he'd go on the Don't Look Back tour of England, where The Times They Are A-Changin' had become an unexpected hit single. Was that two or three Bob Dylan masks ago? No matter. With *Bringing It All Back Home* he had made a map of his future, and ours.

Plugged in: Dylan gives Newport its first ever glimpse of a Fender Stratocaster.

DYLAN GOES ELECTRIC

It had to happen: Bob Dylan ditching his acoustic direction, strapping on a Stratocaster and revealing his new musical direction. Folkies were forced to put their fingers in *both* ears…

JULY 24, 1965
First day of the Newport Folk Festival.

JAC HOLZMAN (*Elektra Records founder*) The event of the folk year was the Newport Folk Festival. George Wein, who was also founder of the Newport Jazz Festival and an accomplished jazz pianist himself, launched it in 1954. I went every year from the first. You'd see all the people you normally would run across in New York or LA, but out of the city there was time for relaxation that transcended business or party loyalties.

JOE BOYD (*festival production manager*) The 1965 Folk Festival came at a time when, on the radio, you were hearing I Got You Babe by Sonny & Cher, which was obviously a Dylan rip-off, Like A Rolling Stone, The Byrds singing Mr Tambourine Man. Things were changing. There was a tremendous anticipation at Newport about Dylan. He arrived rather secretively. He was staying in a luxurious hotel just on the outside of town, and he arrived with Bob Neuwirth and Al Kooper. They were all wearing puff-sleeved duelling shirts, and they were wearing not blue jeans but some kinda trousers. And they wore sunglasses. The whole image was very, very different. They [the festival organisers] were tense because things were happening in the air that summer that they didn't

understand . They were very paranoid about people smoking marijuana, for example.

DONOVAN It was my first big festival, and to be doing the Newport Folk Festival was much more comfortable, obviously. Joan Baez and Pete Seeger had told America that here is an important figure in our folk world arriving, which was marvellous. I can understand now what the shock must have been, for any change, because the audience were in Bermuda shorts and bobbysocks and short hair. I mean, it hadn't happened yet.

JONATHAN TAPLIN (*Dylan's road manager*) Albert Grossman, after hearing that Bob wanted to play electric, hastily put a band together. And the only guys who had electric instruments were Paul Butterfield's band.

AL KOOPER (*organist*) I didn't go to the '65 Newport Folk Festival with Dylan. I went as a regular person who always just bought tickets and went. But Albert Grossman, his manager, saw me walking around and said, "Hey, Bob is looking for you." And so he gave me passes and I sold my tickets.

JB All of the performers did what they called workshops during the day, just small performances on the small stages around the grounds. Dylan was scheduled to sing in the songwriter's workshop. Unlike the previous years, when there was always a good spread of attendance between workshops, this year the crowd around the songwriter's workshop was so immense that it was swamping the others. This was very much against the spirit of what the festival was supposed to be about, and the officials were starting to get tense. The flashpoint came at the blues workshop at the end of the day.

JH On the Saturday afternoon there was a blues workshop. Alan Lomax was hosting the black traditionalists. Alan was the son of John Lomax, two great white musical archivists and collectors, for whom traditional music seemed to freeze-frame about the time of the Tennessee Valley Authority.

JB There had been a lot of pressure from Peter Yarrow [of Peter, Paul & Mary] on adding the Paul Butterfield Blues Band to the line-up. He really put a lot of pressure on the other members of the board to get the invitation, and Lomax was really against it.

JH The second segment of the workshop was slated to be white urban blues, featuring the Butterfield Band. Due to the amazing sales of Born In Chicago on the Elektra sampler, I had arranged for them to perform at Newport. Albert Grossman was in full hover over them [the Paul Butterfield Blues Band] as future clients.

JB Grossman became a focus of hostility for a lot of people. He'd never been popular among these people. Grossman was arrogant, particularly with Dylan now being so big.

JH The crowd at the blues workshop was enormous. Instead of a few hundred this one had nearly a thousand.

> ## "That first note of Maggie's Farm was the loudest thing anybody ever heard."
> **JOE BOYD, NEWPORT PRODUCTION MANAGER**

©David Gahr

MICHAEL BLOOMFIELD (*guitarist, Butterfield Blues Band*) What we played was music that was entirely indigenous to the neighbourhood, to the city we grew up in. There was no doubt in my mind that this was folk music; this was what I heard on the streets of my city, on radio stations and jukeboxes in Chicago and all throughout the South, and it was what people listened to.

JB Lomax gave the Butterfield Blues Band a very condescending introduction at the blues workshop.

PAUL ROTHCHILD (*producer, Elektra Records*) He got up and said something like, "Today you've been hearing music by the great blues players, guys who go out and find themselves an old cigar box, put a stick on it, attach some strings, sit under a tree and play great blues for themselves. Now you're going to hear a group of young boys from Chicago with electric instruments. Let's see if they can play this hardware at all."

JB As the group started to take to the stage, Lomax came off to be confronted by Grossman who, basically, said unkind words about the introduction Lomax had just given. Lomax just pushed him aside and said, "Out of my way, Grossman!". And the next thing you know these two men, both rather over-sized, were rolling around in the dirt throwing punches. They had to be pulled apart.

JH It was Al "If I Had A Hammer" Grossman versus Alan "Mighty Defender Of The Status Quo" Lomax. One very short round, split decision.

JB Lomax called an emergency meeting of the board of the Festival that night – the board voted in favour of banning Grossman from the grounds of the Festival. George Wein, who was a non-voting advisor to the board, had to step in and say, "Look, I don't have a vote, it's up to you, but I can tell you right now that if you do bar Grossman, you have to prepare yourselves for the walk-out of Bob Dylan, Peter, Paul & Mary and Buffy St Marie." So the board dropped the action.

AK Me and Bob and the Butterfield Blues Band rehearsed through the night in the living room of some millionaire's mansion in Newport. By sunrise, we had three songs down.

MB We were all at Newport, Kooper, me, Barry [*Goldberg, keyboardist*], and this guy Jerome [*Arnold*] from the Butterfield Band playing bass and he's fucking up on everything, and we're practising there in a room and we're playing and it's sounding horrible and, finally, it's time for the gig and Barry and me are throwing up in these outhouses at the house.

JULY 25

Bob Dylan is booed off the stage for introducing electric instruments into his music. Donovan and Joan Baez appear at the same show.

JB We had known that Dylan was going to do something with more than just himself. There'd been rumours of secret rehearsals and that he was going to need a soundcheck. I went to Grossman and said, "You guys, we want you to have a soundcheck. Do you want a soundcheck?" And he said, "You bet we want a soundcheck."

JONATHAN TAPLIN We kicked everybody out of the stadium and did a short soundcheck, which Peter Yarrow was mixing.

JB So on came Dylan with the Butterfield Band and Al Kooper on keyboards. We set up the stage the way they wanted it set up. They started playing. We all knew that this was significant. I said, "How many songs are you going to do?" And they looked at each other and said, "Well, we only know three, so that's what we're going to do."

AK We had stayed up all night rehearsing and only got three songs together. I'm not so sure Dylan wanted to play more than that. I think the whole thing was semi-spontaneous about him doing an electric set. He could've gone out and played acoustic, which I think was his original plan when he got in the car to drive up there.

JT The problem was the rhythm section. They were great blues players, but Dylan didn't play 12-bar music. He played very bizarre music in terms of its structure. So they didn't really understand what was going on at all. And Bob refused to do much of a rehearsal.

PETE SEEGER (*folk singer*) It wasn't a real soundcheck. They were tinkering around with it and all they knew was, "Turn the sound up. Turn the sound up!"

JB Dylan wasn't on at the end of the concert. He was on one act before the interval, at around 9.15.

LIAM CLANCY (*folk singer*) I was actually filming at the Newport Festival that year. I was up a 12-foot platform with a telephoto lens. And Dylan came out, and it was obvious that he was stoned, bobbing around the stage.

PR I was at the console, mixing the set, the only one there who had ever recorded electric music. I could barely hear Dylan because of the furore.

JB Care was taken to get Paul Rothschild to mix the sound. Because you didn't want

> **"I saw Dylan backstage and he seemed to be crying."**
> JONATHAN TAPLIN, ROAD MANAGER

some square sound guy fumbling with the dials. You would have had just badly mixed rock'n'roll. It wasn't. It was powerfully, ballsily-mixed, expertly done rock'n'roll, and when that first note of Maggie's Farm hit it was the loudest thing anybody had ever heard.

AK In Maggie's Farm, the beat got turned around so, instead of playing on two and four, [*drummer*] Sam Lay was playing on one and three. That's an accident that can happen, and it did, so it was sort of a disaster.

JB I ran around to the press enclosure and watched at the side of the stage and I thought, This is great! Somebody pulled at

my elbow and said, "You'd better go backstage. They want to talk to you."

JH Backstage, an un-civil war had broken out. Alan Lomax was bellowing that this was a folk festival, you just didn't have amplified instruments.

PAUL ROTHCHILD The old guard... George Wein, Alan Lomax, Pete Seeger. Pete, pacifist Pete, with an axe, saying, "I'm going to cut the cables!"

JB So I went backstage and there I was confronted by Seeger and Lomax and Theodore Bikel or somebody, saying, "It's too loud. You've got to turn it down. It's far too loud. We can't have it like this." And they were really very upset. I said, "I don't control the sound. The sound is out there in the middle of the audience." And so Lomax said, "How

do you get there?" I said, "Well, Alan, you walk right to the back — it's only about half a mile — and then you walk around to the centre thing, show your badge, and just come down the centre aisle." And he said, "There must be a quicker way." So I said, "Well, you can climb over the fence." I was looking at his girth, you know? And he said, "Go out there and tell them that the board orders them to turn the sound down." So I went out. By this time, it was the beginning of the second number.

AK Tombstone Blues was fine, and we did Like A Rolling Stone real good.

JH This was electricity married to content. We were hearing music with lyrics that had meaning, with a rock beat, drums and electric guitars. Absolutely stunning. All the parallel strains of music over the years coalesced for

Man in a van: Dylan prepares for his Songwriter Workshop performance. Note early outbreak of earache.

me in that moment. Then suddenly we heard booing, like pockets of wartime flak. The audience had split into two separate and opposing camps. It grew into an awesome barrage of catcalls and hisses. It was very strange, because I couldn't believe that those people weren't hearing the wonderful stuff I was hearing.

RIC VON SCHMIDT (folk singer) Whoever was controlling the mikes messed it up. You couldn't hear Dylan. It looked like he was singing with the volume off.

JB There was Grossman and Neuwirth and Yarrow and Rothchild all sitting at the sound desk, grinning, very pleased with themselves and, meanwhile, the audience was going nuts. Some people were booing, some people were cheering.

Dylan's hastily assembled band at Sunday's soundcheck: (from left) Mike Bloomfield, Sam Lay, a passing stagehand, Jerome Arnold, Dylan, Al Kooper.

I relayed Lomax's message and Peter Yarrow said, "Tell Alan Lomax…" and extended his middle finger. I said, "Come on, Peter, gimme a break." He said, "Well, just tell Alan that the board are adequately represented on the sound console and that we have things fully under control and we think that the sound is at the correct level." So I went back, climbed over the fence and all I could see of Pete Seeger was his back disappearing down the road past the car park.

JH Pete Seeger was beside himself, jumped into a car and rolled up the windows, his hands over his ears.

BOB DYLAN I did this very crazy thing. I didn't know what was going to happen, but they certainly booed. I'll tell you that. You could hear it all over the place.

AK The reason they booed is because he only played for 15 minutes and everybody else played for 45 minutes to an hour, and he was the headliner of the festival. They were feeling ripped off. Wouldn't you? The fact that he was playing electric… I don't know. Earlier in the festival, The Paul Butterfield Blues Band had played electric, and the crowd didn't seem too incensed. What was I thinking at the time? I was thinking we weren't playing too good.

PR From my perspective, it seemed like everybody on my left wanted Dylan to get off, everybody on my right wanted him to turn it up. And I did. I turned it up.

JB Dylan had been scheduled for 40 minutes – certainly half an hour. People had not come all that way to see 20 minutes of Bob Dylan,

or 15. So Yarrow was all poised to go up on stage and, suddenly, they'd finished.

JH Dylan was hurt, angry and shaken.

AK A large part of that crowd had come especially to see Dylan. Some had travelled thousands of miles and paid a lot of money for tickets, and what did they get? Three songs, and one of those was a mess. They didn't give a shit about us being electric. They just wanted more.

JB There was a huge roar from the crowd. You know, "more" and "boo" sound very similar if you have a whole crowd going "more" and "boo". I think it was evenly divided between approbation and condemnation from the crowd. This roar went on for quite some time.

JH Peter Yarrow took the stage again, very

JB Anyway, finally, Dylan stumbled back out on stage with an acoustic guitar.

JT He says, "Does anybody have a D harmonica?" And all these harmonicas were thrown from the audience.

LC He broke into Tambourine Man and I found myself standing there with tears streaming down my face, because I saw the immense value of what the man was about.

JT The audience thought they'd won. Here was Dylan, no band, back into acoustic folk stuff. And then he sang It's All Over Now, Baby Blue and walked off.

JH And Dylan and folk music and Elektra were never the same again.

JB Right after him were this amazing group of black gospel singers, the Moving Star Singers, and then there was the interval. After the interval, the scheduling misfired and every washed-up, boring old folky left-wing fart you could imagine in a row, leading up to Peter, Paul & Mary in the final thing — Ronnie Gilbert, Oscar Brand, Josh White, Theodore Bikel — they all went on, one after another. It was like an object lesson in what was going on here. Like, you guys are all washed-up. This is all finished.

JT It was unbelievably dramatic. At the party afterwards Dylan was pretty much by himself. It was clear that he didn't like what had happened.

MARIA MULDAUR *(singer)* Dylan was off in a corner, buried, and *[singer]* Richard Fariña told me to go over and ask Dylan to dance.

So I went over to him and said, "Do you want to dance?" and he looked up at me and said, "I would, but my hands are on fire."

MB The next night, he was at this party, and he's sitting next to this girl and her husband, and he's got his hand right up her pussy and she's letting him do this, and her husband's going crazy... so Dylan seemed quite untouched by it the next day.

IZZY YOUNG *(proprietor Folklore Center, New York and friend of Dylan)* Most books on folk music today state that folk music in the USA began with the Kingston Trio in 1958 and ended with Bob Dylan playing electric at the Newport Festival in 1965. But I was there and didn't think that it was important enough to write about in Sing Out!, which everyone read at the time. Who cares if Alan Lomax and Al Grossman fought over being the biggest macho around, or if a few kids booed because they had to wait for an encore?

PR To me, that night at Newport was as clear as crystal. It's the end of one era and the beginning of another. There's no historical precedent. This is a folk festival; you couldn't even say it's blues and the blues has moved to an electric format.

JB The thing I cherish about that evening was that there are a lot of occasions when you can look back and say, "Well, after that night, things were never the same." But it's very rare that you're in a moment where you know it at the time. You knew, as it was happening, that paths were parting.

PR There were two very big passions happening here. And it was an election. You had to choose which team you were going to support. I expected Peter Yarrow to join with the future, because of his peer group and his dedication to Dylan, whose songs had made Peter, Paul & Mary's success so resounding. At the same time it changed Peter's professional life. Peter, Paul & Mary were acoustic folk singers, and Peter had to know that their moment had passed. But Peter's commitment was to the future.

Jac Holzman could just as easily have joined with the Newport board of directors, the Weins, the Lomaxes, the Seegers, and said, "No electric music!" But he didn't. I was very proud of Jac at that moment, watching him choose the unknown rather than the comfort of the known.

JT I ended up working with Dylan, touring all over the world, for two years, and he was booed everywhere. Every time. He would play the first half folk, with just harmonica and guitar, and the second half rock'n'roll, and get booed.

> ## "It was the end of one era and the beginning of another. There's no historical precedent."
> ### PAUL ROTHCHILD, PRODUCER

rattled. He attempted to rally support, urging the audience on until there was enough positive emotion that Dylan could return with dignity.

JB Dylan was hiding in a tent. Grossman didn't want to get involved. He wasn't going to bully Dylan about it.

JT I saw Dylan backstage from a little bit of a distance, and he seemed to be crying. Johnny Cash came up and gave him a big jumbo Gibson guitar, much too big for Bob, and told him to go back out there.

AK I was standing right next to Bob backstage and not only was he not crying, he was feeling good about having played electric. That's when Peter Yarrow came up and handed him an acoustic guitar, because the set was so short he felt there should be more.

"Sign this, would you Bob?" Dylan and Donovan backstage.

The Stories

Just Like A Woman

Folk superstars, tarot readers and
backing singers – he loved
them all. Right from the
start of his career, Dylan
was rarely short of
female admirers. By
Lucy O'Brien

Knock knockin' on
women's doors: Dylan
meets some special
fans, Belfast, 1966.

"Dirt on women is very attractive. It triggers the animal emotions. I want dirty long hair hanging all over the place," Bob Dylan told '60s women's magazine McCall's. Bob rarely went for skinny blonde models. He liked "real" woman he could talk to, could act as his muse. He also went for buxom types and "witchy women" who read tarot cards or, like one squeeze on Rolling Thunder, specialised in tightrope walking.

It's perhaps testament to Dylan's charms that few women have ever bitched about him. According to biographer Clinton Heylin, "Dylan never drops out of somebody's life. He always keeps in touch with ex-lovers."

Dylan has always had a host of lady friends. But apart, maybe, from Joan Baez, he has never had a relationship with someone who could artistically challenge him. "He didn't have a relationship with Joni Mitchell, for example," remarks Heylin. "That would have ended in mass murder."

From the beginning, then…

Greenwich Village, Ja
1962: Suze Rotolo ho
onto her man, but no
long. Below: And you
Joan Baez went to
extraordinary length
impress her old flame

Suze Rotolo

"HE WAS CHARISMATIC. Even though he was one of the imitators of Woody Guthrie, he had something of his own," recalled Suze Rotolo of the first time she saw Dylan at Gerde's Folk City, New York, in 1961.

Rotolo was 17, the daughter of a cultured, left-wing political family. In high school she was involved with the civil rights movement and her heroes were poets rather than movie stars. A central figure in Dylan's life at an important period of his career, she inspired many songs, including Boots Of Spanish Leather.

Dylan "had an impish kind of personality, like Harpo Marx," Rotolo says in Victoria Balfour's book Rock Wives. "He said he was going to be very big. I took it seriously… but had no idea what it meant."

After a short time flirting they moved into a little apartment on West 4th Street and were "very exclusive… in many ways, we kept to ourselves. He would never want anybody to come over… he made me paranoid and distrustful." This, it seems, was bound up with his rising profile. Once he signed to Columbia, Dylan began snubbing old friends. Rotolo's sister Carla and her mother Mary were not amused: Mrs Rotolo's nickname for Dylan was "Twerp".

In 1962 Rotolo had the opportunity to go to take a summer course at the University of Perugia in Italy. During their nine-month separation Dylan was distraught but Rotolo blossomed. She realised that, "I didn't want to be a string on his guitar… I hadn't started yet." When she came back their relationship deteriorated. They appeared as the loving couple on the cover of his 1963 album The Freewheelin' Bob Dylan, but deep down things were amiss.

According to Carla, as Dylan grew famous Rotolo grew "vegetable-like". The situation came to a head in March 1964 when Rotolo had a hysterical row with him about Ballad In Plain D. One of his most autobiographical songs, it brims with regret and desperation.

Rotolo found him "too negative, too pessimistic" with "a death-like quality" that frightened her. At the same time he was very sharp and resilient. "He created an image as the abandoned lover. I'm sure he was having a fine time also," she said ruefully.

In the end Rotolo opted to live her own life, they parted and she eventually married. Dylan called her out of the blue in the mid-'70s but she decided not to see him. She now lives in New York with her film-editor husband and family. And, although there was bitterness when they split, Rotolo has fond memories of Dylan, appreciating the fact that she was the inspiration for so many early songs.

Joan Baez

BAEZ HAS FAMOUSLY been called the Yin to Dylan's Yang. Together they were known as the "King and Queen of Folk", but it was never an easy relationship. Some commentators believe that, on Dylan's side anyway, it was more about a judicious career move than love.

Whatever, there was an attraction between the two that grew during the summer of '63, when Dylan was splitting up with Rotolo. The 22-year-old Baez was content to have Dylan as her protégé, while he seemed to be infatuated with Baez, who already had an established identity. Half-Mexican, half-Scots, Baez had broken through at the Newport Folk Festival in 1959 and, with her silvery voice and political nous, soon became a generational spokeswoman.

Baez first met Dylan when he was playing in New York in 1961, but was reportedly not impressed with his raggedy image. Within two years, though, she had become a convert. They met again after a show in 1963 and the two started a romance. During her appearance at the Newport Folk Festival that year, Baez announced: "This song is about a love affair that has lasted too long," before launching into Don't Think Twice. Suze Rotolo, who was in the audience,

Ken Regan/Camera5, Ted Russell/Polaris/Eyevine

blanched, got up and walked out. Baez then brought Dylan onto the stage to join her singing his With God On Our Side. More than 13,000 people saw Dylan that night. He had gone to Newport as a cult underground artist and, thanks to Baez, left as a star.

On a subsequent mini-tour with Baez the exposure for Dylan was immense, though it was a professional risk for her. "I was getting audiences of up to 10,000 and dragging my little vagabond out onto the stage was a grand experiment," she says in Heylin's biography Behind The Shades. "The people who had not heard of Bob were often infuriated and sometimes even booed him." By the time the tour ended in Queens, though, Dylan won as much applause as Baez.

The royal pair continued their on-off love affair for two years but, by 1964, the strain was showing. as he resisted her overtures to fully embrace political protest. For Dylan, songs such as Maggie's Farm and It's All Over Now, Baby Blue were personal statements of rebellion; he was less interested in aligning him-

self to a particular movement. "Bobby and I are just direct opposites. It took me a long time to figure that out," sighed Baez.

Matters worsened when Baez joined Dylan on his 1965 UK tour (filmed for the movie Don't Look Back). Less well known in the UK, Baez expected Dylan to return the favour and introduce her at his shows. He had no intention of doing so, and spent most of the trip ignoring her. The result was distraught scenes off-camera: Baez broke down, while Dylan's sidekick Bob Neuwirth begged her to go home.

Baez realised it was all over when she called to see Dylan one day after he had a bout of food poisoning and Sara Lownds (his eventual wife) answered the door. They would not sing together again for 10 years, yet in 1969 Baez released Any Day Now, an album of Dylan's songs, and in 1975 sang about him on her own song Diamonds And Rust. Baez criticised Dylan as being a "huge transparent bubble of ego", yet at the same time admitted, "whether or not he decides to join forces with the human race, he's a genius."

By the mid-'70s their relationship had mellowed enough for Baez to join him on the Rolling Thunder tour. Since then she has continued to perform worldwide, and released her first album in six years with 2003's Dark Chords On A Big Guitar. Baez now seems to have adopted a gently mocking view of Dylan. Even if it was a case of two egos clashing, they influenced each other deeply at a key point in both their lives.

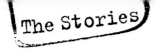

Woodstock, 1968: short-lived domestic bliss with former Playboy bunny Sara Lowds. Below: What first attracted millionaire Bob to "ample" blues singer Dana Gillespie?

Marianne Faithfull

FAITHFULL MET DYLAN during his 1965 UK tour when she was engaged to, and pregnant by, underground impresario John Dunbar. "He came to town wearing Phil Spector shades, an aureole of hair and seething irony," she said in her autobiography. "Dylan was... nothing less than the hippest person on Earth."

Faithfull wangled her way into Dylan's hotel room at the Savoy and spent two weeks hanging out nervously with God and his crew, "trying to look beautiful". When she finally found herself alone with him, he "sat down in a big overstuffed hair and stared at me for so long that I thought I was going to dissolve."

He then went through his new album, *Bringing It All Back Home*, with her track by track. Apparently this was his way of making a pass, but Faithfull was too terrified to respond. He accused her of leading him on, tore up a poem he'd been writing about her and threw her out. "The saddest thing for me was not that we didn't go to bed together," recalls Faithfull, "but that I never got to see that poem."

Dana Gillespie

THE BRITISH BLUES singer first met Dylan on his 1965 English tour when she was 16. "I was about to be slung out of a party by some bouncers. Bob came up, kissed me and saved me by inferring I was with him. He was very chivalrous."

They saw each other whenever he came to England and built up an enduring friendship. In New York in 1973, after finishing a soundcheck at Reno Sweeney's, Gillespie walked out to find Dylan buying a ticket for her show. "I thought that was so nice."

Some suggest Bob was entranced by her 44-inch bust. Gillespie shrugs. "He's supposed to go for buxom women, but most of them have been flat-chested."

In 1998 Dylan rang asking her to support him on tour. When she asked why he said, "You're a great songwriter. And you've always been nice."

Gillespie assigns his dark side to the past. "That was drugs. He's had to confront himself over the years. He said to me, I couldn't carry the mantle of being this massive icon. Last time I saw him he drank fennel tea."

To Gillespie, Dylan will always be the perfect gentleman. "He's amusing, he's spiritual. As for the promiscuity, at least he's honest. Women prefer to be seduced by a brain than a bollock. Brains go a helluva long way."

Sara Lownds

MYTHOLOGISED IN SONG, Sara Lownds (nee Shirley Noznisky) was the only woman that Dylan wrote about directly, as in Sara on 1976's *Desire*. "I had taken the cure and had just gotten through," he sang, "Staying up for days in the Chelsea Hotel/ writing Sad Eyed Lady Of The Lowlands for you."

Lownds was his ultimate muse, his mystic "madonna-like woman". As outlined in Sad Eyed Lady..., Lownds had dark hair, fine features, a graceful body and — yes — sad eyes.

"She is a very private person... she doesn't have to be on the scene, any scene, to be happy," Dylan told biographer Robert Shelton. According to journalist Lynn Musgrave, Dylan's description "junkyard angel" was pretty accurate: "She is not Mother Earth in the heavy way, but just rolls with nature. That is what it must take to sit up in Woodstock, being married to Dylan and never going out much. I don't think she complains much, either. That line, She speaks like silence [from Love Minus Zero/No Limit], that's Sara."

Dylan met Lownds in 1964 through Sally Grossman. A former Playboy bunny, Sara had been married to a Hans Lownds and had a daughter, Maria. Their romance blossomed and by mid-1965 she was his constant companion. Joan Baez once chatted with Lownds about how Dylan had two-timed them both. "I told Sara that I'd never found Bob to be much at giving gifts, but that he had once told me to keep a lovely blue nightgown from the Woodstock house. She said, Oh! That's where it went!"

Part of the attraction for Dylan was that Lownds did not to know who he was. Sally Grossman told Clinton Heylin: "I remember the first time Bobby was ever on television. I watched the programme with Sara. I probably shouldn't say this, but she thought we were going to watch Bobby Darin!"

Lownds was so "un-scene" there was widespread amazement when Dylan married her in a private civil ceremony on 22 November 1965. Although she was pregnant with their first son Jesse, it seems this was no mere marriage of convenience, however. "I wasn't a very good husband," Dylan later admitted, "but I believe in marriage. I first got really married, and then got really divorced."

For a while their life in Woodstock seemed contented. They had a daughter, Anna, and two more sons, Samuel and Jakob (later to form his own rock band, The Wallflowers). But by the early '70s their relationship was breaking down. Dylan spent months on the road and his infidelities put a strain on the marriage. The release of *Blood On The Tracks* in

Forget Me Not...

ECHO HELSTROM

Helstrom was Dylan's high school sweetheart, a working-class girl with a penchant for reading Steinbeck, who apparently looked like a Minnesotan Brigitte Bardot. "Bob wasn't skinny then. He was more cheeky and had a bit of a tummy," she once said. "He was the clean-cut kid, well-scrubbed with rosy cheeks." They talked about having a child, claiming that, whether male or female, it would be called Bob. However, by the time they graduated from high school in 1958, Dylan was moving onto pastures new. When their class held a reunion 10 years later he came back and signed an autograph for her. Helstrom was last heard of living in Los Angeles.

BONNIE BEECHER

Purportedly the Girl From The North Country (though some have claimed the same about Helstrom), Beecher met Dylan in 1960 while a student at Minnesota University. She was from a Minneapolis suburb and anxious to rebel. Dylan fell deeply in love but the feeling wasn't reciprocated. "I fell hard for an actress girl who kneed me in the guts," he said later. Beecher now lives in San Francisco and is married to Hugh Romney, aka former '60s NY hipster Wavy Gravy.

MARY ALICE ARTES

A black actress, referred to as "Queen Bee" on 1978's *Street Legal*, Artes helped convert Dylan to Christianity, and was described by Dylan bandmember David Mansfield as "really powerful. She could look really sexy, while meanwhile being one of those competent mothers who would shower you with all this love and attention... she would have been like the perfect Jewish wife." Dylan reportedly bought her a $25,000 engagement ring in early 1980; later that year he wrote the aptly titled Groom Still Waiting At The Altar. She returned to the East Coast to continue her career as an actress.

CLYDIE KING

Said to be Dylan's second biggest love after Lownds, King and Dylan were inseparable through most of the early '80s. Dylan worked his way through most of the backing singers on his '80s tours, but King seemed to be the favourite. A powerful gospel singer, she appeared on albums by Elton John and Steely Dan, and recorded a solo album, *Brown Sugar*, in 1974.

True to Dylan's taste, glamour was apparently not a priority. Once romantically linked to Mick Jagger, King was a large black woman. She had a very loving nature, and obviously anchored Dylan at a vulnerable time. "Two [more] different people you couldn't hope to meet – her a black, outrageous, hamburger-eating soul singer, and Bob all quiet and white," Rolling Stone Ron Wood told Heylin. She used to boss him around, apparently, but "he needed it at the time".

Dylan and King recorded an album of duets in 1982 but CBS were underwhelmed and the record remains unreleased. King had a child with Dylan, but even though he described their love as one that "surpasses even my understanding", she was eventually superseded in his affections. She now lives in LA.

CAROLYN DENNIS

Another backing singer who toured with Dylan in the '80s, Dennis (sometimes professionally known as Carol Dennis) worked on the studio sessions for *Slow Train Coming* and married him in 1985. The couple had a daughter, Desireé Gabrielle Dennis-Dylan, the following year, and there have been rumours – never confirmed – of a second child. The couple divorced in 1992. Dennis now lives in New York and sings in Broadway musical theatre.

CAROLE CHILDS

Apparently now considers herself "No 1" among Dylan's women. A Geffen Records executive, she met Dylan in 1985 at Jakob's bar mitzvah. A wisecracking New Yorker, she soon became extremely close to the star, getting a Special Thanks credit on 1990's *Under A Red Sky*. Dylan has had affairs over the years, including one with Britta Lee Shain, the girlfriend of his personal assistant Gary Shafner (which Childs reportedly tried to quash), but Childs has remained determinedly close to him. Despite his Christian(ish) beliefs and his support of marriage ("Everyone should have a wife somewhere in the world," he famously once said) Dylan is like that horned goat Pan. He will always flit on to the next paramour – while keeping an eye on those he left behind.

1975, an album stuffed with bitterness, sorrow and spite, fuelled speculation about a split. He was spending time with several lady friends, including the actress Sally Kirkland and CBS A&R executive Ellen Bernstein (supposedly the subject of You're Gonna Make Me Lonesome When You Go).

Things came to a head during the second leg of the Rolling Thunder Revue in 1976 when, according to Baez, Lownds showed up before a gig one night "looking like a madwoman, carrying baskets of wrinkled clothes, her hair wild and dark rings around her eyes". She lambasted Dylan in the car park, but that still didn't put a stop to his adulterous activity. Stoked full of drink and drugs, he was going off the rails.

In March 1977 Lownds filed for divorce. "I can't go home without fear for my safety... He has struck me in the face, injuring my jaw... My five children are greatly disturbed by my husband's behaviour and his bizarre lifestyle," Lownds stated at the time. After the divorce there was a bitter custody battle, which was finally settled at the end of the year.

It took a long time for Dylan and Lownds to be reconciled but now, 23 years later, the two are said to be friends; she even occasionally goes to his shows. At one point they even rekindled their relationship, and in 1983 he reportedly seriously considered remarrying her. Lownds now lives in Los Angeles and has always refused to give interviews, maintaining that Zen-like detachment to the last.

Clydie King: the Buzz Aldrin of Dylan's ladies.

The Road To Glory

Saluting the past and celebrating the future, after *Highway 61 Revisited* Dylan and rock'n'roll would never be quite the same again.

DESCRIBING THE BEGINNING of *Highway 61 Revisited*'s opening salvo, Like A Rolling Stone, Bruce Springsteen ventured "that snare shot sounded like somebody had kicked open the door to your mind." Dylan contemporary Phil Ochs said of the album, "It's impossibly good... how can a human mind do this?" Hyperbole aside, *Highway 61 Revisited* remains one of rock'n'roll's sacred texts, widely regarded as the base metal from which all subsequent poetic, transcendent rock music has been wrought.

An intoxicating swirl of beat poet hip and biblical allegory, visceral rock'n'roll and cerebral balladry, contemporary wit and old weird America, the album captures a 24-year-old Bob Dylan at the moment of his ascension from needle-sharp folk provocateur to visionary rock deity. It's an album that simultaneously looks backwards and gallops forwards, dragging popular music into the modernist age with it.

Dylan had shunned politicised folk songs on 1964's *Another Side Of Bob Dylan*, and gone even further on the subsequent *Bringing It All Back Home* by adding electric instruments and symbolist poetry-inspired lyrics, much to the disdain of Greenwich Village's puritanical folk intelligentsia. Dylan was consciously stepping into the pop spotlight, but he was taking his literate songwriting with him. If this was pop, it was some way from the sunny love songs still favoured by The Beatles. Indeed, with the August 1965 release of *Highway 61 Revisited* the competition suddenly began to look distinctly frivolous.

The album was recorded at Columbia's Studio A in New York, initially with *Bringing It All Back Home* producer Tom Wilson at the controls, later replaced by Bob Johnston. Many of the musicians who had graced its predecessor were recalled, including bassist Harvey Brooks, pianist Paul Griffin and drummer Bobby Gregg. Key additions were Paul Butterfield Blues Band guitarist Mike Bloomfield and session man Al Kooper who turned up simply to watch before joining in on Hammond organ – an instrument he'd never touched before.

The competition suddenly began to look frivolous.

Early sessions yielded a landmark: Like A Rolling Stone. Musically it may have stolen from Richie Valens' La Bamba, but lyrically it came from an entirely different universe. A raging, vituperative epic whose venom-spitting lyrics were edited down from pages of what Dylan dubbed "vomitific" scrawling, its rhetorical chorus ("How does it feel/To be without a home/With no direction home/Like a rolling stone?") made an anthem out of existential angst. The song chimed with the album's overarching sense of restlessness, substituting logical narratives for surreal juxtapositions, sardonic put-downs and elliptical symbols. In June, Like A Rolling Stone was released as a single, racing to Number 2 on the US chart where it threatened to dislodge Sonny & Cher's I Got You Babe.

Work continued after July's Newport Folk Festival at which a leather-jacketed Dylan had fronted the all-electric Butterfield Blues Band, deepening the gulf between him and the folk caucus still further. Emboldened, Dylan and collaborators cut the remainder of *Highway 61 Revisited* in a whirlwind six days at the beginning of August.

IF LIKE A ROLLING Stone signposted Dylan's conversion to unfettered rock'n'roll, then the amped-up, meta-rockabilly of tracks such as Tombstone Blues and From A Buick 6 confirmed it in spades, Bloomfield's wild lead guitar punctuating Dylan's hipster delivery like a sparking knife blade. Contrast came by way of Queen Jane Approximately's stately folk rock – rippling cascades of piano and organ offsetting Dylan's yearning, opaque lyrics.

The ennui of It Takes A Lot To Laugh, It Takes A Train To Cry owes something to the tradition of Dylan heroes Hank Williams and Jimmie Rodgers. Part weary lament, part swaggering country-blues, it manages to seem both earthy and esoteric. Ballad Of A Thin Man, lead by Dylan at the piano, is musically more sophisticated. An elegant, jazzy ballad, it's another of Dylan's withering put-downs – his wounding, anti-critic barbs simultaneously hymning the generation gap: "You know something is happening/But you don't know what it is/Do you, Mr Jones?"

The album's title track transplants the biblical story of Abraham and Isaac to the Mid-west. Highway 61 runs from Louisiana right up to Dylan's home town Duluth, Minnesota and on to the Canadian border. Between the wars it was a major artery taking African Americans – and with them the blues – north in search of industrial employment.

BOB DYLAN HIGHWAY 61 REVISITED

It serves Dylan as a resonant metaphor for his own migration from folk piety to electric provocation and beyond.

Just Like Tom Thumb's Blues finds Dylan in stoned, road-weary limbo, initially lost south of the Mexican border, then ranging over the landscape from "Rue Morgue Avenue" to "Housing Project Hill", before heading "back to New York City". He drops numerous drug references along the way ("I started off on burgundy/But soon hit the harder stuff"), while the band turn a slow 12-bar blues into a thing of heavy-lidded beauty.

On the closing Desolation Row the electricity abates. As if cocking a snook at the naysayers, Dylan returns to the folk form, ably abetted by West Virginian Charlie McCoy's liquid guitar runs, saving his most outlandish lyrics for this 11-minute disquisition peopled by an exotic cast of heroic grotesques, from Cain and Abel to Ezra Pound and TS Eliot. Desolation Row remains one of Dylan's signature works, an epic of moral bankruptcy; an apocalyptic troubadour ballad as imagined by surrealistic filmmaker Luis Bunuel.

It closes an album whose sound is as exhilarating and whose lyrics remain as potent as they did on release. A critical cause celebré and a Number 3 hit in October 1965, Dylan would move on again with the following year's *Blonde On Blonde*, but by then the folk-rock floodgates would be open and his groundbreaking days numbered. It's easy to overlook just how fast Bob Dylan was moving in the mid-'60s; luckily he lingered long enough to commit *Highway 61 Revisited* to posterity. He would never be quite so 'in the zone' again. *David Sheppard*

EYEWITNESS

MAY 2-28, 1966

DYLAN'S 1966 TOUR

The press speculated about his drug use and the fans called him Judas, but Dylan's 1966 jaunt turned him into a bona fide rock star.

IT WAS MAY 3, 1966, one day after the spokesman for his generation arrived in England for the first time since plugging in. A year earlier, Dylan had unveiled the first version of his electric group, effectively the Paul Butterfield Blues Band, at the Newport Folk Festival. The folkie crowd had booed and jeered until, according to some reports, Dylan left the stage in tears. The response was even more violent at Forest Hills Tennis Stadium a month later, where cries of "Traitor!" and the mocking "Where's Ringo?" greeted his rock set.

Before too long, he had replaced the Butterfield Blues Band with The Hawks (later to become The Band), with whom he faced hostile audiences all across America, Australia and Scandinavia. In December 1965, Hawks leader and drummer Levon Helm dropped out. "We got up in the morning and Levon was gone," recalls road manager Bill Avis. "It shook us up for a minute, but it was also understood. No one liked the booing. No one liked having stuff thrown at them."

The pressure was intolerable. On a plane to Denver during March 1966, well after midnight, Dylan told writer Robert

Shelton, "It takes a lot of medicine to keep up this pace. It's very hard man. A concert tour like this has almost killed me."

Replacing Levon Helm for the UK leg was Mickey Jones, unaware of the controversy surrounding the electric part of the set.

Having already sold over 10 million records worldwide, Dylan was not just a popular fellow but a priority act for CBS. As well as record sales, he was generating publishing revenue at an unheard of rate. In one fortnight at the end of 1965, 80 cover versions of Dylan songs were released as singles. Huge wads of company money were invested in him but, as he arrived in London, doubts about his health were beginning to surface.

> ## "Dylan finally removed his dark glasses, but somehow managed to look exactly the same."
> **KEITH ALTHAM, JOURNALIST**

MONDAY MAY 2

London, Mayfair Hotel. The Dylan entourage settles in. Bob meets with Paul McCartney, Keith Richards, Brian Jones and a host of other London hipsters.

PAUL McCARTNEY It was a little bit An Audience With Dylan in those days. You went round to the Mayfair Hotel and waited in an outer room while Bob was in the bedroom, and we were getting ushered in one by one. Occasionally people would come out and say, "Bob's taking a nap", or make terrible excuses, and I'd say, "It's OK, man, I understand, he's out of it, you know?"

MICKEY JONES (*drummer*) I've been told that he carried a drug store of prescription medicine with him, but I never saw it.

TUESDAY MAY 3
Mayfair Hotel press conference.

DERMOT PURGAVIE (*Daily Sketch reporter*) Publicity men with urgent voices had summoned us for gin and tonic, cocktail onions and, principally, for group analysis of Mr Bob Dylan... He wore a blue suede tunic, blue-and-white butcher-stripe pants and dark glasses. His tangled, woolly hair looked as if it had been pitch-forked onto his head.

KEITH ALTHAM (*NME journalist*) For some 15 minutes photographers exposed innumerable rolls of film at Dylan looking bored, slumped on a window sill. Finally, he removed his dark glasses as a bonus to the cameramen, but somehow managed to look exactly the same. As the reporters filed out of the suite, I took one of Dylan's undercover agents to one side and enquired why a man with Dylan's obvious intelligence bothered to arrange this farce of a meeting. "Man," he extolled, "Dylan just wanted to come along and record a press reception so we could all hear how ridiculous and infantile all reporters are."

London, Blaises Club. Dylan takes Dana Gillespie to see John Lee Hooker.

KEITH RICHARDS They had to carry him into Blaises, and then I went over to him, and I was pretty frightened of him.

He doesn't believe you. Dylan and The Band scare the bejesus out of the Manchester Free Trade Hall.

THURSDAY MAY 5
Dublin, Adelphi Theatre

NORMAN BARRY (*reviewer, Sunday Independent*) The barrage of amplification equipment completely drowned Dylan's nasal voice, which requires the utmost concentration at the best of times. His beat arrangements were monotonous and painful, as folk, useless, and as beat, inferior.

FRIDAY MAY 6
Belfast, ABC Theatre

UNNAMED (*Cityweek*) The door of the

drab dressing room was ajar. A fuzzy golliwog in a tight diamond-pattern suit stood staring at me with wide-open eyes. "What d'ya want?" asked Bob Dylan. His lips hadn't moved. The sound seemed to emit from somewhere in the inner regions of the thick, dark curls. Eventually, he invited me inside. "This isn't an interview," he emphasised. "We're jest gonna have a li'l talkie."

DA PENNEBAKER *(filmmaker)* We had previously filmed him in England in 1965 for my Don't Look Back film and it seemed to me that it had been a drag for him, out on his own like that. In 1966, in the second half of each show, he had all these guys with him and from the minute he got out there he was enjoying himself. He was almost dancing with Robbie *[Robertson]*.

TUESDAY MAY 10
Bristol, Colston Hall.

NICHOLAS WILLIAMS *(NME reviewer)* Dylan ambled onto the stage and opened the first half by singing She Belongs To Me, one of his well-known LP tracks. He continued in the same style, accompanying himself on guitar and harmonica. For the second half of the show, Dylan changed to an electric guitar, and a five-strong backing group mysteriously appeared.

JENNY LEIGH *(fan)* They buried Bob Dylan, the folk singer, in a grave of electric guitars, enormous loudspeakers and deafening drums. It was a sad end to one of the most phenomenal influences in music.

ROBBIE ROBERTSON *(guitarist)* At the time, people were pissed off because they had this purist attitude about Dylan. We did not see what was wrong musically. We were treating the songs with great respect.

ANTHEA JOSEPH *(music promoter/ friend of Dylan)* I was the only one that drank. They were all dropping pills and eating acid and generally misbehaving. Anything that was going to tear my mind to pieces, I had no interest in whatsoever. So I was happy smoking dope in a corner while they ate things.

WEDNESDAY MAY 11
Cardiff, Capitol Theatre. Johnny Cash arrives backstage.

JC HOPKINS *(fan)* I saw Bob Dylan in Cardiff, and though slightly disappointed in him as a person, he's certainly one of the greatest artists I've seen.

THURSDAY MAY 12
Birmingham, Odeon Theatre. The Spencer Davis Group turns out for the show.

GRAHAM ASHTON *(fan)* The show was late starting—Dylan came on dressed in black, and someone even screamed. By the time he reached the mic he was already into She Belongs To Me. He didn't speak between the songs until just before Desolation Row, when he looked down and, in slow motion, picked something up, stared at it, and drawled into the mic: "Dirt. Dirt on the *stage.*" Everybody hooted. Dylan grinned.

MUFF WINWOOD *(Spencer Davis Group)* While we were backstage after the show, he was telling me and my brother Steve how he was really into ghosts, and we knew of a very old, massive house in Worcestershire, near Kidderminster, that had been burnt and blackened. And we told him how the guy that had lived in the house had died with his dog and how, if you went there, you could see him walking around with his dog. He was absolutely fascinated and he said, "You've got to take me to this place."

Well, we got there—Dylan, the band, girlfriends and hangers on, in four bloody stretch Princess limos—and we started wandering around. The house looked magnificent, it was a clear night with a great moon and everything, and, of course, somewhere a dog barked! Now, this is likely to happen in the countryside in Worcestershire at gone midnight, but Dylan is convinced he's heard the ghost of the dog. He was like a kid. Really child-like enjoyment of the whole thing. It was great fun.

SATURDAY MAY 14
Liverpool, Odeon Theatre.

VICKI REES *(fan)* Dylan was at his best. Those people who walked out saying they wanted the real Dylan really meant they wanted the old Dylan.

MJ He always seemed to have a lot of energy. On a number of occasions, Bob and I would jump in a limo after the concert and find an all-night hot dog stand. We would then go back to the hotel and talk about everything under the sun until the sun came up. He would make up for it by sleeping a lot during the day, but no one slept more than Garth Hudson. I said to him once, "Garth, you're sleeping your life away". He just looked straight at me and said, "Don't you know about dreams?"

SUNDAY MAY 15
Leicester, De Montfort Hall.

CHRISTINE KYNASTON *(fan)* I was absolutely disgusted at the narrow-mindedness displayed by some of the audience at Bob Dylan's Sunday visit to Leicester. Never before have I seen such an exhibition of childish mentality; they booed and slow-handclapped a man who was merely proving how amazingly versatile he is.

"I still remember thinking, God, that's really him. In the flesh."
PAUL KELLY, FAN

MONDAY MAY 16
Sheffield, Gaumont Theatre.

MJ I've been told there was a bomb threat at the Gaumont but if there was we were totally unaware of it. It certainly didn't affect us or our performance.

HARRY MURRAY *(Gaumont manager)* We decided to sweat it out. If I had thought for one moment that the audience were in danger I would have cleared the theatre.

JEAN-MARC PASCAL *(journalist, Salut Les Copains)* Later on, the entire group meets in a suite. Five musicians, four filmmakers and sound technicians, one sound man, Tom, the driver of the Rolls who is also acting as Dylan's bodyguard, Henri, who looks after the guitars, Al Grossman, Bob Neuwirth, Fred Perry (the tour manager), Bob Dylan and myself plus a few girls picked up at the end of the show. Twenty people altogether. They have to listen and choose the recordings made of the concert. It's a

daily routine — Bob is having a film made of the tour for American television and these recordings have to be synchronised later with the pictures. At 6am there are only three or four people left: Bob, myself and a couple of musicians. We talk about John Lennon, Mick Jagger and trends in cinema.

TUESDAY MAY 17
Manchester, Free Trade Hall.

J-M P At noon the next day, we're off to Manchester. When we arrive, Dylan goes to

Bowling for Calderstones: Dylan enjoys some time off in Liverpool.

Sweating it out: the audience puts Dylan's new direction in the spotlight.

his bedroom to sleep until the concert. The others go to the theatre to set up the sound system Bob has brought with him from America – Ampex, the very best.

MJ As I remember, we all walked down to the Free Trade Hall from the hotel for the soundcheck.

J-M P 45 minutes before the show is due to begin, Dylan arrives and he rehearses briefly with his musicians. Two cameramen and soundmen are around him.

MALCOLM METCALFE *(fan)* The Free Trade Hall, it was sold out. I'd long since perfected the art of getting into cinemas via the back door, so I went looking round the side of the theatre and found a door and kicked it in. It led onto a corridor which led right through to the side of the stage. From there, by pushing another door open a crack, we could get a view of the show.

RICK SANDERS *(fan/usher)* Dylan coming to Manchester was the biggest thing of that time. There was more excitement about it than any other gig I've ever been to. I was a student but I used to get evening jobs ushering at the Free Trade Hall for 15 shillings a time, but the Dylan show was the first proper rock gig I'd worked at.

MJ The atmosphere backstage at Manchester just before we went on was no different than at any of the previous shows. We always laughed and had a great time.

CHRIS LEE *(fan)* He walked onto the stage in Cuban boots, with a black shirt and this Edwardian-style, yellow-brown tweed jacket, and started off with She Belongs To Me. The main thing, though, visually, was that great big unruly mop of long curly hair. That came as a shock, because all the publicity shots we'd seen were about two years old.

PAUL KELLY *(fan)* I'd decided to take along my camera – a Yashica – to the gig, because there was never any problem about taking pictures at concerts in those days. We'd managed to get seats just four rows from the front and, as soon as the house lights went down, and the spotlight came on, I started taking pictures. I can still remember the moment he came on stage for the acoustic set. I was thinking, God, that's really him. In the flesh.

KEVIN FLETCHER *(fan)* During the acoustic set he seemed very different from the way we'd seen him in 1965. Then, he'd been chatty, joking, very open and fresh, but

now the set was more intense. He seemed slower and slurred and very stoned.

CL People were quiet and attentive but you could feel the tension about whether he would play electric. We'd heard about the booing in Dublin and Liverpool and people assumed he'd have learned his lesson.

RS During the intermission after the acoustic set, Albert Grossman, an imposing figure in a cream suit, came round and told me he wanted me to be a bodyguard up on the stage. I was plunked right in front of Richard Manuel. To be honest, though, I didn't feel very threatened up there. The band seemed a million times cooler than anyone else in the building.

CL When they came on, just before 9 o'clock, The Hawks were a rainbow of coloured velvet suits; maroon, purple, green, beige and blue, very Catskills. They had white shirts, and their hair was just starting to grow long. Then Dylan came out with a black Fender and plugged it in.

RS There at my feet was a surging mass of flesh-crazed fans, howling, cheering and screaming, waiting for the spark. I don't think Dylan said anything. Just a glance at the band and suddenly the music started.

MJ He would set the rhythm and the tone before we would come in. He gets the rhythm going, and then Robbie turns it around. He goes, "One, two, one, two, three", and it was completely turned around from the rhythm Bob set.

RS I never heard such an apocalyptic roar. It took your breath away, like a squadron of B-52s in a cathedral. There was wicked crackling guitar over a vortex of sheer noise, with snatches of Captain Nemo organ and mad piano occasionally surfacing.

CL They kicked off with Tell Me Mamma and right away people were stunned by the sheer volume. That got polite applause but by the time they were into I Don't Believe You the audience was divided. It was an affront to the traditionalists. I was used to seeing these people around the folk scene in Manchester, but it was quite bewildering and frightening to see them going apeshit like that. It's hard to convey to people now just how profound the shock was of Dylan going commercial. To those people it seemed he had betrayed all their values, their left-wing principles, the CND movement, their traditionalist sentiments.

STEVE CURRIE *(fan)* I wasn't too impressed by the velvet suits, but I was even less impressed by the dickhead sat next to me who decided to start booing and shouting along with the others who were scattered around the hall. I told him to fuck off home if he didn't like it. Well, that shut him up and he stayed, but the protest carried on elsewhere.

STEWART TRAY *(fan, seated behind Dylan on stage)* I got the feeling there was something going on. The noise, the booing, the slow hand-clapping and all the rest of it.

I mean, this was supposed to be like going to a pop concert. People threw jelly babies at pop concerts, they didn't do this kind of stuff. There was fear where I was sat that Dylan would just walk off.

CL At the end of Just Like Tom Thumb's Blues, a young, long-haired woman walked up to the stage and passed a note to Dylan. He bowed and blew her a kiss which brought thunderous applause. Then he looked briefly at the note and put it in his pocket. Everyone wondered what the note said, but no one knew until I managed to track the woman down when I was writing my book, Like The Night, about the Free Trade Hall gig. Her name was Barbara and her note said, "Tell the band to go home", but it was done with the best intentions. They had been embarrassed by the way the crowd was behaving, and worried that he would think they didn't like his music when, in fact, it was just the band they didn't like.

MJ Frankly, we didn't care. We were playing our music for us and not for the audience. Bob's attitude was: the first half of the show is for them, the second half is for us. And we truly enjoyed ourselves.

CL After Leopard-Skin Pill-Box Hat, there was a delay, during which the hecklers started up again. As the slow-handclaps and the booing got louder, Bob went into a routine. It was an old carny sideshow technique where he mumbled incoherently into the microphone, which had the effect of making people strain to hear what he was saying.

MJ He did that on a lot of occasions. He didn't end with the same thing, he'd say something different. But that really got their attention and they'd stop and all of a sudden they'd pay attention.

KF The mumbling completely floored us. We thought it was brilliant and totally effective, because as he did it the crowd just got quieter and quieter.

CL Once he knew he had everybody's attention, Dylan delivered one single coherent phrase, "If you only wouldn't clap so hard", which had the desired effect of making everybody laugh and briefly winning them over to his side again.

KF The infamous shout of "Judas!" came from in front of us and a bit more to the centre and, as soon as it happened, a kind of hush fell over the crowd. I'd say Dylan was definitely responding to the Judas shout when he said, "I don't believe you." That shout was probably the nastiest knock that Dylan ever got.

CL The implication of "Judas!", obviously, was that he had sold out the folk movement. There was a long gap as he mulled it over before he said, "I don't believe you", in a voice full of scorn and disdain. He turned to the band and said, "Get fucking loud!"

J-M P Suddenly *[during Like A Rolling Stone]* a man behind me whispers, "This is really good. It's Number 1 in the States." I turn around to agree and – surprise – realise that he's a policeman. The British police are wonderful.

RS Before anyone realised what was happening, it was suddenly over. I have a memory of Dylan brushing past me and vanishing down a corridor with Grossman.

MM We'd watched the whole thing through the door from the corridor, terrified all the time that somebody would find us and throw us out. After Like A Rolling Stone, we weren't sure if it had ended because there was just this sudden silence, but then the door beside us blasted open and Dylan and some heavies rushed past us and I remember thinking, My God, he's so small. He was sweating profusely and looked exhausted, really wasted. He was practically being carried by his minders with one hand under each arm. They completely ignored us, so we followed them down the corridor and out into the street where they jumped into this big black limousine.

PK By the end, I'd banged off all 36 shots and, as it happened, about 26 turned out to be useable. During the show, we'd noticed the sound recordist from CBS who had his gear just set up right at the front of the stage. When it was all over we went up and asked him if he would give us the tape. He said, "No way, man, but it's coming out on an album at the end of this year."

RS People started approaching me, furiously demanding their money back, thinking that somehow I'd be able to give it to them, but the whole thing was finished. As the hall emptied, the band came back on without Dylan, and played some great old rock numbers, Bo Diddley and Little Richard stuff, while the clearers-up moved around them. Dylan by now would be back in the Midland Hotel, I suppose. When it was finally over, we humped the gear back outside for them, collected 30 shillings each for the night's work, and went home. Not one of them had said a word to me, but it was an unforgettable, fabulous night to have been Bob Dylan's bodyguard.

MJ After that show we did talk about the Judas thing, but it didn't seem that it had affected Dylan one bit. We were just convinced that nobody had got it.

when he came on in the second half, dressed in black and accompanied by a five-man beat group, that the trouble started. There were shouts of "Rubbish" from the purists and "Shut up" from the beat fans. To cries of "We want Dylan", he replied, "Dylan got sick backstage and I'm here to take his place." Then he walked off stage unperturbed by the boos and cheers that followed him.

MJ There's no doubt in my mind as to why they were reacting the way they were. They felt that the one person in the world who would remain true was Bob Dylan. They felt betrayed. I understand that more today than I did then.

FRIDAY MAY 20
Edinburgh, ABC Theatre. Dylan encounters so many tuning problems that he throws away his harmonica.

ANDREW YOUNG *(fan)* You could tell there was something wrong with Bob's harmonica, so I just walked onto the stage and handed him my own 12/6d mouth organ.

SATURDAY MAY 21
Newcastle, Odeon Theatre.

MIKE HARNON *(fan)* The acoustic set was brilliant, really well received. Then he came out with an electric band and there was real astonishment. They sounded very raw and the crowd split into two camps. After five minutes in shock the diehards started slow handclapping, booing and some eventually walked out. Dylan walked to the front of the stage and flicked them the V-sign. The booing got even worse, but only about a third of the purists walked out. The band warmed up and stopped sounding so rough. It carried on being a brilliant show and was very well applauded. I've never seen anything like it.

JEAN McWILLIAMS *(fan)* All in black, Dylan looked very aggressive. As the booing increased he didn't say anything, just stuck his fingers up. I was shocked.

MJ The first half of those concerts he was absolutely bored to tears. He would come back to the dressing room and put that acoustic guitar down. Then he would put that black Telecaster on and you could see the adrenalin running through his veins. He was ready to rock. He would jump around in the dressing room. He could not wait to get on that stage. It's true, sometimes Bob would hardly face the audience in the electric set. He played to the band. That was where his focus was, on us. The audience was only there so we could get paid to do what we loved to do. We were all in a zone.

WEDNESDAY MAY 18
Dylan and entourage travel to Scotland.

MJ We went everywhere by coach, but Bob had his own car. Now, there were parts of the tour that Bob Dylan was on the coach but, when we went up to Scotland, he went in the car, and we went on the bus. I've long been a collector of Nazi memorabilia, so that morning I went shopping and bought a large German flag. As we left the Midland Hotel to get on the bus for Glasgow, I unfurled the flag in the middle of the street to show it to the guys

on the bus. Man, I was almost run down on the spot by about a dozen drivers. I was still just a kid and it really hadn't dawned on me how powerful those feelings left over from the war were in England. I guess it was a stupid thing to do.

THURSDAY MAY 19
Glasgow, Odeon Theatre.

ANDREW YOUNG *(reviewer, Scottish Daily Mail)* Dressed in checked suit, he stood alone on stage and gasped out the protest songs which have made him a millionaire. It was

Dylan and Françoise Hardy, Paris: "Nice box. Of records."

SUNDAY MAY 22

Touring party flies to France, where Dylan spends the night boozing in Parisian niteries with Johnny Hallyday.

MONDAY MAY 23

Paris, George V Hotel press conference.

Q Are you a happy person, Bob?

A Oh yes, I'm as happy as an ashtray.

TUESDAY MAY 24

Paris, Olympia. The electric set is performed in front of a huge Stars & Stripes on Dylan's 25th birthday.

MJ We were not very happy in France. We thought everyone there had an attitude towards Americans. And they did! I don't remember whose idea it was but we loved the reaction of the audience when the curtain opened and we were dwarfed by the biggest American flag that I had ever seen. It made me and Bob very proud. As you know, Bob and I were the only Americans on the show. The rest of the band was Canadian.

WEDNESDAY MAY 25

London, Hyde Park. Back in Britain, Dylan is filmed by DA Pennebaker during an early morning limo cruise with John Lennon.

BOB DYLAN Oh man, you shoulda been around last night, John. Today's a drag.

JOHN LENNON Oh, really, Bob?

THURSDAY MAY 26

London, Royal Albert Hall. The Rolling Stones are in the audience.

BRIAN CARROLL (*sound engineer*) I was backstage and another engineer and I stared in disbelief as we saw Dylan walk up the stage stairs. This man seemed so out of it that we saw him talking to a fire extinguisher and we both thought that there was going to be a riot when he either failed to appear or stumbled around the stage. Suddenly, a man in a suit led him to the bottom of the stairs and we watched in amazement as he walked up into the lights and cranked out one of his best performances on the tour.

STEVE ABRAMS (*fan*) The most interesting part came in the first half of the concert when Dylan was about to sing Visions Of Johanna. He said, "Now, this next song is what your English newspapers would call a drug song, but I don't write drug songs and anybody who says I do is talking rubbish."

SUE MILES (*fan*) In the first half he was just earnestly twanging away. Out for the intermission, and The Band appeared and

I remember thinking, This is great. This is wonderful. This is proper stuff. Dylan had frizzy, slightly blue hair. He and Robbie Robertson rubbed up against each other all the time. It was great. Half the audience pissed off — all the ones that had rucksacks.

DANA GILLESPIE (*singer/friend of Dylan*) After the Royal Albert Hall show, Dylan and I did talk about how he felt, though, and, although I never heard him say anything derogatory about British fans, I knew he was very surprised by the response because he had felt that England was far ahead of any other country in pop music. When the audience booed and jeered in London, he just rocked more to annoy them.

JOHNNY BYRNE (*writer*) I happened to be staying in the flat where Dylan came back later. He was visibly vibrating. I should imagine it was the exhaustion and a good deal of substances. He was totally away. There was a yawning chasm between him and any kind of human activity.

FRIDAY MAY 27

London, Royal Albert Hall. The Beatles are in the audience.

MJ I do think the best set we did was probably the Albert Hall, the last night. Everybody was lookin' forward to goin' home and we wanted to kinda leave with a bang.

NORMAN JOPLING (*Record Mirror*) After the interval, he returned with his group and launched into an ear-splitting cacophony. The hecklers were in full force and just about everything possible was hurled at Bob (verbally — no missiles were seen).

PETER WILLIS (*reviewer, Peace News*) Dylan remained beatifically unaffected by this; during one of the few enfeebled bursts of slow-handclapping he simply made faces, giggled and remarked, "This isn't English music, this is American music."

NJ The highlight came when Bob sat down at the piano and did Ballad Of A Thin Man, which silenced even the folksier elements. He ended up with Like A Rolling Stone, jumping and yelling all over the stage and looking (as all the girls said) very sweet.

DP I'm not sure how badly the British audiences affected Dylan. During that tour, we were with him, often filming all night long, and at no point did Bob indicate he felt these audiences hated him.

GEORGE HARRISON (*Beatle*) All these people who'd never heard of folk until Bob Dylan came around, two years later they're staunch folk fans and they're walking out on

him when he was playing the electric songs. Which is so stupid. He actually played rock'n'roll before. Nobody knew that at the time but Bob had been in Bobby Vee's band as the piano player and he'd played rock'n'roll. And then he became Bob Dylan The Folk Singer so, for him, it was just returning back. I felt a bit sad for him because he was a bit wasted at that time. He'd been on a world tour and he *looked* like he'd been on a world tour. He looked like he needed a rest.

MJ I've heard people say he did it for the money. The reality is he made less money on that tour than any tour he'd ever done. To take that many people and all that equipment, and all that air freight cost so much more than if he had done the tour alone. By himself, he would have tripled the money he made so, obviously, he did not do it for the money. He did it because his musical tastes were changin' too.

RR Dylan had every opportunity to say, Fellows, this is not working out. I'm going to go back to folk music or get another band where they won't boo every time. Everybody told him to get rid of these guys, that it wasn't working. But he didn't. That was very commendable.

> "As the booing increased he didn't say anything, just stuck his fingers up."
> **JEAN McWILLIAMS, FAN**

SATURDAY MAY 28

Dylan and Sara fly to Spain for a holiday.

MJ I don't remember Bob being any more tired and wasted than the rest of us. We were all beat to hell. Garth and I decided to take a ship home instead of flying. It was a way of catching up on some well-earned rest. We sailed from Southampton on the SS New Amsterdam, the Dutch Line to New York City.

RICK DANKO (*bass player*) We came back from that English tour with Bob pretty fried, man. Then, late in July, Albert Grossman's office called and said Bobby had a motorcycle accident in Woodstock and had hurt his neck.

Compiled by Johnny Black. Photos: © Barry Feinstein

"Everybody Must Get Stoned..."

Between 1963 and 1966 Bob Dylan's music was fuelled by opium, speed and LSD. Andy Gill charts his path from folk preacher to psychedelic visionary.

BOB DYLAN WAS not the first songwriter to write about – or under the influence of – drugs, though you could be forgiven for assuming otherwise judging by the furore that greeted his more risqué mid-'60s work. When Rainy Day Women #12 & 35 flew up the charts in 1966, preaching that "everybody must get stoned", the reaction suggested he had not only invented the drug song but the drugs themselves. Dropped from radio station playlists as an incitement to depravity, in actuality of course it was simply the latest example of a noble, if jolly, tradition stretching back decades.

Pop music and drugs have been a volatile combination ever since the days jazz pianists like Fats Waller and Jelly Roll Morton were playing bordellos for beer money. And for much the same reason: hedonism. Before drug addiction became acknowledged as an illness, drugs were just another means whereby folks could glean a few moments' illicit pleasure to stave off the drudgery and boredom of their working lives.

Listen to one of the anthologies of early-20th century "reefer songs" – such as Trikont's marvellous *Dope & Glory* and *Drug Songs High & Low* – and you'll find celebrations of getting out of your head, from some of the most famous names in music. The Ink Spots' That Cat Is High, for instance, is fairly straightforward about a habit that few at the time regarded as dangerous, as were Louis Armstrong's Kickin' The Gong Around and Gene Krupa's Feeling High And Happy. And it wasn't just cannabis that was considered fun, either: Ella Fitzgerald and Chick Webb's Wacky Dust was one of many songs about cocaine, while even amphetamines were considered chuckle-worthy – witness Harry 'The Hipster' Gibson's Who Put The Benzedrine In Mrs Murphy's Ovaltine?

THE PURITAN ZEAL of post-war America's "back to work" ethic buried this feelgood attitude towards recreational drugs, with the Eisenhower administration and Hoover's FBI keen to establish '50s America as the squeaky-clean land of mom, apple pie and Doris Day. The drug subculture still thrived among musicians but it was more covert, an underground affiliation that would only burst back overground in the '60s through the attentions of Dylan and those he influenced, most notably The Beatles.

The first drug song Dylan performed was probably Rev Gary Davis's Cocaine, one of several numbers he played with Richard Fariña and Eric Von Schmidt at London's Troubadour Club early in 1963. It has been said it was Von Schmidt who taught Dylan the song, though the former seems hazy about this. "Anyone could have taught it to Bob," he told MOJO. "I may have played it to him in my Cambridge apartment but it was definitely common knowledge among folk singers from the '50s onward."

It's unlikely that, at this point in his career, Dylan had much personal knowledge of cocaine. Marijuana, though, was another matter: the aforementioned performance of Cocaine was probably done while stoned, Fariña and he having gone through plenty of weed during their time in London.

Dylan had first encountered the drug during his short spell as a college student in Minneapolis, courtesy of local scenemaker Dave Whitaker, a big influence on Dylan's youthful attitudes. When he migrated to Greenwich Village shortly after, he found a subculture in which cannabis was commonplace, and used it to help in his songwriting. John Herald of The Greenbriar Boys recalled getting turned on by Dylan at the latter's West 4th Street apartment in the early '60s, the pair of them toking furtively in the toilet, after which Herald fell asleep on Bob's sofa. "When I woke up, 20 minutes, half an hour later," Herald told Dylan biographer Howard Sounes in Down The Highway, "Bob was playing guitar and singing what sounded to me like gibberish, just stream of consciousness. Every time he heard himself say something, he'd sort of lean over. He had a little pad and he'd write things down."

In his first major magazine profile, in the August 1962 issue of young women's title Seventeen, Dylan described his songwriting technique as almost a matter of collaging images: "I seem to draw into myself whatever comes my way, and it comes out of me. Maybe I'm nothing but all these things I soak up. I don't know."

The rather serious nature of Dylan's early songs afforded little scope for playful imagery, a restriction the songwriter had grown to resent by the time of *Another Side Of Bob Dylan*. After the furrow-browed earnestness of *The Times They Are A-Changin'*, the unbridled fun of All I Really Want To Do and Motorpsycho Nitemare seemed like self-sabotage. The pivotal My Back Pages reacted against the dominant folk-protest culture in more vivid, oblique manner, its very complexity an affront to the proletarian singalong simplicity of the movement. Dylan had realised social liberation could only grow out of personal liberation. "I've conceded the fact that there is no understanding of anything – at best just winks of the eye," he told Nat Hentoff in The New Yorker, "and that is all I'm looking for now, I guess."

PERHAPS NOT UNCOINCIDENTALLY, a few months before recording *Another Side Of…*, Dylan had taken a road trip with a few friends from New York to San Francisco via New Orleans, with a jar labelled "Marijuana" perched on the dashboard, periodically replenished from packages sent ahead to post offices along the route. It was on this trip that he wrote several of these new kinds of songs, including Mr Tambourine Man, the number that would become the most misinterpreted 'drug song' of the era. The song's exultant imagery and urge for transcendence were widely regarded as analogising the psychedelic experience, an interpretation verified for some by the reference to "smoke rings of my mind" and the invitation to "take me on a trip upon your magic swirling ship".

Most listeners' first encounter with the song came via The Byrds' hit single, and it's easy to understand how the sleek, euphoric rush of their version might lead one to such a conclusion. In Dylan's own more haunted delivery, the desired transcendence is always slightly out of reach, a poetic ideal rather than a narcotic indulgence.

However, it was *Bringing It All Back Home*, Dylan's fifth album and the one on which Mr Tambourine Man eventually appeared, that first included overt drug references, especially in the depiction of drug chemist Johnny "mixing up the medicine" (probably bathtub amphetamine) and the paranoid references to drug busts and police surveillance in

Subterranean Homesick Blues. As with My Back Pages, the message was as much in the style as the language itself, a Gatling-gun stream of images rattled off in a jittery delivery that evoked the edgy nature of speed psychosis.

By this time, too, Dylan had experimented with LSD. According to producer Paul Rothchild (who would later become famous as The Doors' producer), he and Victor Maimudes had introduced Dylan to the drug a few months earlier, following a spring 1964 concert at the University Of Massachusetts in Amherst. "I looked at the sugar cubes and thought, Why not?," Rothchild told Dylan biographer Bob Spitz. "So we dropped acid on Bob. Actually, it was an easy night for Dylan. Everybody had a lot of fun. That was the beginning of the mystical '60s right there."

But Dylan remained equivocal about this most powerful of hallucinogens.

"I wouldn't advise anybody to use drugs," he told Nat Hentoff. "Certainly not the hard drugs; drugs are medicine. But opium and hash and pot – now, those things aren't drugs; they just bend your mind a little. I think everybody's mind should be bent once in a while. Not by LSD, though. LSD is medicine – a different kind of medicine. It makes you aware of the universe, so to speak; you realise how foolish objects are. But LSD is not for groovy people; it's for mad, hateful people who want revenge."

It was, perhaps, mere coincidence that Dylan should begin the famous sequence of excoriating revenge songs – Like A Rolling Stone, Positively 4th Street, Ballad Of A Thin Man, etc – shortly after being introduced to LSD, as he followed up *Bringing It All Back Home* with his second masterpiece of 1965, *Highway 61 Revisited*.

Though her judgement was perhaps clouded by personal issues – having been dumped by him – Dylan's former lover Joan Baez disliked the nihilism of his new material, greatly preferring the social conscience of his earlier straightforward protest songs. "He criticises society, and I criticise it," she complained to folk critic Robert Shelton, "but he ends up saying there is not a goddamned thing you can do about it, so screw it. I'm afraid the message that comes through from Dylan in 1965 is, Let's go home and smoke pot, because there's nothing else to do – we might as well go down smoking."

OVER THE NEXT 12 months, Dylan would rewrite the pop song rulebook, introducing elements such as disdain, contempt and despair into the normally happy-go-lucky environs of the Top 10. The visionary imagery introduced in Mr Tambourine Man would build through *Highway 61…*'s epic Desolation Row into the suffocating, surreal whirl of *Blonde On Blonde*. The sudden lyrical disjunctions, weird interjections and fantastical non sequiturs of songs such as Stuck Inside Of Mobile With The Memphis Blues Again and Absolutely Sweet Marie evoked both the suggestibility of the acid experience and the creeping paranoia induced by speed, the "medicine" Dylan was taking to meet the increasingly strenuous demands placed on him.

But it was Rainy Day Women #12 & 35 that caused the biggest furore, mainly because it was the most blatantly drug-influenced. Supporters and detractors could argue about the possible drug undertones of Dylan's more oblique lyrics, but this one left little room for doubt: quite simply, "everybody

---

When I Met Bob...

SINGING POET LEONARD COHEN

"The last time I met Bob was after a concert he'd done in Paris. We met in a café and we had a real good writers' talk. You couldn't meet two people who work more differently. He said, 'I like the song you wrote called Hallelujah. How long did that take you?' And I said, 'Oh, the best part of two years.' He said, 'Two years?' Kinda shocked. And then we started talking about a song of his called I And I from *Infidels*. I said, 'How long did you take to write that?' He said, 'Ohhh, 15 minutes.' I almost fell off my chair. Bob just laughed."

L·S·D

PARTNERS

LICENSED BETTING OFFICE

"LSD is not for groovy people. It's for mad, hateful people."

BOB DYLAN

must get stoned". Cited as a drug song in the Gavin Report sent out to radio stations, the single was pulled from playlists but still managed to reach Number 2 in the US charts.

Recording the song had been one of the more enjoyable duties for the Nashville session crew that worked on *Blonde On Blonde*. Primed with powerful cocktails and weed, they swapped instruments around to get the desired rough-and-ready Salvation Army band effect. Bassist Henry Strzelecki lay on the floor to operate Al Kooper's organ pedals, his stoned laughter picked up inadvertently by a nearby microphone. Presuming this was just a guide run-through, they were surprised when their shenanigans turned out to be the finished song – and even more surprised when it furnished Dylan with his best-selling single. For Dylan himself, it would also be the high-water mark of his association with drugs.

The excesses of his 1966 world tour with The Hawks were such that DA Pennebaker, filming his second Dylan tour, doubted at times that the singer would ever make it back home. But from this point on, drugs would begin to ebb out of his life, even as the youth culture he spawned latched on to them with alacrity. Some drug songs, such as The Byrds' Eight Miles High and Jefferson Airplane's White Rabbit, were well crafted and reasonably literate; others, such as The Smoke's My Friend Jack, were less subtle. And as the drug culture grew, fewer and fewer could be bothered to employ allusion when referring to narcotics. Where Dylan had punningly invoked oppression in his use of "everybody must get stoned", others

were more blunt: Have A Marijuana. Or even just... Heroin.

Meanwhile, Bob Dylan sat out the hippy explosion up in Woodstock, re-evaluating his life and art and working towards a more condensed lyrical style. Ironically, even as Dylan was disassociating himself from drug culture, obsessive fans strove all the harder to discern drug 'messages' in his lyrics. Foremost among their ranks was the self-proclaimed "Dylanologist" AJ Weberman, who had himself been jailed for dealing marijuana back in 1964. Weberman's attentions led him to trawl through the Dylans' garbage for evidence to support his bizarre theory that Bob was a heroin addict, a hunch he had developed through his idiosyncratic reading of the lyrics to *John Wesley Harding*.

Having initially failed to dissuade Weberman's (literal) muck-raking by lacing his garbage with copious quantities of dog shit, Dylan eventually confronted his persecutor early in 1971, going so far as to roll up his sleeves to show his arms were free of hypodermic track-marks. Weberman just assumed, as you do, that Dylan was snorting heroin rather than injecting it, and carried on his harassment. But Dylan had once more set his face against prevailing cultural attitudes.

Over subsequent albums, it would become clear he was drawing inspiration from a much wider range of influences – theatre, art, cinema, religion, current affairs, and not least his own life. Drugs, as he had asserted years before, were not integral to his writing, but simply helped bend the mind a little. And, having broadened his mind, he knew there were no limits to where he could go next.

DYLAN GETS OUT OF IT!

In conversation with a Swedish DJ in 1966, Dylan gave fans a stark glimpse of his confused, agitated state of mind.

APRIL 28, 1966

A hotel suite in Stockholm: Bob Dylan is playing Swedish radio journalist Klas Burling the as-yet-unreleased *Blonde On Blonde* and answering a few questions. "He was totally out of it," Burling recalls today. "When he took his shades off, his eyes were like raisins. I was so aggravated that by the time he played Sad-Eyed Lady Of The Lowlands and asked what I thought of it, I just replied, 'Long...' We did not part friends. It was the worst interview of my life."

KB: Very nice to see you in Stockholm, Bob Dylan, and I wonder now that you're in Stockholm if you could explain a bit more about yourself and your kind of songs. What do you think of the protest song type?
BD: Um... er... God... No, I'm not going to sit here and do that. I've been up all night, I've taken some pills and I've eaten bad food and I've read the wrong things and I've been out for 100mph car rides and let's not sit here and talk about myself as a protest singer or anything like that.

The first things you did which got really famous, for example in England The Times They Are A-Changin', that was supposed to be a protest song, no?
Oh my God, how long ago was that?

A year ago. Yeah, well, I mean, c'mon, a year ago... I'm not trying to be a bad fellow or anything but I'd just be a liar or a fool to go along with all this. I mean, I just can't help it if you're a year behind, you know.

No, but that's the style you had then, and you changed to Subterranean Homesick Blues with the electric guitars and things. Is there any special reason? No.

No? No.

What would you call yourself? A poet? Or a singer? Or do you write poems and then you put music to them? No, I don't know. It's so silly. I mean, you wouldn't ask these questions of a carpenter would you? Or a plumber?

It wouldn't be interesting the same way, would it? I guess it would be, I mean, it's interesting to me; it should be just as interesting to you.

Well, not as a disc jockey, anyhow. What do you think Mozart would say to you if you ever came up to him and asked him the questions that you've asked? What kind of questions would you ask him? Tell me, Mr Mozart, er...

Well, first of all I wouldn't interview him. Well, how come you do it to me?

Well, because I'm interested in your records and I think the Swedish audience is also. Well, I'm interested in the Swedish audiences too and Swedish people and all that kind of stuff, but I'm sure they don't want to know all these dumb things.

No, well they've read a lot of dumb things about you in the papers and I suppose you could straighten them out yourself. I can't straighten them out, I don't think they have to be straightened out. I believe that they know. Don't you know the Swedish people? They don't have to be told, they don't have to be explained to. You should know that. You can't tell Swedish people something that is self-explanatory. Swedish people are smarter than that.

You think so? Oh, of course.

You know many Swedes? I know plenty, I happen to be a Swede myself.

Oh yeah, certainly. In fact, I come from not too far away from here, my friend.

Shall we try to listen to a song, then? You can try.

Yeah. Which one would you suggest then? Oh, you pick it out, anyone you say. You realise I'm not tryin' to be a bad fellow. I'm just tryin' to make it along, to get everything to be straight, you realise that?

Yeah, and that's why I asked you and you had a chance to do it yourself. No, I don't want the chance to do it myself.

OK. I don't want to do anything by myself.

[Tape lapse]

For what or against what? Well, you know what it's against and what it's for, I'm not going to tell you that... My songs are all mathematical songs, now you know what that means, so I'm not going to have to go into that. So this specific one here happens to be a protest song and it borders on the mathematical, you know, idea of sayings, and this specific one, Rainy Day Women, happens to deal with, er, a minority of, you know, cripples and Orientals and the world in which they live, you realise and you understand. It's sort of a Mexican kind of thing, very protesty, very, very protesty and one of the protestiest of all things I've ever protested against in the protest years.

You really believe it? Do I believe it?

Yeah. I don't have to believe it, I know it. I'm telling you I wrote it, I should know.

So why that title? It's never mentioned in the song. Well, we never mention things that we love. Where I come from that's

© Corbis. Words: Johnny Black

"I've been up all night, taken some pills, eaten bad food and been out for 100mph car rides."

Nowadays what is it you want to do? Nothing.

Nothing? No.

Do you enjoy travelling? Performing? Yeah, I like performing, I don't care to travel, though.

What about recordings? I like to record.

You've got a group now, which you didn't have at the very start. Yes, I had a group at the very start, but you must realise I come from the United States. I don't know if you know what the United States is like. It's not like England at all, you know. People at my age now, 25 to 26, everybody has grown up playing rock'n'roll music, you know.

Did you do that? Yes, because it's the only kind of music you heard. Everybody has done it, because all you heard was rock'n'roll and country and western and rhythm and blues music. At a certain time the whole field got taken over into milk, you know, to Frankie Avalon, Fabian, this kind of thing. Now that's not bad or anything, but there was nobody that you could look at, and really want anything that they had, or want to be like them, so everybody got out of it. But nobody really lost that whole thing, and folk music came in and was some kind of substitute for a while, but it was only a substitute, that's all it was. Now it's different again because of the English thing, and what the English thing did was that they proved that you could make money at playing the same old kind of music that you used to play. And that's the truth, that's not a lie, it's not a come-on or anything, but the English people can't play rock'n'roll music.

Well, what do you feel about The Beatles then? Oh, The Beatles are great but they don't rock'n'roll.

You met them quite a few times as well? In the States and in England... Yeah, I know The Beatles.

You don't think they play rock'n'roll? No, they're not rock'n'roll. Rock'n'roll is just four beats, an extension of 12-bar blues. And rock'n'roll is white, 17-year-old kid music, that's all it is. Rock'n'roll is a fake attempt at sex, you know.

But what do you call your style, then? Well, I never heard anybody that plays and sings like me, so I don't know.

There's no name you would try to put on it yourself? Mathematical music.

blasphemy, blas-puffer-me, you know that word? It has to do with God.

Shall we have a listen to the song? OK.

...Which is selling quite well in the States and how do you feel about that? It's horrible, because it is a protest song. People shouldn't really listen to protest songs.

A lot of people buy the record and listen to it on radio stations. So a lot of people could get the message. Yeah, they do get the message, I'm glad they're getting the message. That was a good record, too, huh?

How do you feel about earning a lot of money if you're not really concerned about it all? I like earning a lot of money.

In the start you didn't have much but now you've got a lot. What do you do with it? Nothing.

Not concerned? No, somebody else handles it for me, you know. I just do the same old things.

When you write a song, do you write the melody or the words first? I write it all, the melody and the words.

At the same time? The melody is sort of unimportant really, it comes naturally, you know.

At the very start, other artists used your songs and recorded them and got hits. How did you feel about that? Well, I didn't feel anything really. I felt happy, you know.

Did you like to suddenly get famous, first as the songwriter, and then afterwards as the singer? Er, yeah, it's sort of all over, though. I don't have any interest anymore, I did have interest when I was 13, 14, 15 to be a famous star and all that kind of stuff, but I've been playing on the stage and following tent shows around ever since I've been 10 years old. That's 15 years I've been doing what I've been doing. I know what I'm doing better than anybody else does.

Tired and emotional: a worse for wear Dylan attempts to stay coherent, fails.

Forever Young

Don Hunstein captured Dylan for the sleeve of his very first album and watched the young folk singer turn from an unknown into one of the biggest stars in popular music.

DON HUNSTEIN FIRST tried his hand at photography while stationed in London with the US Air Force. "It started out simply," he recalls. "I was taking holiday snaps of Buckingham Palace and the Changing of the Guard to show my family back home."

His life changed, however, when he saw a book on the photography of Henri Cartier-Bresson. "I was smitten by his reportage style. After that I spent my days off traipsing around the capital taking pictures. The air force set-up was quite relaxed. We could have digs off site, so we'd rent rooms in the city centre and the photo opportunities became endless. The results became my makeshift portfolio."

Returning to America, Hunstein holed up with a friend in New York and landed a job in a commercial studio.

"It was a crash course," he says. "The studio was great, and the work ranged from serious journalism to women's clothes catalogues. I was pushing lighting rigs around, loading films for photographers... It taught me everything I needed to know."

But it was as a staff photographer at Columbia Records that he honed his craft. "I was lucky. I landed the job purely through getting to know people. I initially started off in the publicity shots library, filing photos. The woman who ran the department quickly recognised the importance of rock'n'roll so she'd have me taking pictures of the artists at their recording sessions for the archives.

"As Dylan's career grew, so did mine. That period was so extraordinary, Dylan went from playing tiny clubs in Greenwich village to topping the charts. I ended up with a portfolio that included shots of Duke Ellington, Ramsey Lewis, Billy Taylor, Sarah Vaughan and Martina Navratilova. It was a time of flowering talents."

For more information, see www.donhunstein.com

Interview by Lois Wilson

Packing Them In

Carnegie Hall, October 1963

There were four of us at the soundcheck: me, two engineers and Dylan's producer, Tom Wilson. My instinct was that this was the shot. It didn't matter that you couldn't see Dylan's face; he was instantly recognisable from behind with those bowed legs of his.

Sittin' On Top Of The World

February 1963

We were upstairs in Bob's apartment. These were taken on the morning we shot the front cover of *Freewheelin'*... Dylan just perched on the chair and I said, "Hold it right there" and took the shot. I took a roll of film in the flat, but a lot of it was just him and Suze snuggling on the chair.

All Over You

Dylan & Suze Rotolo, February 1963

I'd already taken the front cover for the *Freewheelin' Bob Dylan* album, although of course I didn't realise that at the time. It wasn't a spontaneous pose. We were walking around and I just said, "Stop, have a look around, talk to Suze about what you are seeing" — and he pulled the pose. He was incredibly natural in front of the camera.

For The Record

Columbia Studios, New York, August 1963

Bob Dylan was a somebody by now, his career had zoomed and I had to capture everything he did on film, especially any recording dates. I went to most, if not all, of them. Columbia's studio was great. It was dubbed the 30th Street Studio, and was the best natural space for recording in New York. The acoustics were fabulous. It was an old church and had remained virtually untouched. He's sat here with that pensive look listening back to the playback. They had huge speakers on rollers so you could do that rather than have to go into the recording booth and break what you were doing. In those days he'd be in the studio alone. Later on, friends and hangers-on would always be there.

All Fired Up

February 1963

I just wanted a close-up to capture his features. He was very amenable to being photographed, he'd move around if I asked him or hold a pose when I needed him too. In that respect he was great to photograph. I didn't go out of my way to get to know him. I was there to do a job and just did it. I wasn't there to be his pal.

A Sell Out

Outside Carnegie Hall, October 1963

I didn't frame this shot very well and if I had my time again I'd get the top of *The Freewheelin'*... cover in the picture as well, and perhaps some people looking at the posters, too. It's on the night of Bob's Carnegie Hall show. I was down there to take pictures of the crowd queuing up; just wanted the atmosphere before the show.

Wild In The Country

He'd gone electric, sculpted countless classics and come to embody rock'n'roll cool. Then Dylan went to Nashville to record the double album that revealed his genius: *Blonde On Blonde*. By Andy Gill

THERE WAS NO stopping Bob Dylan by 1966. Creatively he was on fire, his commercial profile was equalled only by The Beatles, and in September 1965 eight of his songs were in the US Top 40, half of them covers.

By any reckoning, 1965 had been Dylan's *annus mirabilis*, the year he transformed music with two extraordinary albums that brought a new literacy to rock'n'roll and an electric verve to poetry. *Bringing It All Back Home* had been

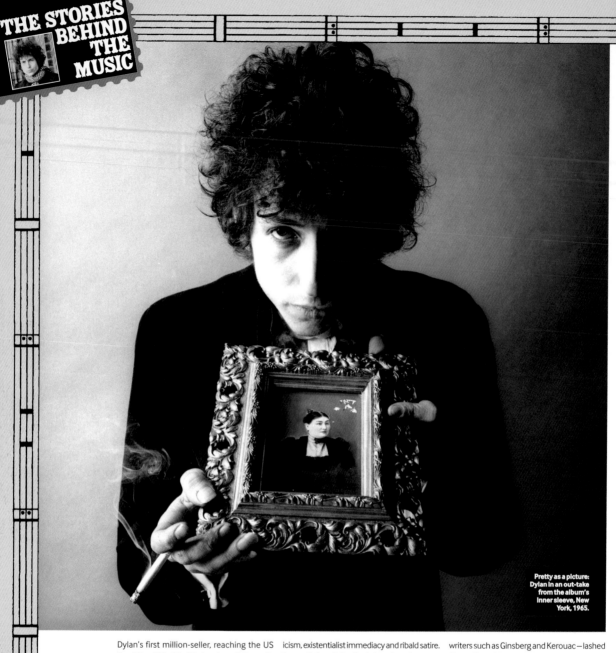

Pretty as a picture: Dylan in an out-take from the album's inner sleeve, New York, 1965.

Dylan's first million-seller, reaching the US Top 10 and No 1 in Britain, where Bob-mania reached such a pitch that in May 1965 he achieved the rare feat of having three of the Top 10 albums (*...Back Home*, *Freewheelin'* and *The Times They Are A-Changin'*).

He had effectively transformed himself over that period too, metamorphosing from a tousle-haired protest troubadour to the electric dandy street punk peering enigmatically out of the sleeve of *Highway 61 Revisited*.

His 1965 songs were packed with images that bounced between anti-authoritarian cynicism, existentialist immediacy and ribald satire. It wasn't that Dylan had abandoned protest songs; he had broadened the scope of his art to more accurately reflect the disconcerting hyper-reality of western culture. A reviewer wrote: "Dylan used to sound like a lung cancer victim singing Woody Guthrie. Now he sounds like a Rolling Stone singing Immanuel Kant."

The truth was that Dylan had devised an entirely new mode of expression which took his primary poetic influences – the Symbolist poetry of Rimbaud and Verlaine, the folk vernacular of Guthrie and the immediacy of beat writers such as Ginsberg and Kerouac – lashed them all to a driving rock beat, and blasted the results into the minds of an entire generation.

The culmination of all these influences and changes would be *Blonde On Blonde*, rock's first double album and a huge step beyond what had been considered possible in music.

Though mostly comprised of love songs (Dylan secretly married Sara Lownds in November 1965), *Blonde On Blonde* evoked a dark urban netherworld that reflected the New York demi-monde of Warhol Factory "stars", dodgy drugs and late-night clubs into which Dylan had recently been sucked.

He had cemented his new electric style by hooking up with a full-time R&B band, The Hawks, with whom he toured through late '65 and the first half of '66. Recording sessions were less successful: attempts at Seems Like A Freeze-Out (later re-titled Visions Of Johanna) failed to convey the song's crepuscular mood.

Accordingly, when producer Bob Johnston suggested going down to Nashville to record, Dylan agreed, taking only organ player Al Kooper and Robbie Robertson to augment the finest session crew money could hire. It was founded around a nucleus of guitarists Wayne Moss, Jerry Kennedy and Joe South, drummer Kenny Buttrey, multi-instrumentalist Charlie McCoy and blind pianist Hargus "Pig" Robbins.

This was an extraordinary decision. Nashville was the home of country, a redneck Mecca whose locals were as likely to attend a Dylan show as they were a Malcolm X rally. But Johnston knew the musicians were good. So, at sessions snatched in between further tour dates in February and March, Blonde On Blonde was recorded at Columbia's Nashville studio.

To facilitate proceedings, Al Kooper served as musical director, translating Dylan's ideas for the local musicians. "Bob had a piano put in his hotel room," Kooper recalls. "And as there were no cassette machines in those days, I would sit and play the piano for him while he sat and wrote. We did this to prepare for the sessions at night, as well: he'd come in an hour late, and I would go in and teach the first song to the band. Then he would arrive and the band would be ready to play. These guys knew how to play together, and were incredibly versatile."

Their versatility proved invaluable when recording Rainy Day Women #12 & 35 during the final session. Dylan wanted to try something different and suggested recording it in the parking lot with a Salvation Army band. Drummer Kenny Buttrey felt the local Salvation Army band might be more disciplined than Dylan needed and suggested that, for a more ramshackle sound, the studio musicians could "play pretty dumb if we put our minds to it".

So, Buttrey dis-assembled his drum kit and deadened his snare drum to approximate the sound of a marching band drummer. A trombonist called Wayne Butler was drafted in, while McCoy performed his remarkable ambidextrous party piece of playing bass and trumpet simultaneously, one in each hand.

VISIONS OF JOHANNA was nailed on the first day of the sessions – a high watermark of Dylan's career. It was cut between successful takes of 4th Time Around and Leopard Skin Pillbox Hat, songs whose widely contrasting styles – elegant acoustic picking and searing Chicago electric blues respectively – give some indication of the musicians' skills.

John Lennon thought 4th Time Around was a parody of The Beatles' Norwegian Wood. "I asked Dylan about it," recalls Kooper. "I said, 'It sounds so much like Norwegian Wood', and he said, 'Actually, Norwegian Wood sounds a lot like this! I'm afraid they took it from me, and I feel that I have to record it.' Evidently, he'd played it for them and they'd nicked it. I asked if he was worried about getting sued by The Beatles. He said, 'They couldn't sue me!'"

The inordinate length of some of the songs never fazed the musicians, even the 11-minute Sad Eyed Lady Of The Lowlands, which took up the whole fourth side of the album. In 1976, Dylan finally confirmed the common knowledge that the song was about his wife Sara, when he admitted, "Stayin' up for days in the Chelsea Hotel/Writin' Sad Eyed Lady Of The Lowlands for you", in Sara, from Desire.

Rock critic Lester Bangs poo-pooed this explanation in Creem: "I have it on pretty good authority that Dylan wrote Sad Eyed Lady, as well as about half of the rest of Blonde On Blonde, wired out of his skull in the studio, just before the songs were recorded, while the session men sat around drinking beer."

Certainly, Charlie McCoy recalled wondering "what in the hell this guy was trying to pull" as they sat around in the basement recreation room, playing ping-pong and drinking coffee. By four in the morning they would be half asleep when Dylan called them upstairs to play.

As the song progressed, they wondered if it would ever finish. Dylan had given them only the sketchiest of outlines and, as each verse moved towards its chorus, they instinctively wound up the power for a conclusion, only to have to rein it all back in again as he began yet another verse. Extraordinarily, the song was cut in one perfect take, a glowing testament to the abilities of these Nashville veterans.

I Want You was the last song cut for the album. "When we were running the stuff down in his hotel room, I went fucking mental over that track," recalls Al Kooper. "I kept saying, 'Let's do I Want You', and Bob just kept putting it off, just to piss me off! Finally, on the last night, I taught it to the band before he arrived. When he came in, I said, 'I took the liberty of teaching them I Want You', and he just smiled at me and said, 'Well, yeah, we could do that'.

RELEASED IN MAY 1966, while Dylan was in the middle of his European tour, Blonde On Blonde was a triumph, its ambition setting new benchmarks for progressive pop music.

"It's an amazing record," reckons Al Kooper. "I know that at one time, one of the jokier things considered was putting a paper band around the album saying Recorded In The South, because it was a bizarre move for Dylan to go to Nashville to record that album. He was the quintessential New York hipster – what was he doing in Nashville? It didn't make any sense. But you take those two elements, pour them into a test-tube, and it just exploded.

The shock waves from that explosion are still being felt today. Within weeks of Blonde On Blonde appearing, pop groups on both sides of the Atlantic were emboldened to forge ahead with the kind of lyrical and musical experimentation that their management and labels had previously tried to stifle – a hugely short-sighted attitude which soon changed when it was realised that the new rock music had spectacularly opened up the extremely profitable LP market.

Just as Dylan and The Hawks' tours had arguably heralded the era of stadium rock, so Blonde On Blonde ushered in the burgeoning counter-culture and its evil twin, the growth of rock music into a huge commercial industry. But the true measure of its greatness is that, even today, Blonde On Blonde's music sounds truly, splendidly visionary.

> "HE WAS THE QUINTESSENTIAL NEW YORK HIPSTER. WHAT WAS HE DOING IN NASHVILLE?" AL KOOPER

THE ENFORCER

Dylan's manager Albert Grossman had a reputation for leaving record company executives and hotel doorman trembling in his wake. By Clark Collis

ONE OF THE great non-fiction books of all-time, Tom Wolfe's The Right Stuff, tells the story of America's early space programme and, in particular, the seven Mercury astronauts. But the undoubted star of the book is Chuck Yeager.

A World War II fighter pilot with 13 kills to his name, Yeager was the first man to reach the speed of sound, an achievement made all the more remarkable by the fact that two days earlier he had broken two ribs after falling off a horse while drunk. According to Wolfe, though, his real influence was not on the record books but on the following generations of pilots who found themselves imitating Yeager's reassuringly laconic Appalachian vocal mannerisms, no matter how hairy the situation might get. Board any commercial flight in the United States today and you can still hear 'that voice': the self-same voice that Yeager used when, as the rapidly increasing G-force began trying to tear his plane apart screw by screw, he reported, "Had a mild buffet there... Jus' the usual instability."

Wolfe's contention that a single man can, by sheer force of character, influence an entire profession would not have come as news to Albert Grossman. Bob Dylan's first real manager, Grossman was also the first real rock manager full stop - a man whose softly-walking, big stick-carrying persona has had an impact on virtually all who came in his wake, from Led Zeppelin's generalissimo Peter Grant to ex-Spice Girls guru Simon Fuller.

Unlike Yeager's airborne followers, though, Grossman's spiritual protégés have the opportunity of scrutinising the man up close and very personal, thanks to his appearance in DA Pennebaker's Don't Look Back. Indeed, it could be argued that you can learn pretty much everything you need to know about rock management from Pennebaker's movie.

Although a largely silent presence throughout Don't Look Back, Grossman is seldom more

©Jerry Schatzberg/Corbis

Who's the boss?
Dylan and Albert
Grossman, 1965.

Paris, 1966: Dylan and Grossman go right over the head of Johnny Halliday (centre).

than a step away from Dylan and ready to swoop if anyone looks like getting in the face of his client.

One unfortunate hotel employee crosses the line when he claims that there is too much noise coming from the singer's room. "There's been no noise in this room," Grossman rumbles, chasing the poor schmuck out into the corridor. "And you're one of the dumbest assholes I've ever spoken to in my life. If we were someplace else I'd punch you in your goddamned nose, you stupid nut."

It leaves you in no doubt that Grossman was capable of balling people out with the best of them. But he was also the first manager to insist that his acts be taken seriously as artists rather than merely marketable products. His was an anti-commercial ethic which not only put Dylan on the cultural map but also, ironically, ensured that both manager and artist would become among the wealthiest people in what Grossman doubtless never referred to as "showbiz".

"Al Grossman probably ended up making more money out of Bob Dylan at that point than Bob Dylan," claims Izzy Young, a music entrepreneur who, prior to Grossman appearing on the scene, had attempted to help the young Dylan's career. "He was smarter than Dylan. He was managing Dylan, then he was managing Peter, Paul & Mary, then he was owning the company that had the copyrights to the songs that Dylan was writing and they were singing, then he owned the company that was recording everybody. Every time there was a move he was getting a slice out of it."

BY 1968 GROSSMAN'S power in the US music industry was virtually without peer thanks to a roster of clients that also included Janis Joplin, The Band, Gordon Lightfoot and Todd Rundgren. As Fred Goodwin argues in his superlative rock business tome The Mansion On The Hill, it was a stable that made him more powerful than the record company presidents he negotiated with, bullied and taught.

Yet, just a decade earlier, Grossman had been working as a public housing administrator in Chicago. It was there that he first began attending folk gigs. Soon he had opened his own club and began to represent a number of artists. Even in those early days he was garnering a reputation for hard bargaining.

"Albert was a strong one-way street," recalls George Wein, one of his early business partners. "He was a brilliant man and a good man in his own way. But a tough son of a bitch."

Grossman believed that artists needed to be masters of their own product if they were going to sustain careers longer than just a couple of years. It was a view which initially aided Peter, Paul & Mary who, thanks to Grossman, retained creative control of both the packaging and recording of their

music. This revolutionary approach soon attracted the attention of Dylan, then looking for someone who could help him break out of the less than lucrative folk circuit.

It didn't take long for Dylan's wallet to widen thanks to Grossman's pairing of his songs with Peter, Paul & Mary's voices. Grossman also renegotiated the songwriter's publishing deal to his advantage, and by 1963 he was acting as Dylan's sole line of communication with the music business from his new offices in Manhattan.

Despite the singer's relatively small fanbase, Grossman convinced him to play not more but less gigs – a situation that made those concerts which Dylan did perform real events rather than just another date in the folk calendar. Meanwhile, two decades before Michael Jackson's handlers insisted that journalists refer to him as "The King Of Pop", Grossman was essentially pulling off the same trick, insisting that hacks that wrote pieces about his star use the phrase "spokesman for a generation".

All things considered, it's difficult to over-emphasise quite how much influence Grossman had on Dylan's career and life during the mid-'60s.

"I think Albert was one of the few people that saw Dylan's worth early on," says Pennebaker. "And he played it without equivocation or compromise. He refused to let him go on any rinky-dink TV shows or let Columbia do bullshit things with him."

Another person impressed by Grossman was The Rolling Stones' manager-to-be Andrew Loog Oldham, who briefly worked as Dylan's publicist when the singer appeared on a BBC drama called Madhouse On Castle Street in 1962.

"Grossman was ahead of the game, turning the quick buck into the long buck," says Oldham today. "His devotion to Dylan, even then, was apparent. That impressed me – the fact that he was sitting in a hotel room, giving all his time to just one artist. They were both very happy together. They acted like they knew something we didn't know yet."

It was a relationship that irked many of Dylan's supporters from the folk circuit, who regarded Grossman as pretty much Mammon incarnate.

"He'd never been popular amongst these people," says producer Joe Boyd, who worked at the 1965 Newport Festival. "He'd always been seen as one of the money changers at the gate of the temple, not a priest. Grossman was very cool, but Grossman's way of being cool got up a lot of people's noses."

One of those noses belonged to Atlantic Records chief Jerry Wexler. "Grossman had people buffaloed," he says. "He would talk in tongues. He had a habit of going on and on and not actually saying anything. And cryptically he'd look at you. The suggestion was that, if you're a cogent-enough person, you'll understand what I'm getting at. If you don't dig me you're some kind of insensate asshole."

Given Grossman's evermore powerful position as The Man With Dylan's Ear, he could afford to make enemies – just as long as those enemies did what he wanted. Yet, as the '60s drew to a close, that position began to look increasingly precarious. In part, the problem appears to have been about money: Dylan was starting to resent Grossman's sizeable 25 per cent commission.

WITH DYLAN ESTABLISHED as one of the biggest acts on the planet, it would seem that the singer concluded he had no need for his one-time mentor.

"The ultimate destiny of the manager who breaks the act is to get blown off," says former Grossman business associate Vinny Fusco. "It's almost irrevocable. Unless the artist is going to continue to grow and needs a grower, anyone can do the job for a lot less money. Get a fucking bookkeeper."

When Grossman's contract ended – on the weekend of the Woodstock festival – Dylan declined to renew it.

Actually, many believe that Dylan had already made his feelings toward Grossman known on Dear Landlord, from *John Wesley Harding*, which found him pleading with a third party not to place a price on his soul – or, it would seem, at least not a price as steep as 25 per cent.

Despite the loss of his principal act, Grossman's management company should still have been in good shape. Soon, though, the usual instability had transformed into something approaching hurricane weather as, one by one, clients such as Paul Butterfield and Janis Joplin succumbed to either the bottle or the needle.

Joplin's heroin-induced death in October 1970 appeared to have been the final straw, Grossman abandoning his New York offices altogether to set up camp permanently in Woodstock. There, he formed his own record company, Bearsville, and

"Dylan and Grossman acted like they knew something we didn't."

ANDREW LOOG OLDHAM, ROLLING STONES MANAGER

built a recording studio and theatre of the same name.

From now on, Grossman's relationship with Dylan was almost entirely conducted through lawyers as manager sued artist for unpaid commissions. The suit would finally be settled in 1987 to Grossman's advantage – but by then he had been dead for almost two years after suffering a fatal heart attack, aged 59, while flying to London.

Dylan attended neither the funeral nor the memorial service, yet, without Grossman, many argue that he wouldn't have made it much beyond New York's coffeehouses.

"There never would have been a Bob Dylan who could have survived and made it without Albert Grossman," concludes Peter, Paul & Mary's Peter Yarrow. "Personally, artistically and in a business sense, Albert was the sole reason Bob Dylan made it."

Back In The Saddle

Holed up in Woodstock, on *John Wesley Harding* Dylan journeyed into the wilderness, invented country rock and revealed some home truths.

THE RELEASE OF *John Wesley Harding* came as a slap in the face for the dominant hippy culture. At a time when everything was getting louder and more flamboyant and colourful, this album sounded almost diffident — one of the most quietly recorded albums ever, it sort of shuffled in modestly with the title track and never bothered straining for the listener's attention. The tales are here to hear, it suggested, but you'll have to pay attention.

Psychedelia was at its floral peak, with countless sleeve designs — *Sgt Pepper*, The Incredible String Band's *5000 Spirits Or The Layers Of The Onion* and, most recently, Jimi Hendrix's *Axis: Bold As Love* — illustrating the era's rococo tendencies. In the face of this cosmic maelstrom, *John Wesley Harding* offered a design of quite striking understatement: accompanied by a motley trio of characters, a hunched, thinly-bearded Dylan peered shyly out of a plain black and white snapshot set into a beige-grey frame. No bright colours. No fancy curlicues. Some funny hats, but no cosmic intentions. Dylan was deliberately distancing himself from the imperatives of an era he himself had done so much to define.

Photographer John Berg took the cover photo in the garden of Sally Grossman, wife of Dylan's manager and the woman accompanying him on the cover of *Bringing It All Back Home*, when the temperature was below freezing. It explains Dylan's hunched pose: he and the others — Lakhsman and Purna Das Baul, of the Bauls Of Bengal musical group, and Charlie Joy, a local carpenter-cum-stonemason who happened to be working at the Grossmans — would pose for a few frames, dash back inside for a few warming slugs of brandy then go back out for another frame or two.

Snatched between slugs, the sleeve came to represent a turning point in pop — the moment at which psychedelia, having reached its furthest extent, retreated to the comforting confines of country-rock.

The sleeve photo summed up the woolly western atmosphere of the album, populated with drifters, immigrants, hobos and outlaws.

One of the most revealing of all Dylan's albums.

This, Dylan seemed to be saying, would be a journey into the wilderness. Dylan's own journey into the outback had begun 18 months earlier, with the July 1966 bike crash. Recuperating at his Woodstock home, he underwent several life-transforming changes, retreating from the hectic, drug-fuelled world tour with The Hawks into a cosier, family-oriented lifestyle.

After such a close brush with death, the birth of his children Jesse and Anna in 1967 affected his outlook profoundly, as did his growing interest in the Bible. His musical direction, as later revealed with the release of The Basement Tapes, had also shifted towards more instinctive, throwaway songs.

IN AUTUMN 1967, he visited Nashville to record his new album with a stripped-down version of the session crew that played on *Blonde On Blonde*, hoping to emulate the sound that Canadian folk singer Gordon Lightfoot had recently achieved using the same players. After the relatively disorganised *Blonde On Blonde* sessions, the musicians were shocked to find the material written and Dylan ready to record; in three swift sessions, the album was finished — a total of six hours recording, according to drummer Kenny Buttrey.

Not that anyone realised it at the time but, following the jovial singalongs recorded in The Band's basement, *John Wesley Harding* contained no choruses at all. It was as if such whimsical, user-friendly business had been ruthlessly swept aside in pursuit of a simpler, more ascetic notion of songwriting. And, with the sole exception of the lengthy Ballad Of Frankie Lee..., all the songs were condensed, three-verse miniatures.

In sharp contrast to the prolix surrealism of his "electric trilogy", Dylan's new LP offered a series of brief, cryptic parables which both in form and, in some cases, content reflected the time he had spent studying the Bible. Indeed, he himself later referred to it as "the first biblical rock album". And despite his subsequent scornful dismissal of those who saw the album as some kind of psychologically revealing "ink-blot test", *John Wesley Harding* does seem to contain various musings upon the singer's own situation, transmuted through a style that married American myth to religious allegory.

At least two of the songs contain direct scriptural references. The Wicked Messenger comes from Proverbs 13:16-17: "A wicked messenger falleth into mischief; but a faithful ambassador is health" —

BOB DYLAN
JOHN WESLEY HARDING

easily read as a comment upon Dylan's own earlier fecklessness. All Along The Watchtower, meanwhile, offers a condensation of the passage (Isaiah 21, 6-9 and 11-12) in which a horseman brings news of the fall of Babylon and the approach of the apocalypse.

The album was further stuffed with scourging critiques of materialism, from the way that America tempted immigrants with promises of "wealth itself" rather than spiritual contentment (I Pity The Poor Immigrant) to the difficulties of "saving" members of a society who had already sold their souls to a variety of temptations (I Dreamed I Saw St Augustine). The general rejection of materialism in favour of a more spiritual outlook is brought into more personal focus by a brace of songs that appear to be see-through allegories about Dylan's relationship with Albert Grossman. Dear Landlord (Dylan had previously lodged at Grossman's places in Woodstock and Gramercy

Park, New York) criticises the manager's attempt to shoe-horn the artist's creativity into a materialist agenda, while The Ballad Of Frankie Lee And Judas Priest places the two men in a parable comparable to the Devil's tempting of Jesus, Dylan reflecting on how close to disaster he was brought by the blandishments of fame and fortune.

These subtexts only became clearer as the years passed. At the time, it was enough that Dylan had returned at all, let alone with songs that offered such scope for textual analysis. In the meantime, John Wesley Harding offered a much-needed oasis of calm contemplation in an era of loud, gaudy excess.

However, with the gift of hindsight, and notwithstanding the competing claims of Another Side Of Bob Dylan and Blood On The Tracks, it's probably true to say that John Wesley Harding is the most personally revealing of all Dylan's albums. Andy Gill

After The Fall

Nursing a hardcore drug habit, and with violent reactions to the '66 tour still ringing in his ears, Dylan needed rest. So he took a nice ride to clear his head. Stuart Bailie picks through the wreckage of the legendary bike crash.

IN MID-1966, Bob Dylan looked like an especially savage cartoon by Ralph Steadman. He was all angles and attitude, the cheeks collapsing, the hair a dreadful shock, the famous cowboy mouth drawn more thin and twisted. He was dispensing with sleep, smoking like a laboratory dog and barely eating. His body was literally consuming itself.

All the time, he was launching his music into the midst of hatred and ignorance. The audience at his European dates howled down the electric songs; reporters were still asking sloppy questions about protest music and the identity of Mister Jones. A year earlier, there was a kind of grim amusement to be had from this carry-on, but such fun was spent now.

There was a psychotic edge to the Dylan entourage, partly due to the availability of drugs (Allen Ginsberg would later call this incarnation of Dylan a "methedrine clown"). In the opening minutes of the '66 documentary Eat The Document, keyboard player Richard Manuel has a swift toot to steady himself for the day. He looks rotten. Dylan notices the disapproving expression of a nearby hotel waiter and cackles, nastily.

"It takes a lot of medicine to keep up this pace," Bob told biographer Robert Shelton in March that year. "It's very hard, man. A concert tour like this has almost killed me. It's been like this since October… it really drove me out of my mind."

Dylan swore that he'd escape his intense work rate in the forthcoming year. But first there was a matter of some shows in America, Australia, England, Ireland, Italy, Sweden and France. His book, Tarantula, was overdue. His contract with CBS was coming to an end, requiring intense re-negotiation.

Manager Albert Grossman was fixing up some further dates, beginning in August, including the Yale Bowl in New Haven and possibly New York's Shea Stadium. In total, he planned as many as 60 extra gigs, pushing Dylan through the autumn, aiming to lift his sales and profile close to those of The Beatles, who had triumphed at Shea Stadium in '65 then quit live performance.

Dylan was all mortgaged out, physically and mentally. "I've been at it longer than a 55-year-old man," he told Shelton. "Hey, death to me is nothing, as long as I can die fast…I've been living under a suicidal hex now for the past six months."

The singer used the line "I accept chaos" as a mission statement back in 1965. Now it seemed as if crippling turmoil was taking up his hospitality. In London, Dylan shared a ride across town with John Lennon. DA Pennebaker was also in the car, capturing the moment for the new documentary. On this rare occasion, Dylan wasn't able to uphold his usual dominant pose. He was distracted, pushing away the hipster shades, rubbing at his eyes, losing the conversational edge, increasingly nauseous. The Beatle was amused to see him. As Dylan hunched over in pain, Lennon turned to the driver and gave an impression of a strung-out spaceman: "Permission to land, Tom..."

DYLAN CAME DOWN on June 29, 1966. The rear wheel of his Triumph locked, throwing him off, damaging several vertebrae and causing lacerations to the head and neck. He had been joyriding in Woodstock: according to Shelton, Dylan had been up for three days and was taking his bike for repairs when he lost control.

The crash took place on Striebel Road, near his home. Dylan was taken to Middletown Hospital, where they checked for concussion and put on a neck brace. Little was revealed to the public, so the rumours grew more fabulous: Dylan was paralysed, disfigured, silenced by government agents, even dead. Bob had gone the way of James Dean, Hank Williams, Robert Johnson or Arthur Rimbaud, making an early exit, leaving great art and a reckless image behind. Fans looking for clues in his work could point to the Triumph T-shirt on the cover of *Highway 61 Revisited* and song titles like Motorpsycho Nitemare (from *Another Side Of Bob Dylan*). The theme of death had been streaked through his debut album and a regular

The rumours grew: he was paralysed, silenced, disfigured, even dead.

feature afterwards. The ceremony was all primed.

Richard Fariña, who married Joan Baez's sister Mimi, had died in a bike crash in April. Folk singers Peter La Farge and Paul Clayton committed suicide the same year. Was this Allen Ginsberg's vision in Howl, in which a generation of untamed individuals are sacrificed to regimented consumer society?

"I always pictured Bobby with a skull and crossbones on his forehead," Baez told writer Anthony Scaduto. "I guess it's because I've seen him be destructive to himself and other people. I would say he was on something of a death trip."

But reports of Dylan's crucifixion were premature. On May 8, 1967, the New York Daily News ran a report from Woodstock. Journalist Michael Iachetta doorstepped the singer and came away with some remarkable quotes.

"What I've been doin' is mostly seein' only a few close friends," Dylan said. "Readin' little 'bout the outside world, poring over books you never heard of, thinkin' about where I'm goin' and why am I runnin' and what am I takin'."

Iachetta noted that Bob was bearded and wearing a bandana, possibly to hide the scars of the crash. His shirt collar was turned up to cover the back of his neck, and the speed jive of '66 had slowed down to a more measured vernacular: "Mainly what I've been doin' is working on gettin' better and makin' better music, which is what my life is all about."

DYLAN'S MARRIAGE TO Sara Lownds on November 22, 1965 had successfully weathered its difficulties, and a new dynasty came swiftly: Jesse (1966), Anna (1967), Samuel (1968) and Jakob (1971). By the following year,

photographer Elliott Landy was allowed to take photos of the chubby, bespectacled patriarch as he balanced a series of kids, feeding bottles and other signs of domesticity.

He was sampling other art forms as well. As early as 1962, Dylan had talked about quitting music for a life of painting, and now, with the help of a neighbour, he was getting his chance. Dylan's visuals later appeared on the covers of *Self Portrait*, *Planet Waves* and The Band's *Music From Big Pink*.

Dylan is rarely hailed as a paint-pusher, although he has received a few sympathetic comparisons to Van Gogh. Yet Elliott Landy, quoted in The Telegraph fanzine in 1987, insisted that the impact of the Big Pink painting was more impressive when viewed directly ("the original is stunning"). He also disclosed that, back in Woodstock, Dylan had been working on a stained glass representation of a clown, a sculpture of a cream pitcher with a weird handle and other "mindblowing stuff".

Consciously or not, Dylan was acting like a born-again nature boy, tending to his creative soul in a rural environment. Yet Bob didn't just go soft in the country. Even after the crash, when he was supposedly getting spiritual, he was fixing up business deals, reading the revised galleys of Tarantula and editing the documentary footage for Eat The Document. The crash freed Dylan from the corporate loop, enabling him to attend to business while avoiding the worst of it.

Music was still an option, but when Michael Iachetta came knocking, Dylan revealed a resentment that was stymying his creative flow: "Songs are in my head like they always are. And they're not goin' to get written down until some things are evened up. Not until some people come forward and make up for some of the things that have happened."

The go-slow had a simple cause. Dylan and Grossman were trying to score a better record deal, possibly by leaving CBS for MGM. After dirty tactics and bluff on each side, Dylan secured an improved deal. At the same time, the singer and his manager began to pull apart, as detailed in Dear Landlord on *John Wesley Harding*. They split in '69, just as Dylan was plotting his route back to MacDougal Street, Greenwich Village.

BACK IN 1967, The Hawks were on a retainer, helping Bob with the documentary. They had already missed their deadline with the ABC TV network by a long way. Things were complicated by the fact that Dylan didn't want a repeat of Don't Look Back, set for release in '67.

Dylan decided that the second instalment should be more figurative, as if the musicians were actors, each playing a role.

With the help of Woodstock film-maker Howard Alk (who had worked alongside Pennebaker on the European dates), the requisite unusual editing job was done. It was fascinating stuff, but never a candidate for mainstream viewing.

Still, Dylan was reunited with his backing band. They too had been resting up, getting over that last tour, as Robbie Robertson told the Saturday Evening Post: "We did it *[the tour]* until we couldn't take it anymore. We were so exhausted that everybody said it was a time to rest. We stopped listening to music for a year. We didn't listen to anything but what you didn't have to listen to, like opera."

Dylan revealed a similar condition in a Rolling Stone interview in 1969. "I still didn't sense the importance of the accident until at least a year after that. I realised it was a real accident. I thought that I was just gonna get up and go back to doing what I was doing before... but I couldn't do that anymore."

Eight years later he spoke again to Rolling Stone about this era and put even more emphasis on the aftershock. "Since that point, I more or less had amnesia. Now, you can take that statement as literally or as metaphorically as you need to, but that's what happened to me. It took me a long time to get to do consciously what I used to do unconsciously."

Nonetheless, Dylan and the group that would become The Band spent the early summer of '67 jamming at Dylan's house. It relieved the boredom and they lost some of their aversion to rock'n'roll, even if the main drift was more folksy. They set up a "clubhouse" in the basement of Big Pink, The Band's place on 2155 Stoll Road, in nearby West Saugerties. As at Dylan's

Born to be wild: the pre-bike crash Dylan on a Triumph Tiger 100.

place, they were taping the sessions, although this time keyboard player Garth Hudson had put in a reel-to-reel recorder, several microphones and stereo mixers for a better quality sound. Over 100 tracks were put down, many of them cover versions, which would later surface as *The Basement Tapes* (see story, beginning page 118).

DYLAN WAS FEELING his way into a field that he had previously described as "historical traditional" music. He explained it best in a 1966 interview with Playboy: "Traditional music is based on hexagrams. It comes about from legends, Bibles, plagues and it revolves around vegetables and death... all these songs about roses growing out of people's brains and lovers who are really geese and swans that turn into angels – they're not going to die."

Though the release of *John Wesley Harding* in February 1968 allayed many fears, fans wanted to hear more material. There was considerable intrigue about his rural lifestyle, even if The Beatles, Beach Boys and sundry acid-eaters were at their best.

Many people have their theories about Dylan's late '60s retreat. Patti Smith's version is more poetic than most, supposing that Dylan quite simply put his personal life before his art and ambitions. "He's like the Duke Of Windsor – how he gave up his crown for the woman he loved, y'know."

When he steered into Woodstock in summer '66, he was a mean-faced proto-punk on the road to annihilation. By the time he left three years later, his music was meditative, riddling and uniquely resonant. Bob Dylan had become a man.

The Bard Stripped Bare

LOST CLASSIC

Dylan goes country, reveals his new voice and bares his soul. *Nashville Skyline* is better than the critics of the time would have you think.

WHILE HARDLY REVILED at the level of the following year's *Self Portrait* ("What is this shit?" asked Rolling Stone's review) *Nashville Skyline* has nevertheless been similarly cast as the album when Bob Dylan lost touch with the streets and the campuses, finally setting himself adrift from the roots that had made him great. Worse, he seemed to be embracing the very redneck – ie Southern – values that had exercised his pen so poisonously on songs such as The Lonesome Death Of Hattie Carroll.

Thankfully, *Nashville Skyline* was much better than such talk suggested. In a sense prefaced by the relaxed coda on *John Wesley Harding* – I'll Be Your Baby Tonight – this was, yet again, a new Dylan: more direct, more overtly musical, a Dylan who, by the way, noted that, "Nashville Skyline is the best record I've ever done".

Still, it was not well received. The New York Times fussed: "Dylan is a businessman first and a prophet some time later. There's old Bobby Dylan, fat and sassy, grinning out from the album cover. Just him and his guitar and the Columbia Records logo saying, Howdy folks. Want to buy some whacky-do songs for sitting and toe-tapping? Come by the shop and I'll give you a free listen."

With time, this proved to be self-serving nonsense. *Nashville Skyline* can take its place with the very greatest of Dylan albums. It has all the hallmarks: like many Dylan classics it was recorded fast and haphazardly ("It was just manip-ulated out of nothing," he said); lyrically it may swap the communal language of blues for country music, but its roots are still clear and true; and it features largely the same band that drove *John Wesley Harding*, so the continuity's there.

Crucially, though, it's Dylan's most direct album. This is central – and the reason why many hardcore Dylanologists wrongly dismiss it. On *Nashville Skyline*, everything is laid bare: there's no need for analysis, no emotional garbage cans to root through because, for the first time in his recorded life, Bob Dylan throws out all the usual obfuscation and means exactly what he says.

Look at the song titles. I Threw It All Away, Tell Me That It Isn't True, To Be Alone With You – utterly unambiguous, and a direct line to Dylan. Subterranean Homesick Blues, Sad Eyed Lady Of The Lowlands, even Jokerman may be more fun to dissect and theorise about – and they may sound more important – but this is the real thing: pure Dylan.

And it's what makes *Nashville Skyline* so perfect. The only lyrical debate worth having is whether or not "Once I had mountains, in the palm of my hand" is a double entendre. Otherwise, it's the soul laid bare.

IT KICKS OFF with the laziest of campfire songs, Girl From The North Country, a duet with Johnny Cash. He'd stopped by the studio and the pair knocked out this and a couple of other tracks, just two good ol' boys fooling around on guitars. It's all a bit raggedy-arsed (they don't even re-take the fluffed final verse and chorus) but the timbre of Dylan's singing is immediately amazing.

The voice that thundered out Positively 4th Street or billy goat-gruffed its way through Maggie's Farm has been transformed into this marvellous syrupy honk with a vocal range previously unheard on Dylan records. Listen to how he swoops down to "she once was, a true love of mine" and soars up to "see for me, when the snowflakes fall"; he's like an old-school singer.

Whether it was giving up the smokes that did it, or a conscious decision to mimic country heroes like Hank Williams and the Carter Family, the effect is electric. Moreover, this "new" voice (some said it was a throwback to his pre-fame days in Hibbing) gives him the tonal repertoire to handle his chosen subjects.

By turns, the songs are romantic, regretful, sorrowful and plain old fun-seeking. The old Dylan snarl wouldn't have made songs such as One More Night and Tonight I'll Be Staying Here With You work – they demand honesty, not irony.

That year he told the Nashville Banner, "I love children, I love animals, I am loyal to my friends, I have a sense of humour, I have a generally happy outlook. I try to be on time for appointments. I have a good rela-tionship with my wife. I take criticism well. I strive to do good work. I try to find some good in everybody."

> ### Everything is laid bare. Dylan means exactly what he says.

This lack of complexity permeates *Nashville Skyline*. Even Elliott Landy's wonderful cover shot, in which Bob smiles down as if to a child, contrasts markedly with the monochrome tones of *John Wesley Harding*. One is a straight arrow, the other a curveball.

The music is also marvellously economical. By the time Dylan asks producer Bob Johnston if the tape is rolling before track three, To Be Alone With You, there are just 20 minutes left. But how well the time is used. Instruments that powered through *Blonde On Blonde* here submit meekly to the songs: Peggy Day is bright as a new pin, Lay Lady Lay rides on one of the most original chord sequences of all time, modulating effortlessly down the scale from major to minor to major to minor again as Dylan pins that glorious melody seamlessly over the top; One More Night contains one of his finest middle eights ("I had no idea what a woman in love could do"). Then there's Tell Me That It Isn't True, the central song: an effortless tune, gorgeous skittery pedal steel and the most affecting performance on the album.

Above it all is that voice. Folk singer Eric Andersen recalls: "He said he had learned to sing for the first time in his life. Now he knew something about music, knew how to play and sing, and he was very proud of it."

Nashville Skyline is important for many reasons. The music speaks for itself, the lyrics illuminate the fact that despite everything gone before, Bob Dylan's brain is wired the same as ours, and that accessibility is pure joy. Such is Dylan's canon that should you ever hear a crappy Dylan album, all you have to do is go back and revisit a great one. Even decades later, it's all still there, humming away. *Another Side Of Bob Dylan*, *Blood On The Tracks*, *Oh Mercy*. And *Nashville Skyline*. *Rob Beattie*

DYLAN PLAYS THE ISLE OF WIGHT

Breaking cover for the first time since his bike crash, Dylan wowed The Beatles, Eric Clapton *and* the inmates of Parkhurst prison.

JULY 17, 1969

Dylan agrees to play at The Isle Of Wight Festival.

RAY FOULK *(festival organiser)* We came up with the idea of making it a holiday for him and his family, in a farmhouse at Bembridge with a swimming pool and a recently converted barn, suitable for rehearsing in. We were offering Dylan a fortnight stay there, no expense spared, car with driver. Also, we would have him come over on the QE2. The fee offered was $50,000.

AUGUST 13

Dylan's son Jesse falls ill and is rushed to hospital soon after boarding the QE2.

FOULK It was dreadful news. I was, at this stage, in daily contact with *[Dylan's agent]* Bert Block. He telephoned me with the news that Dylan had left the ship to go to the hospital and was still in New York. It brought home to us the vulnerability of our position. The event all hinged upon this one human being. It shook us up a bit.

AUGUST 25

With Jesse recovered, Dylan arrives at Heathrow.

FOULK He arrived on a regular flight at about 10pm. Sara was with him as well as Al, Aronowitz *[a journalist in Dylan's entourage]*. Block and myself were there to meet them. We drove down to Portsmouth in two cars, which took about two hours. It was nearly 1am

when we arrived at Portsmouth seafront, and very cold.

I wanted to keep Dylan happy, but I was getting word back from our office that ticket sales were slow and we had to get more publicity out of Dylan. I thought that if we could arrange one main press conference, rather than set up individual interviews, Dylan may well agree to do it.

AUGUST 26

George Harrison travels to Forelands Farm, Bembridge, Isle Of Wight.

JUDY LEWIS *(housekeeper)* One of the first things Bob asked me to get him was some honey. He was quiet. He came over as a very well-mannered person. Most of his time he spent playing guitar with George Harrison.

FOULK I remember walking through the living room one day and Dylan and Harrison were sitting on a sofa singing The Everly Brothers' All I Have To Do Is Dream together. It sounded incredible... just like The Everly Brothers. There was not a lot of rehearsal going on there, though.

> ## "It was audible to the monks in Quarr who hadn't heard music since the war."
> **RIKKI FARR, PROMOTER**

JL I was forever supplying endless cups of tea to him and Harrison. I think Harrison was in awe of him. They got on very well, but I got the impression Dylan felt he was a bit pushy... wanting to play all the time.

AUGUST 27

Press conference at Halland Hotel, Seaview, Isle Of Wight

PRESS Why did you come to the Isle Of Wight?
DYLAN I wanted to see the home of Alfred, Lord Tennyson.
PRESS Why?
DYLAN Just curious.

AUGUST 28

John Lennon flies in.

FOULK Lots of helicopters were landing and using a field next to the farmhouse. The grounds were well kept by a gardener and they were immaculate. Then this helicopter landed right on the lawn, blowing all the flowers away, much to the gardener's rage. Out of the helicopter strolled John Lennon.

AUGUST 31

After a day of rehearsal with The Band, Dylan tops the bill.

TONY BRAMWELL *(Beatles aide)* I was up in London, hanging out with Eric Clapton and some others. Early in the afternoon, Eric said, "Let's go to the Isle Of Wight to see Bob Dylan." He organised a coach and we trundled down with all of Cream and Jackie Lomax, singing and drinking all the way.

RIKKI FARR *(co-promoter)* We had been trying to convince The Beatles to get back together and play, but it never quite came together. What did happen, though, was a kind of spontaneous superstar jam session in the afternoon at a mock tudor house where Bob Dylan was staying.

The Beatles *[Lennon, Harrison and Starr]* came down to watch the show, but in the afternoon they all got together in the house and I saw the most incredible supergroup you could imagine: Dylan, The Beatles, Eric Clapton, Jackie Lomax, all just jamming. Ginger Baker would get off the drum stool and Ringo would step in. Eric Clapton would

take a solo, and then George Harrison would take the next one. It was amazing.

AL ARONOWITZ Dylan invited The Beatles to a game of tennis on the Forelands Farm courts. The game ended at 5.30 and Dylan piled into a white van along with Sara, Ringo, Maureen and me for the five mile drive to the festival site.

JULIE FELIX *(folk singer)* The Band had gone on and they were going down really well. It was the first big gig they had done on their own. And so they just stayed out there for an extra hour or something. Meanwhile, poor Bob Dylan was getting more and more nervous about going on.

FARR The PA system was 2000 watts, huge for the time, so as well as being heard by the audience, the music was clearly audible to

the inmates of Parkhurst prison and the monks in Quarr monastery, who hadn't heard live music since the Second World War.

ERIC CLAPTON Dylan was fantastic. He changed everything. He used to have a blues voice but he changed voices, and then suddenly he was a country and western singer with a white suit on. He was Hank Williams. They *[the audience]* couldn't understand it. You had to be a musician to understand it.

JOHN LENNON He gave a reasonable, albeit slightly flat, performance but everyone was expecting Godot, or Jesus, to appear.

GEORGE HARRISON The concert was marvellous… he gave a brilliant performance.

LEVON HELM *(The Band)* Bob had an extra

Dylan and a forest of microphones, Isle Of Wight Festival, August 31, 1969.

list of songs with eight or 10 different titles, with question marks by them, that we would've went ahead and done had it seemed like the thing to do. But it seemed like everybody was a bit tired… the festival was three days old by then.

TOM PAXTON *(singer-songwriter)* What astonished me was the negative reaction in the British press, including downright fabrications, like saying he had run off the stage halfway through the set. It was a magical performance and, afterwards, I went with him and The Beatles to the farmhouse where he was clearly in a merry mood, because he felt it had gone so well. The Beatles had brought a test pressing of their next album, Abbey Road, and we listened to that and had quite a party.

Setting the benchmark: Dylan at his Byrdcliff home, Woodstock, 1968.

Into The Woods

Holed up in a basement with The Band, Dylan crafted some down-home rural sounds for fun. By 1969, those songs had changed the way The Beatles, The Rolling Stones and others set about making music. By John Harris

ON JANUARY 3, 1969, The Beatles were at Twickenham Film Studios, two days into the filming of Let It Be. The soul-grinding misery that would rapidly define the experience had apparently yet to exert its grip; sound-reels of their conversation that morning suggest they were still occasionally capable of a very Fab-ish bonhomie. That said, John Lennon — accompanied, as was the norm, by Yoko Ono — had yet to arrive, so Paul, George and Ringo could just about pretend it was like the old days. They joked about Paul's new beard, raved about Wilson Pickett's version of Hey Jude, and fell into a brief exchange about Bob Dylan.

Mere weeks before, George Harrison had spent time in Woodstock with Dylan and The Band, marvelling at their apparently idyllic life. Soon enough, the contrast between the Woodstock experience and the increasingly bad vibes coursing through Twickenham Studios would be enough to force him to temporarily quit; for now, he simply seemed driven to tell his colleagues about what he'd found.

"The Band is too much," George enthused. "They're just living, and they happen to be a band as well. The drummer is fantastic. He plays guitar, really: he's not really the drummer. Levon Helm, he's called. He's really like Coates Comes Up From Somerset – those people."

The reference was to an advert for Coates' cider, then all but inescapable on TV. It featured three cartoon yokels, bawling the jingle in fluent bumpkin: "Coates comes up from Somerset, where the cider apples grow." Hindsight suggests that the comparison was a little misplaced...

"He's got, like, no neck, and all these whiskers, and... a happy smiling face," Harrison went on, as if the latter feature beggared belief. "And their scene is just singing all those songs. [To Ringo] You'd go down a bomb with them."

Starr emitted a self-deprecating "Mmm"; Paul McCartney laughed.

"Cos it's all that country western [sic]," George went on. "Their favourite track was Ringo's track. That's their scene completely." He was referring to Don't Pass Me By, the country-ish song from The White Album that had taken Ringo a good five years to put together.

"Are you going to write another?" said McCartney, falling into a speeded-up reading of the song. Bashfully, Ringo admitted that he was trying to write something in a similar vein. He had only one line: "Taking a trip on an ocean liner/I got to get to Carolina."

A few minutes earlier, Harrison had played a snatch of an unreleased Dylan song, Please Mrs Henry, and asked Ringo a question about some coveted items he had recently passed the drummer's way: "Did you play those tapes?"

Harrison was referring to his copies of the music recorded by Dylan, Robbie Robertson, Rick Danko, Richard Manuel, Garth Hudson and Levon Helm two summers before: songs by turns apocalyptic, comic, gracefully poetic and absurdly throwaway. What linked them all was the sense that they tapped into an America that had long since been lost, and in doing so, beat a path away from the star-gazing gaudiness of psychedelia. One of Dylan's few analyses of what he and The Band were up to, delivered in characteristically terse words in 1978, certainly says as much: "At the time, psychedelic rock was taking over the universe, and so we were singing these homespun ballads... or whatever they were."

JUST HOW MUCH of the music had been passed Harrison's way remains unclear; all that is certain is that The Beatles were surprisingly late on the case. Much of the material had begun to circulate in London from late 1967 onwards. By the spring of 1968, when the group were cloistered in India, cover versions – which, as far as the public was concerned, amounted to the premiere of the material – had started to appear. The deluge began with Manfred Mann's camped-up reading of Quinn The Eskimo; by early 1970, it seemed that every cred-hungry British artist had recorded a Basement Tapes cover.

Thanks to acetates produced by Dylan's publishers, and reel-to-

reel tape copies run off by those who wanted to spread the word, the original material was eddying around London's hipper households.

"People were intrigued," says Joe Boyd, then in charge of the talent-heavy roster of Witchseason Productions. "The power of those things was tremendous. There was a time when you could go down the King's Road, go into people's houses, and hear those songs a lot: Dylan singing This Wheel's On Fire or Quinn The Eskimo. They had a huge circulation."

What became known as The Basement Tapes represented the first fruits of Dylan and The Band's time in Woodstock. They had arrived there two years after their paths first collided: in the wake of Highway 61 Revisited, Dylan had been alerted to the roadworn quintet then known as Levon & The Hawks, who were seeing out a club residency in New Jersey. Having been recruited as his sidemen, they made their first appearance with him on August 28, 1965 at the Forest Hills Stadium in New York. Thus commenced the nine months of borderline insanity during which they would play some of the most glorious live rock'n'roll ever heard, only to have it greeted by endless deluges of abuse. Unable to stand it, Levon Helm vacated the drumstool that November; after a spell making money as an oil worker, he was only reunited with his colleagues a couple of months after The Basement Tapes sessions began.

A breath of fresh air: Dylan with George Harrison, Woodstock, 1968.

In their wake, Dylan would tumble into the austere, biblical music that made up the lion's share of John Wesley Harding, while The Band poured their side of the Woodstock experience into Music From Big Pink. Taken as a trilogy, these three sources form one of the most influential corpuses of work in rock music's half-century history; a body of music that, when it drifted into the world, caused rethinks and about-turns that, taken as whole, amounted to an artistic revolution.

It's a matter of record that, having spent months under the spell of acetates containing both Dylan's material and The Band's Music From Big Pink, Eric Clapton decided to call time on Cream and strip down his art. "When I heard that music," he later reflected, "I felt we were dinosaurs and what we were doing was rapidly

"WHEN I HEARD THAT MUSIC, I FELT THAT WE WERE DINOSAURS... OUTDATED AND BORING."

ERIC CLAPTON

Mad for it: Dylan and The Band, Manchester Free Trade Hall, 1966.

becoming outdated and boring." In turn, Clapton apparently passed taped copies to future Blind Faith compadre Stevie Winwood: listening to Traffic's 1970 album *John Barleycorn Must Die* – and the title track in particular – one hears a singularly English take on the music Winwood had been handed.

Perhaps most interestingly of all, it's certain that, at the end of 1967, with *Their Satanic Majesties Request* having anti-climactically collided with the world, Mick Jagger and Marianne Faithfull took copies of *The Basement Tapes* on holiday with them to Brazil. Four months later, the Stones began the back-to-the-roots exercise that was *Beggars Banquet*, whose sleeve would feature the back-handed acknowledgement "Music From Big Brown". The point has rarely been made, but it is not hard to draw lines between Dylan and The Band circa 1967 and the Stones a year later: *Dear Doctor* shares its air of burlesque ribaldry with the likes of *Odds And Ends* and *Please Mrs Henry*; *Jigsaw Puzzle* sounds of a piece with the doomy magic oozed by *This Wheel's On Fire*; *Salt Of The Earth*, in terms of its back-to-the-land pastoralism, is archetypal post-*Basement Tapes* stuff.

In short, the music that Dylan and The Band created from 1967 to '68 played the key role in wrenching London's musical aristocracy out of the glassy-eyed reverie of psychedelia, and pointed the way back to an altogether more timeless approach. Those whose youth had been marked by an enthusiasm for blues or folk (or both) found their old selves being stirred; suddenly, the quest for endless novelty, lysergic visions and ever-more-strange sounds seemed strangely behind-the-times.

LONDON WAS PARTICULARLY well suited to the propagation of this new approach. As of 1964, the art-school mindset that had started to pervade the more ambitious end of English rock provided the perfect context for Dylan. Moreover, the reverence in which he had been held since the release of *The Freewheelin'...* had been boosted both by the 1965 UK tour portrayed in *Don't Look Back* and the frenzies surrounding the electric shows that took place the following year (not to mention the raptures prompted by *Bringing It All Back Home*, *Highway 61 Revisited* and *Blonde On Blonde*). On both occasions, his monarchical place in hip London's psyche was amply demonstrated

by the fact that even The Beatles and the Stones were forced – in Marianne Faithfull's gorgeously worded recollection – to "sit meekly on the couch as the mad dauphin came in and out, talking of Apocalypse and Pensacola".

When news of 1966's motorcycle accident crossed the Atlantic, Dylan's status seemed only to increase. News of his fate was now the stuff of wild rumour and borderline lunatic speculation; as with many an absent prophet, his followers seemed to be hanging on his every word. In October 1967, Disc And Music Echo printed a letter from one Elaine Batten of Whitmoor, near Leeds. "Can you please, please, for the sake of my sanity, tell me what is happening in the world of Bob Dylan?" she wrote. "Is he ill, well or in jail?"

"There were people who thought the CIA had got him," says Mick Farren, then an integral member of London's underground elite. "It was, 'How the CIA fixed the brakes of Bob Dylan's motorcycle.' And don't forget that soon enough, with Bobby Kennedy and Martin Luther King, the Left was starting to look like the last act of The Godfather. So that became another point of view; that it had been, 'Don't shoot me, I'll just retire'."

Courtesy Michael Gross, Mark Makin/Retna

121

House band: Robbie Robertson (left) and Levon Helm at Rick Danko's Zena Road home, Woodstock, 1969.

"IT WAS CLEAR BOB WASN'T GOING TO LEAD US TO THE PROMISED LAND. THE PROPHET HAD QUIT."

MICK FARREN

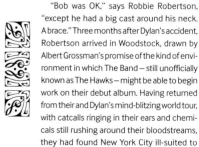

"Bob was OK," says Robbie Robertson, "except he had a big cast around his neck. A brace." Three months after Dylan's accident, Robertson arrived in Woodstock, drawn by Albert Grossman's promise of the kind of environment in which The Band – still unofficially known as The Hawks – might be able to begin work on their debut album. Having returned from their and Dylan's mind-blitzing world tour, with catcalls ringing in their ears and chemicals still rushing around their bloodstreams, they had found New York City ill-suited to

festooned with stereo equipment and checkerboards; outside was a huge yard where people could throw a football around. "It was like a clubhouse," says Robertson. "And we would go, every day, to the clubhouse, the same way as guys in the Mafia would go to their clubhouse. Or a street gang: I remember in those old movies like The Dead End Kids, they always had a clubhouse. It resembled that to me — except that it was out in the woods. Downstairs in the basement, we started putting some of our gear. And then Garth hooked up this little tape recorder that we had — a little quarter track model. And we had a mixer: just the most basic things, some of the microphones from the tour, whatever we could put our hands on, just slapped together.

"It was everything that you're not supposed to do in putting together a place to record something," he marvels. "It was all concrete blocks, and a cement floor, and this big metal oil furnace for heating the house — all these hard surfaces. Whenever you went to a studio, they always had things baffled, and corked, and soundproofed. This was the opposite."

ROBERTSON, DANKO, MANUEL and Hudson began casually working on some of the music that would eventually make up *Music From Big Pink*. Meanwhile, in the course of a few visits, Dylan began to surmise that the homely, hassle-free environs of the basement might form the ideal backdrop for the first music he would put to tape since *Blonde On Blonde*.

"By this time," says Robertson, "he was well recuperated; [maybe] a little bit stiff. He liked the vibe of the place; he couldn't hang around his house all day. So he came there, and heard some of the things we started recording — we were just having some fun, it wasn't like we got real serious yet — and said, 'Well, I wanted to write some songs for other people to record'."

Such, it seems, was the genesis of the core songs on *The Basement Tapes*. Given Albert Grossman's past success in "placing" Dylan's compositions with other artists (doubtless motivated by his 50 per cent share in Dylan's publishing receipts), and Dylan's retreat from public view, Grossman seemed to be nudging his charge into writing potentially lucrative new hits — though Dylan hardly seemed to take the enterprise very seriously.

"Sometimes we would record things," says Robertson, "and he'd say, 'OK, well that one would be a good one for [country singer] Ferlin Husky'. The mood was never real serious. We

did a lot of laughing putting down those songs. We would lay something down, and then he would, in fun, say, 'OK, that's a great one for The Everly Brothers. Let's send that to them.' Sometimes it would have nothing whatsoever to do with that artist: it was just a funny idea."

It was also an easy way to fill up miles of tape. *Basement Tapes* bootlegs attest to the never-ending reels that mounted up: aside from the album's-worth of songs that would be issued eight years after the sessions drew to a close, there were pantomimic skits such as See You Later Allen Ginsberg ("After-while, croc-a-gator"), All American Boy ("Well, I know a boy, yesterday/He become a guitar and he floated away") and Don't Know Why They Kick My Dog ("Dog dog dog/Why why why?"). More promising were the charming, half-finished doodles Rocks Off and Bourbon Street. Better still were at least two strokes of wonderment, mysteriously never taken to completion: the beautifully gospelised Sign On The Cross and I'm Not There (1956), a song as ghostly and mournful as any in Dylan's oeuvre.

There were also reams of cover versions: songs from sources as diverse as Hank Snow, John Lee Hooker, Curtis Mayfield and the folk canon in which Dylan had immersed himself circa 1960-61. Robbie Robertson says that this ad hoc repertoire was the upshot of Dylan acquainting The Band with his formative sources, while they turned him on to the soul, rockabilly and R&B that formed theirs; Levon Helm, who took his place in the basement sessions after his belated arrival in Woodstock, says that casually tumbling through such songs gave The Band the chance to find their musical feet. "We were [learning] how to sound good together. All of a sudden, we had to come up with all the vocals. We had never learned how to blend our voices. So that was a lot of what we were doing. We would take standard songs — like In The Pines — and we would take turns singing the lead, and the others would practise the harmonies, and we would try to come up with harmony blends that we could put behind Bob's voice... and we had our hands full (laughs). We certainly weren't Crosby, Stills & Nash."

Helm also claims that two-thirds of the music put to tape in the basement featured his contributions. Both existing accounts of the period and the bootleg CD set *The Genuine Basement Tapes* rather suggest otherwise, but his memories of the period attest to his lengthy presence — as when he is evoking the spirit of knockabout joviality that defined the sessions.

creative endeavour. "We couldn't find a place where we could make enough noise," says Robertson. "Or we couldn't afford anywhere. We were at a real point of frustration."

Robertson temporarily moved in with Dylan, Sara Lownds and their new family, and assisted in the editing of Eat The Document. He was soon joined by Rick Danko, Richard Manuel and Garth Hudson — who set up home in an ugly West Saugerties house, painted the colour of strawberry ice cream. The living room of the house, known locally as Big Pink, was soon

"Our nature at the time kept us from ever thinking about it seriously," he says. "We had to have some laughs, and that's why we all were getting together. And I was just learning to be around Bob, and enjoy the guy. I hadn't really ever had the chance to get to know him that well. We were waiting for Bob to get better. It was a busy time, without it feeling too serious. No fun, no work was our policy."

To the outside ear, *The Basement Tapes* suggest hours of tomfoolery – "Reefer run amok," to use Robertson's phrase – punctuated by the focused periods that gave rise to the cream of the material. Robertson, however, claims that even the sessions' seemingly intensive moments were characterised by a devil-may-care looseness. "We had no idea that anybody was ever going to hear this stuff," he says. "It was strictly for the publishing company. There were no arrangements, as such: nothing was worked out, it was just whatever happened. Sometimes we would play songs two or three times, just to get a complete take, or try something in a different rhythm – just anything to make us feel like, OK, that's good enough."

Fourteen original songs were eventually extracted from the *Basement Tapes'* all-pervading murk and cut on to an acetate. By that

(aka Mighty Quinn), Open The Door, Homer and Nothing Was Delivered. It was these songs that would be transported to the Old World, where they would work their strange magic.

The results were often surreal in the extreme. Take You Ain't Goin' Nowhere. It had been put to tape as a stoned survey of Dylan and The Band's new circumstances: "Look here, you bunch of basement noise/You ain't no punching bag/I seen you walkin' out there and you're the one to do it/Pick up your nose... You ain't goin' nowhere." The song had then mutated into the elliptical hymn to the country life that would be covered by The Byrds on *Sweetheart Of The Rodeo* – and, thanks to a visit to London by Danish impresario Johnny Reimar, a Scandinavian group called The Floor. Their version was released in 1968, backed by a version of Open The Door, Homer that – as improbable as this sounds – betrayed the influence of Cliff Richard

Satisfaction: Faithfull and Jagger enjoyed the Tapes on holiday, 1967.

Faithfull, thanks to ties with Dylan's camp, was slipped taped copies of the 14-track acetate, which she duly took on a trip to the Caribbean – where Jagger was considering buying either a big house or a small island – and Brazil.

In such songs as Down In The Flood, I Shall Be Released and Too Much Of Nothing, Faithfull heard earth-shaking tidings indeed. "I took it as if the apocalypse was coming," she says. "I couldn't stop playing it. I was in tiny aeroplanes, while Mick was looking at islands. And so I was quite scared. I just felt it was like the end of the world coming. That sense of doom.

It's not in all the songs, some of them are very funny. But the side that I liked was the more doomy one. There's a lot of stuff about water and... something coming. This Wheel's On Fire, Lo And Behold! – that one was crucial.

"It was one of the first times that Dylan started talking almost in sort of ancient tongues. I always felt that the place where the great horrors were going to come from was America. And when I listened to these things, I felt that he knew that too. It was a Watch Out record."

Such was one of the tangled threads that led the Stones to *Beggars Banquet.* "I'm sure those songs were an influence," says Faithfull, "but a very unconscious one. Poor Mick was driving in a small plane for two weeks with me playing *The Basement Tapes.* I was playing them all the time. That can't not be an influence."

While Faithfull heard the imminent end of the world, others could make out the much more comforting sound of hit records. On that front, once he had donated Too Much Of Nothing to Peter, Paul & Mary and allowed The Byrds to cover You Ain't Goin' Nowhere and Nothing Was Delivered (as well as donating Down In The Flood to the bluegrass duo Flatt & Scruggs), Grossman's next point of contact was Manfred Mann. The latter's talent for turning Dylan compositions into cash-dripping hits had been demonstrated by covers of With God On Our Side, the unspeakably rare If You Gotta Go Go Now (only issued by Dylan as a Belgian B-side, for some reason) and Just Like A Woman. The two parties duly met at the London Charing Cross Road offices of Feldman's, Dylan's British music publishers.

"IT SOUNDED KIND OF SUBTERRANEAN. THERE WAS THIS STRANGE CLOAK OF WEIRDNESS COVERING THEM."

ASHLEY HUTCHINGS, FAIRPORT CONVENTION

point, Dylan had set his sights on the Nashville recording of *John Wesley Harding*, and The Band were readying themselves for *Music From Big Pink*. And so, with most of the *Basement Tapes* songs suddenly lying fallow, Albert Grossman – then still Dylan's manager – began spreading the word.

The acetate's tracklisting ran as follows: Million Dollar Bash, Yea! Heavy And A Bottle Of Bread, Please Mrs Henry, Down In The Flood (aka Crash On The Levee), Lo And Behold!, Tiny Montgomery, This Wheel's On Fire, You Ain't Goin' Nowhere, I Shall Be Released, Tears Of Rage, Too Much Of Nothing, Quinn The Eskimo

And The Shadows circa Summer Holiday.

Over in Britain, meanwhile, the acetate's arrival was made all the more enticing by the idea that some blessed people would be given the chance to – no, really – introduce these songs to the world. Thus, in the shadowy booths of the Speakeasy and Ad-Lib, or over sticky formica tables in some wee-hours M1 transport caff, the news soon spread: those Dylan tapes, those songs – have you heard?

AT THE TAIL END of 1967, among the first to hear what had been recorded in the basement were Marianne Faithfull and Mick Jagger.

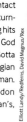

Heading into the
past: The Band, at
Rick Danko's house,
Woodstock, 1969.

"Grossman came to London with what we understood as Dylan demos," says the band's then-guitarist, Tom McGuinness. "We were given what amounted to a private viewing. I recall seeing this guy walking along ahead of me: quite a tall, broad-shouldered guy with long grey hair and a suit. Up to his neck he looked like your average businessmen, but he had long hair. That was Albert Grossman.

"He was a businessman. I don't recall any great warmth on his part. It was, 'Here are some tunes by Dylan – see which ones you like.'"

The band duly listened to these strange, largely drum-free, echo-filled songs, on which the Dylan who had barked out the material with which the band were most familiar was nowhere to be heard. Recalls McGuinness, "Manfred said to Albert, 'Why does Dylan get that fella with the funny voice to do his demos?' Albert looked at him with a slightly quizzical expression, trying to figure out whether it was a wind-up or not, and said, 'That is Bob'."

Despite that unfortunate misunderstanding, and the bizarre tenor of the music, the group soon came to the conclusion that they might well turn some of the songs into the hits Grossman was evidently after.

"We thought there was a lot of great material there," says McGuinness. "My recollection is that almost immediately we were sent four one-sided acetates: The Mighty Quinn, Please Mrs Henry, You Ain't Going Nowhere... and I Shall Be Released, which was written on the label as 'I Shall Be Relieved'. I got the impression that we were the first to hear them."

Manfred Mann recorded the first two songs, leaving them to one side for a period of weeks before returning to Mighty Quinn. Whereas at least one of the *Basement Tapes* takes – later released on *Biograph* – had sounded rather bleary-eyed, Manfred Mann had managed to imbue it with an endearing mixture of innocence and energy. Initially, however, it had sounded sluggish – until, by chance, singer Mike D'Abo discovered that his rather more positive opinion was based on the fact that his home stereo played the record slightly fast. It was duly sped up, embellished with Klaus Voormann's flute part, and released in January 1968. Grossman was doubtless cheered by the fact that it reached the top of the UK singles chart; in the States, an impressive Number 10.

In hindsight, the single sits precariously on the faultline that The Basement Tapes were about to open up. Though Dylan and The Band were blazing a trail away from the psychedelia that reached its apogee with The Beatles' *Sgt. Pepper's Lonely Hearts Club Band* (released the same month that they entered the basement), Manfred Mann turned Mighty Quinn

Looking rosy: The Band outside Big Pink, West Saugerties, Easter Sunday, 1968.

Elliott Landy/Redferns

into a primary-coloured pop song that fitted perfectly into *Sgt. Pepper's* slipstream.

As if to prove it, the song was soon subject to a reading that marked it down as a de facto companion piece to the Small Faces' Here Come The Nice: an ecstatic hymn to the kind of friend who would bring pleasure in the form of pills and pot. It was an amusingly neat theory, seemingly focused on a perfectly reasonable interpretation. When Quinn The Eskimo got there, sang Dylan, everybody was gonna jump for joy, or wanna doze. What else could he mean?

The point was duly raised in an interview by Happy Traum and John Cohen, in Sing Out! in October 1968. "For years now," said Traum, "people have been analysing and pulling apart your songs. People take lines out of context and use them to illustrate points, like on Quinn The Eskimo... I've heard some kids say that Quinn is the 'bringer of drugs'. Whatever you say doesn't matter... the kids say, 'Dylan is really into this drug thing... when the drugs come, everybody is happy.'"

"Well," considered the song's ever-voluble author, "that's really not my concern."

IN THE MEANTIME, *John Wesley Harding* – the first public notice to be served of the changes wrought by Dylan's move to Woodstock – had arrived. "This is Dylan's quietest, most modest album in years," said Rolling Stone. "It's an intensely religious record, one that owes almost as much to country as it does to rock." In London, Mike D'Abo was played the album by Disc And Music Echo. "I definitely get the feeling he should be using more production," he said, perhaps rather missing the point.

"For me, it was a kind of wistful disappointment," says Mick Farren. "There wasn't a son of *Blonde On Blonde*, just when we could have used one. *John Wesley Harding* wasn't what we were looking for. It wasn't a big meat and potatoes dinner. He showed up, and it turned out to be a salad. It was clear that Bob definitely wasn't going to lead us to the Promised Land. The prophet had quit."

In time, however, the more sussed elements of Dylan's British public began to cotton on to the album's underlying agenda. "At the same time," says Farren, "there was an element of, 'OK. Maybe I'll dig out the old Robert Johnson albums.' And in that respect, musically, it had its impact. It maybe got the Stones going on the Prodigal Son, Dear Doctor thing; it got Keith digging out his acoustic 12-string again. In retrospect, everybody had kind of psychedelically overreached themselves. Dylan was pointing some of us to Nashville, some of us to Memphis... and there was something in the air. Let's not forget that Elvis Presley staged his comeback that year."

While his disciples slowly decoded the muted signals Dylan was sending, the best British cover of a *Basement Tapes* song arrived that spring. Julie Driscoll, Brian Auger and The

"I had an acetate made – which I've still got – and took it home. Julie really liked the song. But I just couldn't figure out what to do with it. It was more like listening to a jazz duo. It was, 'This is all cool – but what are we going to do?'"

All Auger had to go on was the most basic of arrangements. In the studio, however, he slowly came up with his treatment: This Wheel's On Fire was quickened, its underlying march-time metre was bolstered, and Auger frosted the sound with a string part played on a Mellotron. "At that point," he says, "it took on this very strange atmosphere. And when Julie put the vocal on, the words really came to life. We were kind of stunned: like, Wooah – that's really out there! I knew it was good, but I didn't know whether the record company would want to put it out as a single. When it was such a huge hit, I was really taken aback."

"WHY DOES BOB DYLAN GET THAT FELLA WITH THE FUNNY VOICE TO DO HIS DEMOS?"

MANFRED MANN TO ALBERT GROSSMAN

Trinity were then being managed by Giorgio Gomelsky, the impresario of French-Russian descent who had briefly seen to the progress of the Stones, before assembling a roster that included The Yardbirds. His clout, unfortunately, was not sufficient to place his charges at the front of the queue for *Basement Tapes* songs. Gomelsky played Auger and Driscoll a mere three songs; luckily, one of them grabbed their attention in an instant.

Auger had been introduced to Dylan's music by London musician-cum-human institution Zoot Money, who would play Dylan records late into the night in the company of the likes of Jimi Hendrix and Brian Jones.

"By the time the tapes got to our office," says Auger, "Manfred Mann had decided they were going to do The Mighty Quinn. I couldn't see Tears Of Rage being part of our repertoire. But we found this strange song: just Dylan singing with a walking bass part. The lyrics were very attractive: really mysterious. The song had this amazing atmosphere: two or three musicians, and Dylan singing these incredibly strange lyrics.

Auger's modesty is misplaced. From its opening piano, suggestive of the opening of some doom-filled box of tricks, their version is little short of stunning. Led by Driscoll's magical vocal, it teases out the phantasmagoric undertones of Dylan's original to the point that they define every aspect of the song.

The authors of the music Auger had first heard, though, seem to have been only barely aware of what he and Driscoll had accomplished. "Julie Driscoll and Brian An... Auger or something?" says Robbie Robertson, sounding as if he is scanning the furthest recesses of his memory. "What did they record? This Wheel's On Fire? That's right! Yeah. And they did it pretty good. *(Pause)* Ab-Fab or something – they were using that again recently..."

BY MID-'68, encouraged by the two British *Basement Tapes* hits, Dylan's UK publishers were taking a proactive approach to his latest material. One Brenda Ralfini was now in the habit of both inviting and allowing curious musicians to hear the 14-track acetate, though it was clear to any visitor that her agenda was

Hideaway: Dylan at his Woodstock home, 1970.

Elliott Landy/Redferns

bassist Ashley Hutchings. "We were an act who might have covered some of those songs, but more than that, we were fans. We wanted to get in there and enjoy it.

"Most of the group went in there and put these white-label copies on. And this strange kind of mish-mash of styles and drawled lyrics came out of the speakers. It sounded kind of subterranean; there was this strange cloak of weirdness covering them. We loved it all. We would have covered all the songs if we could."

Fairport picked three songs: Down In The Flood, Open The Door, Homer and Million Dollar Bash. The second quickly entered their live set, and was recorded for a BBC session. The third was selected for *Unhalfbricking* (on which it joined two other Dylan compositions, Si Tu Dois Partir and Percy's Song), and arranged as an in-the-round hoedown: a verse sung by each member of the group, as if they were drunkenly recalling the revels in question. "You don't get many bright, happy, uptempo kind of songs," considers Hutchings. "Certainly with Fairport, there was a preponderance of sad songs, so something like that was great to come across." *The Basement Tapes* songs are sprinkled throughout the history of both Fairport and their alumni. The only album by Fotheringay, the band built around Sandy Denny and her husband Trevor Lucas, featured a rather prim reading of Too Much Of Nothing; Denny included an endearingly loose Down In The Flood – a duet with Richard Thompson – on her 1971 solo debut, *The North Star Grassman And The Ravens*. In the '70s, Fairport recorded versions of Down In The Flood and You Ain't Goin' Nowhere. One hesitates to use a word like "talismanic", but it surely fits.

IF THE TAPES Dylan and The Band had made in Woodstock had often been ragged, slipshod, and suffused with unfinished music, The Band's *Music From Big Pink* took what had been coursing around the basement to completion. Three songs created either by Dylan or in collaboration with him – I Shall Be Released, Tears Of Rage and This Wheel's On Fire – found their way on to the running order; equally importantly, the record found its authors successfully applying the lessons they had learned in the summer of '67.

"We'd been concentrating on honing this vibe that we had discovered in Big Pink," says Robertson. "The way that we played in the basement had nothing to do with the way we had played with Bob on the tour or any of the

based on strait-laced commerce rather than musical evangelism. "Brenda had sort of a Dusty Springfield, blonde, slightly bouffant perm," says Joe Boyd. "Late twenties, from the Home Counties. She was very much the matter-of-fact businesswoman in the music business. Very straight. She had no countercultural tendencies. Well groomed."

After an approach from Boyd, he and the lion's share of Fairport Convention were then invited to Charing Cross Road. As far as rare Dylan material was concerned, they had form: Jack O'Diamonds, a Dylan poem set to music by an American actor named Ben Carruthers, had been included on their self-titled first album; I'll Keep It With Mine, given by Dylan to Nico, had found its way on to *What We Did On Our Holidays*. Nonetheless, Fairport's main motive for the visit was wide-eyed curiosity.

"It was under false pretences," says Fairport

recordings we had done. It had nothing to do with the way we'd played as The Hawks or with Ronnie Hawkins. It was a whole new persona.

"From playing in the basement, we had to balance the music off of one another. If you played too loud, it was just annoying, cos it was all concrete – the sound hurt your ears. So we learned to play in the room. The vocal had maybe a little bit of amplification, and maybe not, so we had to play so we could hear the voice. And then subtleties came into the music: it had this kind of timeless spirit. And when we would play on acoustic instruments, upstairs in the living room, there was a whole different balancing thing going on. Unconsciously, we took all that, and incorporated it into *Big Pink*. It's played in the same way."

John Wesley Harding had perhaps been a little too muted to decisively spread the Woodstock gospel, but *Music From Big Pink* was bold enough to have a truly revelatory impact. In The People's Music, the late Ian MacDonald wrote: "Among the student audience, the album immediately became an exalted work, regarded with awe as something at once completely new and timelessly old, listened to as reverentially as Dylan's 1965-66 trilogy."

Among musicians, it was no less admired. "In effect," says Joe Boyd, "*The Basement Tapes* had set London up for the tremendous impact that *Big Pink* had. The effect of *Big Pink* was enormous: within a couple of months, you really couldn't move without hearing that record."

Fairport Convention were transfixed. Their admiration for The Band's achievement, however, was tempered by the realisation that the album signalled the end of anyone else trying to capture the America that was central to *Big Pink's* magic. From here on in, Fairport began to realise that they should concertedly apply The Band's approach to the English traditions that had seeped into their music with the arrival of Sandy Denny. "It was *Big Pink* that inspired them to do what they did with *Liege And Lief*," says Joe Boyd. "For Fairport it was, 'OK, we've been trumped. We're not going to look across the Atlantic anymore. We're going to do something as English as *Big Pink* is American.'"

In Theale, Berkshire, blues-rock troupe Spooky Tooth had been billeted in a rented cottage by Island Records boss Chris Blackwell, seemingly keen to repeat the rural experience that had been the making of Traffic. Indeed, Steve Winwood and his band lived mere miles away in Aston Tirrold, and Winwood had been kind enough to pass on the tapes he had been

given by Eric Clapton, leading to an improbably aggressive cover of Too Much Of Nothing being included on their debut album, *It's All About*.

It's telling, however, that the group's recollections of this period tend to focus on music made by The Band. "*Music From Big Pink* had an amazing effect on all of us: we used to learn the songs and play them in the barn," says drummer Mike Kellie. "Whole nights were spent to recreate it. I can remember Trevor Burton hanging out with us. He'd just left The Move: he kept saying he wanted to play some real music. I can remember him endlessly trying to recreate the organ sound from Long Black Veil. That whole Southern image... there was something very authentic about it. That music touched all serious musicians at the time deeply. You can't imagine it now, but the Atlantic seemed bigger than it is now. And unless you had really delved into American folk, you'd never heard anything like it."

THE STONES, MEANWHILE, came upon *Big Pink* during the stay in Los Angeles that saw the final work on *Beggars Banquet*. "We were taking a lot of mescaline and going out to Joshua Tree and playing it in the desert," says Faithfull, who recorded her first version of Sister Morphine on the same trip. "It had a huge effect on all of us: it was fantastic road music. In a funny way, *Big Pink* was very comforting."

"A lot of musicians said, 'Oh my God! This record changed my life'," says Robertson. "We were very much like, (incredulously) What? In a good way? Eric Clapton told me, 'I heard this

being seized on by the hippy multitudes). Eric Clapton was the first, swiftly followed by George Harrison. By 1969, the effects of the music created in Woodstock were everywhere. The Stones were settled into the incarnation announced by *Beggars Banquet*. Even if they had missed out on the music early the previous year, it's hard not to read Paul McCartney's decision to take The Beatles back to their roots for *Let It Be* as his response to the lead set by Dylan and The Band in 1967, and to hear tinges of Woodstock in the likes of Don't Let Me Down, I've Got A Feeling and Let It Be. Meanwhile, cover versions of songs from both *The Basement Tapes* and *Music From Big Pink* sporadically appeared, thanks to the likes of Thunderclap Newman, The Tremeloes, The Hollies... even the dreaded Jonathan King, whose novelty version of Million Dollar Bash rather suggested the party was almost over.

Moreover, those outside London's more charmed circles could now hear seven songs from Albert Grossman's 14-track acetate on the fabled bootleg *Great White Wonder*, furtively bought in head shops and carried back to cast its sepia-tinted spells. Cellophane flowers, mice called Gerald and people who could hear the grass grow now seemed like the totems of an altogether different age.

The revolutionaries at the heart of this sea change still seem a little fazed by the aftershocks of their creation. "We were doing what we thought was honest, and trying to be true to ourselves," says Robertson. "With a lot of these other groups that we were hearing,

"WE DIDN'T WANT TO HAVE ANYTHING TO DO WITH THAT PSYCHEDELIC STUFF."

LEVON HELM, THE BAND DRUMMER

record, and I decided I was going to pack it in with Cream.' I thought, Really? I kind of like Cream. He said, 'No, it doesn't work for me any more.' I thought, That's strange. I hope this thing is a positive thing. It influenced a lot of people, much to our surprise."

In time, a handful of musicians would go to Woodstock, desperate to breathe in whatever had led to the creation of such magic (in effect, the 1969 festival represented the same idea

playing the kind of music you're talking about, it sounded like they had just got their musical instruments for Christmas. It wasn't soulful. It didn't have depth or timelessness. Instinctively – in the heart of our musicality – that's how it struck us. And when we did something we liked, it was because it pushed those buttons."

Levon Helm is a little more direct. "Oh, we didn't want to have anything to do with that psychedelic stuff. We thought it was all bullshit."

Bob Dy[lan]
Stuck Inside Of Mobile
With The Memphis Blu[es]
Rita May

KEITH EMERSO[N]
MUSIC IS THE MESSAGE
Sounds
DECEMBER 15, 1973
7p

DYLAN
SELLS
OUT!

INSIDE
Me[...]

A NEW Bob Dylan LP
recorded with the Band and
featuring 10 new tracks
recorded recently will be
[...]

Chapter Two

WANTED MAN

Dylan's wild years – the sex, the drugs, the divorce, the religious conversion…

Reborn In The USA

Before The Flood found Dylan sparring with The Band, his voice transformed into a wild howl and the lyrics applicable to a troubled America.

A 92-MINUTE OBELISK OF pounding live music, *Before The Flood* shows us what happened in January and February 1974 when Dylan undertook his first US tour for eight years and his audiences realised that the creeping years (he was 32) and Woodstock seclusion had not withered him. Not only is *Before The Flood* the richest and most entertaining of the Dylan live albums, it also deserves a high place in any inventory of the best double-lives of the 1970s.

As a double-live set, *Before The Flood* used its vinyl boundaries to great effect. Each of the four sides had a character to distinguish it from the other three, and by listening to all four in sequence one could get an accurate feeling of the changes and intervals in the original show. The principal criticisms of the album at the time – that there was much too much of it; that Dylan and The Band sometimes went crazily overboard – become less relevant as the years pass. *Before The Flood* is the sound of six men (as another famous live album put it) getting their ya-yas out... singing and playing at close to the peak of their abilities.

The original Side One begins with 45 seconds of the audience clapping and cheering, interrupted by an up tempo riff from Dylan's guitar and a brisk "let's go" from drummer Levon Helm's snare. The first sign of the excitement to come is when Dylan starts singing, revealing a) that this song is Most Likely You Go Your Way And I'll Go Mine, and b) what he intends to do to it. "You say you love me and you're *[brief pause]* thinking of me, but you know you could be WRRRONNGGG..."

If you're listening to the album on headphones, the wild guttural rip in Dylan's delivery of that line seems to be followed by some sort of thickening of the air. You can't hear any sound from the crowd – the full-pelt, full-fat rocking of The Band sees to that – but something has definitely occurred in the room; a vast inhalation or exhalation, perhaps, as everyone reacts to Dylan's bellow simultaneously. This is how he's going to re-work the old tunes? Jesus...

Even the softer tunes on side one (Lay Lady Lay, Knockin' On Heaven's Door) are way more intense than their original versions. Dylan sings the latter as though he is about to weep with the terrible emotion of it all, lending an extraordinary phrasing to one couplet – "Momma put my guns in the ground/I can't shoot them any more" – which begins as a mumble, seems to mislay the tempo, takes three syllables over a word usually verbalised in one ("ground" becomes "gerrounder"), cracks completely on the words "I can't" and then spends more time on "shoot" than some men do on entire verses.

SIDE TWO IS The Band's side. Two of their three singers deliver the songs as though they have made a pact to expel every lyric from their mouths with maximum velocity and at maximum volume. The exception to the brouhaha is keyboard player Richard Manuel, who sings I Shall Be Released like a man who has been crawling through a desert for 15 years and can't remember how his tongue moves. Staggeringly yearning, Manuel's voice has you wondering not so much if the song is in the right key for him, more if it's in the right language. That he is singing it to 20,000 people in an ice hockey stadium is simply impossible to credit. And let us not overlook Garth Hudson, whose baroque organ solos and stirring orchestrations on the synthesizer lend a beauty to this music that cuts right through his colleagues' power and rage.

If there is one moment on *Before The Flood* that does what Dylan was anxious that the tour should do – namely, confirm his importance to America in the '70s and elevate these concerts to a status far above mere nostalgia – it arrives on side three (where Dylan is featured solo with an acoustic guitar), two minutes and 20 seconds into It's Alright, Ma (I'm Only Bleeding). By January 1974, Richard Nixon was hanging on in the White House by his fingernails as his three former aides faced investigation by a special Watergate prosecution force. In March, the House Judiciary Committee would formally address the possibility of impeachment. There was no better time for Bob Dylan – the new, rejuvenated, roaring Bob Dylan – to sing the line in It's Alright, Ma about Presidents of the United States sometimes having to stand naked.

> **Dylan sings as if he is about to weep with the terrible emotion of it all.**

The cheer that explodes in the audience is one of the most colossal sounds ever heard on a rock record.

All the same, it is not side three that authenticates this as a classic and the best live album of Dylan's career. That particular honour belongs to side four. Having supposedly been surpassed by younger stars such as Led Zeppelin and Neil Young in his long absence from the road, Dylan responds by pulling out four nuggets from his catalogue, baring his teeth and letting the audience have it. All Along The Watchtower goes by in an awesome blur. Highway 61 Revisited is a vicious argument between Dylan's lungs and Robbie Robertson's whammy bar. The profound questions of Blowin' In The Wind are bitten out in a fury. But it's the penultimate song on the album, Like A Rolling Stone, which has the most cut-throat vehemence. The verses are punched out, incrimination by incrimination. The four-man choruses are all but screamed. The next time people heard music this bilious, The Clash was making it.

The Clash and their fellow punks would cut Dylan no slack, and maybe rightly so. He earned a reported $2.5 million from Tour '74 and departed soon afterwards from David Geffen's Asylum label, angry that it hadn't sold the requisite billions of his next studio set, *Planet Waves*. Dylan was now demanding one of the highest royalty rates in entertainment, and he would get it. Yet for all his banal money-grubbing in that period, *Before The Flood* has found a place in history as something altogether more extempore. It is the sound of crackling fire, damned insubordination and bloodshot rock'n'roll, and that sound is none the quieter after three decades. *David Cavanagh*

The Special One

As soon as photographer Daniel Kramer cast eyes on Bob Dylan, it was love at first sight — and he went on to help the singer define his visual image.

FOR DANIEL KRAMER, photography started out as a hobby and ended up his very reason for being. "It was like alchemy. I became hooked. I remember the first time I watched a piece of white paper in a developing tray turn into a picture. It was breathtaking. I went to the library straight after to learn everything I could about it."

By 15 Daniel was hosting a one-boy show at his school and the following year he was teaching basic photography at his local YMCA. On leaving college he landed a job as photographer's assistant to Allan Arbus, the husband of iconic camerawoman Diane. His next assignment was with Life photographer Philippe Halsman: "I couldn't believe it. I was working with the likes of Marilyn Monroe for Philippe, getting to travel to wonderful places around the world and also getting paid to do so. Suddenly I was an adventurer, and I liked it. It was really exciting."

It wasn't long before Kramer decided to branch out on his own. One of his first assignments was to document Bob Dylan's monumental transition from folk protest singer to electric rocker. Over a period of 12 months from 1964 to '65 he captured him both live and in the studio. He photographed both the press sessions and the front covers for *Bringing It All Back Home* and *Highway 61 Revisited*.

"The first time I ever saw Dylan, he was on TV in 1963," he recalls. "I didn't know who he was, but when I heard him sing The Lonesome Death Of Hattie Carroll I was mesmerised. Nobody else that I was aware of was dealing with such material in this way and I was impressed by his performance: his face, his physical appearance, the total effect he produced. I had just started out in my own studio, and I was keen to build my portfolio. I immediately wanted to capture him. I called his office but was refused a sitting. I kept calling, but got the same answer month after month."

But Daniel's persistence eventually paid off and in August 1964 he was invited to compose a portrait of Bob Dylan. The setting was at the home of Dylan's manager, Albert Grossman, in Woodstock, and he had one hour to complete the task.

"Well, the hour turned into five or six. We took a lot of pictures, hung out and got to know each other a little. On my return to New York I developed the pictures, and they liked what they saw. Bob invited me to go see him play in Philadelphia the following week. He drove me up there in his station wagon. I saw him play live for the first time and I was astounded. I immediately realised just what a special person he was and how I had to get that on film."

For more information, see www.danielkramer.com

Interview by Lois Wilson

Hi Honey, I'm Home

1965

Sara Lownds, Bob's girlfriend at the time, soon to be his wife, is waiting for Bob to come home *[laughs]*. Sometimes you just take a photograph because it seems like a good idea at the time and this is one of those times. We sat Bob outside the shed and mocked it up to look like a real home with props we found inside — there's a pack of cards, some photos and a mirror.

Into The Void

**Forest Hills Stadium, NY,
August 28, 1965**

This was a pivotal moment in
Bob's career. He'd introduced
the electric guitar on *Bringing
It All Back Home* and he'd
played two or three electric
numbers at the Newport Folk
Festival the month previous,
but this was his first Bob Dylan
commercial concert for his
fans to come to. He was going
to be breaking with his past
musically. It was a tense night
and I wanted to capture the
atmosphere before it all kicked
off – the empty stadium, and
the unknown.

Love Bob

Philadelphia, 1964

This was the first Dylan concert I went to. Bob drove me there. It was a two-and-a-half hour drive, which was very helpful because it gave us the time to get friendlier. When you are locked in a car together, you make do, and we soon started getting to know each other – we compared boyhood stories. Here he is after the show.

Shelter From The Storm

Forest Hills Stadium, NY, August 28, 1965

This is one of those quiet moments before the concert, one when you think about things. Bob's getting himself ready but there's a doubt in the air. How will his electric songs go down? He wasn't negative, but he couldn't predict how fans would react.

News Flash

**Woodstock,
August 27, 1964**

You're in the room, Sally,
Albert Grossman's wife, walks
over to read a section of the
Herald Tribune newspaper,
the door is open, there's this
fabulous light streaming in.
Bob is sitting there, he's
reading his section of the
paper, and reading is
something he does a lot of,
he's always absorbing and it's
an instinctive shot, a true
moment. Click!

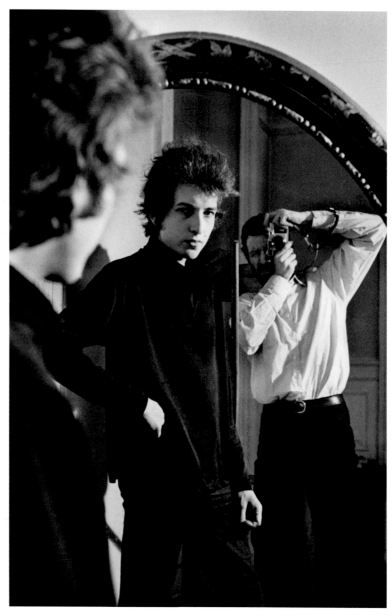

Shooting Stars

New Haven, 1965

I call this one "Cross Lights".
It's a photographer's picture,
because there is a strong
design element. It was a very
dramatic moment; there's
this huge auditorium, the light
is coming from either side,
and you have Bob and Joan
Baez in outline. It captured
the intensity and magic of
the show and them.

Reflective Moods

New York, 1965

This was taken in Bob's
Gramercy apartment and that's
me in the reflection. I'd gone to
do some general photos, and this
one's an important one because
of the statement behind it.
Because we see both sides of
the camera, it expresses that
photography is not a one-way
street. Both the subject and the
photographer are involved.

So Much Older Then...

His reputation sullied, his personal life
in turmoil, Bob Dylan hit middle age
and... delivered the masterpiece that is
Blood On The Tracks. By Andy Gill

AFTER HIS EXTRAORDINARY achievements
of the '60s, there should have been no doubt
about Bob Dylan's position in the rock firmament. After all, he had almost single-handedly
dragged pop music through troubled adolescence to a new maturity. But his reputation
suffered badly as that turbulent decade slipped
uncertainly into the shameless '70s. In the first
place, Dylan's prolonged silence following his
motorcycle accident corresponded with the

Flares for music: Bob Dylan & The Band, 1974.

ascent of the hippy counterculture that he had, to all intents and purposes, spawned. When he eventually broke that silence, with first *John Wesley Harding* and then *Nashville Skyline*, there was widespread bafflement at the more conservative direction he seemed to be pursuing, a perplexity that curdled into outright anger with the release of the feeble *Self Portrait* at the beginning of the new decade.

Subsequent releases did little to dispel this. When Dylan then defected to David Geffen's Asylum Records, his old label Columbia stuck the knife further into his tottering reputation with the indefensible release of *Dylan*, a collection of rags-and-tatters outtakes from *Self Portrait* and its follow-up *New Morning*.

As they surveyed his dwindling career, a few voiced disappointment that Dylan hadn't actually died in the motorbike crash and secured his place in the rock firmament alongside Hendrix, Joplin, Morrison and Jones. Perhaps, some glumly mused, the torch had been passed on to the next wave of singer-songwriters that followed in Dylan's wake — to

Loudon Wainwright, Jackson Browne or Don McLean, or maybe that wordy young chap just signed to Columbia, Bruce Springsteen?

It would be a long haul back to rehabilitation. The first inklings of a comeback came with *Planet Waves*, the first fruit of his new deal with Asylum, and the best album he had made in years. In retrospect, it was a flawed work, but at the time it was enough just to hear Bob back with The Band again, and apparently enjoying himself. Apart from the anthemic Forever Young, the songs were mostly simple, effusive celebrations of love – though the bitter Dirge, with its opening line, "I hate myself for lovin' you and the weakness that it showed", sat uneasily among all the hearts and flowers.

Still, it couldn't be about his own situation, could it? After all, the same album's Wedding Song, with its references to "babies one, two, three" and "you were born to be my bride", clearly referred to his own wife, Sara. And it was the most fulsome of romantic tributes, with lines guaranteed to melt the hardest of hearts, such as, "And if there is eternity I'd love you

there again". What an old softie! As it turned out, the most significant line in the song was the one admitting, "What's lost is lost, we can't regain what went down in the flood", which threw an entirely different light on all the song's other expressions of devotion. Things, it transpired, were far from stable in the Dylans' marriage, and Wedding Song can be viewed in retrospect as the singer's desperate attempt to salvage a relationship heading fast towards the rocks — as if mere words might make up for more destructive shortcomings.

DYLAN'S LIFE, THOUGH, was in the process of changing gear again. Thanks to his late decision to change its title from the original *Ceremonies Of The Horsemen*, *Planet Waves* was released some weeks into his 1974 tour with The Band, which according to promoter Bill Graham was the most over-subscribed tour in history, with over 12 million applicants (more than 7 per cent of the entire American populace) vying for the 658,000 available tickets. It was Dylan's first sustained roadwork since

1966, and alongside musicians whose drug and drink habits had grown more extreme in the intervening years.

To Sara, it undoubtedly posed a threat to their domestic stability by re-acquainting her husband with the rock'n'roll lifestyle from which she had "rescued" him. To Dylan, it may have been undertaken in an attempt to recapture something of the spirit of his youthful endeavours, though in the event he hated the experience; in the seven years since his last stretch on the road, touring had been transformed into a huge, impersonal business enterprise.

When the tour ground to its conclusion, Dylan headed for New York while Sara stayed at their West Coast home near Zuma Beach, north of Los Angeles. Designed by architect David Towbin in consultation with the couple, the house was an elaborate, fantastic structure topped by a copper onion-dome. As costs spiralled out of control, the house apparently became a source of friction between Sara, who relished the opportunity to indulge her artistic side, and Bob, who just wanted a bit of privacy again.

Upon his return to New York at the end of April 1974, Dylan started hanging out at his old haunts in New York's Greenwich Village, catching up with old chums such as Dave Van Ronk and Phil Ochs and even, at the latter's behest, giving a somewhat sozzled performance at the Friends Of Chile benefit Ochs had organised at the Felt Forum. With Sara remaining on the West Coast, rumours soon began to circulate about the state of their marriage, particularly when he started spending time with Ellen Bernstein, a young Columbia A&R executive who was later widely believed to be the subject of the most emotionally upbeat of the *Blood On The Tracks* songs, You're Gonna Make Me Lonesome When You Go. He also started taking a course of classes given by art teacher Norman Raeben, which would have a (literally) dramatic effect on his songwriting.

The son of the Yiddish writer Sholem Aleichem, Raeben was a Russian immigrant whose own artistic ambitions had been side-

lined by his success as an art teacher. When Dylan started attending his classes, Raeben was a 73-year-old with an exotic past, which Dylan further embroidered with characteristic verve: he was, the singer told friends, a former boxer who had roomed in Paris with the modernist painter Chaim Soutine, and had known the likes of Picasso and Modigliani – claims subsequently denied by Raeben's widow Victoria. He did, however, appear to have achieved a kind of guru status among his pupils, wielding his rhetorical gifts with a kill-or-cure indifference to their feelings. As each student worked at their own easel, Raeben would move from one to another, critiquing each in turn, loudly enough for all to hear.

"He would tell me about myself when I was drawing something," Dylan told journalist Pete Oppel. "I couldn't paint. I thought I could. I couldn't draw. And it wasn't art or painting. It was a course in something else. I had met magicians, but this guy is more powerful than any I've ever met. He looked into you and told you what you were. And he didn't play games."

ACCORDING TO ONE former classmate, Raeben was particularly fond of berating his students, including Dylan, as "idiots" for their inability to understand forms in terms of shadow and light – a principle he tested by requiring them to draw an object after viewing it for only a minute or so: real perception, he believed, was a matter not just of looking but seeing.

again: "He put my mind and my hand and my eye together in a way that allowed me to do consciously what I unconsciously felt." In particular, Raeben had brought Dylan to a more fruitful understanding of time, enabling him to view narrative not in such strictly linear terms, but to telescope past, present and future together to attain a more powerful, unified focus on the matter in hand. The immediate effect of this can be heard on *Blood On The Tracks*, most notably in a song such as Tangled Up In Blue, where temporality, location and viewpoint shift back and forth from verse to verse, rather in the manner of montaged jump-cuts in a movie or the fictions of Thomas Pynchon and Don DeLillo, allowing him to reveal underlying truths about the song's characters while letting them remain shadowy, secretive figures.

Armed with his newfound techniques, Dylan retired for a few weeks that summer to his recently purchased Minnesota farm, where he wrote the songs that would make up *Blood On The Tracks*. By July, he was excitedly playing them for friends such as Crosby, Stills & Nash, Tim Drummond and Mike Bloomfield, and behind the scenes his representatives hammered out the details of his imminent return to Columbia. Less happily, the transformative influence of Raeben seems to have driven another wedge between Bob and Sara, as Dylan explained to Pete Oppel: "Needless to say, it changed me. I went home after that and my

"**MY WIFE NEVER DID UNDERSTAND ME. SHE NEVER KNEW WHAT I WAS TALKING ABOUT, WHAT I WAS THINKING ABOUT.**" **BOB DYLAN**

Whether or not Raeben improved Dylan's artistic prowess is a matter of opinion, but he certainly had a radical effect on the singer's songwriting, with which he had been struggling since around the time of his motorbike accident, finding it now took him "a long time to get to do consciously what I used to do unconsciously". Dylan told journalist Jonathan Cott that Raeben had taught him how to "see"

wife never did understand me ever since that day. That's when our marriage started breaking up. She never knew what I was thinking about, what I was thinking about, and I couldn't possibly explain it."

On August 2, 1974, Dylan officially re-signed with Columbia at a considerably more advantageous royalty rate. On September 13, Phil Ramone took a call from Columbia A&R chief

Coming in from the cold: Dylan in 1974, when he returned to Columbia Records.

John Hammond. "Dylan's in town," said Hammond, "and we need to capture something magical about him."

Phil Ramone is one of the industry's top producer/engineers, who since starting his career in 1963 with Lesley Gore's Number 1 hit It's My Party has worked with an impressive roster of artists including Frank Sinatra, Barbra Streisand, Billy Joel, Elton John and Quincy Jones. He had been sound engineer on Dylan's '74 tour and spent the summer with producer Rob Fraboni editing the concert tapes and assembling the performances that would become the *Before The Flood* live album. But it was Ramone's work on Paul Simon's highly acclaimed solo album, *There Goes Rhymin' Simon*, which had marked him out as a producer with a particular sensitivity to the needs of singer-songwriters, and a shrewd choice to work on Dylan's next sessions.

"John said that Bob was going to be in town and was insisting on using the old Columbia A studio on 54th Street, which then was called A&R Recording," says Ramone. "I think there was a feeling of coming back to Columbia, and to his friendship with John."

If Ramone was lined up at short notice, the musicians had even less time to prepare. Even as Dylan entered the studio three days later, his office was still trying to locate Eric Weissberg, the guitarist and banjo player who recorded the hit Duelling Banjos for the Deliverance soundtrack. Weissberg eventually arrived around 6pm with his band (also called Deliverance), though they ultimately appeared on only one track of the finished album. He and his band found working with Dylan a difficult experience, as the singer was playing in an unusual open tuning and was reluctant to explain which key the songs were in, making it almost impossible for the rest to follow him.

"It was weird," Weissberg later admitted. "You couldn't really watch his fingers, cos he was playing in a tuning arrangement I had never seen before. If it was anybody else I would have walked out. He put us at a real disadvantage. If it hadn't been that we liked the songs and it was Bob, it would have been a drag."

The writing was on the wall, he understood, when right in the middle of the playback of the session's first song, Simple Twist Of Fate, Dylan started running through the next song for the musicians. "He couldn't have cared less about the sound of what we had just done," Weissberg realised. "And we were totally confused, because he was trying to teach us a new song with another one playing in the background. I was thinking to myself, Just remember, Eric, this guy's a genius — maybe this is the way geniuses operate."

Ultimately, only bassist Tony Brown was called back for further sessions, and it appears to have been Dylan's intention all along to make a pared-down, acoustic album after the fuller sound of *Planet Waves* and the 1974 tour.

"When I got the call, he said, 'Maybe you need a bass player, but I don't think you'll need drums — we'll just have the bass player figure out the parts'," recalls Phil Ramone. "Well, Bob doesn't rehearse, Bob just starts creating, and these songs start pouring out of him, and the bass player's looking at me like, 'What's wrong with you? Excuse me, but can I write these charts down?' I said, 'He won't do it the same way twice, he might throw a 2/4 bar in there, or suddenly go to the next part of the verse without the normal turnaround song form.' Most songs have some kind of shape, but his shapes were so unpredictable and wonderful that the musicians had to learn a lot on the date." There was no prior consultation about arrangements with either Ramone or the musicians, something that was easier for the engineer to handle than the players.

"My job," explains Ramone, "was to make sure he was comfortable at the mike, make sure his earphones were working, and just start recording. I've been a part of some momentous occasions where you prepare your studio and yourself and then wait and watch, and sometimes what I thought was the rundown turned out to be the performance; so I just let the tape run. I sat the bass player where he could see Dylan's hands, but if Dylan moved his hands to another chord suddenly, the bass part would be wrong at that point so we would punch it in later. I never stopped a take. That's the kind of thing you don't do."

The vital thing, says Ramone, was to let things flow in as comfortable an atmosphere

as he could sustain, and not bother the artist unnecessarily: "A lot of artists work from a freeform attitude, and the discipline is to know where the bass line might be. Then the parts get created, then later you start to add and subtract them. But I think what's incredibly unusual about Bob is the fact that it flows in a most natural way. He's mysterious and very private, and I understood from the people I'd worked with before, like Sinatra, that their privacy is probably the most important thing you get to deal with. Critical to anybody's relationship is how you manage to stay out of the way as the music is coming in — it's not fun to be chatty and silly all over the place. Bob's a serious guy."

OVER THE NEXT three days, Dylan and Tony Brown recorded the rest of the songs, with organist Paul Griffin (whom Dylan had used on *Bringing It All Back Home* and *Highway 61 Revisited*) and pedal steel guitarist Buddy Cage overdubbing atmospheric tints to Idiot Wind and You're A Big Girl Now, the most emotionally moving pieces resulting from the sessions. It was obvious to those involved that these were Dylan's best songs in years. It was also obvious that, in contrast to the songwriter's more oblique works, they were woven from the threads of his fraying personal situation.

"*Blood On The Tracks* was an outpouring of the man's life, in a very troubled time for him, and this was almost cathartic for him in the studio," recalls Ramone. "It was incredible: nobody stopped, nobody said anything, nobody talked very much. It certainly wasn't a social gathering, it was more of a soul being revealed directly to tape. Did I ever think it would become historic? No. I just thought it was a phase in a man's career: it's like running into a painting Picasso did in 1940, as opposed to one he did in 1950 — the essence is what you feel, and when you're in the room engineering it and being part of the production, you definitely come up with

> ## "*BLOOD ON THE TRACKS* WAS AN OUTPOURING OF DYLAN'S LIFE AND THIS WAS ALMOST CATHARTIC FOR HIM IN THE STUDIO."
>
> **PRODUCER/ENGINEER PHIL RAMONE**

**Reels on fire:
Dylan in the studio.**

feelings that are, you know... they were tremendously sensitive areas."

The album came together quickly. Dylan appears to have had a track sequence in mind from the start, and the dozen songs recorded were soon whittled down to 10. Call Letter Blues was discarded in favour of Meet Me In The Morning, which was effectively the same arrangement with new lyrics, and the reassuringly jaunty Buckets Of Rain — with a melody reminiscent of Tom Paxton's Bottle Of Wine — was preferred as the album closer to the more involved Up To Me, which was perhaps considered too close melodically to both Tangled Up In Blue and Lily, Rosemary And The Jack Of Hearts. Both Dylan and Columbia wanted to get the album out within a few weeks, so a cover featuring a sleevenote by New York journalist Pete Hammill was quickly assembled, and half a million printed up. However, after listening to a test pressing, Dylan postponed its release. Something wasn't quite right.

Three months later, Dylan returned to Minnesota to spend Christmas with his younger brother David's family. Although a revised January 3 release date was looming, he was still dissatisfied with several of the *Blood On The Tracks* songs and, as was his way, had continued to revise their lyrics, most notably toning down the more obviously autobiographical parts of Idiot Wind. David, himself active in the Minneapolis-St Paul music scene both as producer of radio and TV jingles and manager of local singer-songwriting talent, suggested re-recording the troublesome songs at a local studio, Sound 80, with some musicians he knew. The only problem was that Bob required a specific, quite rare, Martin guitar for the songs, and had left his in New York. David called up a local singer he managed, Kevin Odegard, and asked him to find one. Secrecy was of paramount importance to Dylan and Odegard, whose own debut album had just been released, had proved his discretion earlier when he had accompanied Bob on some publishing demos.

"He called me the day after Christmas 1974," recalls Odegard. "He was asking for a 1937 0042 Martin guitar, which was a very rare thing. I believe he had Lily, Rosemary And The Jack Of Hearts in mind, which is what he eventually used it on. It's a small-bodied instrument, known in elite Martin circles as the 'Joan Baez model', being the identical guitar she often used on-stage, and which she introduced Dylan to during his tour of Britain in the '60s.

"I had no idea where I might find it, but I checked around and located one at a little store in Dinkytown — where Dylan actually spent a lot of his early years — called The Podium. A friend of mine, Chris Weber, owned the shop, and he had it on his wall. This began a long dialogue along the lines of, 'What do you need the guitar for?', and I couldn't tell Chris anything. David then contacted the rhythm section, *[bassist]* Billy Peterson and *[drummer]* Bill Berg; together we found *[organist]* Gregg Inhofer, and Chris came along to baby-sit his valuable guitar, and wound up playing on the sessions!"

The musicians were all experienced players, particularly Peterson and Berg, able to turn their hands to anything from jingles to jazz. Peterson, who subsequently became Steve Miller's bassist, was up for anything, but Berg had to be persuaded to play, having been literally on the point of moving out West to pursue his dream of becoming an animator.

"He had plans to move to Venice, California," says Odegard. "He had rented an apartment, but when told it was Dylan he was going to be working with, he saw the wisdom in that, and took the session. I would say he and Peterson were Dylan's primary creative foils on the project – they were the synergy that made that record great." (As it happens, Berg did eventually realise his dream, becoming the lead or 'hero' animator for such Disney movies as The Little Mermaid and Hercules.)

SITUATED AT 2709 East 25th Street in the Seward section of Minneapolis, just across the Mississippi River from the bohemian Dinkytown area, Sound 80 Studios was the "best room in town", with two recording studios, a finishing room and in-house disc-mastering facilities. "We recorded everything from classical music, all the way through pop and rock, down to school choirs," says engineer Paul Martinson, who had previously worked with artists as disparate as the St Paul Chamber Orchestra and Leo Kottke.

Like Phil Ramone in New York, Martinson had only a few days' notice to prepare for the Dylan sessions. "They came up very quickly," he remembers. "They were booked at a time of day when there was not very much activity in the studio – late in the afternoon, evening really – and I believe the first date was on a Friday evening. At the beginning of the first session, he settled in slowly, sitting by himself reading a newspaper as we finished setting up. David talked to him a little bit, as did Chris and Kevin, who knew him a little; but once we started doing the music, he seemed to settle down and talked to the other musicians. I think he was just very shy at the beginning. Then once he got the sense that it was gonna work, and that the session was going well, he relaxed."

Kevin Odegard concurs about the relaxed nature of the session. "Dylan was kind and chatty, comfortable to be with, friendly, engaging," he recalls. "All the things you don't associate with Dylan. He schmoozed with Chris over the guitar when we got there; they talked about guitars and songwriting. He asked Chris if he wrote, and when Chris said he did, Bob asked

him to play something he'd written. So Chris played him a little something, then Bob said, 'Here's one of mine!' He started off with a C minor chord, then went rather dissonant – it sounded all wrong at first, then gradually, as he went through it, you understood there was a pattern to it, and that it did work."

The song was Idiot Wind, which Weber then taught to Peterson, Berg and Inhofer. After four or five takes, a more urgent, accusatory reading of the song, quite different in tone to the melancholy fatalism of the New York version, was in the can. "It has a very different feel to the New York session version," concurs Odegard. "It bears a closer resemblance to the '60s work than to anything he's done since, particularly with the organ. He overdubbed that organ himself: he knew what he was going for, how he wanted it to sound – he turned on the Leslie speaker and overdubbed it."

For his part, Martinson was relieved when Dylan expressed satisfaction with his work. "At an early playback, Bob – who was in a separate booth – came into the control room to listen, and commented, 'You have a nice way of picking things up here.' Which of course made me relax right away." After Dylan had punched in a few vocals on Idiot Wind, a new, fuller-sounding but less pained version of You're A Big Girl Now was polished off in a couple of takes; Dylan was so happy with what happened that the musicians were called back for another session the following Monday, December 30.

"IT'S AN EARTH-SHAKING FEELING – YOU KNOW THAT NOTHING THAT YOU EVER DO WILL TOP THIS." **SINGER KEVIN ODERGARD**

When the musicians gathered again on the Monday, Dylan ran them through Tangled Up In Blue, which was still not sounding quite right. "We were playing it in G, and it was just kind of laying there, not doing much, a little tame," remembers Kevin Odegard. "He said, 'How is it? What do you think?', and I said, 'Well, it's passable', and he gave me that look that he gives Donovan in Don't Look Back, twisted his head a little bit: 'Passable?' he said. Well, I just turned beet-red and sweated right through my clothes – I could feel myself being skewered

on the spot. I knew my career was over, then... for at least 10 or 15 seconds.

"He scrunched out an imaginary cigarette on the floor, looked up and said, 'Well, OK, let's have it your way, then' – because I had suggested moving it up to A. So we tried it, and the thing had new life: it made Dylan reach for the notes, and gave it a new energy and urgency. After half a run-through, we stopped and did a take, and that first take is the one that you hear on the record." Odegard was also responsible for the little guitar fanfares which introduce each verse, which had been inspired by a riff he'd heard on a Joy Of Cooking song called Midnight Blues.

HEARTENED BY THE success of Tangled Up In Blue, Dylan elected to try a take of Lily, Rosemary And The Jack Of Hearts. David Zimmerman came out of the control booth to warn the musicians they were about to embark on a lengthier than usual take: "Don't think it's over when you think it's over," he instructed them, "because it's not over. Just keep playing!" In the event, they nailed it in one take.

"It was a lot of fun," recalls Odegard, "like going to the movies for everyone." After Billy Peterson had left early to play a gig at a jazz club, a further version of If You See Her, Say Hello completed the session. Peter Ostroushko, a local mandolin player, was called over from the nearby 400 Bar in order to realise Dylan's desire for a high-register counterpoint to the song's melody line, but in the event Bob surprised everybody by playing it himself. "You can hear a lot of Dylan overdubbing," claims Odegard, rejecting the accepted view of the sessions as being free of such amendments. "He overdubbed on every single song – he even overdubbed the mandolin, borrowed it from Peter to play what's called a 'butterfly' part, in a higher register; Peter played his part, but Dylan played it as well. And Dylan overdubbed the flamenco guitar parts on You're A Big Girl Now and If You See Her, Say Hello."

Troubled tr[...]
Dylan, LA For[...]
Right: with v[...]

The sessions were over. Paul Martinson made a tape copy of the five tracks for Bob and David, and the players dispersed back to their day jobs. It was obvious to all the musicians that they had been part of something special, and equally clear that these were Dylan's best, and most personal, songs in years. "It was obvious what was going on in his private life, that there was some inner turmoil," affirms Odegard. "If you look at the five songs we did, apart from Lily, Rosemary And The Jack Of Hearts — which is arguably a musical version of Renaldo And Clara — everything was marriage-related, and we all knew who he was married to. We were aware of the impact this would have.

"We knew we were part of the best new Dylan album in some time. It was obvious at the time how good it was; as we drifted out of the first session, it was quite a feeling — we knew we had witnessed history. There's a guy named Vinnie Fusco in New York, who is pictured in some of the Dylan biographies just sitting in a chair during the recording of Like A Rolling Stone, and he experienced that same feeling

that I'm referring to, of being witness to history: it's obvious when you're there. It's an earth-shaking feeling — you know that nothing that you ever do will top this, and it's going to be something you tell your grandchildren."

FOR PAUL MARTINSON, though, history was still in the process of being made. Due to the extremely tight deadline, he met up again with Bob and David on New Year's Day 1975, to mix the songs. First up was Tangled Up In Blue.

"We got so far, and Bob said, 'I really don't like this'," recalls Martinson. "I said, 'Oh my gosh, what do you want to hear?' So he pulled out the copy I had made for him of the rough studio mix we had done the night of the session, and said, 'I want it to sound like this!' Because it was the only machine I had available at that time in the room, I had made the mix to our best 2-track recorder at 15ips, so I thought if there was nothing wrong level-wise, we might as well go ahead and release it that way.

"We proceeded to do that with all of them except Idiot Wind, which I had surmised from

the studio playback would be a little tough for the mastering engineer to put on a disc — it just needed a little more control of some levels, and so on. There's a lot of powerful instrumentation in that track, and a lot of dynamics, some high-flying peaks that needed to be brought under control. Bob said, 'OK, go ahead and do that, but don't change the basic sound of it.' So we really didn't mix, in the sense of doing more EQ or compression, like you usually do."

"That's the way *Blood On The Tracks* went to the pressing plant, with four of the songs unmixed — literally, live 2-track mixes," marvels Odegard. "It says a lot for Martinson's abilities — he has the perfect demeanour and personality, and was very talented in his own right." As too was drummer Bill Berg, with whom Dylan had spent a considerable time in conversation.

"There was a story that Dylan had asked Bill to go out on the road as part of his European touring band, but Bill had declined, saying he wanted to be an animator," says Odegard. "Of course, all the rest of us in the studio, thinking he was being recruited, were sitting there drooling with our tongues hanging out – is it our turn next? Is he going to ask the whole bunch of us to go? But that was not to be.

"It was a collaboration of genius, and there's no question in my mind that Bill Berg was a genius. He's especially proud of Tangled Up In Blue: the hi-hat flourish that opens the song is a David Zimmerman production touch – David is really the uncredited executive producer of this masterpiece, both for contracting the sessions, and for the many musical contributions he made. I think his contribution made it a completely different record. It would have been another quiet, sleepy little wonderful Bob Dylan album had it not been reworked; but David Zimmerman is the man responsible for making it a masterpiece. And I do think it is Dylan's masterpiece – it's the most consistent, in-tune recording Dylan has made, top to bottom."

BACK IN NEW YORK, Phil Ramone was surprised to hear about the re-recorded tracks. "Oh yeah, I was shocked. I thought he was quite happy with what he had. I think it was possibly just a time of new confusion, having moved back to Columbia; they didn't release the record in the two weeks that they had promised to do, and I think he had time to sit around with the tapes – and once you do that you reflect and worry and then, typically, you add strings, horns, anything. You'll be playing it and somebody says, 'Wouldn't it be great if there were horns there, or some electric guitar...' Generally, you try ideas out when you're on the road, and either you improve on your album or you don't. But you could tell from the feelings in the room that this guy was touching you and himself and everyone else that would hear this music – and the simpler the better, for me."

The composite *Blood On The Tracks* featuring tracks from both sessions was released later in January, going on to become Dylan's most widely respected work. Because the album sleeves had already been printed crediting the New York session musicians, none of the Minneapolis musicians received their due credit. Even when Dylan's artist friend David Oppenheim later replaced Pete Hammill's sleevenote with a painting, the credits were never revised. The Minneapolis musicians soon acquired a semi-legendary status when, within a few weeks of the official album's release, a bootleg called Joaquin Antique surfaced, featuring some of the un-issued takes. The relative merits of the New York and Minneapolis sessions have been the subject of keen debate ever since, with many regretting the loss of the

more nakedly painful original versions of You're A Big Girl Now and Idiot Wind, in particular. The latter was the most drastically altered lyrically, though the most significant changes were of tone and delivery. In place of the original's air of despair and resignation, the new version was ebullient and vindictive, closer in sound and manner to Dylan's "finger-pointing songs" of the '60s. Despite the retention of the final refrain's crucial switch from second-person singular to first-person plural, it now seemed to be more about blame than regret, the song of someone battling to restore their own self-esteem, rather than lamenting a tragic loss. The original version of You're A Big Girl Now, meanwhile, remains one of Dylan's most harrowing and painful performances. Tangled Up In Blue, though, is clearly superior in its revised version, as too is Lily, Rosemary And The Jack Of Hearts, while the mandolin-sweetened If You See Her, Say Hello has a more complex emotional flavour than the bare original.

"We heard the originals shortly afterwards," says Odegard. "They're quite good – they're wetter, with a slicker New York sound, and I don't know why Dylan didn't like them, because they're plenty good. A lot of people prefer them. But the ones chosen did make it a different record to what it was – it had a certain texture. All the New York work followed that same sonic formula, but we broke away from that in Minneapolis, primarily because of the brilliance of Berg and Peterson."

To many, it appeared as if Dylan had suddenly developed cold feet about revealing too much of his private life; though if that was the case, the changes did little to dispel the widespread impression that these songs were torn directly from his heart. In March, he all but admitted as much when, in a rare radio interview given to Mary Travers (of Peter, Paul And Mary), he responded peevishly to her comment about how much she enjoyed the new album: "People tell me they enjoyed that album. It's hard for me to relate to that – I mean, people enjoying that type of pain..."

But he quickly became just as annoyed with the too-literal interpretation afforded the album: "I read that You're A Big Girl Now was supposed to be about my wife. I wish somebody would ask me first before they go ahead and print stuff like that. I mean, it couldn't be about anybody else but my wife, right? Stupid and misleading jerks sometimes these interpreters are... Fools, they limit you to their own unimaginative mentality..."

FOR ALL HIS protestations, he and Sara were irreversibly set on divergent paths. A reconciliation of sorts was attempted after he recorded the embarrassingly fulsome tribute Sara for his next album, but the couple finally divorced in 1977, with Sara securing a half-share of the rights to all the songs written or recorded by her husband since their marriage in 1965, worth around $36 million. Bob responded with a mixture of desperate jollity – indulging freely in wine, women and fun – and rancorous bit-

> ## "PEOPLE TELL ME THEY ENJOYED THAT ALBUM. IT'S HARD FOR ME TO RELATE TO THAT."
>
> **DYLAN ON *BLOOD ON THE TRACKS***

terness, on one occasion (according to Howard Sounes), visiting Steven Soles and T Bone Burnett to play them a set of new, "scathing and tough and venomous" songs about his marital break-up. The songs were never recorded.

However, it's hard to retain such a pitch of spite and anger for very long, particularly when parental duty necessarily throws the estranged parties together as often as it must for the Dylans and their five children, and relations have long since settled down to a more equable level. Indeed, despite the numerous girlfriends (and a second wife, Carolyn Dennis, also subsequently divorced) that he has squired since their split, it's interesting to note that at the Golden Globe Awards this year, according to Kevin Odegard, the woman accompanying Dylan to the ceremony was none other than Sara.

Going Underground

It was the most mythical bootleg of all time. But even an official release couldn't unravel all the mystery surrounding *The Basement Tapes*.

THE GREAT WHITE WONDER might actually be Dylan's most influential album of all time. Smuggled out under the counter in 1969, it inaugurated a cottage industry that has, according to the music business, been threatening Western civilisation ever since. Besides introducing the illicit delights of the bootleg, it also allowed the public its first exposure to demos cut by Dylan and the future members of The Band in a Woodstock basement two years earlier.

The songs, by turns sublime and scatological, provided hit singles for artists as diverse as The Byrds and Julie Driscoll. They were endlessly recycled on underground releases to the point where Dylan was impelled to make them officially available and — so he naively believed — capsize the bootleg trade at a stroke. Forever restless when it came to confronting his own past, he delegated the task of compiling *The Basement Tapes* to Band guitarist Robbie Robertson. He duly sifted through multiple reels of tapes lovingly preserved by keyboardist Garth Hudson, the sessions' archivist. During his research, Robertson unearthed one previously undocumented Dylan original, Goin' To California, and took the controversial decision to overdub additional instruments onto several songs — adding his own simplistic drum parts to This Wheel's On Fire, You Ain't Going Nowhere and Apple Suckling Tree, for example.

Robertson adopted an equally cavalier approach to the track listing itself. He omitted two of Dylan's more opaque originals from the Basement sessions, the gospel pastiche — or was it meant for real? — Sign On The Cross, and the well-nigh indecipherable I'm Not There (1956). Yet his selection also passed over arguably the two most famous songs from the bootlegs: Quinn The Eskimo (a British No 1 hit for Manfred Mann as The Mighty Quinn) and I Shall Be Released, which by 1975 had already become an all-purpose singalong. The only rational explanation was that Dylan had issued versions of both songs on later albums, but by that reasoning Robertson should also have

dismissed Down By The Flood and You Ain't Going Nowhere, both of which made the cut. That the cover artwork, a surreal line-up of Dylan characters, stray members of the Band and (for no reason beyond a shared love of expensive wine) Ringo Starr, openly depicted the mighty but missing eskimo simply deepened the mystery.

Nor was the decision to split the official release between Dylan (16 cuts) and The Band (eight) any more comprehensible — especially when subsequent bootlegs of the sessions revealed how many additional Dylan titles Robertson could have included, from Get Yer Rocks Off to Santa Fe, Silent Weekend and All You Have To Do Is Dream. Strangely, it emerged later that many of The Band's contributions to the set were cut not during the Basement sessions, but several months later, as demos for their debut album. Weirder still, two of their tracks, Ain't No More Cane and Bessie Smith, were possibly recorded as late as 1974. A cynical observer might have wondered whether these songs had been slipped into the running order to disguise the fact that The Band's most proficient composer in 1967 was not Robertson but Richard Manuel, author of the sublime Orange Juice Blues and Katie's Been Gone.

YET FOR ALL quirks and inconsistencies, The Basement Tapes escaped any sense of nostalgia or anachronism. "We needn't bow our heads in shame because this is the best album of 1975," wrote Village Voice critic Robert Christgau. "It would have been the best album of 1967 too." Time, and timelessness, was one of *The Basement Tapes*' inescapable themes. In his liner notes, Greil Marcus indulged in some inspired myth-making, anticipating his subsequent book on the Basement sessions by unearthing links — in fact or fancy — between Dylan's "discovery of roots and memory" in these songs, and the Americana tradition that stretched back through Elvis Presley and Robert Johnson to banjo-picking hillbilly country pioneer Doc Boggs and beyond. But whether you swallowed his line or not, *The Basement Tapes* represented an elegant sidestep away from the frantic pursuit of modernity that dominated the late '60s.

In place of psychedelia, mind expansion and hippy nirvanas, Dylan's songs offered another kind of freedom. They liberated him from the shackles of significance and meaning, from providing a coherent

> Dylan never sounded more alive or in control of his destiny.

vision of the world that could be decoded into instructional texts for a generation. They allowed him to frolic in a boys' club where the only women were grotesques, alcohol dulled inhibition and filled brain and bladder to excess, and Dylan could slide from bawdiness to divine insight. With music to match — ramshackle, lazy, unerringly right — Dylan had never sounded more alive, or in control of his own destiny.

Yet his subterranean songs also signalled Dylan's distance from the prevailing mood of youth culture. Nothing on the album chimed with the global preoccupations of the age — the Vietnam War, LSD experimentation, guilt-free sexual liberation, the conviction that teenagers automatically understood more than their parents. Tears Of Rage repudiated that idea in a single line: "What dear daughter beneath the sun could treat a father so?" These songs were full of mystery, the

most bewildering being how they could have emerged from an artist regarded as the leader of a generational revolt just a year earlier.

The Basement Tapes would have sounded impossibly intimate and out of phase in 1967. Eight years on, with the idealism of the '60s betrayed, it seemed to come from a more antiquarian but knowing time. By then, it had performed its task. As a shared secret, this material had maintained Dylan's mystique through an era when his official releases were screaming that there was really no aura to preserve. Once Dylan had released *Blood On The Tracks*, and revived the speculative excitement that had surrounded his every move in the mid-'60s, he was free to jettison these intriguing conundrums and let them roam free, eternally out of time, and hence incapable of growing old or stale. *Peter Doggett*

BOLT FROM

Beat Poets, shamen and face paint... an evangelical Dylan was determined to push the envelo

aThe fully rolling Revue: (from left) Roger McGuinn, Ramblin' Jack Elliott, Joan Baez, Dylan, Scarlet Rivera, Rob Stoner, Ronee Blakley and Bob Neuwirth.

THE BLUE

1975's Rolling Thunder Revue. By Phil Sutcliffe. Photographs by Ken Regan.

AFTER THE STUNNING comeback tour with The Band in 1974 and the release of the universally applauded *Blood On The Tracks* the following March, Dylan might have felt entitled to punch the air. But it seems that fundamental restlessness in his nature allowed triumphalism no elbow room.

Taking a spring break in Europe, he decided that The Band's tour had been "nothing but force", a sort of greatest hits steam-roller campaign. So he tried to relax into his true instincts. "I was in Corsica just sitting in a field overlooking some vineyards," he told writer Larry Sloman for his book On The Road With Bob Dylan. "I recall getting a ride into town with a man with a donkey cart and I was… bouncing around on the road there when it flashed on me that I was gonna go back to America and get serious and do what it is that I do."

He meant touring. Nothing grand; theatres or clubs, places he could drive to. Pick up some kind of band of friends, a "gypsy caravan" thing. "It's in my blood," he concluded.

Thinking about the tour back home in Malibu, he watched a thunder storm "boom, boom, boom, boom, rolling from west to east. So I figured that should be the name."

THAT SUMMER, LOOKING to record an album then put the Rolling Thunder Revue together, Dylan resumed his immersion in hip New York – and, incidentally, his part-time separation from his wife. Conveniently, he found that just hanging out at The Other End in Greenwich Village brought

Right: Dylan near Jack Kerouac's grave, Lowell, Massachusetts, October 1975. Below: the Rolling Thunder Revue checks into the Palace Theater, Waterbury, Connecticut, November 11, 1975.

him every connection he needed.

Down there one night in June, he hit it off with Jacques Levy, an off-Broadway theatre director and songwriter. Within a month they had completed much of what became *Desire*: Romance In Durango, Joey, Mozambique, Isis, Oh Sister, Black Diamond Bay, Hurricane. At once, Dylan started recording. Through his usual trial-and-error period – which saw Eric Clapton and British R&B group Kokomo enter, then exit – he built a basic band via friends he saw at the club.

Mick Ronson thought he was passing through, but didn't. Guitarist Bobby Neuwirth joined. Ramblin' Jack Elliott's Mr Fix-It, bassist Rob Stoner, soon became Dylan's de facto musical director because of the rapport and concentration that enabled him to instantly deduce changes of chord and rhythm by watching Dylan's fingers and pounding boot-heel. Dylan encouraged them to recruit musicians they liked, so Stoner pulled in drummer/pianist Howie Wyeth and Neuwirth called up David Mansfield (mandolin and more), Steven Soles (guitar, from Los Angeles) and T-Bone Burnett (guitar, from Texas). Dylan took a shine to Scarlet Rivera when he saw her walking down the street with a violin case in her hand and asked her over for a try-out.

By August, it emerged that the album was done and tour rehearsals had begun. Lou Kemp, a childhood friend of Dylan's taking a break from his Minnesota fish canning business, had suddenly popped up talking road-managerial logistics.

The band joked about doing it in a station wagon. But Dylan was serious. He had a cause: to free Rubin "Hurricane" Carter, a black New Jersey middleweight who certainly couldn't have

"I'm doin' God's work. That's all I know."
DYLAN

been champion of the world, as Dylan's song claimed (he'd won only six of 14 fights after clearly losing his title challenge against Joey Giardello in 1964) but who probably didn't commit the triple murder for which he had been sentenced to life in 1967. Dylan had read his autobiography, visited him in jail, and reckoned "this man's philosophy and my philosophy were running on the same road".

Into October, with the tour opening on the 30th, Dylan sought more big names. Old pals Roger McGuinn and Allen Ginsberg were delighted to sign up. But Dylan knew it would be really something if his ex-star-crossed lover Joan Baez would appear with him for the first time in 10 years. Kemp rang her and she said, "I'm doing my own tour – unless Dylan asks me personally." So he did.

Evidently, Dylan still needed more women and, at The Other End on October 22, he snagged Ronee Blakley, new star of Robert Altman's Nashville. The following night, Dylan announced Rolling Thunder at a Gerde's Folk City bash for owner Mike Porco's 61st birthday. He was still on the pull for additional talent, but Patti Smith turned him down because she saw "no space" for her talents on the bill and Bette Midler, another strong candidate, disqualified herself by

"I got carte blanche"

Photographer Ken Regan recalls the unbelievable access he got for Dylan's tour.

For lensman Ken Regan, Rolling Thunder began when the phone rang at 4 o'clock one July morning: "It's Barry Imhoff, the promoter, and he says, 'What are you doing?' I say, 'Sleeping!'"

Imhoff passed the phone to Lou Kemp, who said he was an old friend of Bob Dylan's and there was a very special tour coming up. Regan snapped that this was a lousy joke, Kemp passed the phone to someone else... and Regan could hardly fail to recognise the voice.

"Dylan had been my idol since I was a kid," says Regan, then 26. "He said he liked my pictures of his last tour [with The Band in 1974] and asked to see my portfolio. A couple of days later I was hired. I couldn't believe it."

A Bronx boy, Regan had both studied photography and served an apprenticeship in sharp-elbowed hustling. As a teenager, he made himself a nuisance to Bill Graham, Imhoff's business partner, gatecrashing the Fillmore East to shoot Janis Joplin, Jimi Hendrix and Jim Morrison – until the hands-on promoter would spot him and throw him out, with a bellow of "You bustin' my balls again?"

But eventually he started to get legitimate assignments covering music, sport, social issues and even wars, starting with Vietnam.

Even so, for him, Rolling Thunder was like nothing else. "Dylan had been reclusive since the motorcycle accident, and yet he put that aside and gave me carte blanche," says Regan. "He'd never let anyone have that kind of access before. I certainly moved cautiously, and I think he appreciated that, but we were always out on the street looking for material. He came up with a lot of the ideas himself – like the one with him standing in front of the crucifix near Jack Kerouac's grave."

So Regan and his camera were the only other parties present when Dylan hunkered down in front of Joni Mitchell for a dressing-room run-through of a duet, or when Muhammad Ali talked with Dylan at Madison Square Garden.

Dylan remained committed to the photographic side of Rolling Thunder throughout. "Every night, Bob and I would go through the contact sheets and choose maybe three shots per roll which might be usable," says Regan.

For many years, though, nothing emerged beyond those pictures that were rather badly reproduced in Sam Shepard's Rolling Thunder Logbook. Regan never signed a contract, but stood by his personal promise to Dylan to release nothing without his agreement – especially touchy as Regan had many shots of Dylan with Sara a couple of years before their divorce (he was surprised that Dylan approved a romantic image shot at Niagara Falls for the original Logbook – it went missing from the recent revamp).

However, after three more decades of shooting big fights, Hollywood stars, wars, famines and many more Dylan concerts, Regan can finally publish more of his Rolling Thunder work. "I talked with Dylan when we did the booklet for the tour live album a couple of years ago and he said I could use all that material anywhere. I did my first gallery exhibition of the pictures in America last year, so at last I can show people what a once-in-a-lifetime event it was."

For more information visit www.kenregan.com. Prints available from www.snapgalleries.com

throwing a glass of beer over Smith for reasons unknown.

Two nights later, in the small hours, Dylan slipped behind the wheel of a cumbersome green and white Winnebago camper van bearing the logo "Kemp Fisheries Co" and headed north to Falmouth, Massachusetts.

Using one of his favoured aliases – either Keef Laundry or Phil Bender – he checked into the Seacrest Hotel, where rehearsal space had been booked, and was shortly joined by the entire tour party. They arrived in two buses: "Phydeaux", a luxury model borrowed from Frank Zappa by Rolling Thunder promoter Barry Imhoff and appropriated by the band, and the significantly named "Ghetteaux", an old banger carrying assorted extras such as Levy, Ginsberg, his boyfriend Peter Orlovsky and Orlovsky's girlfriend Denise Feliu (they worked as baggage handlers). In addition, there was a 15-person crew hired by Dylan to film a fantastical variant of the standard on-tour movie – this to be scripted by the team's latest arrival, hot young American playwright Sam Shepard.

THE TOUR OPENED with two nights, October 30-31, at the 1800-seat Plymouth Memorial Auditorium, then zigzagged its way through Massachusetts, Rhode Island, New Hampshire, Vermont and Connecticut.

Dylan seemed confident from the outset. In Plymouth, he rather startled a People magazine journalist by saying, "I don't care what people expect of me. Doesn't concern me. I'm doin' God's work. That's all I know." Quite why this involved donning white face paint on stage remained unclear. In one interview he related it to commedia dell'Arte (a 16th to 18th century Italian street theatre movement), possibly just to make

"He doesn't know what he's doing half the time."

MICK RONSON

people look it up. Another time he said, "I put it on so you can see my face from far away". When Bruce Springsteen – or "Springfield" as Dylan called him then, not necessarily by accident – visited backstage in New Haven and his girlfriend asked about the slap, Dylan droned, "I saw it once in a movie". At a couple of venues he waved his more wide-eyed disciples in the direction of identity issues by wearing plastic masks on top of the white face – one of President Nixon, the other, eerily, of himself – but he had to cast them aside when it was time to blow his harmonica.

Not surprisingly, at first the band didn't get it. They felt confusion, chaos and the need for more rehearsal. Ronson, used to Bowie's precision, shook his head over Dylan's flightiness: "He's

Hanging in the rigging: Dylan and compadres on the Mayflower. Note passer-by, possibly annoyed at McGuinn talking loudly on his very early mobile phone.

all over the place some nights… being a bit shaky on his timings, key changes and all, he doesn't know what he's doing half the time… plus he never plays anything the same twice." Baez, too, was struggling to follow Dylan during their duets, though Ginsberg suggested, "He's teaching her how to sing those songs by over and over again looking into each other's eyes…"

But outsiders Shepard and Sloman thought the music was great way before the nervous players knew it. Running up to four hours, the shows flowed through a diverse first half as Neuwirth, Burnett, Soles, Ronson, Blakley and Elliott showcased their best material, then climaxed with a few songs from Dylan (among them When I Paint My Masterpiece, A Hard Rain's A-Gonna Fall and Isis). After the break, a small coup de

"What would have happened if we'd married?"

JOAN BAEZ TO BOB DYLAN

théâtre saw Dylan and Baez start singing The Times They Are A-Changin' before the curtain came up. Then they'd reel on through their duets (including The Lonesome Death Of Hattie Carroll, I Shall Be Released), solo acoustic Baez (Joe Hill, Diamonds And Rust) and Dylan (Mr Tambourine Man), a bit of McGuinn (Chestnut Mare), followed by a hoe-down rock-out finish with more of the unreleased *Desire* songs (Hurricane, One More Cup Of Coffee, Sara) rounded off by Just Like A Woman and a singalong closer Pete Seeger himself would have approved, Woody Guthrie's This Land Is Your Land.

The music surely was transcendent at times – as confirmed by just about every track on the *Bob Dylan Live 1975* double-

CD issued in 2002. The film, though… that was more the work of the Jokerman. At least, it left the Revue party with little time for tour ennui to set in. Bizarre events, albeit of utterly artificial contrivance, filled their days.

At Lowell on November 2, a deputation led by Dylan and Ginsberg visited Jack Kerouac's grave to pay their respects arty-Manhattan style. A large crucifix near Kerouac's flat gravestone provoked Dylan into what Ginsberg described as "this funny monologue, asking the man on the cross, 'How does it feel to be up there?' Dylan was almost mocking, like a good Jew might be to someone who insisted on being the Messiah, against the wisdom of the rabbis…"

Here comes the bride: Joan Baez confronts Dylan (with Arlo Guthrie and Ramblin' Jack Elliott, centre left and right) at Mama Frasca's Dreamaway Lodge, Becket, Massachusetts, 1975.

On Rhode Island a couple of days later Shoshone medicine man Rolling Thunder turned up from Nevada (where, aka John Pope, he worked as a brakeman on the Southern Pacific). A friend of Grateful Dead drummer Mickey Hart, Rolling Thunder had lately published a book of autobiography and assorted sagacities which Dylan read, hence the invite. The shaman promptly proved his worth by creating his own movie scene; he summoned the band to the beach at dawn to perform a "Tobacco Ceremony" which McGuinn deemed "very cool".

And the most surreal element of the whole movie farrago was the tale of the Edgar Allan Poe impersonator. When, on November 21, the tour approached Poe's hometown, Boston, someone said it would be a brilliant idea to stage an encounter between him and Dylan. They knew a Lower East Side pool

hustler with a sideline in Poe impressions and had him driven up. At the hotel he donned frock-coat, wig and moustache and, by way of audition, delivered a barnstorming performance of The Raven. But schedules went to hell, they never got to the scene and, permanently out of shot, the Poe impersonator moped back to New York.

Sam Shepard despaired of the movie, saying it had "fallen into smithereens till it has no shape or sense". But one thing it did do was give the women of the tour the chance of some role-play to offset the stress inflicted on them by the confinement of Rolling Thunder and Dylan's eternal ambiguities.

Baez cut loose during a little bar-room improv at the Dreamaway Lodge, Becket, Massachusetts, an idiosyncratic watering hole recommended by Arlo Guthrie. In character as a

Blowin in the wind: (from left) Dylan, Blakley, T-Bone Burnett and Neuwirth.

whore but wearing a wedding dress, she started in on Dylan with "Why did you always lie?" "I never lied. That was the other guy," he said. "What would've happened if we'd got married, Bob?" she curveballed. "I married the woman I love," he said, crushingly. She swiped back, "Didn't you used to play the guitar?" "No, that was the other guy." "Oh, you mean that little Jewish brat from Minnesota? His name was Zimmerman." "Yeah."

The trouble was, Dylan looked as though he loved it. And that was before Joni Mitchell joined the tour in New Haven (November 13) and Sara Dylan in Boston (November 21 – in his book Behind The Shades, Clinton Heylin avers that at this point Dylan had to move a female publicist out of his quarters to make room for his wife). The friction arising from this concatenation of powerful women – Blakley pitched in too – was dubbed The Battle Of The Berets.

Heylin reckons that Howard Alk and Ron Howard, two of the movie's directors, actually asked Sara to join the tour because they thought the marital tension would make good cinema and they probably got the money shot when they persuaded both her and Baez to play whores and "reminisce" about their love lives. It was possibly a relief all round when, on November 26 in Augusta, Maine, Dylan's mother Beattie joined the tour – "The 'mysterious' Dylan had a chicken-soup Yiddish mama," marvelled Ginsberg – and her son had to behave himself.

Meanwhile, Dylan aside, the men had a rather less intense time of it – immersed in their all-night muso jams, distracted by the ministrations of the man with the duffel bag full of cocaine (deductible from *per diem* payments at $25 a gramme), getting their rocks off via the usual horseplay and practical jokes.

And still, as the Revue swung up through Canada before the climactic New York show, almost everyone started to talk of their regret that Rolling Thunder was almost over. McGuinn said, "It was a great big rolling party, out there with all your friends... amazing". Tough cookie Baez retained her positivity: "I've never seen such a spirit among people". And T-Bone Burnett took it as terrific (if ambiguous) therapy: "Dylan's given me reason to live. I only want to be shot about 10 times a day now."

"Dylan had a chicken-soup Yiddish mama."
ALLEN GINSBERG

UNTIL MONTREAL Forum on December 4 – the 29th show in 36 nights – to the band Rubin Carter was just a song. On December 7 they all came face to face with him – oddly enough, at the Edna Mahan Correctional Institution For Women, Clinton, New Jersey, where "Hurricane" lodged among a hundred separately housed inmates.

The Revue did the show right there. Roberta Flack, a late special guest substitute for Aretha Franklin, went down a storm. Dylan could hardly miss with Hurricane, and the prisoners even took a shine to Ginsberg's recitation of his poem Kiss Ass: "Whites will have to kissass Blacks for peace and pleasure". Only Joni Mitchell, in ornery mood, failed to get across – according to Stoner, "Two minutes into her set, hoots and catcalls sailed up over the makeshift stage... That tomcat face of hers puckered into a wicked sneer. 'We came here to give

"Dylan ain't as purty as me, you'll have to admit."

MUHAMMAD ALI

you love,' she lectured them. 'If you can't handle it, that's your problem.'"

The following night at Madison Square Garden, she revealed what was on her mind. Having taken the trouble to talk to Carter on the phone several times, she had decided – quite possibly in error – that he was "faking it" to take advantage of "a bunch of white, pasty-faced liberals". When Baez asked her to introduce Muhammad Ali, who had been campaigning for the ex-boxer long before Dylan got on the case, Mitchell said her line would be, "We're here tonight on behalf of one jive-ass nigger who could have been champion of the world, and I'd like to introduce you to another one who is". Baez said maybe someone else should do the job.

Still, the show went as well as ever, and for four-and-a-half hours. Dylan poured it on inexhaustibly, inspirationally and just

plain affably – calling Robbie Robertson on to play guitar on It Takes A Lot To Laugh, It Takes A Train To Cry and duetting Knockin' On Heaven's Door with McGuinn. When he opened the second half with Baez and The Times They Are A-Changin', she was dressed in exact imitation of him down to the flower-bedecked gaucho hat and the white-painted face.

Even Ali and Carter couldn't stop talking about Dylan. Ali said, "When they asked me to come here I was wondering who this guy Bob Dylan was. He ain't as purty as me though, you'll have to admit." Then when Ali got Carter on the phone live from Clinton, "Hurricane" started quoting It's All Right Ma: "Walk upside down inside handcuffs/kick my legs to crash it off/say OK I've had enough/what else can you show me".

By the time the entire Revue rallied round one last time

for This Land Is Your Land, even this notably apolitical big-time rock crowd probably believed they were in on something.

Sam Shepard saw Dylan just twice more that night. After the finale, he was in the dressing-room when Dylan raced in "ripping the harmonica brace off his neck, make-up dripping in long streams, red eyes popping out" and hollered "Rubin's been acquitted! He'll be out by Christmas!" (this proved a false rumour). Then at the aftershow reception in the neighbour-ing Felt Forum, Dylan grabbed Shepard, Ronson and a few others – mostly women – and they drove off in his Winnebago.

"Now we're hitting the streets and Dylan's starting to crank this monster up to around 50," wrote Shepard in his Rolling Thunder Logbook. "I'm losing track of time and space but it seems we're hitting midtown [when] he brakes the sucker and bails out in the middle of the road… Dylan's gone again and it's only us. Just like it was before we got on."

The Rolling Thunder Revue of 1975 made waves, though not really for Rubin Carter; he was bailed, retried, found guilty again and not finally released until 1985 when an appeal court found "grave constitutional vio-lations" in that second go-round.

For Dylan, the Revue had led to or presaged big changes: The failure of his marriage (Sara started divorce proceedings on March 1, 1977); the less permanently wounding failure of the tour movie, Renaldo And Clara; his whole-hearted embrace of playing live which eventually became The Never Ending Tour. Rolling Thunder had been a grand affair. As New York Times critic John Rockwell wrote after the MSG concert, the tour had "kept the flames of artistic involvement in political causes alive for the 1970s… Mr Dylan has rein-vigorated the flagging New York folk-rock scene… Most important of all, however, he has reinvigorated himself."

Clockwise from above: meeting gaoled Rubin Carter, December 7; the nightly white face preparation; Rolling Thunder's stage backdrop.

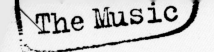
The Gypsy King

Carousing in France and bar-hopping in New York, Dylan partied hard making *Desire*, the seductive prelude to The Rolling Thunder Revue.

WITH HIS RETURN to the top of the tree following universal acclaim for *Blood On The Tracks*, the remainder of 1975 should have been a time of consolidation for Bob Dylan. Yet instead of helping Robbie Robertson compile *The Basement Tapes* or cementing his apparently encouraged reconciliation with wife Sara, the emotionally battered singer headed to France and a two-month bender with painter David Oppenheim.

Veering from moments of deep self-examination and daily calls to his faraway wife to bawdy nights drinking, shagging and hanging out with gypsies, his time with Oppenheim (who painted the sleeve portrait for *Blood On The Tracks*) suggests an internal struggle between the 30-something family man and the freewheelin' youth. The family man, of course, was on a hiding to nothing from the troubadour. While hitching a lift on the back of a donkey cart, Dylan decided it was time to get back on the road, to "get serious and do what it is that I do, because by that time people didn't know what it was that I did".

The details weren't specific – hell, who needs details when you're Bob Dylan? Other people will jump at the chance to fill in the blanks – but there was no way the songs from *Blood On The Tracks* could form the backbone of a new live set. They were too painful and personal for what he had in mind; the carousing caravan he'd later dub The Rolling Thunder Revue.

Under no particular pressure from Columbia (both *The Basement Tapes* and *Blood...* were selling healthily), Dylan returned to New York and spent time bar-hopping, playing alongside old friends and taking the pulse of the city. Meeting an impossibly exotic violinist, Scarlet Rivera, he invited her to jam. They clicked instantly, and although her playing would dominate the eventual album, another random meeting would prove even more inspirational.

One night in the Other End, Dylan met Jacques Levy, former psychologist, Broadway director and occasional songwriting partner of Roger McGuinn. Levy became the only person ever to totally collaborate with Dylan, taking co-writing credits on all but two of *Desire*'s tracks (One More Cup Of Coffee, written in France, and Sara). Levy brought discipline – the pair retreated to a house in the Hamptons for several weeks to finish writing when New York proved too distracting – and a sense of theatre. Dylan wanted to return to story-based songs, and Levy re-taught him how to write in cinemascope.

The songs ranged from the epic 11-minute tale of Brooklyn gangster Joey Gallo, the travelogue pop of Mozambique, and the twisting tale of Black Diamond Bay's hotel guests killed by an erupting volcano, through to the gunned-down lovers of Romance In Durango, seduction by a gypsy princess in One More Cup Of Coffee, and Sara, a rose-tinted ballad wistfully – if belatedly – recalling his love for his wife.

FOR THE RECORDING sessions Dylan invited just about every musician in New York to sit in. As the studio filled some of the cast became disillusioned: Eric Clapton bailed early, the scene far too loose for someone with his endless capacity for overdubs, as did British pub rockers Kokomo. Eventually, a tiny band of just Dylan, Rivera, Rob Stoner (bass) and Howie Wyeth (drums), with Emmylou Harris on backing vocals, sat down to see what they could find.

They found "it" quickly. Astonishingly, after one wildly improvising all-night session on July 30, they had an album.

"We all felt great because it was intimate," recalled Stoner. "We started running through the tunes, bam, bam, bam, just getting every complete take. Just like that." Wyeth was more cosmic. "There was a lot of ESP that night."

Only Harris was unhappy. When she'd improvised with Gram Parsons he'd allowed her to correct mistakes, but with Dylan there were no such fripperies. Privately, she hoped the session would be binned, but in fact only two songs on the album weren't recorded that night: Romance In Durango survived from the extended band jams, while Sara was taped the following night.

> ## After one all-night session, they had an album.

Leading *Desire* are two Dylan classics: Hurricane and Isis. When he visited Ruben "Hurricane" Carter in the New Jersey prison where the boxer was serving life for a triple murder he denied, Dylan was bowled over by both the man and the huge injustice visited upon him. Hurricane, his first protest song in nearly a decade, claims that an innocent man had been framed by a racist police force and convicted by a jury fearful of an uppity nigger, the strident, swinging melody

carrying the spat out, damning lyrics along at breakneck speed. And it worked: the song directly contributed to Carter's release in 1985.

Hurricane was designed to agitate, but the most ruffled feathers initially belonged to CBS lawyers. During October's Rolling Thunder rehearsals the suits begged Dylan to re-record the most contentious lyrics, finally succeeding when he and the original little band, minus Harris, returned to the studio. After 11 unsatisfactory takes Dylan got his coat and told the engineer to pick the best one (eventually two were spliced together). Three months after nailing the song, the artist was being forced to look back, and he didn't like it.

Levy first heard the lyrics to Isis when Dylan read them to a table of people that night in the Other End. Transfixed by this magical tale of "pyramids embedded in ice" and places of "darkness and light",

Levy invited Dylan to his nearby apartment to iron out some lyrical creases. Dark and foreboding, with Rivera's violin again winding its way throughout, Isis has been claimed as a metaphor for his marital breakdown, but is probably every bit as fanciful as Black Diamond Bay.

Desire's exotic lyrics are counter-balanced by the simplest of music. Stoner's snaking bass and Wyeth's pitter-patter drums escort Dylan's melodies, while Rivera's raggle-taggle violin is the instrumental equivalent of his nasal twang. *Desire* is not always easy, but the music is as seductive as One More Cup Of Coffee's Romany princess, and it became his only album to simultaneously make No 1 both sides of the Atlantic. It may have been responsible for inventing Hothouse Flowers but, as a foil for *Blood On The Tracks*, *Desire* stands proud beside it at the pinnacle of Dylan's '70s regeneration. *Andy Fyfe*

The Soul Of Bob Dylan

Before he went on to direct Hollywood legends, photographer Jerry Schatzberg helped to define Bob Dylan's idiosyncratic visual image.

LENSMAN JERRY SCHATZBERG is one of just a few photographers in the mid-'60s who can truly lay claim to defining Bob Dylan visually. His portfolio not only includes the photograph that was used on the front cover of Dylan's 1966 *Blonde On Blonde* album but a number of more intimate and personal shots taken at Jerry's 333 Park Avenue South studio from 1965 to 1967.

"I'd always spend time with my subjects before snapping them. I wanted them to be as relaxed as possible in front of the camera. It didn't always work. Some subjects were impatient and uncooperative, but even that gave me an angle to capture them from," Jerry explains.

It was a technique that reaped rewards with Dylan, whom Jerry first met through his friend Sara Lownds, who would later become Bob's first wife. "She got to hear I was interested in photographing him and a couple of days later she gave me the address of the studio where he was recording *Highway 61 Revisited*. The next day I went there and that became my first photo session with him."

"He was a dream subject," Jerry enthuses. "I just had to point the camera at him and it seemed I had captured something remarkable. My first impressions: he was shy, intelligent and challenging. As he started to trust me and feel more comfortable he would relax. We had a very good relationship, we talked, laughed and hung out together."

Like Dylan, Jerry calls himself a "storyteller" and after a brief spell in the '60s as a fashion photographer working for Vogue and Esquire, he turned his attention to the silver screen, directing 1970's Puzzle Of A Downfall Child (an innovative vehicle for Faye Dunaway), 1971's The Panic In Needle Park, a stark portrayal of heroin addiction starring Al Pacino, and its follow-up, Scarecrow, with Pacino and Gene Hackman, that won the Palme d'Or at the Cannes Film Festival in 1973.

But it is Jerry's portraits of Dylan that capture best the photographer's vibrancy, imagination and sense of fun: "I like to think that I was getting something below the surface. Something that gives the viewer an insight into Dylan, the musician and the man."

For more information, see www.jerryschatzberg.com

Interview by Lois Wilson

Black Magic

New York, 1965

I asked Bob if I could spend some time with him in my studio at Park Avenue, just to take shots for myself. There was no brief or commission; we were just having fun. He wandered around the studio picking up objects and playing with them. The crucifix sculpture was made by Paul Von Ringleheim. The cat was given to me after I took a cover shot for Vogue magazine. Her name was Cha Cha.

Lighter Moments

Schatzberg's studio, New York, 1965

Just a further look into the way Bob's mind worked. We were throwing ideas back and forth. He took out his keys and just lit a match to see if they'd catch light. They didn't. Then he sat on a stool and tossed the harmonica up in the air and caught it a few times. I didn't have to get him to pose. He knew what to do.

Hair Raising

Backstage, Mineola, Long Island, NY, 1965

He was just about to go on stage and I caught him fixing his hair before he went out. I just caught the moment. It brings out the humanity in him.

Playing With Fire

Schatzberg's studio, New York, 1965

The fact Bob went around the studio picking objects up, like the cigarette lighter, and playing with them, that he was totally relaxed in the studio setting, gave an insight into his personality and attitude.

I liked the way his mind worked and tried to capture that in these pictures. He just decided to lie down on the floor with the drum on top of him so I took an overhead shot to capture it.

He was always very co-operative. Dylan was always such a fantastic subject to photograph.

All photos © Jerry Schatzberg/Corbis

Mr Piano Man

Columbia Studios, 1965

This was taken on the first day I met Dylan. He was recording *Highway 61 Revisited*. I spent about five hours in the studio. He loved people being there – he'd play stuff and get them to listen to the playbacks. He'd also just sit at the piano and write. He didn't change in front of the camera. He just went on with whatever he was doing.

Behind The Mask

Schatzberg's studio, New York, 1965

I exhibit all of the 12 pictures from this roll together as a contact sheet. I call it 'The Soul Of Bob Dylan' because it seems to get underneath his exterior and reveal his inner depths. He does protect himself, but this is one of those moments when he seems to reveal his soul.

Stormy Weather

1976, and Dylan is gorging on groupies and booze. Then his wife turns up. And he has to play a gig in fear of his life. *Hard Rain* captured it all.

THE YEAR 1976 was a pivotal one for rock. The promise of the '60s had congealed into pomposity and bland-out (this was the year that Paul McCartney led Wings around a vast arena tour of the USA which resulted in a triple album); The Rolling Stones went most of the way into self-parody with the thoroughly unremarkable Black And Blue. All told, the music had taken a rum turn; the white-hot energy of its beginnings had dimmed to the faintest glow.

In retrospect, Bob Dylan knew something was wrong. The launch of The Rolling Thunder Revue in October 1975 was his attempt to pull off all kinds of feats — to combine music with theatricality, to reclaim American folklore from those who'd have it locked in a museum — but its chief merit was its air of back-to-the-roots, ragged excitement. Listen to the Rolling Thunder version of Isis on *Biograph*: proof that anyone who wished to combine rock music with intelligence and grand designs need not end up standing in a cape performing songs about King Arthur.

The first leg of Rolling Thunder, featuring such added attractions as Joan Baez, Roger McGuinn and Joni Mitchell, trekked around the North Eastern Seaboard to rave notices. Dylan then decided to prolong the fun. The idea was to tour the Gulf Coast, starting in Florida, which seemed like a good idea until Dylan showed up for rehearsals.

He was grumpy beyond belief. Some of his decisions made precious little sense: Rolling Thunder guitarist Mick Ronson, plucked from David Bowie's Spiders From Mars to become one of the Revue's most interesting features, found himself sidelined — he would spend a great deal of the tour sitting on the bus, waiting for a stage-call. Most importantly, Dylan's marriage to Sara was hurtling towards termination; he duly dropped most of the material from *Desire* and updated songs from the altogether more angst-wracked *Blood On The Tracks*, giving them a new vituperative edge. This was the tour as a soundtrack to divorce — art and life colliding to nobody's great benefit.

This was the tour as a soundtrack to divorce.

Four days after Rolling Thunder Part Two's beginning, Dylan led the troupe into a TV studio in Clearwater, Florida, to film a TV special promised to the ABC Network. Though the results were impressive enough, he vetoed them, leaving him no option but to film the Revue's penultimate show a month later: a gig in front of 25,000 at Fort Collins, Colorado.

To say that circumstances were less than ideal would be an understatement. A week or so prior to the gig, with Dylan drinking and philandering as if the world was about to end, Sara turned up unannounced with their children, demanding to know what he was playing at. As it turned out, imminent divorce was only half the problem.

COME THE DAY of the gig, it was peeing down. Dylan had only made things worse by spending the two-day warm-up period in a mountain retreat, getting endlessly drunk. This would be Rolling Thunder's last word to the world — and it looked doomed. "Everybody's soaked," remembered bassist Rob Stoner. "The stage canopy's leaking, the musicians are getting shocks from the water on the stage. So everybody is playing and singing for their lives, and that is the spirit that you hear on that record."

After all the dysfunction, Dylan and his band delivered something absolutely incredible. The film, never commercially available, shows them facing down the elements; wearing Arab-style head-dresses (for some reason), they pound through the songs with such force that even a meteor shower would have only momentarily put them off.

And, remarkably enough, you can draw lines from Fort Collins to the musical insurrection that finally shook the flab off '70s rock music. The version of Shelter From The Storm played that day sounds eerily like The Clash's lopsided take on reggae, a good year before it was unveiled to the world.

Hard Rain has a number of unfortunate omissions. Joan Baez is nowhere to be heard. Neither is the McGuinn-enhanced reading of Knockin' On Heaven's Door included. Contractual fascism, the bane of so many '70s multi-artist enterprises, must have been the problem. Either that, or Dylan was still grumpy.

Instead, there are nine tracks that flip over countless themes but keep returning to Dylan's marital tear-up. No sooner have the band — aided, for one track only, by Mick Ronson — exited a 200mph, Chuck Berry-esque version of Maggie's Farm, than Dylan leads them

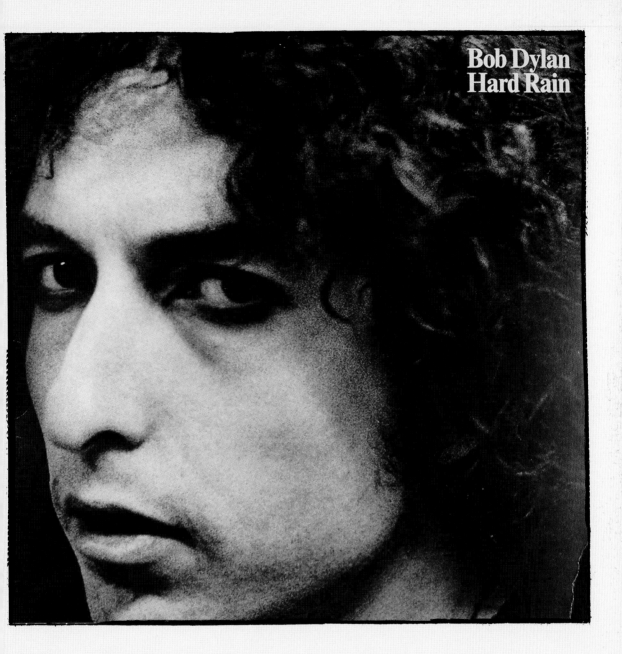

**Bob Dylan
Hard Rain**

into One Too Many Mornings: as concise a summary of the end of an affair as Dylan ever wrote. Here, it has a new coda: "I've no right to be here/If you've no right to stay/Until we're both one too many mornings/And a thousand miles away."

Lay Lady Lay, once a hymn to the love that coursed around the house in Woodstock, receives arguably the cruellest re-write of all. Now, it's a hymn to the bawdy abandon of drunken adultery. "Forget this dance," Dylan yells, "let's go upstairs!/Let's take a chance – who really cares?" If, as some witnesses claim, Sara really was waiting in the wings, this was shitty behaviour indeed.

Four songs on, after sounding a note of contrition and self-pity by playing *Nashville Skyline*'s I Threw It All Away – delivered in a veritable howl – the record closes with Idiot Wind. This is vicious: its spite is

balanced by regret on *Blood On The Tracks*, but here it's allowed to mutate into something almost wholly hateful. "Visions of your chestnut mare" becomes "visions of your smoking tongue".

All that said, it is that Clash-esque reading of Shelter From The Storm – featuring Dylan playing hands-of-concrete slide guitar – that exercises the most addictive spell. It is, quite simply, one of the most exciting things Dylan has ever recorded – proof that his endless re-tooling of his songs can result in completely fresh inventions, and that strife and discord are often great music's meat and drink.

"Bob was really hitting the bottle that weekend," said Stoner. "That was a terrible fuckin' weekend. There was a lot of stuff that makes *Hard Rain* an extraordinary snapshot."

"It was," he surmised, "like a punk record or something." *John Harris*

In full flight:
Dylan's Picnic
at Blackbushe
Aerodrome, Surrey,
July 15, 1978.

Redemption Song

Dylan's 1978 year-long tour would take the recently divorced singer from confrontations with Sid Vicious to concerts at Nuremberg and, eventually, some kind of salvation. By Richard Jobes.

Danny Clifford

Standing on stage in San Diego's Golden Hall on November 27, 1979, three weeks into his first series of gospel shows, Bob Dylan is facing crowds that include a volatile mix of true believers, the inquisitive and the outright hostile. His world tour of the previous year little more than a distant memory, Dylan's new material not only appears to be a rejection of the artist's profound life scepticism, but also the Jewish faith in which he'd been raised.

In a manner eerily similar to his 1966 electric shows, this tense blend of audience devotion, anger and protest has resulted in some of Dylan's most empowered, confrontational performances. In those weeks, Dylan would meet audience cries of "I believe in Highway 61!" and "Praise the Lord with puke!" with lengthy, impassioned diatribes. Yet, as he now gazed out at the audience, he embarked upon a far more personal narrative, from an earlier hectic schedule.

"I was here about a year ago," he says, "...coming from someplace and feeling real sick. Towards the end of the show, somebody out of the crowd knew I wasn't feeling too well, and threw a silver cross on the stage. Usually, I don't pick things up that are thrown on the stage. But I looked down at this cross and I said, I gotta pick that up.

"I brought it with me to the next town," he continues, "where I was feeling even worse, so I said, Well, I really need something tonight. I didn't know what it was – I was using all kinds of things – and I said, I need something tonight that I never had before. And I looked in my pocket and I had this cross..."

THE YEAR-LONG 1978 world tour that had brought Dylan to this point stands as one the most dynamic periods of his career, in which the singer had proven himself to be anything but an anachronism, reinventing his legacy before an audience of close to two million fans before turning his back on that sound and that world completely.

As Dylan himself would recall, "I was doing fine. I had come a long way in just the year we were on the road..."

Among the offices and warehouses of Santa Monica's industrial district, the former gun factory that would subsequently become Rundown Studios is, somewhat predictably, neither an impressive nor inspiring sight. In December 1977, musicians began to gather in this disused factory space to sketch out the basic elements of a live repertoire. Dylan's previous outfit, the Rolling Thunder Revue, had clattered out, raw and drunken, in the spring of 1976, after which Dylan had withdrawn from public performance. With commitments for a year-long world tour now pencilled in, an embryonic group began to form around a few remnants from The Rolling Thunder Revue, among them bassist Rob Stoner.

"His office called and told me to show up and bring whoever else I thought would make a good core band," says Stoner. "I showed up with Walter Davis Jr, who'd played with Charlie Parker; I knew Bob was always looking for new things, and I thought that would be an interesting element. Dylan had already decided he wanted guitarist Steve Soles and multi-instrumentalist David Mansfield from the Revue. So, we got there and...Bob didn't show up for a week and a half. We didn't even hear from him...There wasn't a whole lot to do, but eventually I hit on this method of rehearsing his songs without him being present. He seemed quite distracted."

For anyone willing to look, Dylan could be found at Burbank Studios, watching and re-watching reel after reel of footage from

Leaving on a jet plane: Dylan, Hong Kong International Airport, March 1978.

the film he had spent almost two years crafting, Renaldo And Clara. For a man accustomed to achieving his musical intentions within a matter of days, his filmic aspirations had proven more demanding. Much of the past year had been spent in the editing suite, splicing together what was either a deeply personal or wholly reticent meditation on the state of his marriage to Sara Lownds. Yet even as the process ground on, the relationship itself was playing out its final, painful moments.

The custody battle that surrounded his children had degenerated into little more than an ugly squabble. It would culminate in a highly wrought scene at the children's school when Sara allegedly tried to kidnap her brood. She would ultimately be fined for assaulting one of the teachers.

While Dylan felt he could palm off the role of "Bob Dylan" to someone else in his celluloid reality – the Dylan role was, bizarrely, taken by Ronnie Hawkins – the full weight of his legacy was about to be forcibly placed back on his shoulders.

"We had a list of songs given to us," Rob Stoner remembers. "The Japanese promoter sent us a telegram, saying they

"How many singers feel the same way 10 years later? A lot of my songs don't work now." BOB DYLAN

expected – or rather, I guess, parenthetically demanded – that he would perform a certain number of greatest hits."

Yet many of the songs on the list had not been played for many years. It seemed entirely possible that such material, so endlessly evocative of a certain period in history, might never survive the transition into the new decade.

"How many singers feel the same way 10 years later?" Dylan would ask Ron Rosenbaum, clearly uncertain of his untested repertoire. "Now there's a certain amount of act you

can put on, you know. You can get by on it, but there's got to be something to it that's real, not just for the moment. And a lot of my songs don't work. I wrote a lot of them just because my gut told me to write them – and they usually don't work so good as the years go on."

Every aspect of Dylan's career had brought forth its own legion of devotees, each eager to impose their own set of pre-conceived notions upon him, and throughout the '70s he'd found interesting ways to deflect the full glare of his fame.

"Prior to this he'd shared the stage with The Band," says Stoner. "They took up a large portion of the evening's festivities in 1974, and in the Rolling Thunder Revue there were several acts. But now he's faced with doing an entire 'Bob Dylan' show."

No matter how creatively drained or emotionally raw he may have felt, Dylan had no intention of being reduced to a nostalgia act just yet. "Although Bob didn't verbally communicate what he wanted, he clearly had something in mind," recalls David Mansfield.

As a ceaseless stream of musicians came and went, Dylan searched for the combination that would fit his latest intentions. "It was a long creative process," recalls Stoner of the steady rotation of drummers, guitarists, vocalists and pianists who passed through the rehearsal space. "We had a goal in mind, we just didn't know what it was."

Keyboardist Alan Pasqua recalls: "I showed up for the first day and there were two bands there: two drummers, four piano players and a bunch of people singing… it was bedlam. Every day I'd come back and there would be one less person, until we got down to one drummer, one bass player. I was there with one other keyboard player, and when I went back the next day I was the only keyboard player. That was when I realised I had the gig."

IF DYLAN WAS now being straitjacketed into the role of living legend, at least he had the ideal man in his corner. With large parts of his wealth vanishing into his divorce settlement and movie project, Dylan had signed managerial contracts with Jerry Weintraub, the man who'd nursed the autumnal careers of Frank Sinatra and Elvis Presley. "I'm sure Weintraub would have had his ear," believes Stoner, "saying, Hey, if you want to make some money, here are the top acts: Elvis, Frank – this is what you gotta do."

However, the perils of a life at the top had recently been demonstrated with the death of Elvis himself, an event that shook Dylan deeply. "I broke down," he'd later recall. "I went over my whole life. I didn't talk to anyone for a whole week after Elvis died. If it wasn't for Elvis and Hank Williams, I wouldn't be doing what I do today."

Once seen as his usurper, it was perhaps only Dylan who'd come close to matching Elvis's intuitive understanding and re-presenting of American roots music, with that rude mix of blues, country, pop, gospel and R&B. Yet, to the 36-year-old Dylan, that mantle seemed to be exerting a significant pressure.

With his attention largely focused upon the impending premiere of Renaldo And Clara, Dylan's appearances at rehearsals proved spasmodic.

According to Stoner, now acting as bandleader: "Bob would show up at some of these sessions and others we would just tape, and he'd arrive later that night." What became clear from the outset was that there'd be no attempt to recapture former glories. The rootsy charms of the Rolling Thunder Revue

were now strictly outlawed. Indeed, Dylan now toyed with every musical texture around, from heavy metal to pop, reggae to gospel, even going as far as attempting to insert some Egyptian folk-singing into proceedings.

"One day at rehearsals he called me into his room and handed me some records by [acknowledged queen of Egyptian music] Oum Kalsoum, telling me that was what he wanted from me," says Mansfield. "God knows what he meant or if he was putting me on. Regardless, I took them home and listened. It was wonderful to hear that woman's voice for the first time, but I never had any idea how Kalsoum's music related to Bob's, or mine."

As the first dates of the extensive tour grew closer, Dylan became a more permanent fixture at the studios, sleeping in one of the complex's converted office spaces and working with Stoner on a new incarnation of If You See Her, Say Hello.

No longer informed by the bittersweet warmth of the original, the song was now driven forward by a funk-lite rhythm and occasional touches of baroque pop. Extensively rewritten, the tone was no longer one of consolation but indicated an individual long past the point of reconciling himself with his past: "If she's passing back this way most likely I will be gone/But, if I'm not, just let her know it's best that she stay gone." It sat well with the now extensively retooled songbook, sharing space with a pop rendition of Tomorrow Is A Long Time, while You're A Big Girl Dylan had arrived at a sound built around an uncharacteristic blend of female vocalists and horns, with the likes of Elvis's own sax man, Steve Douglas, and Motown percussionist Bobbye Hall on board.

"I broke down... I didn't talk to anyone for a week after Elvis died."
BOB DYLAN

Anaesthetised to the emotional weight they once carried, the songs now took on an oily, urbane quality.

Surrounded by 10 musicians, this was Dylan's very own big band, an ambition he'd harboured for many years. Stoner remembers the eager delight as the final pieces were put in their place. "We were ecstatic. When we had our final private listening session, where we realised that the whole thing had come together, Bob suggested that he 'do an Elvis' and give me a new car as a bonus. Nothing ever came of it, but I was moved by the suggestion. We knew we were really on to something."

The tour opened at the Nippon Budokan towards the end of February, marking Dylan's first performance in front of a Japanese audience. It was quite an entrance. As the sleek rhythm and blues of Lonesome Bedroom began to uncoil, a sight came into focus quite unlike anything the crowd could have bargained for. The musicians were decked out in black-and-white silk uniforms, along with a generous amount of make-up.

"The costumes were an attempt to do something other than the Rolling Thunder approach of everyone wearing denim," says Stoner. "He wanted to look slick." Dylan: "I just got too depressed having to go on in my street clothes all the time."

Dylan himself revelled in the show's wild histrionics. Next to Bob's name, among the credits in the tour's souvenir programme, was a single word: Entertainer. "There's more than a little Wayne Newton in all of us," smiles Stoner, alluding to the notoriously gaudy Vegas entertainer. Dylan's exuberance extended off-stage, where he fixed his charms on the youngest of the backing vocalists, Helena Springs. Now back on the road, returning to the territory in which he was most certain, he delighted in its "opportunities". His fiery, larger-than-life lover Mary Alice Artes would eventually join the entourage, an addition he artlessly balanced with his affair with Springs. Clearly not one to be deterred by an awkward situation, once the tour reached New Zealand Dylan would lose himself in the company of a Maori princess called Ra Aranga.

While the musical mix remained in a state of flux during the opening shows, Dylan at least seemed happy, retreating into the comforting surrounds of his band. "He didn't rely on his solo format, alone with the acoustic guitar and harmonica," says Stoner. "Instead he relied upon the piano accompaniment of Alan Pasqua, which was sensational."

"Words were few," remembers Pasqua. "I believe I shared

"Jesus put his hand on me. It was a physical thing. I felt my whole body tremble." BOB DYLAN

a special musical connection with him, even though it wasn't really spoken. When we did our duets, there were some really magical things that happened."

For Stoner, accustomed to the mercurial brilliance of the Rolling Thunder Revue, the pattern adopted for these shows came as a shock: "It became a well-oiled machine. Like doing a Broadway show; the same tunes, in pretty much the same order, every night. It was very consistent. If anything, that was the single musical drawback, but I think he settled on that."

Further band tensions would arise from Dylan's relationship with Springs, especially among those band members who would offer advice on Springs' unschooled talents. Rob Stoner's bids at constructive criticism did little to calm the situation. "Rob's a great player, but he got out of hand; he started

playing lead bass," claims guitarist Billy Cross. "We were in one of the Australian cities and Bob called me up to his room. He said, 'I've got to get rid of Rob. He breaks my heart on stage, because he played all over the music.' Then he asked me if I'd tell him..."

While it never fell to Cross to do the dirty work, by the time the first leg wound to its conclusion in Sydney, Stoner was no longer in the band. "There was a mutiny," Cross now says. "The musicians really resented that they had to go through me with any grievance. My job was to insulate Bob from situations that he didn't want to be directly involved with, so I had to make decisions on his behalf... But the timing wasn't the greatest."

STONER'S DEPARTURE COULDN'T have been more inconvenient. With more dates ahead, the now road-tested band had limited opportunities to record new material. Only days after walking off the Sydney stage, the band now found themselves back in the Santa Monica rehearsal space, attempting to plug the holes. There was the addition of Carolyn Dennis to the roster of backing singers, following the departure of the then pregnant Debbie Dye (though rumours abounded that friction between her fellow vocalists had played a significant part in her exit). Jerry Scheff, yet another member of Elvis's Las Vegas outfit, took over on bass. With only a matter of days in which to familiarise themselves with their new roles, they were about to receive a crash course in Dylan's unique working methods.

Unable to find a studio capable of housing them, the band were reduced to recording in the cavernous rehearsal area. David Mansfield: "On the first day of the sessions the crew spent a lot of time choosing mics, placing baffles between musicians and doing all the things one usually does to get good recording sound. But the process must have tried Bob's patience, because suddenly he asked us to push everything out of the way and drag our instruments around in a big circle, and then he just launched into the songs. The crew frantically scrambled to reposition the microphones, but from then on it was a live album, not a studio one."

Pasqua remembers Dylan doing little to conceal his exasperation. "After the first day of recording he fired the whole band. But the next day we all got a call saying we'd been rehired. It was out of control. There was no clear producer, so Bob was in charge and it was pretty disorganised. I remember him singing his vocals in one of the bathrooms. It was just this big, open, tiled room and the sound was awful."

While the songs that would eventually form Street Legal had been with Dylan for many months, he seemingly possessed no wish to capture definitive versions of them.

"I see that it's badly mixed and it doesn't sound very good, but what can you do?" Dylan would say. "Every time you make an album, you want it to be new, good and different, but personally, when you look back on them – for me – all my albums are just measuring points for wherever I was at a certain period of time. I went into the studio, recorded the songs as good as I could, and left. Basically, realistically, I'm a live performer and want to play onstage for the people and not make records that may sound really good."

"It went really fast," recalls Cross, who'd initially hankered for a more polished production. "He said to me, 'It is these songs, recorded by these musicians, on this day.'"

also quite happy to lose himself in the city, visiting cinemas and shops, hunting out gifts for his family, seemingly unaware of the growing mania that surrounded his six shows at Earls Court.

Album charts that summer sagged under the weight of the Saturday Night Fever and Grease soundtracks, while the Patti Smith Group's Because The Night rubbed shoulders with Abba's Take A Chance On Me in the Top 40.

A great deal had changed in the 12 years since Dylan was last on a London stage, yet, if anything, the interest that surrounded him had intensified rather than dissipated. The faintest rumour of his return often fuelled the music press into wild speculation, and now – amazingly – it was actually happening. That spring queues formed around ticket outlets days in advance of sale, snaking down streets and around blocks for what seemed like miles. It was only a matter of hours before all 94,000 tickets for the London shows were gone.

The evening before their European debut, Dylan and his band soundchecked one last time before going on to a CBS industry party in Covent Garden. But Dylan soon grew bored and, with several band members, flitted off into the night. Moving from club to club, they eventually settled at the Music Machine (now the Camden Palace) to catch Robert Gordon. Despite the new-wave hype, Gordon possessed a pounding rockabilly heart, a fact underlined by the presence of one of Dylan's heroes, Link Wray, in his band. The teenage Robert Zimmerman had seen Wray share a stage with Buddy Holly.

Dylan had another reason for turning up. Also in Gordon's band was Rob Stoner. "He was a big rockabilly fan, especially of Link Wray," says Stoner, "and he wanted to confirm there was no lingering animosity between us."

Among those backstage was one Sid Vicious, eager to check out Gordon, a legend of the CBGB New York punk scene. He hadn't, in his wildest dreams, expected to encounter Bob Dylan, the man who surely encapsulated the dying hippy ideals that punk had raged against. Vicious drunkenly circled the group before firing off the single witticism: "Aren't you Bob Dildo?"

"I don't know how he got in," says Stoner. "He was just this sad, drunken, drugged-out guy, waving his arms around. Bob kept his cool, he's a tough little guy. Sid had this switchblade knife, but before he could even open it Steve Soles hustled him out of the room." They moved on to the 100 Club before returning to Dylan's hotel, joking and singing far into the morning.

Yet, somehow, this gypsy raggedness does much to enhance a deeply personal portrait of where Dylan found himself. During the final verse of Where Are You Tonight? he lets out a howl. Equal parts epiphany and pain, he sings, "There's a new day at dawn and I've finally arrived.../I can't believe I'm alive, but without you it just doesn't seem right." There was little else he could do but forge ahead.

ON JUNE 13, 1978, the eighth floor of the Royal Garden Hotel on London's Kensington High Street reverberated with the sound of waking musicians and ringing phones. Yet the man around whom it all revolved was absent. As became his customary London routine, Bob Dylan was at the Swiss Cottage public swimming baths, eager to try the Olympic-sized pool, his spindly frame unrecognised. He was

Lost in translation: Dylan, Osaka Station, Japan, February 27, 1978.

The carnival atmosphere arranged by the promoters at Earls Court on that opening night in June, with clowns and Punch & Judy shows dotted around the outer concourse, had done little to dispel the mounting tension. Proceedings opened with an instrumental rendition of A Hard Rain's A-Gonna Fall, Dylan nowhere in sight. He would eventually emerge, for the first time in the capital since the Royal Albert Hall in 1966, the drainpipes and Cuban heels look of that era replaced by a billowing flared outfit, customised with a rather striking metallic lightning flash.

This was Dylan anew, fresh with unfamiliarity, an audacious reinvention. Tangled Up In Blue smouldered as a torch ballad, while One More Cup Of Coffee clutched wildly at the coattails of its Bo Diddley beat. It's Alright Ma (I'm Only

Bleeding) leered and spat in its new heavy metal guise before the twinklingly hymnal Forever Young. It was everything fans and the critics could have hoped for, yet nothing they would have expected. "All these luminaries came backstage to pay respects," says Mansfield, "Mick Jagger, George Harrison…"

"He had a great time," remembers promoter Harvey Goldsmith. "He was chatty and enjoyed himself. He even met Princess Margaret." Among the throng was Michael Gray, author of what many hold to be the first serious study of Dylan's work, Song And Dance Man. Led into the dimly lit area, with his nine-year-old son Gabriel, Gray was presented before Dylan, who was flanked on either side by Jack Nicholson and Bianca Jagger. "Jack was standing there beaming, glad to be in his presence," says Gray, "and Bianca was fuming at being ignored… [Bob] was saying, 'The old songs really do stand up, don't they?'"

AS THE TOUR rolled through Europe that summer, Dylan appeared happy and eager to sample the cultural life that surrounded him, such as visiting the homes of Rembrandt and Anne Frank in Amsterdam. "We had Goebbels' train; it was an Art Deco Nazi train," says Cross of the private train carriages used for their tour. "He said he'd book us into the finest hotels available, told us to bring our wives, and he paid for everything. It was incredible."

Following a performance in Rotterdam, the band moved on through Dortmund and Berlin, before eventually reaching Zeppelinfield, Nuremberg, the site of Hitler's infamous rallies. Dylan insisted on the stage being constructed at the opposite end of the stadium. Before an audience of 80,000, emotions ran high, as drummer Ian Wallace remembers: "Fritz Rau, the German promoter, just broke down. Here was this huge audience looking away from where Hitler had once stood, towards this little Jewish guy."

Shelter from the storm: waiting for Dylan, Sydney Sports Ground, April 1978.

When I Met Bob…

ROLLING STONE RONNIE WOOD

"At The Last Waltz, Neil Diamond came off stage and Bob's just about to go on. And as he came off, Diamond said, 'You're really gonna have to go some to follow me, man. I was so great.' And Bob says, 'What do you want me to do, go on stage and fall asleep?'

"Another time we were in the studio, my studio time, in New York with the Al Green band. All these guys from Memphis couldn't understand Bob's chord sequences. Every time he started off a new song, he'd start in a new key, or if he were doing the same song over and over, every time it would be in a different key. Now, I can go along with that with Bob, but the band were totally confused, and one by one they left the studio. Only a couple of them stayed. They said, 'You're OK, Woody, but who's your friend?'"

"It was a larger-than-life moment," adds David Mansfield, "playing Masters Of War as we stared at the podium where Hitler had delivered his famous speeches. From it we could see a line of torches far in the distance as twilight fell."

Following the success of Dylan's Earls Court residency, one final performance was arranged for the British masses on July 15, 1978. Under the banner of "Picnic at Blackbushe" Dylan would face the largest crowd of his career, bringing the European tour to a conclusion at the old, crumbling Blackbushe Aerodrome on the borders of Surrey. His last appearance before such a crowd had been at The Isle Of Wight Festival in 1969.

"It was a bright, clear day, and the crowd stretched out for miles," remembers Graham Parker, who performed that afternoon, sharing a bill with Eric Clapton and Joan Armatrading. As the crowd continued to gather, someone who'd encountered Dylan during his first visit to England in 1962 was weaving his way through backstage security. "He told me to come along that day, but it took me three hours to get to him," remembers Martin Carthy, the source of many of Dylan's earliest folk melodies. "I had a friend working backstage who got me a pass. There were just a few people around his caravan, and he was very relaxed, very funny. Just the same bloke, but 16 years on."

Dusk was settling over the audience, now a staggering 250,000 strong, as Dylan took to the stage, thick plumes of bonfire smoke eddying in from the peripheries. The sheer enormity of the event wasn't instantly apparent, even to Martin Carthy watching from the stage. "I didn't realise until he started playing Like A Rolling Stone," recalls Carthy. "You could see these little Bic lighters being raised into the air, and it just rolled back in a gigantic wave as far as you could see."

That night the songs of *Street Legal* would dominate the show in a manner unlike any other during the tour, lending the concert a darker hue. Blackbushe proved to be a unique union between the classic songbook and the man of that moment. He played for three hours, and as The Times They Are A-Changin' reverberated in the darkness for one last time, it felt to many that this would be the last time they'd ever see him.

Amid the hubbub that surrounded the Earls Court shows, Dylan had turned to biographer Robert Shelton and confided, "I feel at home in America, because, as primitive as it is, I can still create from America. All my feelings come out of America." Yet, when he took to the stage in Augusta, Maine, three months later, that bond would be stretched to breaking point. The 18 shows played that summer in Europe were cast into sharp relief by a touring schedule that would see Dylan play 65 concerts over a gruelling three-month period in the US and Canada.

Slowly the grand conceit – this glittering, travelling music box of hits – began to slip. While the shows remained largely unchanged, previous elements of richness and warmth were lost as Dylan drove himself and the band on. The deadening routine of grey sports arena upon grey sports arena began to grind them down. Unlike their European counterparts, American journalists were unwilling to come to terms with this latest incarnation of Dylan. Having tasted blood during the Renaldo And Clara feeding frenzy, they saw little reason to relinquish their grip now.

"Some of the comments were very cruel," recalls Ian Wallace. "One critic likened Dylan's show to a Las Vegas cabaret act."

"I saw one review that accused me of going 'Vegas' and copying Bruce Springsteen because I was using Steve Douglas, a saxophone player," Dylan later told Cameron Crowe. "The Vegas comparison was, well, you know, I don't think the guy had ever been to Vegas, and the saxophone thing was almost slanderous."

By the time he reached his hotel room in Tucson, Arizona, Dylan felt utterly adrift. Alone and road-weary, yet still possessing the little silver cross that had been thrown on to the stage a few nights before, something shifted. "There was a presence in the room that couldn't have been anybody but Jesus," Dylan would recall. "Jesus put his hand on me. It was a physical thing. I felt it all over me. I felt my whole body tremble... Being born again is a hard thing. We don't like to lose those old attitudes and hang-ups."

It didn't take long before his experience channelled itself into his songs. "I was sat next to him when he wrote Slow Train Coming," says Billy Cross. "But he'd always used biblical references in his lyrics, so... I didn't pay it that much attention." Dylan's entourage remained largely unaware of the man's new concerns.

"I didn't know anything about it," claims Mansfield. "I didn't notice any big changes that one could attribute to a religious epiphany." What it did do, however, was instil a new sense of purpose to those final weeks of touring. Dylan's humour once again broke forth, with many songs now prefaced with long, bizarre tales of geeks, circuses, bearded ladies and bedevilled old men.

THE TOUR WOULD conclude in Miami, after 10 months. As the show wound towards its close he debuted Do Right To Me Baby (Do Unto Others), the first public airing of his new Christian message. Yet this wouldn't be the note on which the night, and the entire year, would end. Returning for a second encore, one last honky-tonk through I'll Be Your Baby Tonight, the band reprised the song's coda again and again, refusing to let it end. It felt like nothing more than the summation of a yearlong promise to posses, delight and indulge the wishes and fantasies of every member of his audience.

After the concert, Dylan remained awake for much of the night, numbed with exhaustion, yet flushed with excitement. "He was telling us all about these plans he had for next year," says Ian Wallace, "a new album, a new tour... I think we were all pretty devastated when we never heard from him again."

The Bob Dylan that was to publicly emerge nearly a year later was a markedly changed figure. The songs he wrote early in 1979 were, even to their author, striking in their intensity. "I didn't like writing them," he would later say. The message that coursed through this new material would, he realised, be too much for his own audience. Instead these songs would, it was proposed, be recorded by backing singer Carolyn Dennis, with a possible Dylan production credit.

Yet he came to realise that there was nowhere to hide from the direction in which his instincts were pushing him. He immersed himself in the communal faith-based existence of the Los Angeles Vineyard Fellowship, to the great surprise even of those members of his touring band who possessed such beliefs themselves. "I went through a similar awakening myself after the tour ended," says David Mansfield, "as many people

"The critics were very cruel. One likened Dylan to Las Vegas Cabaret."

DRUMMER IAN WALLACE

did in the late '70s. When I started attending church, I was shocked to find that there was Bob at the back of the room. It was the first I knew about it."

As he'd done before, Dylan embraced the possibilities, his work energised with this new, deeply personal revelation. If Elvis's ghost had stalked him throughout the previous year, it seemed that Dylan had finally found the spiritual escape route from the weight of his own mythology that had been so crucially denied to The King. Billy Cross, having worked so closely with him throughout the world tour, sensed a certain inevitability as Dylan shed one skin for another. "The guy is a huge talent, who would have to go off in whatever direction he felt he had to," he says. "He was following his muse."

Missionary Zeal

LOST CLASSIC

In 1979 Dylan converted to Christianity, got nasty, recruited two of Dire Straits and created the spellbinding *Slow Train Coming*.

GETTING BORN AGAIN was the most unpopular move Bob Dylan ever made. By comparison, the controversy over going electric in 1965 was pretty low-grade – the real "Judas" shout from the mass of Dylan fans went up when he turned to Christ. Philosophically, fundamentalism stood his world on its head. Dylan abandoned tolerant liberalism. He even stopped being enigmatic. Instead, there was mean-spirited certainty.

He twisted his Jewish heritage and his just-discovered American chauvinism into a new take on global politics. On stage, he preached that Russia and China were about to start Armageddon in the Middle East, expounding the notion outlined in *Slow Train Coming*'s title track of, "Sheikhs walking round like kings/Wearing fancy jewels and silver rings/Deciding America's future from Amsterdam and Paris". Bloody foreigners, eh?

During the album's tour, he would preachify against all manner of "sinners", homosexuals being a favourite target at one particular point. Bloody faggots, eh?

The whole rationale was irrational; stupid, vicious and cruel. There again, great music rarely flows from purity, sweetness and light, and Dylan's bug-eyed rage at the world made *Slow Train Coming* a great album.

The weight of it bears down from the moment Barry Beckett strikes the opening notes of Gotta Serve Somebody: electric piano has never sounded more spine-chilling. Then Dylan introduces himself, sneering and wagging of finger, admonishing one and all – ambassador to rock'n'roll star to barber – that their visions of personal grandeur are but temporal vanities because they all "gotta serve somebody", be it "the Devil or the Lord".

Every note is crisp, Mark Knopfler's down-mix guitar figure relentless, Pick Withers's drumming basic and black, and Dylan sings fit to kill, everything poured into loathing the lot of us.

Dylan's bug-eyed rage made *Slow Train Coming* a great album.

For sure, it's calculated to offend, but it's a hell of a drama, intensified by the work of the most disciplined and astute studio team Dylan ever pulled together. At Muscle Shoals, Beckett co-produced with Atlantic legend Jerry Wexler – who rebuffed Dylan's evangelising attempts to recruit him with a tart, "Bob, you're dealing with a 62-year-old confirmed Jewish atheist. I'm hopeless. Let's make an album."

Dylan handpicked more non-believers in Knopfler and Withers from the emergent Dire Straits. Then, perhaps mindful of widespread comments that his previous album, *Street-Legal*, was musically sloppy, he told Wexler, "I've been making, like, home records, but I wanna do a professional record." He got it: his fired-up fanaticism was brilliantly counterbalanced by the surrounding team's cool objectivity.

The title track, Gonna Change My Way Of Thinking and When You Gonna Wake Up all share Gotta Serve Somebody's rocking ferocity, Dylan's singing even angrier than in his protest days.

Despite his mindset, his artistic instinct does allow for some range of tone and pace. I Believe In You, with its purr of electric piano, is almost meek. Do Right To Me Baby (Do Unto Others) strolls breezily along to redemption. Man Gave Names To All The Animals is a dark reggae nursery rhyme.

The concluding track, When He Returns, comes straight from church, stately piano and burning voice only. The lone dull track is Precious Angel, a dutiful tribute to Mary Alice Artes, the girlfriend who, after his religious revelation, led him to Bible study.

AT THE TIME, of course, most Dylan lovers simply couldn't believe his conversion to Christianity had happened. Yet his writing had always been riddled with religious allusions, Dylan himself describing *John Wesley Harding* (1968) as "the first Biblical-rock album".

Then the mid-'70s pitched a heap of problems into the path of his spiritual search: the drug-strewn turmoil of The Rolling Thunder Revue (1975), followed by the diverse emotional uproar of his profound grief over both Elvis Presley's death and his bitter divorce from Sara (1977), then the critical and commercial failure of his grotesquely egocentric movie Renaldo And Clara (1978). Finally, in autumn 1978, American audiences gave a cool reception to

SLOW TRAIN COMING
BOB DYLAN

his *Street-Legal* album and its accompanying comeback tour.

Another girlfriend, backing singer Helena Springs, advised him to pray his way out of this slough of despond and, after a Tucson, Arizona gig on November 17, he experienced what he later called a "born-again experience" when "the glory of the Lord knocked me down and picked me up" right there in his hotel room. Within days he introduced the first rudimentary instrumental drafts of Slow Train Coming and Do Right To Me Baby (Do Unto Others) at soundchecks. When the tour finished he obediently immersed himself in the Vineyard Fellowship.

The aftermath of *Slow Train Coming* played out through three more albums of gradually diminishing religiosity in *Saved* (1980), *Shot Of Love* (1981) and *Infidels* (1983). Springs suggested a couple of explanations for his fervour cooling. "He found a lot of hypocrisy in those

Jesus people that he had gotten involved with," she reported. But she added an observation that draws the plot back to perceptions of Dylan as a rock'n'roll chameleon: "When he'd learned all he could learn, he went on to something else." None of which, of course, implies that he didn't believe absolutely at the time.

Whatever, *Slow Train Coming* stands as the born-again movement's one great gift to music, despite all the hellfire rhetoric ("The Devil has taken rock'n'roll music and used it for his own purposes," he told one audience). In 1981, he reflected, with a gentleness atypical at the time: "I just have to hope that in some ways this music that I've always played is a healing kind of music." But, for the born-again Bob, healing could hardly be balanced and holistic – more a matter of cauterising wounds with Jehovah's white-hot branding iron. *Phil Sutcliffe*

Chapter Three

ON THE ROAD AGAIN

The fall,
the rise
and that
never-ending
tour...

The 1980s was a strange decade for Dylan. He almost ruined Live Aid, made bad films and wore even worse clothes. Then he came to his senses. By David Sheppard

Oh Mercy!

If you want to know if Bob Dylan is having a good decade, examine his wardrobe. In his '60s prime Bob was the epitome of boho chic. In the less certain '70s there was the wilfully conservative flannels and reading-specs image (he was so far ahead of the game by this point he'd probably lapped himself), later superseded by the mystical gypsy who led the Rolling Thunder Revue. Only as his muse grew shaky at the decade's end did flared jump suits make an appearance.

© Ken Regan/ Camera 5

Leather jacket *not* required: Dylan, 1983.

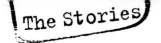
So it's unsurprising to look back on Bob Dylan's 1980s – a decade generally regarded as his musical worst – and find the one-time avatar of cool cavorting around the world's stages in a skimpy vest and driving gloves. If the '80s were the Decade That Style Forgot, Bob had 90 per cent amnesia.

Sartorial pointers notwithstanding, Dylan and the 1980s were always going to be incongruous bedfellows. He was the enduring symbol of all things mythical, poetic and sublime, plunged into an era of conspicuous consumption, Lionel Richie schmaltz and Linn drum machines. This, all told, was no place for a wrinkling folk iconoclast.

In retrospect Dylan should have taken the '80s off and hibernated. Artistically at least, that's almost exactly what he did.

But not immediately. First he had the Born Again period to see out, via *Saved* (1980) and *Shot Of Love* (1981). Though his live concerts began the decade stuffed with Christian proselytising and new material, it wasn't long before his live sets became dissipated under an influx of his blue chip '60s work and Dylan – with, no doubt, a heavy hint from CBS – began to take his foot off the evangelical pedal.

Unfortunately, his creative motor was now beginning to stutter. Sure, there was 1983's reasonably well-received *Infidels* album, on which reggae rhythm-gods Sly & Robbie slugged it out with ex-Rolling Stone Mick Taylor and producer Mark Knopfler (Knopfler was only third choice – earlier approaches to Frank Zappa and, of all people, Giorgio Moroder, proved fruitless). The trouble was, he left off all the good songs.

Something was clearly amiss. What other major artist in need of a critical fillip would omit songs as deep, dark and truly resonant as Blind Willie McTell or achingly honest as Lord, Protect My Child, in favour of lumpen dirges such as Neighbourhood Bully or Union Sundown?

Veteran Dylan accompanist Al Kooper, a mainstay of Dylan's 1982 live shows, recalls similar errors of judgement. "The shows were brutal. One of the first nights, we played Like A Rolling Stone so slow it must have taken 20 minutes to go through the whole song."

Even a more robust 1984 tour found Dylan's form still plummeting, while that year's *Real Live* album did little but confirm that his performing talents were bottoming out. With his old, wilful ways coming in for strong criticism, Dylan once more took stock. Surveying the musical universe of the mid-'80s was a chastening experience. Although the Subterranean Homesick Blues sequence that began *Don't Look Back* was retrospectively hailed as the "first video", the era of MTV seemed antithetical to Dylan's entire being.

STILL, **DYLAN'S ENDURING** status and the reverence with which his earlier work was still held made him a must for 1985's We Are The World single and Live Aid – themselves partial proof that the rock fraternity had not been totally subsumed by the self-serving spirit of the age. At the videoed recording session for We Are The World, Dylan looked decidedly uncomfortable amid a gaggle of over-emoting platinum-sellers: Stevie Wonder had to coach him through his cameo because he wasn't sounding "Dylan enough".

Equally, Live Aid should have been a re-affirmation of Dylan's Lordly status. Certainly, concert promoter Bill Graham thought so, giving Dylan top billing at the US show. Alas, Dylan

Dylan was the enduring symbol of all things mythical, plunged into the era of Lionel Richie schmaltz.

blew it. There was no vest but, instead of reminding the watching millions of his mercurial songwriting genius or onstage magnetism, Dylan, having spent the day boozing with Keith Richards and Ronnie Wood, murmured distractedly through three lifeless acoustic dirges (Ballad Of Hollis Brown, When The Ship Comes In and Blowin' In The Wind), while his drinking buddies stumbled about lost.

Dylan put the embarrassing farrago down to dodgy stage monitors: "We couldn't even hear our own voices, and when you can't hear, you can't play. It's like proceeding on radar."

Ronnie Wood elaborates: "Bob says, 'I'm playing Philadelphia the day after tomorrow.' I didn't even know about Live Aid. He says, 'It's a big charity thing and I have to go along with it.' Then he says, 'Do you think you and me could play together sometime?' I said, 'Sure, let's do the gig on Saturday.' So I rang up Keith and I said, 'Get over here because Bob wants us to do Live Aid with him.'

"When we got to the stadium he [Dylan] was saying, 'I wonder what Bill wants me to do?' We were going, 'Do what you want to do, Bob!' Even going up the ramps, we'd

Like a Rolling Stone: Dylan flanked by Ronnie Wood and Keith Richards, Live Aid, Philadelphia, July 13, 1985.

decided what songs we were going to play and he turns and says, 'Hey, maybe I should do All I Really Want To Do!' We were going, 'Aargh! Oh my God!'"

Over in London, Bob Geldof was aggrieved, to say the least. The music wasn't so much the problem as Dylan's blurted last words: "It'd be nice if some of this money went to American farmers."

This was a pretty pass indeed: pipe-smoking US corn-belt agriculturalists being placed in the same bracket as emaciated Ethiopians. Still, things weren't about to get any better.

Dylan's on-stage observations lit the flame for Farm Aid, yet another televised charity jamboree, co-organised by Willie Nelson and Neil Young. Rather than risk further humiliation, Dylan decided to go in mob-handed with Tom Petty & The Heartbreakers and spent a week rehearsing. The results, in all fairness, were palatable.

Much of the next two years was spent touring in tandem with Petty and his compadres. Dylan blew hot and cold: many noted his new-found ability to recast all his songs in the same, droning two-note "melody", others wondered who exactly had sanctioned his latest garb: raccoon-tail hat and silver cape. The dodgy clothes were once again inauspicious omens.

His next album, 1985's *Empire Burlesque*, proved to be another curate's egg. Mixed by electro pioneer Arthur Baker, it was at least a sign that Dylan was engaging with the technology of the age. It contained both satisfactory and shockingly dull songs, but neither strand benefited from the angular keyboards and thwacking snare drums Baker had employed so fruitfully with New Order.

Simultaneously, Dylan found time for another good cause, adding his voice to (I Ain't Gonna Play) Sun City, Steve Van Zandt's 1985 anti-apartheid single. Engineer Jay Burnett was charged with the apparently onerous task of finding a place for Dylan's singular efforts. "He sang the whole song and we had to pick out one line that sounded good. That was a big problem because we couldn't find a line that a) sounded like Dylan, b) was in tune, c) was in time. Good old Bob!" It seemed everyone knew how Dylan should sound except the man himself.

AS IF TO BALANCE his increasingly erratic output, CBS released *Biograph*, a 53-track retrospective that anthologised two decades of Dylan's sporadic genius, including many rarities. Typically, the maestro dismissed the whole affair: "I didn't put it together and I haven't been very excited about this thing. All it is, really, is re-packaging, and it'll cost a lot of money."

What it actually did do was throw Dylan's less-than-scintillating '80s oeuvre into stark relief. The inclusion of out-takes such as the brilliant Caribbean Wind (omitted from *Shot Of Love*) only reinforced the impression that Dylan's judgement was hopeless.

Dylan and Garcia: "Hey, this cat looks even worse than me!".

Still, Dylan wasn't completely done with the contemporary zeitgeist. In August 1985, he appeared – for reasons never fully explained – on hip hopper Kurtis Blow's Street Rock, making quite a fist of rapping. Meanwhile, hooking up with Eurythmic turned in-demand producer Dave Stewart looked like a contrived attempt to reap the benefits of his beardy Midas touch. "I was excited to work with Dave. I've always liked his work a lot," Dylan announced, somewhat unconvincingly.

In fact, Dylan saw Stewart as a potential foil, deciding to record some tracks at Stewart's Church Studio in Crouch End, London. Yet the geography of the N8 area evidently messed with Dylan's radar. Stewart recalls: "When we were recording in London, Dylan arrived at my house an hour late, looking flustered. I asked what had happened, and he said, 'Well, I rang the doorbell of number seven and this woman comes to the door and I said, Is Dave here?, and she said, No, he's at work, do you want to wait?' So, Dylan waits and thinks, That's strange, he told me to come round. And the woman's thinking, this is weird, he looks like Bob Dylan. So she rings up her husband and asks him, Did you invite Bob Dylan to come round to our house? The husband doesn't know what she's talking about and it turns out that Dylan has got the right number but the wrong street."

Regrettably perhaps, the Stewart sessions came to nothing, while two Stewart-chaperoned videos for Emotionally Yours and When The Night Comes Falling From The Sky – two of *Empire Burlesque*'s better tracks – bulged with "lonesome rocker" clichés and found Dylan looking wan and uninterested.

All of which made Bob's next move grindingly depressing. Essentially a turgid re-telling of the Star Is Born story, 1986's tawdry Hearts Of Fire was a movie with "straight-to-video" etched between every line of its banal script. Without Dylan as the – wait for it – "reclusive rock legend" Billy Parker, it would never have reached a cinema at all.

As journalists gathered at London's National Film Theatre for a pre-filming press conference on August 17, 1986, expectations were decidedly mixed. Dylan gave a glimpse of his old witty self as he wrestled sardonically with The Times' Philip Norman, who was hell bent on warning him off the whole project.

Norman was right. Hearts Of Fire proved to be worse than feared – the sight of Dylan's wooden, mumbling performance was only marginally less embarrassing than the arch over-acting of foppish co-star Rupert Everett, playing the convincingly named English star "James Colt". It all pointed to Dylan's lapsed sense of his own worth.

Soon he was removing his toe from the '80s current altogether as he swiftly banged out an album, *Knocked Out Loaded*, with the Heartbreakers in the old, first-takes-will-do style. It was another grim collection, not helped by children's choruses, steel drums and lethargic 12-bar blues work-outs.

Only one effort bucked the weary trend, the sprawling,

When I Met Bob...

JON BON JOVI:
"Dylan's not the most forthcoming of conversationalists so I'm thinking, What can I talk to him about? So I asked him about his boxer. I heard this rumour – well, it's not a rumour, it's true – that Dylan carries a boxer with him on the road, to work out. I must know about 50 people that have seen him working out with this boxer, so I said, 'I hear you have a boxer on the road with you.' And he said, 'I haven't got a boxer. Don't believe everything you hear.' Just like that. Played dumb. And I'm like, Sure Bob. If that's what you want to tell me, then it's gospel to me."

cinematic Brownsville Girl, co-penned with playwright Sam Shepard – and even that could have been better. As New Danville Girl it was inexplicably left off *Empire Burlesque*, allowing Dylan two years to write ever more bewildering verses about Gregory Peck, abandoned cars and the Corpus Christi Tribune.

1987 WAS PERHAPS the oddest year of an odd decade. In February, Dylan duetted with Michael Jackson at Elizabeth Taylor's 55th birthday party. In March he performed, incongruously, at the Brooklyn Academy Of Music's George Gershwin tribute. In September he played his first ever concerts in Israel – to mass indifference – and appeared wary and taciturn on the BBC's Omnibus special, Getting To Dylan.

He also joined forces with the Grateful Dead for a short run of concerts that are generally widely regarded as the worst artistic decision of both parties' entire careers.

With the Dead's Robert Hunter he penned some songs destined for 1988's barely half-hour long *Down In The Groove* album – the majority being dour cover versions of songs about death. Things were looking bleak again.

Salvation came, oddly, by way of George Harrison. Looking for somewhere in Los Angeles to record a quick additional B-side, Harrison alighted on Dylan's Malibu garage studio in

On We Are The World, Stevie Wonder had to coach him as he wasn't sounding "Dylan enough".

the company of producer Jeff Lynne and pal Tom Petty. The quartet had a ball. Dylan even fired up his barbecue.

Thus, The Traveling Wilburys were born and Dylan's songwriting juices started flowing again. The Wilburys album duly sold by the truck load. Emboldened, Dylan went back-to-basics once more and kicked off his Never Ending Tour in mid-1988 with a raw enthusiasm that left fans happily stunned.

As the Berlin Wall tumbled and the '80s breathed their last, Dylan was even working studio magic again, under the astute guidance of U2 producer Daniel Lanois. Not unreasonably, 1989's *Oh Mercy* even drew favourable comparisons with the best of his '60s and '70s benchmarks.

Incredibly, Dylan was back on message. Somewhere in the back of his Malibu wardrobe, the vests were neatly folded.

Praise Be

After threatening to retire from recording at just 48, somehow *Oh Mercy*, Bono and Daniel Lanois managed to salvage Bob Dylan's career.

WERE IT NOT for the intervention of U2's Bono *Oh Mercy*, Bob Dylans' most celebrated album since *Blood On The Tracks*, might never have been made at all. By 1988, Dylan's recording career had reached a nadir, with May's weary, covers-strewn *Down In The Groove* dash-off attracting critical opprobrium and predictions of an imminent retirement. At roughly the same moment, Daniel Lanois was completing a meteoric evolution from small town studio engineer to stellar international record producer. Destiny decreed that these very different trajectories would soon collide.

'Discovered' by musician/producer Brian Eno, Lanois was a mixing desk boffin who was also a gifted musician with an ear for the melodically sublime. Eno invited Lanois to assist with the production of U2's 1984 album, *The Unforgettable Fire*, having registered the Canadian's ability to generate modern sounding recordings that still oozed arcane mystery. When, during a boozy summer dinner in 1988, Dylan hinted he might never record again, Bono insisted he meet the producer.

Lanois was in New Orleans with The Neville Brothers, capturing the Louisianans' soul gumbo magic in a makeshift studio set up in a rented apartment block. At Lanois' behest the band cut two Dylan songs for the album: Ballad Of Hollis Brown and With God On Our Side. Dylan duly dropped by that September and was impressed not only by the relaxed environment but also by the sound of his old songs given Lanois' tremulous, ethereal imprimatur. Intrigued, Dylan agreed to meet up with the producer again the following spring to begin tentative sessions for a new album.

In February Lanois rented a large, blue-shuttered Victorian mansion on Soniat St and installed his recording gear, along with New Orleans musicians, including Neville Brothers regulars Cyril Neville (percussion), guitarists Brian Stoltz and Mason Ruffner, bassist Tony Hall and

drummer Willie Green. Dylan arrived at the end of the month.

Work began on the song Political World, but quickly fizzled out. They tried again with Most Of The Time, but that also ground into the sand. "I thought I'd left all this recording aggravation in the past," Dylan later admitted. Matters improved markedly as March rolled on, with Dylan slowly warming to Lanois' instinctual production style and the producer learning to cope with his charge's tetchiness. It was rarely plain sailing, though, with Dylan at one point pronouncing that the tracks sounded "like demos", so aggravating the mild-mannered Lanois that the producer smashed an expensive Dobro guitar.

For all the teething troubles, what emerged after two months of intense recording was a sultry, hallucinatory, but above all timeless sounding record, superficially unlike anything else in Dylan's canon. Lanois' signature halo of valve reverbs and shimmering tremolo guitars hung across it like Spanish moss, sympathetically couching Dylan's cracked, semi-spoken, but always grippingly intimate vocals.

The once knotty Political World opens the album, emerging from a mist of ambience on a torrent of dystopian rhyming couplets and careering guitars, like a train speeding out of a nightmare. The similarly themed Everything Is Broken is Vince Taylor's Brand New Cadillac as re-imagined by a hellfire preacher; an apocalyptic litany set to an exotic rockabilly swagger. "Take a deep breath/Feels like you're chokin'/ Everything is broken", Dylan barks, as if he really is about to gag.

> **Dylan so aggravated Lanois that he smashed a guitar.**

Splitting the two is the genteel ballad Where Teardrops Fall, cut in one take with local accordion hero Rockin' Dopsie and his combo. Dylan insisted on its inclusion, mainly, it seems, because its sobbing sax solo was played by a man – one John Hart – who bore a striking resemblance to an early Dylan hero, bluesman Reverend Gary Davis.

THE ALBUM'S CENTREPIECE is the spectral Man In The Long Black Coat, a song Dylan likens to Johnny Cash's I Walk The Line. Written quickly in the studio, the song ranges over the same dark, mythic landscape as Charles Laughton's chilling cine masterpiece Night Of The Hunter; its stygian, Southern gothic allure ushered in by agitated percussion and fragmentary guitars, with Dylan's vocal the most engaged he had mustered in years.

BOB DYLAN

OH MERCY

Elsewhere, the lurching Most Of The Time, and eggshell-delicate What Good Am I show off Lanois' luminescent sound, while the hymn-like Ring Them Bells is a beautiful piano spiritual, albeit one riddled with apocalyptic imagery ("The last firetruck from hell"). The portent lifts on the closing Shooting Star, its aching country soul arrangement framing crooned, self-examining lyrics that are among the most candid and poignant in Dylan's oeuvre, "Seen a shooting star tonight/And I thought of me/If I was still the same/If I ever became/ What you wanted me to be."

To Lanois' chagrin, Dylan insisted on leaving a brace of outstanding tracks off the album. The breezily sardonic Dignity and the churning, surrealistic Series Of Dreams would eventually see the light of day, but their exclusion here seemed like a perverse act of control on Dylan's part, evidence that his notorious obstinacy was still at work; a defiance that meant Oh Mercy was a very good, but not quite great album.

Released in September 1989, it was greeted with press hosannas nevertheless — and sighs of relief from fans. Coupled with the firebrand urgency of Dylan's late-'80s touring show, Oh Mercy was almost universally recognised as proof of an unlikely creative renaissance for the 48-year-old Dylan.

Almost a decade later Dylan and Lanois would reunite for Oh Mercy's looser limbed cousin, Time Out Of Mind. Perhaps he'd come to realise the magnitude of Bono's 1988 intervention, tacitly acknowledging what the vast majority of fans had long concluded; that, back in that blue-shuttered mansion on Soniat Street, Daniel Lanois had saved Bob Dylan's recording career. David Sheppard

He's With The Band

Driving across the States with Bob and working as his official tour photographer, freelance cameraman Barry Feinstein built up a special relationship with Dylan that still endures today.

AS A PHOTOGRAPHER and designer, Barry Feinstein has been responsible for some of the most memorable album covers in rock history – among them The Byrds' *Mr Tambourine Man*, The Flying Burrito Brothers' *Gilded Palace Of Sin*, Eric Clapton's debut LP and George Harrison's *All Things Must Pass*. But his enduring personal relationship with Bob Dylan produced perhaps his most celebrated work, striking for both its access and its intimacy.

Feinstein was working for Columbia Pictures as a production internee when he began taking photographs, and drifted easily into a freelance career. "I started out working for magazines, taking portraits of stars," he says from his Woodstock home, "and then began working on album covers in the '60s." His introduction to Dylan came via the singer's manager, Albert Grossman. "I'd known Albert since the '50s, in Los Angeles," he explains. "We were best friends for years. I met Bob in his office one day, and we hit it off from the start. We became friends, and we still are today."

In 1964, Feinstein and Dylan drove Albert Grossman's Rolls-Royce from Denver to New York City. It was one of Dylan's last adventures before he became prohibitively famous. "It was the car that people noticed," Feinstein laughs. "There weren't many Rolls-Royces in middle America."

Besides shooting the cover photographs for two Dylan albums, *The Times They Are A-Changin'* and *Before The Flood*, Feinstein was also the official photographer on two epic Dylan tours with The Band; in Europe in 1966, and in the US eight years later. By then he had also directed the counter-culture movie You Are What You Eat, and worked on the documentary films Monterey Pop and The Concert For Bangladesh – an involvement with the movie business that continued for many years afterwards.

Dylan occupies a unique place in Feinstein's affections, however. "The man's a poet," he says, "maybe the Poet Laureate of our times. He puts it all out there, every time he goes on stage, and leaves you to figure it out. If you can't, then you shouldn't be in the theatre!"

For more information contact camouflage2@hvc.rr.com

Interview by Lois Wilson

On The Road Again

May 26, 1966

That was taken during a soundcheck at the Royal Albert Hall in London. I don't think he knew that I was taking his photo, so the shot is very natural. Most of my photos of Dylan were taken unawares, as he trusted me and I trusted him. But this really captured how he was at this stage of his life: the loneliness and isolation of being Bob Dylan.

Poster Boy

May 24, 1966

He was signing a poster with the words 'God bless'. I think it was in the dressing room of the Olympia Theatre in Paris. He had a confrontation with the audience there, which started when he put up this 30-foot American flag. That got them going, and it all built up from there.

Tour Blues

UK, May 1966

An amazing tour. Dylan was easy to photograph, because we were friends, but there was all this other stuff going on during the tour. He had a hard time at the shows – Scotland is the one I recall – because the audiences were waiting for their god and didn't want to hear him with an electric band. So there was a lot of booing and tension in the air.

Oh Mersey

May 14, 1966

This shot has never been seen before. It was taken in Liverpool. I call it The Giant. I could see the potential, so I quickly told Bob, 'Hold it', and I got down on the ground to take the shot. Liverpool was a wonderful place to take photographs – that incredibly grey, overcast sky.

The North Country

May 14, 1966

That was Liverpool again. Dylan loved talking to the kids, because they were so natural, and probably because they didn't know who he was, so there was no pressure from them. So I asked them to pose together for this picture. It's like two different worlds colliding.

The Man In Me

UK, May 1966

Dylan had an attitude back then, for sure, but he was never difficult with me. We'd known each other for several years by this time, and he knew that I would never use a photo where he looked bad. He appreciated that, and just let me be around him, so I could do what I do. He had a very strong visual presence, but there was never the sense that he was trying to manufacture an image. The photos show him exactly the way he was.

The Hands Of Bob

UK, May 1966

He always had expressive hands, and as I watched them, I could see that they looked like a photograph – so I took the picture, as simple as that. The cigarettes were always around back then, for all of us. Bob gave up later, I think, and so did I.

Motorpsycho Nightmare

Paris, 1966

The French press followed Bob everywhere; here's a paparazzi on the back of a motorcyle on the way to the George V Hotel for a press conference. Bob had just been to the flea market and bought a marionette. Each time an interviewer asked a question, he would whisper to the puppet and listen before answering. He drove them crazy.

Born Again

After years foundering in the wilderness, 1997's *Time Out Of Mind* sounded like its creator had acquired a new lease of life.

THE CHALLENGE OF Bob Dylan's Time Out Of Mind – his first collection of self-written songs since 1990 – is to take it at face value. There is no point searching for autobiographical confessions ("It's a break-up album, right?" said a friend, referring to all the tunes about lost love and a broken heart) or messages of hope. This is as bleak and blasted as any work by any major artist in any field (and by major artist I mean an artist with something – a reputation, an audience – to lose) has offered in ages. *Time Out Of Mind* is hedged only by craft, by the performer's commitment to his material. The world may be meaningless, but he has no choice but to try to shape that void.

AT FIRST THE MUSIC is shocking in its bitterness, in its refusal of comfort or kindness. Then it settles in as something like a conventional set of songs, and then a curve in one of them – the finality of a life left behind in the way Dylan gets rid of the seemingly traditional lines "I been to Sugartown I shook the sugar down" in Tryin' To Get To Heaven, perhaps, or the quiet drift of Highlands, a nearly 17-minute number so unassumingly mysterious you feel it could have unwound its ball of string over the entire length of the record without exhausting itself – upends any casual listening and throws every bit of wordplay or quiet testimony into harsh relief, revealing a tale seemingly complete and whole.

The story opens with the singer, the tale-teller, walking dead streets and ends with him walking the streets of an almost deserted city: "Must be a holiday," he mutters to himself, as if he could care less whether it is or not. Images of homelessness and of endless wandering drive song after song. Sometimes that motif suggests a man who doesn't want a home ("I know plenty of people," he tells you at one point, "put me up for a day or two"); sometimes it calls up the tramp armies of the Great Depression, or the film director in Preston Sturges's 1941 Sullivan's

Travels, disguised as a hobo, riding the boxcars like a railroad bum in order to meet the masses, the dispossessed and the defeated – and finding that the rags of poverty and anonymity are easier to put on than take off, that they don't merely hide the signs of wealth and celebrity but dissolve them.

As in that old movie, made as the Depression was about to disappear into the maw of World War II, when *Time Out...* plays, another country comes into view. It's less the island of one man's broken heart than a sort of half-world, a devastated, abandoned landscape where anyone might end up at any time, so long as that time is now.

This is a land as still as the plains, its flatness broken only by a violence of tone or the violence of syncopation, of hard truths or a band's rhythms rushing up on each other like people running out of a burning house. "I thought some of 'em were friends of mine, I was wrong about 'em all," Dylan sings in Cold Irons Bound, letting the whiplashed rhythm carry his words around their corner. But on that rhythm, the word "all" isn't really underlined at all; the drama of *Time Out Of Mind* is in its moments of queerly shared vehemence, when a solitary seems to speak with 50 states and 400 years in his voice, but that vehemence is never obvious. Here the whole line is not stressed but swung – "Wrrrrrong about 'em alllll" – with the first word tipped up, the last tipped down, an organ sweeping up the song like wind. For a moment the landscape – which from song to song takes names, "Missouri," "New Orleans," "Baltimore," "Bostontown" – is erased by the movement taking place upon it, and the singer moves out of earshot; when he returns, nothing has changed.

The country that emerges is very old, and yet fresh and in sharp focus, apparently capable of endless renewal. At the same time the place is very new, and all but worn out: "I got new eyes," Dylan sings coolly, in one of the deadliest lines of his writing life: "Everything looks far away." Verbal, melodic and rhythmic signatures from ancient blues and folk songs fit into the songs on *Time Out Of Mind* as naturally, seemingly as inevitably as breaths – say in the way Dock Boggs, standing on the railroad platform in his Danville Girl in 1927, passes the song's cheap cigar to the singer on the platform in Standing In The Doorway. That the reappearance of the forgotten past in an empty present is a talisman of *Time Out Of*

> This is as bleak and blasted as any work by any major artist in any field.

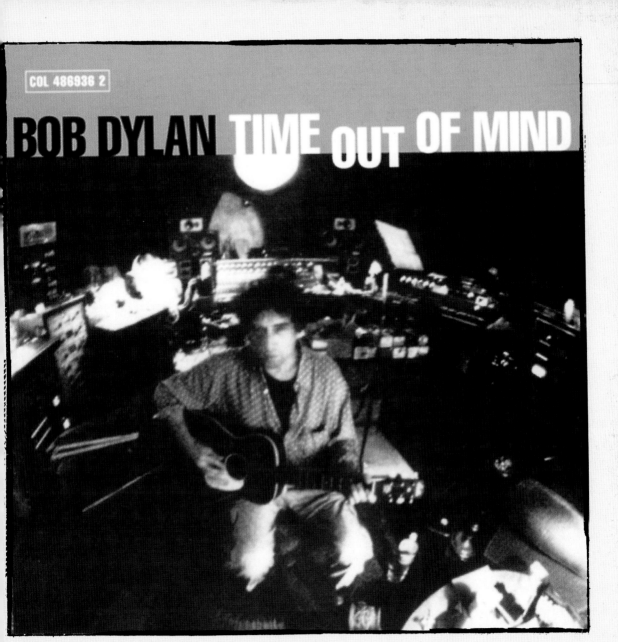

BOB DYLAN TIME OUT OF MIND

Mind is sealed by the art Dylan has chosen to be imprinted directly onto his disc: the classic "Viva-tonal/Electrical Process" Columbia label from the late '20s, a label that ran one series for "Race" or negro recordings, another for "Old Time" or country.

DYLAN'S RECORD SPINS on that label in the way certain of its choruses and verses seem to write themselves, tossed off with a throwaway gruffness that suggests Dylan knows that after hearing half of a line the listener will automatically complete it even before he, Dylan, has sung it: "That's all right, mama, you/Do what you gotta do," as he drawls in Million Miles. But the label also spins backwards, until nothing on it can be read. As many incidents in the music seem to come out of nowhere, the nowhere that

is both the present and the future of the country where the story Dylan is telling takes place. "Maybe in the next life," Dylan says elsewhere in Million Miles, "I'll be able to hear myself think." Over and over, with resignation and sly, twisting humour, with the flair of a Georgia string band or the dead eyes of a gravedigger, the tale-teller poses the same question, sometimes almost smiling when he asks "if everything is as hollow as it seems".

So often, listening to the songs on *Time Out Of Mind* is like watching people pass through revolving doors: the ambience is that abstract and vague and untouchable. You have as much right to expect someone to reappear as quickly as she vanished as to expect never to see her again. That's how it is in the central incident in Highlands, where a man walks into a restaurant, empty except for a

On the road again:
New York, 1997.

waitress. They banter, almost flirt, and in an instant – an instant of fatigue, of boredom, of his or her memory of too many instants just like it, any of that or just a single word uttered with an edge it shouldn't carry – the mood dies. The room, the city outside, the nation around it, its entire history and all of the pieces of music and dramatic scenes that so quietly enter and depart from this one – One Meat Ball, Skip James's 1931 Hard Time Killin' Floor Blues, Jack Nicholson's diner dialogue in Five Easy Pieces, Dylan's own Desolation Row cut down by Robert Burns's half-original folk song Farewell To The Highlands – all of that, from song to nation, turns hostile and cold. For a moment the waitress turns her back, and the air in the restaurant is now so mean you're as relieved as the singer when he quietly slips out of his chair. You can feel yourself tensing your muscles as he tenses his. Yet the singer barely has to go out the door, or the song down its Boston street, for you to imagine that this might have been the last conversation the tale-teller ever had – or, in Boston, on the ground where the nation began, the last conversation that could even begin to suggest the possibility of a story that hadn't been told before.

That is what is new in *Time Out Of Mind*, and in the country it traces as if it were a map you can read once and then throw away, because you won't be able to forget it whether you want to or not. Though crafted out of fragments and phrases and riffs far older than anyone living, bits of folk languages that joke and snarl as if for the first time, this is a picture of a country that has used itself up, and the peculiar thrill of *Time Out Of Mind* is in its completeness, its absolute refusal to doubt itself.

And the winner is: Bob Dylan, who picked up three Grammys for *Time Out Of Mind*, February 25, 1998.

THIS NEW STORY does not come out of nowhere, or at least it is not quite a solitary voice in the wilderness. The same cynical, damaged, sardonic, absolutely certain acceptance of one's own nihilism has been all over Bill Pullman's face in recent years, in The Last Seduction, Malice, Lost Highway, in Wim Wenders's The End Of Violence – for just as *Time Out Of Mind* is an end-of-the-American-century record, closing with a fantasy of a retreat to the Scottish Highlands, to the border country where the oldest ballads first came to life, Bill Pullman, in these films, is the ultimate end-of-the-American-century man. His face may have the cast of knowledge as a movie begins, or it may take most of a movie for the sheen of unsurprise to settle over his features. He may walk with the looseness of the already dead, as in The Last Seduction, or shatter before your eyes, as in Lost Highway – regardless, as in The End Of Violence and as with the narrator in *Time Out Of Mind*, the fact that in some essential way the story he has to tell ended before he even took the stage only increases his wariness.

In The End Of Violence, Pullman is a movie producer whose life, not unlike that of Preston Sturges's director John L Sullivan (played by all-American boy Joel McCrea), is turned upside down. We first see him in his eyrie looking down over all of Los Angeles, surrounded by computers and mobile phones; soon he is dressed in rotting clothes, part of a crew of Spanish-speaking gardeners, hefting his leaf-blowers, moving invisibly through the perfectly groomed estates where, only days before, he looked past his own gardeners as a lord. With an old baseball cap on his head, his eyes squint against the sun; weirdly, they also squint inwardly, as if it's only with a squint that he can bear to look at himself. Unseen by everyone else, a drifter, unshaven and penniless, he misses nothing, but the more he understands, the

less need he has to say anything to anyone. Who would listen?

Blowing his harmonica through passages in Tryin' To Get To Heaven until the song builds on itself like a folk version of The Ronettes' Be My Baby, it's not a question Bob Dylan has to ask himself. Though most often spoken of today as a figure from the past, as someone now marginalised along the dimmer borders of the pop world, Dylan might well answer that when the music is as uncompromised as it is on *Time Out Of Mind*, it's the old songs and the people in them that listen; the dead streets of his new songs, as depopulated, somehow, as the streets of his 1963 Talkin' World War II Blues, will have to take care of themselves. And Dylan may be far less marginalised than he seems; he may be less of a crank, or pop outsider, than an embodiment of the sort of cultural memory he plays with in *Time Out Of Mind*.

Last May, in the college town of Iowa City, on the Dubuque Mall, a soul band set up its amplifiers, and soon a woman was belting out Chaka Khan imitations, driving the afternoon street singers into the corners, where acoustic guitar-and-harmonica versions of Prince's Purple Rain and The Replacements' I Will Dare could barely be heard. As night came on the crowds got younger, the basement bars noisier, the street singers more numerous – by 10pm, there was one every 20 feet or so, each looking bereft and ignored, each with a girlfriend in idolising attendance – and the repertoires more ambitious: These Foolish Things, You Belong To Me, Railroad Bill, something that must have been by Phil Ochs, The Rolling Stones' Singer Not The Song. Every singer seemed to want nothing more than to sound like Bob Dylan, and in his own way, every one did. *Greil Marcus*

The peculiar thrill of Time Out Of Mind is in its completeness.

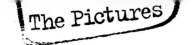
The Other Sides Of Bob Dylan

From the stories behind those famous early Dylan album sleeves to the images that didn't quite make the cut...

WHETHER FRESH-FACED AND clutching an acoustic guitar on his debut album or strolling down a Manhattan street with his girlfriend Suze Rotolo on *The Freewheelin' Bob Dylan...*, the covers of Bob Dylan albums are often as iconic and resonant as the music they contain. Dylan may look like he habitually dresses in the dark but, like almost all great artists, he has always possessed a finely developed visual sense.

Behind every picture lies a story, and every photographer who has worked closely with Bob Dylan has a tale to tell. It's amazing how many of the seminal early Dylan album covers came together through pure happenstance. A short-and-snappy or even perfunctory session would yield a legendary image that would soon find its way into millions of homes around the globe.

"The whole thing took less than 10 minutes," says Barry Feinstein of the session that produced the unforgettable cover shot of *The Times They Are A-Changin'* – a typical experience for the cameramen who shot Dylan in the '60s. Yet many of these same photographers went on to build a strong working relationship with the star and work with him on numerous repeat assignments.

So what happened on the days that history was made? Over the next few pages the photographers who shot the talismanic images that grace the early Dylan albums share their memories of the creative process. What emerges are tales of chance and spontaneity, shots snapped on a whim – appropriately, both singer and snappers busking their way towards posterity.

Also included here are out-takes from those highly rough-and-ready sessions, the images that could just as easily have passed down into rock'n'roll history. Rarely seen, these pictures serve as a fascinating insight into what it was like to be around Bob Dylan in those early days. Things, as you might expect, were rarely quite as they seemed...

Interview & words: Lois Wilson

Bob Dylan

PHOTOGRAPHER DON HUNSTEIN: It wasn't a big deal at the time – a very casual commission. I was working in the Columbia publicity photo studio, capturing recording sessions and taking some head shots. Then one day they needed someone to shoot Dylan for an LP cover. Dylan came by one Saturday morning; it was very casual. I didn't even have any lighting equipment with me. But it was a sunny day and we wandered around the offices until I saw a window with some good light coming through. I positioned him in front of it and took the snap. I took two rolls of 120-size film. Today you'd shoot about 100 rolls. They actually used the shot the wrong way round on the sleeve, I have no idea why, but luckily there were no clues that gave it away.

The Freewheelin' Bob Dylan

PHOTOGRAPHER DON HUNSTEIN: There were no guidelines. It happened quite by accident. I went round his scruffy apartment in the Village. Unlike the first album shoot, I took some lights along this time. We trudged up four or five flights of stairs. Suze Rotolo was there, too. We spent about two hours in the apartment. I took mostly black-and-white pictures, although I did do some colour, too. When I'd taken what I thought we needed, I decided to leave. I asked Bob and Suze to come out to do some shots outside before the light went. It really was that casual; we all went downstairs and stood on Jones Street, which dead-ends 4th Street where he lived. I just said, "Walk away from me then turn around and walk towards the camera", and that's exactly what you see, that's *The Freewheelin'*... front cover. I took just one roll of film on it.

The Times They Are A-Changin'

PHOTOGRAPHER BARRY FEINSTEIN: It was one of the easiest and quickest sessions I've ever done. We went up to somebody's balcony on the Upper East Side of Manhattan, and the whole thing took less than 10 minutes. Bob and Columbia Records wanted a really strong image, and when I saw his face against the sky, which was all whited out, I knew we had something that would endure.

People have placed all sorts of interpretations on the photo, that Dylan was trying to put across a particular image, or was trying to look like Woody Guthrie. But we never took a single premeditated picture in all the time we spent together. Bob had a strong visual sense, but he was never consciously trying to imitate somebody or something else. So it wasn't a conscious statement on anyone's behalf – it was just a moment that was so striking that it was simply asking to be captured for posterity.

For years, Columbia Records wouldn't give me back the negatives, but finally they were returned to me. And this picture became the signature photo in the Dylan exhibition at Seattle in 2004. It turned out to have an amazing lifespan for something that was done so quickly.

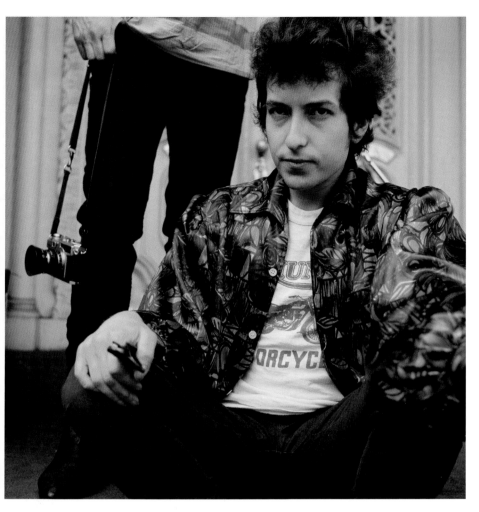

Highway 61 Revisited

PHOTOGRAPHER DANIEL KRAMER: I'd planned out the sleeve to *Bringing It All Back Home* before its execution but we approached *Highway 61 Revisited* in a different way. We didn't want a big set-up with lots of lights and props, so we spent a day wandering around New York taking pictures. We tried out various locations and stopped at a clothes store and bought outfits for Bob, though the ones he wears on the cover are his own. We took shots there and others by O'Henry's, a sidewalk café in Greenwich Village where we stopped for refreshments. We ended up on the stoop outside Bob's apartment in Gramercy Park and that's where the cover shot is taken. I put someone *[Bob Neuwirth]* behind him in the picture to give it extra colour – a small touch, but one that works well. The camera that he is holding, a Nikon Rangefinder SP, is the one I took all my major shots of Dylan on. The final picture was shot on a two-and-a-quarter format rather than on 35mm film. Bob chose the cover shot, and such was his clout that he only gave this one to the record company.

Bringing It All Back Home

PHOTOGRAPHER DANIEL KRAMER: We drove to Woodstock to Dylan's manager Albert Grossman's house. Sally Grossman (she's the lady in red on the cover) and Albert were there. I wanted to do something utterly different and break with tradition – not just for Dylan, but for album sleeve design in general. I wanted Dylan still and motionless in the midst of swirling chaos, to reflect how perceptive he was; as the world changed he could not only see it but understand it too. To the rest of us, it was just a blur.

I devised a technique to do this that created the circular turning effect around him by turning the film 360 degrees on a slow exposure. That shot blacked out Dylan and Sally, then there was a second exposure that kept him still while the rotating of the camera created the blur around him. The point was for him to look

elegant. He could be a businessman, a professional, an educated person, a leader, a captain of industry, a senator; any of these people. I felt that he was a special person and I wanted to convey this in the picture.

The photo was taken on a 4x5 camera rather than a 35mm. There really was no smudging or putting Vaseline on the lens. You have to remember, great portraiture is really great furniture moving. We had to drag in all the lights, make the set and find the right clothes. I took a Polaroid of a mock-up and showed Bob, who liked it. Then we rearranged a few things in the photo. We spent an hour collecting objects around the house that looked good – the fallout shelter sign, a Robert Johnson album, Time magazine – and then we executed the photo. It was nominated for a Grammy, which pleased me very much.

Blonde
On Blonde

PHOTOGRAPHER JERRY SCHATZBERG: Dylan and his manager were very enthusiastic about my photographs. They asked me if I would photograph the cover for *Blonde On Blonde*; it was my first ever commission.

There were only two frames from the session that were out of focus and Dylan chose one of them to be the cover shot. We were shooting at the Meat Market district of Manhattan. It was very cold that day and we were both shaking. There was no brief. I just wanted to get an interesting photograph of Dylan outdoors, in New York, and really the shoot went very smoothly.

Dylan also chose the interior photographs, one being a portrait of myself. While he was in my studio he also saw a photograph of *[Italian actress]* Claudia Cardinale. He liked it and included it on the inner sleeve, too. Claudia's people were not too happy, so they contacted Columbia and complained about it. They and Columbia eventually came to an agreement, and on the second run the photo was eliminated from the jacket.

Nashville Skyline

PHOTOGRAPHER ELLIOTT LANDY: Bob, in this photo, is not the Dylan that everybody was used to seeing – this is the everyman Bob Dylan, your down-to-earth country guy. He was trying to continue the same visual theme seen on the *John Wesley Harding* cover. The brown suede jacket he wore for our sessions was the same one on he wore on the *John Wesley Harding* and *Blonde On Blonde* sleeves.

"Do you think I should wear this?" he asked, starting to put on his hat, smiling because it was a goof, and he was having fun visualising himself in this silly-looking traditional hat.

Bob was really open and in a good mood. It was sunny and we just followed our instincts. It was the first picture of him smiling and, in my opinion, it reflects his inner spirit, the loving essence of the man behind all the inspiring music he has given us.

Black Comedy

Love And Theft makes the dark worlds of moral ambiguity, salvation and the simple business of growing old sound like so much fun.

NOT LONG AFTER its release, Bob Dylan was asked to explain the themes of *Love And Theft.* "The whole album deals with power," he said. "If life teaches us anything, it's that there's nothing that men and women won't do to get power." Its other strands took in "wealth, knowledge and salvation... If it's a great album – which I hope it is – it's a great album because it deals with great themes."

There's something to all that, of course, but in making *Love And Theft* sound like some rock'n'roll version of Machiavelli's *The Prince,* Dylan was perhaps indulging in his customary sense of eloquent elusiveness. As with just about all his best records, this one was indeed streaked with elemental ideas. On occasion, they were made explicit, as in the most compelling passage of Lonesome Day Blues: "I'm gonna spare the defeated... I'm going to speak to the crowd/I'm goin' to teach peace to the conquered/I'm gonna tame the proud." But even in those words, one could hear *Love And Theft*'s most satisfying undercurrent – a skewed humour that served to somehow lighten up even its most heart-stopping moments. When pushed, Dylan conceded that the record was "funny *and* dark"; with a smirk creeping across his face, he also claimed that his new songs were bound up with "business, politics and war – and maybe love interest on the side".

The record's rib-tickling aspects were all the more remarkable given where the record sat in his career. In 1997 *Time Out Of Mind* may have served notice of a talent once again in full flight, but its themes fused with his subsequent life-threatening illness to couch the album in terms of some funereal death-trip. Four years on, Dylan may have been pacing through a similar landscape – morally ambiguous, altogether not-quite-right – but it was some way from silence.

For a start, there were no end of burlesque distractions – Tweedle Dee And Tweedle Dum, Othello And Desdemona, Romeo And Juliet, Groucho Marx, characters hoisted straight from F Scott Fitzgerald. The scenes through which they – and Dylan – passed were sometimes doom-laden, but often lit up by flashing neon, blinding headlamps, and the tantalising promise of A Good Time. And if the narrator sometimes found his brushes with such excitement strangely unsettling ("I'm standing in the city that never sleeps/Some of these women, they just give me the creeps"), there were times when he was only too happy to jump straight in. One minute, he was "standin' on the table, proposing a toast to the King"; the next, he had exited the party and joyously taken to the road. "*I got a cravin' love for blazing speed, got a hopped up Mustang Ford,*" went High Water (For Charley Patton), "*jump into the wagon, love, throw your panties overboard.*" One hesitates to use a phrase like "old devil", but really...

IF *LOVE AND THEFT* was a great record – one of the most confident, consistent albums Dylan has ever recorded – the explanation at least partly lay in the pared-back, straight-ahead methods with which it was put to tape. A production credit for "Jack Frost" turned out to refer to Dylan himself. He also took the inspired decision to simply park his tour bus outside the studio, and – give or take keyboard and percussion parts – use the band that had been accompanying him since June 1999: guitarists Larry Campbell and Charlie Sexton, bassist Tony Garnier, drummer David Kemper.

Anyone who saw him play a series of drooled-over shows in Britain in Autumn 2000 could hear the same empathetic spirit and kinetic energy that frequently materialised onstage, whether in the spiked attack of Lonesome Day Blues, the easy grace that defined Mississippi or the wondrous acoustic sparkle (Campbell's work, in the main) used for High Water. Better still, the band's innate confidence seemed to have allowed Dylan to nudge at least some of the songs into music that sounded both age-old and vivaciously new: if he wanted pre-rock jump-blues (Summer Days), or croonsome ballads (Bye And Bye, Moonlight) they could meet the demands.

Its air of assured excellence was only compounded by Dylan's voice: raddled and shot, perhaps, but so suited to these songs that more toned-up vocals would have waylaid their defining spirit. Such was his mastery of the trick that has eluded so many of his generation: building age into his music as capably as he once conducted the swirling currents of his youth. So, though wealth, knowledge and salvation may have numbered among the album's themes, the notion of hard-wrought experience underpinned almost every note. When it alighted on love-gone-bad, there was the clear sense that life was always fated to go

> ## Dylan conceded it was "funny *and* dark".

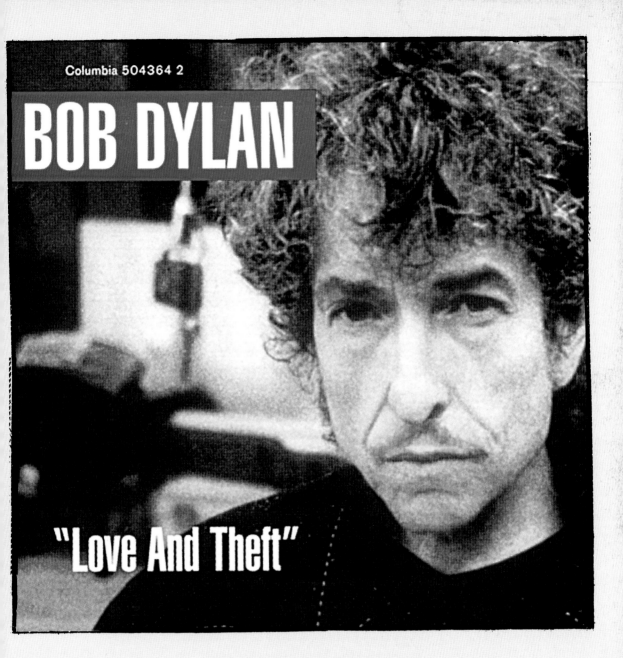

Columbia 504364 2

BOB DYLAN

"Love And Theft"

that way; in the album's more rib-tickling moments, you could hear the laughter of a man so acquainted with life that what might once have delivered a shock could now prompt droll amusement. On both counts, one of baldest lines in Mississippi spoke volumes: "Say anything you wanna/I have heard it all."

If Dylan came close to voicing some eternal kind of wisdom, that sense was only furthered by *Love And Theft*'s abiding location: the place that, with reference to both *The Basement Tapes* and *Harry Smith's Anthology Of American Folk Music*, writer Greil Marcus called The Old, Weird America. On this album, there were moments that could have come straight from Clothes Line Saga or Lo And Behold. Elsewhere, Tweedle Dum And Tweedle Dee seemed to live in much the same world as Tiny Montgomery And Mrs Henry. And therein lay a

crucial part of *Love And Theft*'s magic: the lines one could draw went back not only to Woodstock in 1967, but the half-remembered past which Dylan and The Band had so wonderfully revived.

Such was another, rather more coincidental aspect of the album's wonders. It is one of the stranger aspects of its story that its release date fell on the morning of the attacks of September 11, the moment that found some Americans responding with raised voices and flag-waving belligerence while others wondered whether their trumpeting of American values was treading an altogether more sympathetic set of traditions into the dust. *Love And Theft*, in its own gentle, fatalistic, wonderfully funny way, sounded like that other America incarnate.

"A great album that deals with great themes," reckoned Bob Dylan. In context, he was almost painfully right. *John Harris*

My Back Pages

The first instalment of Dylan's autobiography, Chronicles, offers an all-too tantalising glimpse into its writer's formative years.

ON ELECTION NIGHT, November 2, 2004, in Oshkosh, Wisconsin, Bob Dylan played Masters Of War, his 1963 protest song against arms merchants. It sounded obvious, self-righteous and strident even when Dylan was first performing it; why, this night, was the song so frightening, the singer's delivery so deliberate, with Dylan's voice shaking on the last phrases?

Why is the song still so alive? There's a hint of an answer in Dylan's Chronicles: Volume One, the book he published last fall. It's not a memoir, where the world revolves around the author; it's a *bildungsroman*, where a questing person relates the tale of his or her education in art, life, and the ways of the world. Chronicles is an account of learning and discovery, most deeply in Minneapolis in 1959 and 1960, then in Greenwich Village in the early '60s, and an account of frustration and failure in the decades to come. The old man looks back at his younger self less to find out where he took the wrong road ("The mirror had swung around and I could see the future," Dylan writes of himself in 1987, "an old actor fumbling in garbage cans outside the theater of past triumphs") than to begin again, from the beginning. It's not a tease that Dylan's '60s glory years and the startling breakthroughs since the early '90s are ignored: the book revolves around those poles where the writer knew nothing and where he could do nothing.

So it is modest, humble, squinting, doubting, carefully written, with the writer giving the phrases that leap from his mind free rein ("The mirror had swung around" – my God, what happens when the mirror swings around?) but also reining them in to serve the story, to push it forward or pull it backward – and the story is that of someone with a gift to live up to, if he can figure out what it is. That's what the book is about. The tale-teller is a detective ("I cut the radio off, crisscrossed the room, pausing for a moment to turn on the black-and-white TV," Dylan writes in perfect Raymond Chandler pitch, walking Philip Marlowe around his apartment in Los Angeles in 1947, trying to get a fix on the killer. "Wagon Train was on"), a pathfinder, looking at other people's footprints on the forest floor. He watches the world from a distance; he watches himself only as a reflection of the light the world gives off.

Because he is a musician, the reflections are sometimes echoes, and some of the echoes are words. "My father," Dylan writes of Abraham Zimmerman, "wasn't so sure the truth

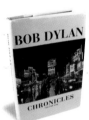

would set anybody free" – and those words sound down through the book. This isn't just the stiff-necked Jew turning his back on Jesus's truth – and it's that truth, and none other, that in John 8.31-32 Jesus says "shall set you free" – it's the truth as, again and again in Chronicles, Dylan applies it to songs. Folk songs. Old songs. Songs that resist the singer, that change shape as soon as he thinks he knows what they are. Songs that may force the singer to exchange facts for mystery and knowledge for ignorance.

"The singer has to make you believe what you're hearing and Joan could do that," Dylan says of Joan Baez and her 1960 rendition of Silver Dagger, an ancient ballad about a mother who carries a knife to keep men from her daughter, and of the Kingston's Trio's 1958 version of Tom Dooley, about a North Carolina man who murdered his lover in 1866. "I believed Joan's mother would kill someone that *[Joan]* loved… Folk music, if nothing else, makes a believer out of you. I believed Dave Guard in the Kingston Trio. I believed that he would kill or already did kill Laura Foster. I believed that he'd kill someone else, too."

"I didn't know what age of history we were in nor what the truth of it was," he writes of the folk culture of Greenwich Village and the mainstream culture that surrounded it. "If you told the truth, that was all well and good and if you told the untruth, that's still well and good. Folk songs taught me that… whatever you were thinking could be dead wrong." Folk music opened the door to a "parallel universe": "a culture with outlaw women, super thugs, demon lovers and gospel truths… landowners and oilmen, Stagger Lees and Pretty Pollys and John Henrys – an invisible world."

"Folk music was a reality of a more brilliant dimension. It exceeded all human understanding, and if it called out to you, you could disappear and be sucked into it. I felt right at home in this mythical realm made up not with individuals so much as archetypes, vividly drawn archetypes of humanity, metaphysical in shape, each rugged soul filled with natural knowing and inner wisdom. Each demanding a degree of respect. I could believe in the full spectrum and sing about it. It was so real, so more true to life than life itself."

Songs that say I am true, but there is no truth: Figure that out, buddy.

It was, Dylan recounts, the dare behind his whole career: the poker game he's still playing. And that is why, on a certain night, an old protest song like Masters Of War can change shape, swing the mirror around, and dare the singer to sing it, to make it true – "the truth about life", as Dylan writes of folk songs, even if "life is more or less a lie". No, it wasn't going to set anybody free, except, for an instant, maybe the singer. Probably not. But of course you never know. Never mind. *Greil Marcus*

It is modest, humble, squinting, doubting, carefully written.

The fag end of his career?
Dylan at Hammerstein
Ballroom, New York,
August 2001.

After years in the wilderness, Bob Dylan rediscovered his muse in the '90s and entered the new millennium on a creative high. Nick Kent charts his comeback.

THE SECOND COMING

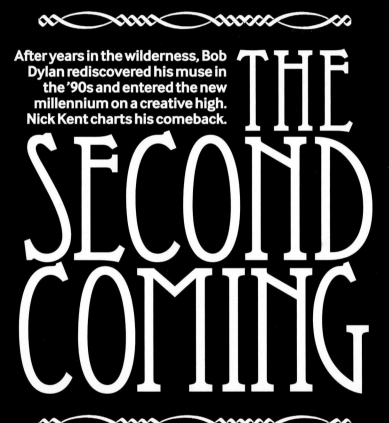

AS BOB DYLAN himself clearly indicates in Chronicles, he experienced several powerful epiphanies during 1987 that would ultimately change his artistic destiny and set him on the path to realising his second creative golden age – something that continues to this day. In a chilling passage recalling the year in question, Dylan writes unflinchingly about the condition of creative impotence that had engulfed his spirit throughout most of the decade: "Everything was smashed. My own songs had become strangers to me. I didn't have the skill to touch their raw nerves, couldn't penetrate the surfaces. It wasn't my moment of history anymore. There was a hollow singing in my heart and I couldn't wait to retire and fold the tent."

He was similarly bereft of inspiration for new songs even though he'd shackled himself to an ongoing deal with Columbia/Sony records to release a record a year. Two albums put out during this period – *Knocked Out Loaded* and *Down In The Groove* had found him struggling in vain to conjure up memorable new material with a mind-boggling array of co-helpers, ranging from Sex Pistol Steve Jones to playwright Sam Shepard and Grateful Dead lyricist Robert Hunter. In order to best exploit his current standing, Dylan's handlers had hit upon the idea that he would be best served working with others high-profile rock acts – if only to ensure his live shows would be well-attended.

IN 1987, DYLAN'S manager Elliot Roberts booked him to do a tour supported by Tom Petty & The Heartbreakers, then as now big stars in their own right. Dylan had performed at the first-ever Farm Aid with the Heartbreakers in 1985 and the group had quickly proven themselves adept at replicating the wild mercury sound of Dylan's own mid-'60s electric period during that performance, so it made sound commercial sense to continue the association.

Petty's hard-working players were certainly prepared for these shows – or at least as prepared as any musicians about to confront Dylan's often bewildering loose-canon agenda as a live performer – but Dylan himself was not. "Tom was at the top of his game and I was at the bottom of mine", he would later remark in his autobiography. "Benmont Tench [*the Heartbreakers' keyboard player*] would always be asking me, almost pleadingly, about including different numbers in the show… and I'd always be making some lame excuse… The problem was that after relying so long on instinct and intuition, both these ladies had turned into vultures and were sucking me dry."

Even so, the first part of the Dylan/Heartbreakers tour – which ended up lasting, on-and-off, for almost 18 months – was well attended and kindly received by most critics. Then, in June, Elliot Roberts got Dylan to link up with the Grateful Dead for a summer stadium tour. Dylan had first seen the Dead at the Fillmore East in New York during 1971 – promoter Bill Graham had even located a throne-like chair for Dylan to sit on during the show – and had performed with them on the same bill at a 1975 benefit concert that had been presented by none other than Marlon Brando.

More importantly, when Dylan was in San Francisco in 1979 performing his born-again Christian songs and facing both dwindling audiences and aggrieved critical responses, Jerry Garcia had made the effort to show some solidarity by bringing his guitar along to one show and performing with Dylan's gospel band. Throughout the early '80s Garcia had been struggling with deteriorating health issues brought on by a chronic addiction

to both heroin and cocaine but, after surviving a diabetic coma in 1986 that almost killed him, he'd briefly cleaned himself up so that both he and the rest of the Dead were fit and focused for these six special shows.

Dylan, meanwhile, was lost in a fog somewhere. Arriving at the band's rehearsal space in San Raphael, suddenly he "felt like a goon and didn't want to stick around" after various band members started suggesting he perform some of his lesser-known compositions during this short tour. Excusing himself from the session, Dylan ended up in a nearby bar nursing a gin and tonic and listening to a small jazz combo when he had his first spiritual wake-up call. "The singer reminded me of Billy Eckstine. He wasn't forceful but he didn't have to be; he was relaxed, but he sang with natural power. Suddenly and without warning, it was like the guy had an open window to my soul… I used to do this thing, I'm thinking. It was a long time ago and it had been automatic… This technique was so elemental, so simple and I'd forgotten. I wondered if I could still do it. I wanted at least a chance to try."

RETURNING TO THE Dead's company, Dylan felt suddenly ready to partake in some kind of creative challenge. "At first it was hard-going, like drilling through a brick wall. All I did was taste the dust. But then miraculously something internal came unhinged… I played these shows with the Dead and never had to think about it. Maybe they just dropped something in my drink, I can't say, but anything they wanted to do was fine with me. I had that old jazz singer to thank."

Of course, it should be added that the Grateful Dead and their organisation have markedly different memories of these 1987 shows. According to group biographer Dennis McNally, during the shows Dylan was so drunk and generally loaded that he often forgot his lyrics and sometimes performed songs in a different key to the rest of the group. Later on, he and Garcia almost came to blows while listening to rough mixes of a live album that had been put together from their shared concerts.

In Howard Sounes's Dylan biography, Down The Highway, Dead guitarist Bob Weir is quoted as claiming that Dylan himself petitioned the group to be taken on as a permanent member around this time but that bassist Phil Lesh voted against the idea. No matter: even though their concerts together had been mostly frustrating exercises for the Dead, Dylan himself had learned much from being in their company and witnessing first-hand the effortless way they could sow every disparate thread of classic American music – from Appalachian folk ballads to Bing Crosby songs to free-form jazz – into one singular sonic tapestry.

"[*With the Grateful Dead*] I really had some sort of epiphany on how to do those songs again, using certain techniques," Dylan told Rolling Stone's Mikal Gilmore. "When I went back and played with Petty again, I was using those same techniques and found I could play anything." A further enlightenment occurred in Locamo in Switzerland when

> ## "With the Dead I had some sort of ephiphany on how to do those song again."
> **BOB DYLAN**

Born again: Dylan with the Grateful Dead (Jerry Garcia, front left), 1987.

Dylan – backed by Petty and co – suddenly lost his voice in front of 30,000 people. While fixating on the phrase, "I'm determined to stand whether God will deliver me or not", Dylan had somehow willed himself into finding a new voice – or at least a new vocal technique – in order to carry on performing. The evening suddenly transformed itself into a sustained moment of revelation for him. "I found out I could do it effortlessly – that I could sing night after night after night and never get tired. I could p roject it out differently."

By the outset of 1988, Dylan had started making radical changes to the direction his career was heading in. He decided to stop working with other big-name groups like Petty and the Dead and form his own combo instead. He got rid of the four-piece gospel choir he'd been toting around for years also, even though it meant effectively sacking both his wife Carolyn Dennis and his mother-in-law. He also immersed himself in re-learning a guitar technique first taught to him by blues/jazz guitarist Lonnie Johnson back in 1964: "It had to do with the mathematical order of the scale on a guitar and how to make things happen, when it gets under somebody's skin and there's really nothing they can do about

it, because it's mathematical." This only came to halt when he hurt his arm in a domestic accident.

Still, he was back on stage in the spring of 1988 playing guitar for the first date of the aptly named Never Ending Tour. He had Saturday Night Live band leader GE Smith on guitar, Kenny Aaronson on bass and Christopher Parker on drums – a capable bunch of musicians who nonetheless sounded tentative and ill-at-ease at having to constantly second-guess their leader's every deeply eccentric gesture. Dylan threw a lot of old non-original songs (from Barbara Allen to Nadine) into the repertoire but these new techniques – both vocal and guitar-wise – had yet to fully impact on his still wayward singing capacities.

An even more grievous problem was his general inability to communicate with a band that struggled along manfully behind his clanging rhythm guitar like the high-priced garage band they effectively were.

It's telling that Dylan chose not to include Smith, Aaronson and Parker on the New Orleans-based sessions that gave birth to *Oh Mercy*, letting producer Daniel Lanois instead piece together various line-ups for him. It's even more telling that

One man and his dog: Dylan and friend, Telluride, Colorado, 2001.

Dylan should devote so many pages of his autobiography to painstakingly describing the genesis of the songs and the general ambience of the sessions themselves, because this is the first tentative step into the second golden age right here. "We live in a political world/Where everything can be bought", he crooned with a barely concealed disdain on the opening track, and everywhere else the singer was wearily confronting unfaithful lovers, fragmenting cultures, doubting believers and the numberless victims of the "disease of conceit".

There were three or four really first-rate songs – the authentically skin-crawling Man In A Long Black Coat, Everything Is Broken, Political World and What Is It You Wanted – and the rest were rescued by Lanois' smoky, slightly sinister production atmospherics. Not since the *Infidels* sessions had Dylan

come up with new songs of such potent substance. Now approaching 50, he was starting to find a new identity and purpose for himself for the first time since entering middle age. *Oh Mercy* sold well but not quite as well as either *The Traveling Wilburys Vol 1* or *Dylan And The Dead*, the appalling live album culled from the 1987 shows, which were both released not long before it.

THE WILBURYS HAD been a brainchild of George Harrison: while recording at Dylan's home studio at Point Dume, he'd invited Dylan, Tom Petty, Jeff Lynne and Roy Orbison – whom Lynne was then producing – to record a song, Handle With Care, and the project had swiftly grown into an album. Dylan had jovially partaken in the whole musi-

I didn't care to record anymore. Recording was too mental. I'd rather play on the road."

The *Red Sky* sessions in particular had been strange events, with Dylan forever hiding his face behind various hooded garments and rarely communicating directly with the many guest musicians who'd been invited by producers Don and David Was to contribute. "There were times when he looked absolutely beleaguered," David Was later recalled. "It occurred to me that it was a continuous burden having to be 'Bob Dylan' after all these years."

JUST HOW MUCH of a burden it was for Bob Dylan to support the onerous weight of his mystique after so many years became clear to anyone who happened to watch the Grammy Awards show televised live on February 20, 1991, right in the middle of the First Gulf War. Dylan – looking both battered and slightly bloated – was clearly not in good health as he struggled through a garbled version of Masters Of War before accepting a Lifetime Achievement award from Jack Nicholson. He then delivered an eerie speech referring to his deceased father, who had once informed him: "Son, it's possible to become so defiled in this world that your own mother and father will abandon you."

Many interpreted this as Dylan's admission that he had lost his way in the world spiritually, but 10 years later he explained to Mikal Gilmore what had really transpired that night. He'd been suffering from a fever that had pushed his temperature up to 104°, and had been further dismayed by the fact that four other leading singer/songwriters originally booked to sing Dylan songs in his honour had suddenly backed out at the last minute.

"I got disillusioned with all the characters at that time – all the ones that have the gall to thrust their tortured inner psyches on an outer world, but can't at least be true to their word.

> # "I'd had my fill. Recording was too mental."
> **BOB DYLAN**

From that point on, that's what the music business and all the people in it represented to me. I just lost all respect for them."

Still, Dylan managed to make an appearance the next year when Columbia hosted a special 30th anniversary concert in his honour at New York's Madison Square Garden that featured artists such as Neil Young, Lou Reed and George Harrison performing his songs. Unfortunately, the event was over-shadowed by fellow guest Sinead O'Connor's dramatic career meltdown: scheduled to sing Dylan's I Believe In You, she launched instead into Bob Marley's War in front of 20,000 jeering audience members.

Throughout the first half of the '90s, Dylan steered his own haphazard course through the music industry, neither as a blazing star of the new grunge dynasty (Neil Young had

cal charade – he was Lucky Wilbury – but recorded little worth storing in a time capsule. After that, though, he was still touring tirelessly, found himself on a musical treadmill once more, and ended up recording a deeply disappointing follow-up to *Oh Mercy* entitled *Under The Red Sky*, as well as an uninspired sequel to the Wilburys' platinum-shifting debut, the oddly named *Traveling Wilburys Vol 3*.

"Looking back on it now, it seems kind of unthinkable," Dylan later confessed to Mikal Gilmore. "I would leave the Wilburys and go down to Sunset Sound to record *Under A Red Sky* simultaneously, all within a set schedule, because I needed to be in Prague or someplace at a certain date. And both records – the Wilburys' and *Under The Red Sky* – I'd just left them hanging and see the finished product later… I'd really had my fill.

The 30th Anniversary Concert Celebration: which included Ronnie Wood, George Harrison, Johnny Cash, Roger McGuinn, Tom Petty, Neil Young and Chrissie Hynde, Madison Square Garden, New York, October 16, 1992.

grabbed that role) nor as a washed-up '60s has-been. He had a new manager – Jeff Kramer – and a new backing band that at one point boasted two drummers and a pedal steel guitarist (named Bucky Baxter) just like the Grateful Dead. He previewed no new compositions of his own but recorded two albums, 1992's *Good As I Been To You* and 1993's *World Gone Wrong*, that captured him alone in his Point Dume home studio lovingly reinterpreting old American traditional songs he'd first encountered in his excitable youth.

Neither disc was a classic Dylan record *per se*, but it was still refreshing to hear the grouchy-voiced maestro performing songs again in such a simple and natural way. His version of Elvis Presley's Tomorrow Night was delightfully melancholy, for example, while his excellent liner notes to *World Gone Wrong* were a first indication of the remarkable prose writer who would be fully unveiled with the publication of Chronicles 11 years later.

In 1993, Dylan performed at Bill Clinton's presidential inauguration at Washington's Lincoln Memorial and a year later, he was an unexpected success at Woodstock II. In 1995 he sang Restless Farewell to an 80-year-old Frank Sinatra at a special tribute concert and allowed The Times They Are A-Changin' to be used in ad campaigns for both the Bank of Montreal and accountancy giant Coopers & Lybrand. In other words, it was still business as usual, as anyone who witnessed the underwhelming live show he performed in 1996 in London's Hyde Park would have been acutely aware.

Yet little more than 12 months after that concert, Dylan's creative stock would suddenly skyrocket into the stratosphere

and he would be feted as the new comeback king of contemporary music. What prompted this startling change of perspective was the release of *Time Out Of Mind*, his first album of new songs in seven years.

RECORDED IN 11 days in Miami during January 1997, with Daniel Lanois back behind the controls, the songs of *Time Out Of Mind* had actually been started while Dylan had been snowed in at his Minnesota farm in the winter of 1995. During the summer of '96, he'd recorded demos of many of them while staying at Ronnie Wood's Dublin mansion. Reconnecting with Lanois that same year, he played the Canadian-born producer his old Slim Harpo and Otis Rush records and indicated that he wanted to capture the same raw bluesy sound on his own up-coming sessions.

Both Dylan and Lanois gathered a plethora of gifted back-up musicians – Memphian pianist Jim Dickinson, blues guitarist Duke Robillard, Asleep At The Wheel pedal steel player Cindy Cashdollar, famed session drummer Jim Keltner and – a personal favourite of Dylan's – Texan organist Augie Myers, formerly of the Sir Douglas Quintet, to participate in the recordings.

The sessions themselves were often intense, argumentative affairs with Dylan feeling throughout that his more up-tempo compositions hadn't been captured correctly on tape. Yet after listening to the songs sequenced together for the album, he must have at least sensed that the record he and Lanois had created was a work of rare substance.

Not every song of *Time Out Of Mind* is particularly brilliant but the performances always are. Dylan's brittle, aged voice had never sounded so vivid and penetrating, his phrasing equally astonishing as he lurked ominously amid the complicated shadows the music behind him was creating.

More crucially, however, *Time Out Of Mind* contained two of the most extraordinary songs Dylan has ever written. Not Dark Yet is nothing short of genius, the most remarkable meditation on approaching death that's yet been captured in song. But Highlands was even more fascinating, as Dylan seductively enticed his audience to step into his own psyche for 17 minutes and try to perceive the world through his eyes. The song – a floating country blues that sounds like it's being played by musicians in an hypnotic trance – found Dylan walking disconnectedly through his life, staring with envy at others who enjoyed the liberty of being anonymous, and suffering an intrusive, vaguely flirtatious conversation with a fame-smitten waitress. Yet somehow he could contain the feeling of gloomy isolation that had become second nature to him. "I've got new eyes – everything looks far away." Time creates new distances: thus the album title.

WHEN *TIME OUT* Of Mind was released on September 30, 1997, all hell broke loose. Just after the January sessions, Dylan had contracted pericarditis, an inflammation of the sac around the heart preventing the organ from functioning correctly, and had almost died. Leaving the hospital in June, he was back on the road in August, although still looking puffy and not fully recovered. In September, he serenaded Pope John Paul II at the World Eucharistic Congress in Bologna, Italy, and in December Clinton gave him the Kennedy Center medal in Washington alongside Charlton Helston and Lauren Bacall. By then, the album had garnered rave reviews and was well on its way to selling more than a million copies in the US alone. Its sounds of spooky, wistful dislocation were all over the airwaves anyway and Dylan suddenly really mattered again to many who'd virtually forgotten he ever existed.

Time Out Of Mind even won the Best Album award at the 1998 Grammys – Dylan's son Jakob's group, The Wallflowers, also picked up an award, as did Harry Smith's Anthology Of Music, a collection of old folk songs he'd extensively plundered from throughout his career. After that, he was on a roll.

He brought Larry Campbell and – slightly later – Texan Charlie Sexton into his line-up as guitarists, alongside drummer David Kemper and long-time bassist Tony Garnier. Suddenly he had his all-time dream-come-true support unit.

Here was a band that could effortlessly re-ignite all the old

"It was a burden having to be 'Bob Dylan' after all these years."

DAVID WAS

The President's man: Dylan playing at Bill Clinton's Inauguration, January 16, 1993.

R&B, folk and roots rock refrains that Dylan had grown up adoring, while at the same time forging solid arrangements to all the disparate material that Dylan suddenly had no problem adhering to. His live concerts with this band rank with the best of his entire career: finally, those new techniques first glimpsed in 1987 were making a meaningful impact on his music. As a consequence, he looked re-energised, younger and thinner, and sounded genuinely delighted to be in their company.

It was obviously a good time to be Bob Dylan again, although sad tidings inevitably still loomed from time to time (his beloved mother Beattie passed away in January 2000). And he was still chillingly clued into the contemporary zeitgeist, as his song Things Have Changed mordantly demonstrated: "I used to care/But things have changed". It didn't get any colder or more real than that. It ended up winning an Oscar for him – he wrote Things Have Changed for the soundtrack to a film about mid-life crisis called Wonder Boys – and for a while he proudly placed it on his amplifier during live shows.

A YEAR LATER, HE wisely gathered his magic band in the studio and recorded a set of feisty new songs that ended up becoming the album entitled *Love And Theft*. Here was another masterpiece, more playful and joyous in spirit than *Time Out Of Mind*, and with more potent songs too: Dylan at his most sardonic and wickedly witty. There are several extraordinary numbers here, not least Po' Boy, which captures Dylan spinning wonderful poetic lines off a jaunty Django Reinhardt-inspired melody with effortless grace.

But *Love And Theft* works best when listened to in its entirety as the defiant, exuberant statement of a 60-year-old man who intends to stick around creating and generally having a good time for many, many years to come. If anything, it stands in stark contrast to the sentiments expressed on *Time Out Of Mind*'s foreboding Not Dark Yet. Death may be out there lurking but it's clearly going to have to wait a while longer before Bob Dylan gives up the ghost.

And he still has the capacity to astonish us in all the right ways. Look no further than his 2004 Chronicles, which exposed us finally to his mighty gift for writing vividly about his own singular life. In a Newsweek interview to promote the book, Dylan made a remarkable confession: he felt that the years between 1967 and 1997 had been spent in a personal creative wilderness, and that he'd only relatively recently become re-connected to the essence of his calling. He also spoke of six new songs he'd laid aside for a forthcoming album.

Most recently, Dylan has lost both Campbell and Sexton but located adequate replacements. He has even begun performing his songs while playing an electric piano – a guitar laying on the stage for him to use is seldom picked up. In short, the man is simply unstoppable and, most remarkable of all, still at the top of his creative game. Bob Dylan's future promises to be as eventful and challenging as it was at any other stage of his long and illustriously winding career.

The Hard Way

The soundtrack to Martin Scorsese's Dylan documentary, *No Direction Home*, offers a wealth of brilliant, unreleased music.

L ET'S START AT the end. "It was wet and cold and very isolated," said the photographer Barry Feinstein. Though he could have been referring to Bob Dylan's mindset in mid-1966, but was actually describing the location for the shot that adorns the cover of *No Direction Home*, the latest instalment in Dylan's official Bootleg Series of CDs and the two-disc soundtrack to Martin Scorsese's documentary of the same name. It was taken at the Aust Ferry, Gloucestershire, the means of transport from England to Wales rendered redundant by the opening of the Severn Bridge (which stands, mistily, in the background behind cameraman Howard Alk). Dylan made the crossing on May 11, just prior to his second electric show on British soil. The first, at Bristol Colston Hall, found the molten racket he made with The Hawks greeted by very English shouts of "Turn it down!"; by the time he arrived in Manchester, the jeers would be combined into that famous, hateful noise.

The photograph perfectly represents the conclusion of this story: Dylan both stoic and frazzled, only one hardy associate minding the car, the suggestion that – as one of his more recent songs puts it – the emptiness is endless. Stare at it while playing the second CD's closing track, the Live 1966 version of Like A Rolling Stone, and everything coheres. The song, seemingly by its very nature, stands as the summation of the story: "Once upon a time," Dylan begins, having jumped into the music after an intro that sounds positively valedictory. Once you've put something so unstoppable on a record, where else is there to go?

So, that's the final chapter: the point at which Dylan is as adrift from the world as any musician probably ever has been, and on the verge of an exhausted retreat. Compare it to the pictures evoked by the first few tracks – the traditional Rambler Gambler, put to tape on a Radio Shack tape recorder in 1960; a reverent version of Woody Guthrie's This Land Is Your Land, recorded a year later at Carnegie Hall – and the mesmerising nature of the tale becomes clear. How on earth, in only

half a dozen years, did he get from there to here? We know the answer, of course – it takes in the civil rights movement, and electric guitars, and the performance at Newport on which much of the story turns, and countless elements besides. The wonder of this record, however, is that it maps out the saga using music that hasn't been dulled by familiarity. Like A Rolling Stone and the Bob Dylan album's Song To Woody aside, the 26 unreleased tracks build a whole new vantage point from which to view Dylan's whirlwind years.

Dylan's catalogue handlers have worked similar tricks in the past. Volumes 1-3 of *The Bootleg Series* appeared in 1991, beating a path from 1961's Hard Times In New York ("live in a Minnesota Hotel Room", said the credits, announcing just how close to the source we were), to Series Of Dreams, the sublime 1989 outtake from *Oh Mercy*. It was, needless to say, a collection of jaw-dropping richness; all that seemed untoward was how little space was given to that crucial phase of Dylan's progress from *Bringing It All Back Home* to *Blonde On Blonde*. A mere nine songs were taken from that period (the same number as from the slightly less eventful 12 months of 1962), only four of which featured a full band. In subsequent years, *Live 1966* plugged part of that gap, and the instalments of the series devoted to the Rolling Thunder tour and his 1964 concert at New York's Philharmonic Hall were hardly disappointing, but still – wasn't something missing?

T HE 10 UNRELEASED tracks on *No Direction Home*'s CD2 answer that question at a stroke. There will be Dylan aficionados who cast their eyes over the running order and announce that they have owned the lot for centuries. They may even be right, but none of the studio offcut collections available under the counter approach the clarity and quality of what's here. On *Highway 61 Revisited Again*, for example, there's the same first take of Desolation Row, on which the delicate acoustic riff is replaced by a doleful blues figure and Al Kooper plays an electric guitar like the young Lou Reed – but relative to the full-blooded treatment here, it's a trebly makeweight. Similarly, *Acetates On The Tracks Vol 2 (1965-1974)* contains two rickety, tentative versions of Visions Of Johanna – but neither is a patch on the barnstorming *No Direction Home* take, recorded with The Band and built on a martial backbeat that sounds like the very essence of the opening line ("Ain't it just like the night/To play

> ## How on earth, in only half a dozen years, did he get here?

BOB DYLAN

NO DIRECTION HOME : THE SOUNDTRACK

A MARTIN SCORSESE PICTURE

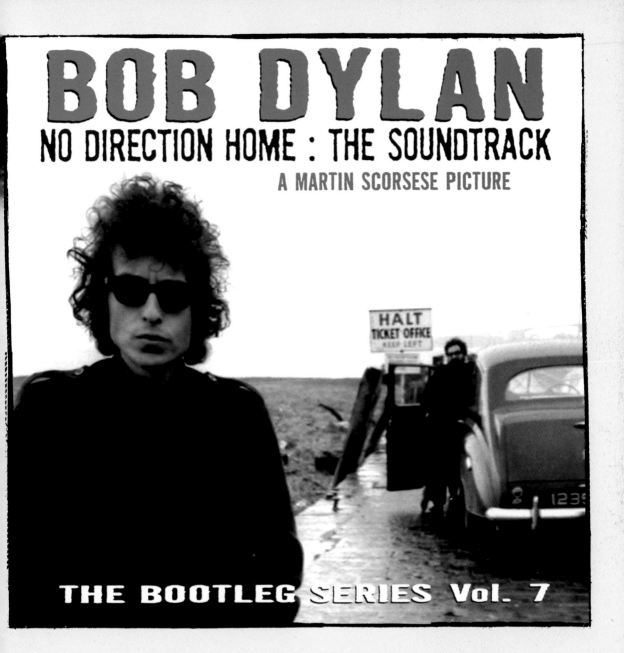

HALT
TICKET OFFICE
KEEP LEFT

THE BOOTLEG SERIES Vol. 7

tricks when you're trying to be so quiet"). Besides, neither bootleg contains the more pointed, punchier – perhaps plain better – reading of Just Like Tom Thumb's Blues here (take 8, for those wondering).

If you only know Dylan's watershed performance at the 1965 Newport Folk Festival from black and white news footage suggesting Dylan simply yelped along with a stinging Mike Bloomfield guitar part, go straight to Maggie's Farm: half-rehearsed, but so tight, fast and fleshed-out. To have an instant understanding of exactly why slipping out of his work shirt and into a leather jacket created such brouhaha, refer to the first, all-acoustic CD. "I don't mind the 10 command-ments," he tells the audience at New York's Town Hall. "I believe in the 10 commandments. The first one, I am the Lord thy God, is a great commandment, if it's not said by the wrong people." The thought is

less remarkable than the flood of applause that greets both the oration and the Masters Of War that follows. It's the sound of frenzied adulation that would soon send Dylan elsewhere.

Let's finish at the start. No Direction Home begins with a 90-second extract of a self-penned blues entitled When I Got Troubles, recorded in 1959 by a high school friend called Rick Kangas, played with a guitar technique best described as rudimentary and sung in a mannered half-whisper. It might pass for a pre-war field recording, or a hilariously lo-fi off-cut from Harry Smith's Anthology Of American Folk Music. You certainly wouldn't identify it as the work of the same mind that created the musical cyclone that brings this record to its glorious close. Seven years later, then, Bob Dylan could be forgiven for standing precariously on that jetty and looking kind of tired. Wouldn't anyone? John Harris

Chapter Four

LONG TIME GONE

All the Dylan
albums, songs and
further reading
you'll ever need…

100 BEST DYLAN SONGS

He has one of the most awe-inspiring back catalogues in contemporary popular music, but what are the best Dylan songs of all time? MOJO writers and a host of musicians list the Top 100 tunes of Bob Dylan's superlative career.

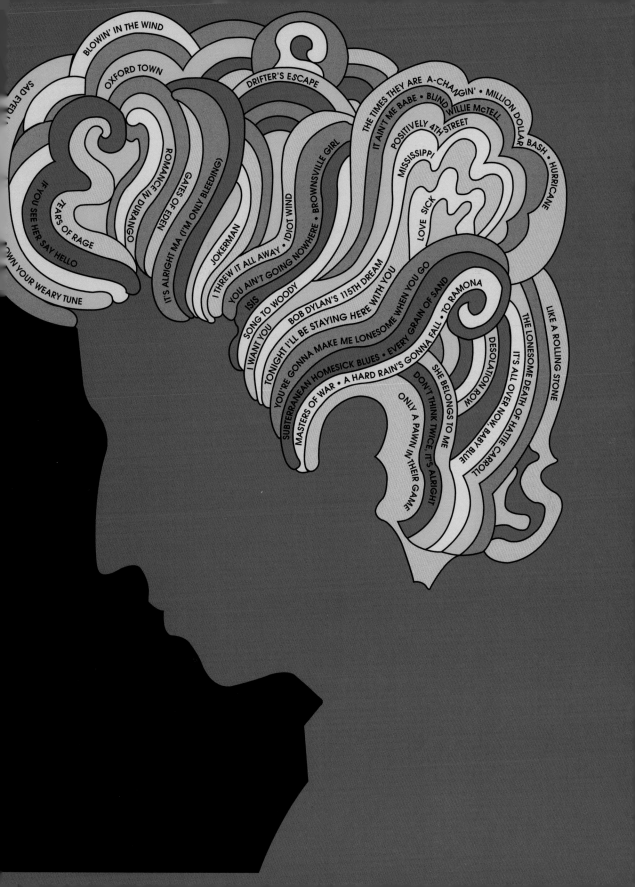

© Jim Marshall

100 Oh, Sister
DESIRE, 1976

Girl From The North Country redux.

Andrew Bird (songwriter and multi-instrumentalist): "I like this because it stands out from Dylan's more typical torrent-of-words type of song. It's only the surface of the story, and you're left wondering what the nature of this relationship is. What has this guy done to lose his sister's affection and why is he giving her this moral-religious guilt trip? It's mysterious and kind of creepy and also quite simple. It's the same thing that draws me to Charlie Patton or an old Childs ballad.

"One thing that Dylan managed to pull off which I admire a lot is that he is able to tell a story and send a message without sacrificing the beauty of language. Can you imagine a rousing, populist protest song today that wouldn't just sound ludicrous? Sure there've been some noble, artful attempts, but nothing like Maggie's Farm. I was also drawn to this tune because of Emmylou's gorgeous vocal harmonies of the original, and I really wanted to hear my friend Nora O'Connor's singing on that song, which she did, just right, as always."

99 This Wheel's On Fire
THE BASEMENT TAPES, 1975

Watch out! Mean ol' Dylan's goin' to confiscate your lace!

Siouxsie Sioux: "I chose this for our covers album because I thought Julie Driscoll had written it. I'd seen her perform it on Top Of The Pops as a kid and I loved her Joan Of Arc look. Then I found out it was by fucking Bob Dylan! I liked the song so it stayed on anyway. Have I heard his version? No, never! He wasn't someone who captured my imagination back in the mid-'70s."

98 My Back Pages
ANOTHER SIDE OF..., 1964

Year Zero for post-protest Dylan.

Accepting, if that's quite the word, an award presented by a New York liberal institution called the Emergency Civil Rights Committee on the evening of December 13, 1963, Dylan made a febrile speech that, among other things, appeared to express empathy with Lee Harvey Oswald. "It's took me a long time to get young," he said, amid the boos, "and now I consider myself young." Out of that evening came My Back Pages's "I was so much older then" refrain, and its rejection of well-meaning lefty rhetoric, killing off the old Dylan who'd feared "not that I'd become my enemy / In the instant that I preach". Judas's rapid journey

97 Sign On The Window
NEW MORNING, 1970

Street-wise raconteur wrestles with his Family Man alter ego.

Rich Robinson (The Black Crowes): "It's just Bob on piano at first, then his band are trying to catch up. It comes off in such a great way. Lyrically there's a lot of reflection on city life. He's trying to figure out the world and ends up looking for the simple things. "Build me a cabin in Utah/Marry me a wife, catch a rainbow trout." That's beautiful and concise but it has meaning on a greater level. Musically, it's textured to the point where it sounds like it has earth in it. I covered this song live when I did some solo touring and it made me think that whatever artists you're talking about it's all about the

96 Goin' To Acapulco
THE BASEMENT TAPES, 1975

Dionysus clinks mugs with Our Lady Of Guadalupe.

Bob Dylan's most straightforwardly beautiful voice was the one he shared with The Band's Rick Danko and Richard Manuel – a soaring banshee wail embracing fear and joy and heartbreaking sadness.

Goin' To Acapulco, meanwhile, is its apotheosis, gilding the song's outlaw ribaldry with a patina of the divine. "It's a wicked life," shrugs Bob, "but what the hell/Everybody's got to eat," while the turnarounds of Robbie Robertson simply tumble down and Garth Hudson's organ takes it to church. Surely the

The tyres they are a-changin': Dylan New York, 1963.

93 Chimes Of Freedom

ANOTHER SIDE OF..., 1964

Spokesman For A Generation disappears.

If Dylan was caught at divergent roads in '64 – the narrow path of the protest singer or an ascent to skies of super-real impressionism – then this is his moment of epiphany. In a city doorway, waiting out an electrical storm, Dylan and companion marvel as thunder and lightning "*[seem]* to be the chimes of freedom flashing". Musically spare, sung as if trying to remember a dream, it's the sound of protest song and songwriter fragmenting in awesome nature. And what of those bells of lightning tolling for the luckless? Nature's just rage or clangorous futility? Maybe the freedom is in the not knowing. (AM)

92 The Ballad Of Hollis Brown

THE TIMES THEY ARE A-CHANGIN', 1964

As bleak and powerful as the troubadour gets.

The song began life as a newspaper item – in common with other contemporary pieces such as Only A Pawn In Their Game. Unlike some of these social comment songs, however, Hollis Brown does not point the finger but rather, from the very first line, plunges you into the cumulative desperation of the starving poor. This accords with the fatalism that comes from the song's melodic source: the murder ballad Pretty Polly, recorded in 1927 by Dock Boggs and tackled by Dylan himself in Minneapolis during May 1961.

This relentless modal drone is the engine that powers you through the song: it begins tough, and doesn't stop. Over 11 stanzas, Dylan uses two modes of address – the third party descriptive and the more direct "you" – to ram home the fact that, for Hollis Brown and his family, there is no money, no friend, no escape, no future. Each detail piles up and up until there is no way out except seven deaths. This fated, fatal mood of pre-determination is highlighted by the ambiguous promise of reincarnation in the song's cosmic ending: "Somewhere in the distance/There's seven new people born".

The Ballad Of Hollis Brown was a highlight of Dylan's first major TV appearance, on Folk Songs And More Folk Songs, in May 1963. Its compulsive dread is best heard on an extraordinary live version from Philadelphia in November '64, where Dylan spits out the stanzas like machine gun bullets and his guitar makes the noise of a full rock'n'roll band. In its length – over six minutes – and intensity, The Ballad Of Hollis Brown now sounds like a precursor to the great psychological/perceptual epics – It's Alright Ma (I'm Only Bleeding), Desolation Row – that would

95 Lily, Rosemary And The Jack Of Hearts

BLOOD ON THE TRACKS, 1975

"There's something funny going on," says the backstage manager. He's right.

Ron Wood: "I first heard this when I was making my first solo album and it strikes me now as it did then – a mini-novel with twists and dark turns like something Ray Bradbury would have written, like Something Wicked This Way Comes. I love that it gathers momentum and the lyric makes you picture mysterious mining town incidents, bank robbers and hookers. Dylan's very impressionistic as a painter as well as a songwriter, and fun to play live with. You never quite know where you are – which suits me fine! Before going on stage, he always says to the MD, 'Just give Woody the keys to the songs and once

94 Tombstone Blues

HIGHWAY 61 REVISITED, 1965

Fast-cut symbolist fun in the bleaching sun.

Norman Blake (Teenage Fanclub): "It's just relentless; a six-minute torrent of surrealistic images. You can tell it was written at the height of Pop Art, with these incredible iconic characters: Galileo, Cecil B DeMille and Beethoven all thrown together. And there's a lot of humour in it – all that stuff about knitting a bald wig for Jack The Ripper. There's a real punk quality to it, too – Dylan has youthful energy pouring out of him and the band are missing cues. I was listening to it this morning and it struck me, for the first time, how much Dylan had influenced the early Velvet Underground – especially a song like Hey, Mr Rain. There's a really

91 Spanish Harlem Incident

ANOTHER SIDE OF..., 1964

Bob's in thrall to a gypsy gal "too hot for taming".
Howie Payne (Liverpudlian folk rockers The Stands):
"I heard that it was recorded in one night with a
couple of bottles of wine and you do get the feeling
of being there with him. He bursts out laughing
or forgets his words, or knocks the mic stand
or rambles some nonsense; but it's the human
element that Dylan gets through whatever persona
he's donning. This has that semi-drunken, 4am feel
of a sailor in New York, staggering up First Avenue
while the dawn's rising over the East River, following
a girl who's leading him into dangerous territory.
It's so perfectly delivered, and almost feels like it's
falling to pieces at times. The riff, too, is striking '
cos it doesn't quite fit and is attacked really harshly,
which makes it seem rockier. It's got a lot of Irish
in it, even though it's about a girl from Harlem, it
has a raucous Clancy Brothers feel."

90 Señor (Tales Of Yankee Power)

STREET LEGAL, 1978

**Dismissed by Greil Marcus as "a pastiche of the
best moments of the Eagles' Hotel California".**
A grim, era-shifting adventure that seems to
bounce between frontier America, first century
Jerusalem, and a futuristic netherworld, the song is
Dylan's attempt to convey the widescreen majesty
and redemptive themes of the films of Peckinpah
and Ford. Metaphorically rich lyrics foreshadow his
looming Christian phase; the song is rife with
apocalyptic imagery. Guided by a mournful Latin-
flecked groove, expansive sax, soul choir and a
creaking lead vocal to capture the drama of the
narrative ("Let's overturn these tables/Disconnect
these cables"), It's both epic and inscrutable. (BM)

89 Talkin' Bear Mountain Picnic Massacre Blues

TIME OUT OF MIND, 1997

Woody Guthrie-indebted disaster movie rap.
Badly Drawn Boy: "It's Bob Dylan's funniest song, all
about how he buys tickets to a picnic but ends up
corralled onto this ship, which sinks. He wakes up
on the shore: 'My arms and legs were broken/
My feet were splintered/My head was cracked/
I couldn't walk, I couldn't talk, smell, feel/Couldn't
see, didn't know where I was. I was bald.' He was
bald! Dylan's great at going that one step further
than anyone else. When it was his 60th, I was doing
David Letterman, and they time everything
perfectly in rehearsal. But I did a little intro: 'I'd like
to wish Bob Dylan a happy 60th birthday.' The
floor manager went barmy but it was worth it."

88 Lonesome Day Blues

LOVE AND THEFT, 2001

Wry, rolling blues that laughs in the face of death.
Ian McNabb (former Icicle Works): "I think Dylan is
better now than he's ever been. I wasn't into all that
'The sun ain't yellow/It's chicken... Napoleon in
rags' period. It sounds cool and witty, but the last
two albums are some of the best he's written. He
sounds like he's been through everything and is
resigned to his fate. Somebody of that age with that
wisdom, it's inspirational because it just says you
get to the end of the game and you still don't have
the answers. On Lonesome Day Blues he's resigned
to everything, prepared to admit his failures... but,
you know what? 'They're doing the double shuffle/
Throwin' sand on the floor...' And at the end of the
day, it's all about doing the double shuffle. Life
sucks, but it's better that we're here and it sucks
and we can do the double shuffle than we never got
a chance. And some of it's so funny. *(Sings)* 'Well, my
pa he died and left me/My brother got killed in the
war/My sister she ran off and got married/Never
was heard of anymore.' You can tell now he's just
having fun with these tales of mortality. He's
getting smaller and smaller, and dealing with failure,
age and ill-health and writing about them in a
humorous and entertaining way. Who else is doing
that? Neil Young? No! All we have left is Dylan."

"Dylan's great at going that step further."

BADLY DRAWN BOY

© David Gahr

87 It Takes A Lot To Laugh, It Takes A Train To Cry

HIGHWAY 61 REVISITED, 1965

**Dylan rides a coal-blazin', whistle-wailin',
yakety-track loco all the way to gloryland.**
It's Dylan showing off. Proving that he knows the
blues, knows that roots equate with routes that
find their way via rails just four-foot eight-and-a-
half-inches apart. And it's a great ride as he recalls
stanzas from old 12-bars — "Don't the moon look
good, mama, shining through the trees", lines that
blues-kids were fed at birth. He's having fun even
though it's a mail train, a slow train that's forever
getting flagged down by brakemen. Woody rode
the trains, Jimmie Rodgers rode the trains... and
here's Bob doing it musically, and doing it with
such panache that you pray the terminus will
never loom into view. (FD)

86 Fourth Time Around

BLONDE ON BLONDE, 1966

**"Everybody must give something back/For
something they get." Is Dylan responding to
Lennon's borrowings?**
Win Butler (Canadian avant gardists The Arcade
Fire): "I've probably listened to it 50, 60 times trying
to figure out exactly what's going on. The melody is
really similar to Norwegian Wood and I love the
repetitive classical guitar lick, the machine-gun
drum beat, and the bass line that just keeps driving.
Dylan can talk about real emotions, and then go
way off and say something completely aesthetic.
The end result is this rich, interesting piece that you
can dig into forever. This one's kind of a warning.
The new girlfriend is being told how it ended with
the last one. That line is really hard: 'I never asked for
your crutch/Now don't ask for mine.' Or maybe it
really is about The Beatles after all."

85 Corrina, Corrina

THE FREEWHEELIN' BOB DYLAN, 1963

Gently swinging billet-doux discreetly unveils Dylan in combo mode.

Corrina, Corrina's almost throwaway insouciance might have stood out amid the protest polemics and mordant anti-love songs of Freewheelin', but Dylan's wholesale refurbishment of a traditional British folk ballad (previously looted by everyone from Red Nichols to Big Joe Turner) bears distinctive hallmarks. The loose-limbed backing of bass, drums and the tumbling guitar lines of future collaborator (and Mr Tambourine Man inspiration) Bruce Langhorne anticipates the sound of Dylan's still two-year off folk rock pomp, though his vocals would rarely, if ever, match the relaxed ingenuousness of his delivery here. And still arguably the prettiest song in Dylan's canon. (DS)

84 Tomorrow Is A Long Time

GREATEST HITS VOL 2, 1971

Premiered by Odetta in '65, later essayed by Rod Stewart—Bob at his most crushingly forsaken.

Samantha Parton (Be Good Tanyas): "I was 19 when I first heard it. This guy I had a big crush on played it on guitar for me. It's such a love song, but it's also a strange, philosophical song, talking about the great mystery of life: 'I can't see my reflection in the waters/I can't speak the sounds that show no pain.' Then, I took it to be an existentialist song but now I just see him tortured by an unrequited love. I've always been inspired by what Dylan draws from traditional song, which itself draws from old English poetry. His songs have a sense of story, with a beginning, middle and end, and all the disturbing, mysterious qualities, the sickness and danger. He's like a shaman, reaching outside this world into the next, and bringing things back for us to wonder at."

83 The Man In Me

NEW MORNING, 1970

Tipsy bucolic finds normally cagey guy caught off-guard.

"La la la la lalala la la!" Singing like he's adrift in some joyous, three-beers, summer-evening, fire up the barbeque euphoria, a knocking-on-30 songwriter finally 'fesses up: he can't go it alone: 'Take a woman like you/To get through to the man in me.' If New Morning found Dylan ditching obfuscation and polemic for a shimmering everyday world (eavesdroppings, birdsong, bakery trucks) here's why: he's found himself, because someone found him. And oh, what a wonderful feeling. All woozy organ and jake-leg drums, it's a stoned surrender to companionship; but still cautious, like a junkyard dog offering a nervy paw. "The man in me will hide sometimes to keep from bein' seen." Quite. (AM)

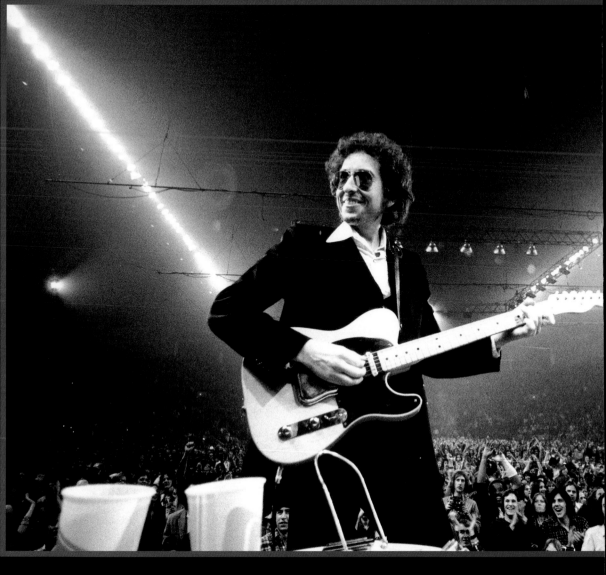

82 I Believe In You
SLOW TRAIN COMING, 1979

The perpetual trial of religious faith... or the labour of love?

Many Dylanites' problem with his Christian period is a trading of lyrical subtlety/ ambivalence for 2000-year-old biblical dogma. This song, written with the convert's fervour still freshly blazing in his heart (note the passionate vocal delivery), is a worthy exception. Here, a believer affirms their faith in the face of doubting jibes and ostracisation. However, the faith's exact nature is never explicitly stated – this could easily be a Dark End Of The Street-type lover, especially given the line "I believe in you, even on the morning after". Jack White's a fan – check the melodic "referencing" on 2005's As Ugly As I Seem. (AP)

81 Standing In The Doorway
TIME OUT OF MIND, 1997

All Bob needs is love.

Jonathan Rice (Virginian singer-songwriter): "My favourite line is: 'Last night I danced with a stranger/But she just reminded me you were the one'. He's in the twilight of his life and it's like love is still a total mystery to him. In a previous verse he says: 'I would be crazy if I took you back/It would go up against every rule,' but he's not saying that he wouldn't... That's part of being a romantic, isn't it – setting yourself up for a kicking? Dylan's connected with his muse in such a permanent way that it must prevent people getting close. It's like he holds the music and the message in such high regard that he would sacrifice his health and happiness for it. In his writing there's just this constant loneliness."

80 Changing Of The Guards
STREET LEGAL, 1978

Angels, witches and dog soldiers move through the scene as Dylan tells us "Eden is burning".

Patti Smith: "I've always cherished this song. The first time I heard it was when I'd just moved to Detroit. I put on Bob's new record, and Changing Of The Guards was the first song... it just moved me to tears. I would never presume to know what his songs are about, but it has such a mix of tarot card and Joan of Arc imagery. The song starts, 'Sixteen years...', and Joan of Arc was 16 when they shaved her head and burned her at the stake. I'm actually hoping to record this song, so perhaps I'll have the chance to speak to him about it. No matter how bitter or melancholy his songs are, there's always so much resilience, a sense of him striking back."

"They're behind you!": Dylan, LA Forum, 1974.

© Barry Feinstein

78 With God On Our Side
THE TIMES THEY ARE A-CHANGIN', 1964

Masterful protest – written at only 21 – that echoes down the decades.

Linton Kwesi Johnson: "It speaks of the wickedness of the strong against the weak, of powerful nations and what they do – what the American settlers did to the Indians... the First World War. It goes to the heart of how little we value human life, how we kill for power, for greed, and invoke the name of God while doing so. In a way the song explores a kind of helplessness in the face of evil. It's the voice of the weak. He's obviously faced with a conundrum at the end and that's part of the song's power, that paradox – 'If God's on our side / He'll stop the next war'. You have to see it against the background of a world in turmoil – the proliferation of nuclear weapons, the Cold War at its height... – but the strength of the song is that it's relevant and still speaks to the conflicts of our time. That's why Dylan is the greatest protest lyricist ever."

77 You're A Big Girl Now
BLOOD ON THE TRACKS, 1975

Gut-wrenching honesty as Dylan accepts blame for the break up.

Richard Hell (ex-Television guitarist): "Talking about Dylan is too complicated for just a few words. You can see why everybody writes books about him. It seems that anyone who likes him at all has a relationship with him, whether they admit it or not. He's been that useful, meaningful and exasperating all your life long. No wonder he resents his fans. And this song is the one for me that's the most revealing of his bewildering powers because it's the one that has the greatest distance between its emotional impact and its actual words. How does he make those silly words so affecting? 'Time is a jet plane, it moves too fast.' Where is the poetry in that? The metaphor is obvious and the observation commonplace. But in the song it breaks your heart.

I think maybe it's something about both his openness and the way his mind skips around in his condition, somehow indicating the shape of everything, and I mean everything. It's how the lines turn into each other. For instance, the whole beginning of that stanza goes, 'Time is a jet plane, it moves too fast/Oh, but what a shame if all we've shared can't last/I can change, I swear.' No one line is much more than banal, but it's how they follow from each other that makes that 'I can change, I swear' choke me up every time. Or is it his delivery? Or the melody? Or the weird way saying 'You're a big girl now' is inherently sarcastic, when obviously what's going on is he wants her more than anything? It's all the currents, in something apparently so simple and ordinary. There's no explaining it."

79 Po' Boy
LOVE AND THEFT, 2001

Farce, tragedy, Shakespeare and old glorious love garnish the only Dylan song named after a sandwich.

The voice creaks like an unoiled hinge, but Po' Boy sashays dapper and so warm of heart, you know something's happened... kicking open the door to his years of age maybe (after all, his Chronicles autobiography followed). Dylan's quietly rioting imagination leaps from Othello to a beloved uncle, a call to room service to send up a room – and this: "Time and love has branded me with its claws", and "All I know is that I'm thrilled by your kiss". So life – even the "Washin' them dishes, feedin' them swine" part – is OK. Like the man said, thing of beauty equals joy forever. (PS)

76 I Dreamed I Saw St Augustine
JOHN WESLEY HARDING, 1968

Muted hallucinatory tale in which Dylan's visions of the saint lead to feelings of guilt.

Joseph Arthur: "When I heard this it blew my mind. First it was the production, so stripped down. Then there was the lyric which revealed him to be so vulnerable. I took St Augustine to be a metaphor for Dylan himself, him feeling this immense guilt and this was killing him somehow. The song is so short yet contains so much lyrical complexity, but then in contrast and out of necessity to house such a lyric, the melody is so sweet and simple. And the lyrics, they read like a psalm. 'I put my fingers against the glass/And bowed my head and cried' – like he's trapped behind a window, maybe a comment on the trappings of fame, how he can't escape it."

75 Talkin' World War III Blues
THE FREEWHEELIN' BOB DYLAN, 1963

Post-Cuban missile crisis political point-making masked by a daydream ramble.

Robert Plant: "(Sings) 'Some time ago a crazy dream came to me/I dreamt I was walkin' into World War Three.' I love where he goes: 'And I drove 42nd Street in my Cadillac/Good car to drive after a war'. For a guy who wanted to be in The Teddy Bears with Phil Spector, he's certainly moved some minds and mountains, hasn't he?

I've got his autobiography, but I don't want to read it. I read something about him being a piece of work who lied and danced with Mimi Fariña a bit too often. I thought, I don't need to know this; I just need to know A Hard Rain's A-Gonna Fall."

74 Things Have Changed
THE ESSENTIAL BOB DYLAN, 2000

Missing link between *Time Out Of Mind* and *Love And Theft*.

Tacked onto the latest hits-and-more compilation by way of the soundtrack to Michael Douglas-as-stoner-author vehicle Wonder Boys, this is a perky, mid-paced and decidedly wry shrug of ambivalence from the edge of old age, as informed by Dylan's brutally dry humour and a fleeting mood of teenage abandon. Our "worried" protagonist "used to care but things have changed", so he considers taking dancing lessons, dressing in drag and steering a female stranger around in a wheelbarrow. Also contains, in the confessional spirit of his recent songs, the telling line: "I've been trying to get as far away from myself as I can." (TD)

73 Simple Twist Of Fate
BLOOD ON THE TRACKS, 1975

The bard stripped emotionally bare.

Neko Case (alt-country siren): "There are some moments here that you can feel as he's having them. The way he sings the lines – 'She looked at him and he felt a spark tingle to his bones / 'Twas then he felt alone and wished that he'd gone straight' – is just devastating. There's so many moments like that which are so painful, but they're really honest and they're said in a way that I don't think anyone had said before... or since. I don't think Dylan even knows where songs like that come from. A lot of his songs seem born of that spirit."

71 Tonight I'll Be Staying Here With You
NASHVILLE SKYLINE, 1969

Superior country soul with a lascivious edge proving that Dylan had the hips.

Beck: "I didn't get too deep into his music until I got into the Nashville records. Those are the ones that really got to me, because I was so into country music when I was younger and hearing those records for the first time... I always liked his kind of throwaway love songs. For somebody who's a giant like him, who writes those great cinematic songs like Visions Of Johanna that draw you into a strange world, to just toss out a good little tune... that's an aspect of Dylan I always really appreciated."

never spelt out the identity of his target, typically claiming Jane was a man. But well-known pacifist Joan Baez seems a likely candidate, given the similarity of her first name and the line about the bandits Queen Jane turns the other cheek to. (RU)

"The Nashville records are the ones that got to me." BECK

72 Oxford Town
THE FREEWHEELIN' BOB DYLAN, 1963

Dylan disses racism at the University of Mississippi University, aka Ole Miss.

When Dylan sprang onto the folk scene, he was a commentator on our social ills. James Meredith's 1962 attempt to integrate a public university was an injustice like Hattie Carroll's murder and Emmett Till's lynching. Dylan's adaptation of this tale is less fact-based; offering up two dead bodies basking in the moonlight, it's a glib yet mournful portrayal of the civil rights era on acoustic guitar (AL)

70 Queen Jane Approximately
HIGHWAY 61 REVISITED, 1965

One of his pithiest put-downs. Joan Baez believed to be the target. Again!

Unlike some of Dylan's more vicious odes to stuck-up princesses, Queen Jane Approximately shoots its poison arrows with grace and an insistently singable chorus. The out-of-tune guitar somehow lends a nice touch of garage rock rawness to an arrangement otherwise dominated by the piano-organ blend he did so much to innovate. Dylan

69 Gates Of Eden
BRINGING IT ALL BACK HOME, 1965

Eden: Good. 1960s America: Bad.

Marc Carroll (Dylan-endorsed UK troubadour): "I was initially struck by the sheer weightiness of the song, the Biblical imagery and incessant rhythm. The whole song is so powerful it's unsettling. Bob often refers to the imperfect human state, the fall from grace and exile from Eden. The 'motorcycle black Madonna, two-wheeled gypsy queen', is such a powerful image. Dylan is a very sexy writer who empowers the listener, so women love him."

68 Bob Dylan's 115th Dream

BRINGING IT ALL BACK HOME, 1965

Bob gets comical on yo' ass.

This "dream" might be very hard to interpret for those who didn't go to school in America, saturated as it is in historical and mythological references. If you want to understand how Dylan integrated the disparate cultural influences he cites in Chronicles, this lyric would be a hell of a place to start.

115th Dream also refutes the myth that Dylan abandoned politics when he began playing with rock'n'roll bands. The music here rocks wilder than anything else on *Bringing It All Back Home*, but not one of the song's cultural referents is placed casually. In fact, there's nothing that isn't calculated, including the false start, which gives a hint that he'll play it solo, before the band cuts in on the second take. He also travesties several folk tropes: sea shanties in the first verse, the "three ships a-sailin'" in the last, and all the surreal detail, from the Guernsey cow to the pay-off with the pay phone, harkening to the weird occurrences in traditional ballads.

Wordplay is secondary here, though. The narrative is coherent, even given the dream logic. He carefully scrambles the detail, not the sequence of events (as he pretty much always has).

All of that makes the song and the record great, but here's the capper: humour. Wit has always been Dylan's secret weapon, and 115th Dream ranks with his wackiest satires, looking back at I Shall Be Free and I Shall Be Free No.10, and forward to songs from *Highway 61 Revisited* to All Along The Watchtower. Woody Guthrie would have laughed at this inspired nonsense – after all, it owes as much to Woody, no stranger to inspired nonsense himself, as any song Dylan ever came up with. (DM)

67 One Of Us Must Know (Sooner Or Later)

BLONDE ON BLONDE, 1966

From the The Snidey Bastard Years, a semi-apology to one who got away.

The thankless experience of being dumped has inspired some of Dylan's best – and worst – songs. This kiss-off to a casual-sounding liaison is definitely among the former – a delicious attempt at saying, Look, it wasn't all my fault, you know. In fact, maybe one day you'll realise I had been seeking a deeper connection than you. And, really, how can anybody know each other anyway? Slightly rich, perhaps, but, aided by a sharply stirring band recording, incredibly alluring. Despite flopping as an early '66 single, Dylan wisely took the sound – the half-cut dance between Robbie Robertson's guitar and Al Kooper's organ – as the template for new album *Blonde On Blonde*. (SL)

66 Drifter's Escape

JOHN WESLEY HARDING, 1968

Law and nature do battle.

Joey Burns (Calexico): "Dylan's work is a never-ending process of discovery. Over time certain songs shine through, they have more meaning in different parts of your life. This is one of those. It's a perfect exercise in form, craft and content, the song has this story and there's a moral behind it as well. Then there's the performance: the looseness of his delivery, the band's phenomenal playing. It's not overdone. It's just very organic and beautiful."

65 Lay Lady Lay

NASHVILLE SKYLINE, 1969

A brand new voice – creamy, seductive – and horizontal schemes in mind.

Norma Waterson (Brit folk matriarch): "I love Lay Lady Lay. It's a real working-class song, a really sexy song. It reminded me as soon as I heard it of Lady Chatterley's Lover. 'His clothes are dirty, but his hands are clean' – you can imagine he's a gardener or a blacksmith who falls for this grand lady. He wants to keep her, and it's bridging the class divide.

"Why's his voice so different? Dylan over the years has had trouble with his voice, you can tell. And when a singer has trouble with their voice, they sing from a different area. So here he is singing from his diaphragm for a change. Or it could have been that one day he was in the bath and made a funny noise and thought, 'Ah! I like that noise! I'm going to do a song with that noise...' That happens, too."

64 Song To Woody

BOB DYLAN, 1962

Dylan doffs his peaked cap to his primary influence, as road- and world-weary as his idol.

Donovan (the Scottish Woody Guthrie): "I like this song as I was so influenced by Woody Guthrie before I heard Bob. I was 16 and my best friend Gypsy Dave wrote to me and said he'd found a record of a new American folk singer who was doing what I was doing, singing Woody Guthrie songs and wearing a cap and a harmonica harness. Song To Woody confirmed to me that I was not alone in wanting to bring true poetry and new, meaningful, social lyrics back to popular culture.

"Joan Baez introduced me to Bob. In the famous scene in Don't Look Back where we're both playing our songs, Bob turns to me and I sing To Sing For You. Then I ask him to sing a song and he does *[It's All Over Now, Baby Blue]*. What people miss is that he listens to my song, acknowledges that it's good, but not with too many words. He was amazed that there was another Guthrie disciple, arising out of Europe. But we were no threat to each other. When they used to say I was the British Bob Dylan, I used to quip, 'No, I'm the Scottish Woody Guthrie.'"

63 If Not For You

NEW MORNING, 1970

A plain and simple Valentine to the one Dylan loved most.

"I wrote the song thinking about my wife," Dylan revealed. The lyric was fashioned to mean something to just one person. There were no messages to be imparted, though the world was invited to listen in to what were really whispers meant for Sara's ear. Lyrically, the song came spare and simplistic, Tin Pan Alley-like in its use of "blue...", "you...", "too..." rhymings and lines that almost descended into mush. But the genius of Dylan turned this love poem into something endearing to all who heard it. A triumph of heart over head. (FD)

62 Most Of The Time

OH MERCY, 1989

"I don't even care if I ever see her again," he lies.

David Gray: "I got into Dylan aged 13, and loved the early, simple stuff best. By the time of *Oh Mercy* I'd stopped buying Dylan albums, but when I heard Everything Is Broken, I knew he was back. Most Of The Time is a beautifully simple song. You get this central idea that he's on the case, stronger than the bullshit he has to deal with, but then it becomes a love song by a man thinking of someone he lost long ago. I talked to *[Daniel]* Lanois about making that album and he said Dylan spooked him, he felt Dylan was inhabiting him like some ghost."

61 Quinn The Eskimo (The Mighty Quinn)

BIOGRAPH, 1985

Lovable nonsense about our pigeon-attracting hero making everyone "jump for joy".

Mark Mulcahy (ex-Miracle Legion): "I knew the song as a Manfred Mann song. And then when I was at college in the early '80s I met a very eccentric fella called Roger whose whole record collection was jazz and Dylan, and one day he put on Quinn The Eskimo. Roger and I were 'experimenting' at the time, and a couple of days after hearing the song we were walking round Connecticut hallucinating and we got into this guy's car, turned on the radio and heard Dylan doing Quinn The Eskimo. We just couldn't stop laughing. Then this guy knocked on the window: 'What are you doing in my car?' And we said, 'Dude! Quinn The Eskimo!' At the time I wished I played in a band and Roger got me my first gig a couple of days later. So in a way Quinn The Eskimo was a weird bridge into everything I wanted to do.

"The lyrics make no sense but they stick – that disgusting line about a 'cup of meat', for instance – and everybody comes in when they want. I dig it as a musical piece because to me it represents how he plays. He doesn't play with the people he's with. He's opposite, doing his own thing over the band."

60 Romance In Durango

DESIRE, 1976

Rattling Mexicana propelling a tale of doomed lovers fleeing on horseback.

John Cooper Clarke (punk-poet laureate): "It's a movie isn't it? The mariachi accompaniment (those trumpets!) and even the way he pitches his voice a bit like Alfonso Bedoya, the leader of the bandits in Treasure Of The Sierra Madre) conjures the Mexican desert – 'Hot chilli peppers in the blistering sun' – you're straight there. The picture of him and that girl on the one horse makes me think of Marlon Brando and Pina Pellicer in One-Eyed Jacks. I wonder if the whole Spanish milieu that he likes could be a device by which Dylan can leave the patrician world of North America with its Judeo-Protestant values and enter the more elemental Catholic-Latin world where he's the impulsive doomed hero, in trouble by his own actions.

"He's obviously shot her husband or something, and although he's made it across the desert he's clearly about to die but he's blinded by love (and optimism, and shit-frightened underneath it all) and the present tense is shot through with both this beautiful regret and projections into the future. He's dying not only of a fatal gunshot wound but with the mortal sin of murder on his soul ('the face of God... with his serpent eyes of obsidian'). In Romance In Durango, like all the best westerns, the people are complex, but the morality of the Old World they inhabit is clearly defined."

59 Stuck Inside Of Mobile With The Memphis Blues Again

BLONDE ON BLONDE, 1966

Redneck inbreed picaresque crawling with "neon madmen" sung molto fortissimo by a man having the time of his life.

Frank Black (Pixies): "There's a lot of beauty in this song. I don't know what it's about, and I've never bothered to work it out, but even though it's about being stuck somewhere with the blues, it's a triumphant song, with a really powerful chord progression. So when you've got that going for you, with the killer lyrics and the band going for it, it's defiant blues, very exhilarating.

"At the moment, I'm so in love with the drummer: Kenny Buttrey. Sometimes get choked up, literally, just listening to the drummer, the way he does a little snare roll, or something. I know it sounds silly, but I love that song and how it pulls me in, but once I'm in there I always focus on the drummer. It's a song with so much soul, but the more I listen, I always go back to

58 Rainy Day Women #12 & 35

BLONDE ON BLONDE, 1966

The ultimate party starter and a statement of defiance and rebellion, all in one song.

Bob – being Bob – once described it as "a Portuguese folk song". The symbolic stoning is certainly biblical in nature, and Dylan was getting hit with plenty, be they cast from the press or fans screaming "Judas!". Scholars have come up with various interpretations: one claims it's about Dylan's mother, whose maiden name was Stone. But Bob reportedly heard Ray Charles's Let's Go Get Stoned right before writing it. Time magazine (mistakenly) claimed a "rainy day woman" was a "marijuana cigarette". The 4am recording sounds like one helluva party. So the simplest interpretation remains the world's gonna getcha... so you might as well get stoned. (BH)

57 One More Cup Of Coffee

DESIRE, 1976

Brooding wonder as Dylan contemplates a sleeping lover and her mysterious family before venturing into the unknown.

Rennie Sparks (of husband-and-wife country duo The Handsome Family): "It's a cliché festival of psychic knife-throwing gypsy outlaws and it sounds corny on paper, but when you hear it, it works on this very natural dream-like level, like magical realism. It's almost like a little opera about coffee! He's singing these soaring harmonies with Emmylou Harris and they make this little line about one more cup of coffee seem like the most important romantic statement you could make to a lover.

"I spent a summer of love here in New Mexico 20 years ago with [husband] Brett and there was lots of drugs and not a lot of clothing, and much of it involved running around graveyards and singing this song at the top of my lungs. We came from the generation that had to hate hippies so we never listened to Dylan that much. But this song and this album just transported us to something bigger than everyday life.

"There's no Bob Dylan in it anywhere as such. It's not a page from his diary. It's something more mysterious – a little dream that fell from the sky. He's sitting there drinking coffee in this weird mountain empire of psychics deciding whether to go back down to the valley below. Perhaps the valley below's death but I think he's talking about going back to the real world, which is a kind of death really. I think he decides in the end that he doesn't belong up here in this realm of what seems

56 Tears Of Rage

THE BASEMENT TAPES, 1975

Setting the genius of the Bard to verse.

In May 1967, Dylan told Michael Iachetta, a reporter who'd tracked him down to Woodstock, that since disappearing from public view he'd been "seein' only a few close friends, readin' a little 'bout the outside world, porin' over books by people you never heard of..." Which makes you wonder if Iachetta had the balls to ask, "And exactly which books would those be, Bob?"

A little unlikely, as he was halfway through a world-exclusive interview. Dylan lives! Dylan talks! It's also unlikely that Iachetta hadn't heard of one William Shakespeare, author of, among a few other trifles, King Lear. Many writers have noted the debt owed by several of Dylan's *Basement Tapes* songs (Too Much Of Nothing, This Wheel's On Fire) to Lear. But Tears Of Rage is the song which comes closest to achieving its emotional devastation.

If accounts are to be believed, this is how the song came about: Richard Manuel of The Band was fooling around at the piano one day at Big Pink when Dylan came in with the lyrics already written. Which may explain why the chords have that aching, arching quality. They're not Dylan changes, though they owe a lot to the gospel that always comes out when he sits at the piano.

In Chronicles, the reasons for Dylan's post-motorcycle crash retreat are clarified: he was scared of what his fame might do to his family. He's written other songs to and about his children, but Tears Of Rage captures the terror of being a father. It's my favourite Dylan song because I find it so moving. The American poet Emily Dickinson said, "If I read a book and it makes my whole body so cold no fire can ever warm me, I know that is poetry. If I feel physically as if the top of my head were taken off, I know that is poetry. These are the only ways I know it. Is there any other way?" Is there? (TL)

55 I Threw It All Away

NASHVILLE SKYLINE, 1969

Regretful balladeering of the highest grade.

Nick Cave: "This is my favourite Dylan song. There is such an ease and innocence to Dylan's voice. This is a guy doing the job God put him on Earth to do. This song is about craft; Dylan removes himself, the burden of his history, his myth, to craft a song unparalleled in its gorgeousness. It's mathematics, music by numbers, and all the more affecting for it. It's Mozart man up against the wracked Beethoven of his other work. *Nashville Skyline* was an audacious record, flying in the face of those who thought it was Dylan's moral duty to be the drum major of his generation. I can put this song on first thing in the morning or the middle of a dark night, and it will serve me as it should, lift me up, make me better,

Setting Shakespeare to music? Dylan at home in Woodstock, 1968.

Mississippi learning: Dylan visits Greenwood for a voter registration rally, 1963.

54 To Ramona
ANOTHER SIDE OF..., 1964

Love song to Southern belle – possibly active in the civil rights movement – lost in the metropolis.

Lucinda Williams: "The first time I heard Bob Dylan, in 1965, it changed my life. Here was someone who had taken the worlds I was from – traditional folk music and creative writing – and put them together and made it work. From that moment on, I decided I wanted to write songs like that. I'm still working at it. To Ramona is just a love song, not intensely heavy, but the ultimate love song. There's something about it – the rhyming, the imagery, everything is wonderful. This was Dylan at his inimitable, quintessential best, right there."

53 She Belongs To Me
BRINGING IT ALL BACK HOME, 1965

"She's got everything she needs" – and she doesn't need you, chum.

Bruce Johnston (The Beach Boys): "I heard about Dylan from Jack Nitzsche's wife Grazia who made me listen to *Freewheelin'*. It wasn't his voice, which was difficult to get comfortable with, it was his songs. What we were hearing on the radio at that time was highly polished pop, like Goffin-King kind of songs, but Dylan was 180 degrees in the other direction. Then, when I heard She Belongs To Me, I was struck by the fact that it has such a natural groove. To me, a natural groove record would be something like Little Richard, R&B stuff, but here's this Greenwich Village folkie, who has turned the lyric-writing thought process upside down, and suddenly he's making songs with a natural groove. Dylan's melodies can be hard to digest sometimes, because he's not a singer who writes, he's a writer who sings, but this has a great tune."

52 You Ain't Goin' Nowhere
GREATEST HITS, VOL. 2, 1971

Country-fied existentialism and one of the most melodic glances into the abyss ever.

Roger McGuinn – who's name-checked in Bob's best-known rendition for botching a lyric on The Byrds' version – claims Dylan wrote it while recuperating from his motorcycle accident. It sounds like the Old West, with Happy Traum's banjo and references to mail-order brides (McGuinn claims Zimmy was simply waiting for Sara to come home). Still, characters like Ghengis Khan's brother Don had the hallucinogenic imagery we expected. Some think it's about this mortal coil, a glance into the void... hey, you ain't goin' nowhere. Or it could simply be about being stuck – and stoned – immobile, in that "easy chair". (BH)

51 I Don't Believe You (She Acts Like We Never Have Met)
ANOTHER SIDE OF..., 1964

Dylan sets out to prove that there's more to love than boy meets girl.

John Sebastian (ex-The Lovin' Spoonful): "With this song, Dylan established an unprecedented relationship between man and woman in song. Before Bob, things had been pretty benign between the sexes. It was absolute love or utter heartbreak. What little shading there was usually came from the woman's point of view, laying out the case against her man. Dylan turned the tables in this sense, offering romantic critiques of women, and he did it with a degree of emotional awareness and insight. He made it more real, and opened up vast new territories for songs to explore."

50 I Pity The Poor Immigrant
JOHN WESLEY HARDING, 1968

New England meets Old Testament in Dylan's resigned, ambiguous hymn to the migrant's lot.

This oracular, gravely beautiful highlight of 1968's ascetic album finds a sanctified Dylan at his most ancient-sounding. Borrowing an aching melody from arcane Scottish ballad, Tramps And Hawkers, Dylan imparts lyrics of unflinching solemnity on which neither his rudimentary acoustic guitar, nor spartan, 6/8-time bass and drums, intrude. A slow, quiet song with mighty reverberations, some see it as Dylan playing God, ironically rebuking the white American settler, "Who falls in love with wealth itself / And turns his back on me." A cryptic, allegorical finger to the American Dream disguised as an abstinent hymn. (DS)

49 Only A Pawn In Their Game

THE TIMES THEY ARE A-CHANGIN', 1964

Remembered by a man who knows a good protest song when he hears one…

Pete Seeger: "Back in 1963 I got together with Bob and Theodore Bikel for a voter registration rally in Greenwood, Mississippi. A friend was making a little documentary film there and the mayor told him, 'We never had a nigger problem here, it's outside agitators cause the trouble.' We had a little song festival in a cotton field and Bob sang Only A Pawn In Their Game which he'd just written about Medgar Evers, the Mississippi civil rights activist who was murdered three weeks earlier. The song says just putting the murderers in jail wasn't enough. It was about ending the whole game of segregation.

"Generally, Bob wanted to make a record that would make people think. He told me he'd seen me singing when he was at the University Of Minnesota [1959-1960]. But I must have first met him in New York up in the Broadside magazine's office. I remember sitting there and Bob and Phil Ochs played their songs and I was thinking, I'm in the same room as two of the greatest songwriters in the world! Two weeks later I had Bob on at a Carnegie Hall Hootenanny and there were so many artists on I had to tell everyone they were limited to 10 minutes and he said, 'I've got one song that lasts 10 minutes' – and he did A Hard Rain's A-Gonna Fall. I was always impressed by his independence.

"Bob made records that'd make people think." PETE SEEGER

"I realised he was a genius turning out one great song after another. Blowin' In The Wind is still one of the greatest songs of the 20th century. I used to sing Masters Of War occasionally myself and Hard Rain. Bob had drawn lessons from Woody, he knew a good song tells a story or paints a picture. And he didn't try to be too specific. I have a little skating rink in my yard and when *John Wesley Harding* came out I skated around listening to it on the outdoor speakers thinking, What does this mean?

"There are reports of me being anti him going electric at the '65 Newport Folk festival, but that's wrong. I was the MC that night. He was singing Maggie's Farm and you couldn't understand a word because the mic was distorting his voice. I ran to the mixing desk and said, 'Fix the sound, it's terrible!' The guy said, 'No, that's how they want it.' And I did say that if I had an axe I'd cut the cable! But I wanted to hear the words. I didn't mind him going electric."

48 If You See Her, Say Hello

BLOOD ON THE TRACKS, 1975

A masterwork of emotional turmoil that reveals itself layer by layer.

Robert Fisher (folk-noir group the Willard Grant Conspiracy): "I was a teenager working in an LA record store when *Blood On The Tracks* came out. It's a formative record in my life and this is the stand-out track. The delivery has this amazing transformation, from the opening verse where he's looking at this love almost casually and going, 'It wasn't that big a deal', to the final verse where we see it's a huge deal. It's complex because that lovely fingerpicking carries so much melancholy and undercuts the gunslinger swagger he's affecting. There's anger but the song's opening line is wistful: 'If you see her, say hello, she might be in Tangier.' It's the genius of Dylan that the song contains these conflicting emotions. In the beginning, Dylan's songs were jammed with words. By now, he's allowing more to be filled in by the listener."

47 Jokerman

INFIDELS, 1983

Slippery central character – false prophet? Cult leader? – beset by snaking reggae groove.

Sly Dunbar: "Bob Dylan always do songs in different keys, like he'll change three, four different keys in a song, and he will change the lyrics on the fly, so when we cut Jokerman, we recorded it then had a break overnight. He came in the morning and said, 'Oh, gentlemen, could you just run Jokerman for me again?' Nobody know the tape was spinning; we were just running down the music and he said, 'OK, that's it' – he used the take we didn't know we were taking. It was a surprise; I think we were playing the run-down a bit looser, 'cos it was just a run-through, but he probably liked something about it."

46 Don't Think Twice, It's All Right

THE FREEWHEELIN' BOB DYLAN, 1963

Poignant song of leaving – complete with air of righteousness – for and about Suze Rotolo.

Romeo Stodart (melodic UK hipsters The Magic Numbers): "This is one of the first songs I learned to play on the guitar. It's a really simple song, a simple melody – but the lyrics are really hard-hitting and moving. It's an early morning song, the first song of the day. It also helped the band because it's just acoustic guitar and vocal, and when we write songs we try to do that. Even though we go crazy and orchestrate lots of big arrangements, we come back just to words and one accompaniment. Dylan has helped me as a songwriter, just like he's helped everybody else. He's walked the line and he's shown everybody else how to do that."

45 Lay Down Your Weary Tune

BIOGRAPH, 1985

Written in 1963 with a Wordsworthian lyric: "The water smooth ran like a hymn / And like a harp did hum."

Chris Hillman (The Byrds): "This has always, always been a favourite Dylan song of mine. The Byrds got an acetate because our manager Jim Dickson knew Bob. At the time I didn't like it, but Roger, then known as Jim McGuinn and always an insightful guy, picked it to record on *Turn! Turn! Turn!*. Such a great opening verse, really a beautiful lyric all around. It is kinda like Dylan Thomas poetry, as if he wrote lyrics for popular music."

44 Forever Young

PLANET WAVES, 1974

Dylan waxes simple, sincere. "May you build a ladder to the stars…" Not a dry eye, etc.

Roddy Woomble (Scottish rockers Idlewild): "Forever Young is probably my favourite song. Allen Ginsberg said this song should be sung every morning by every child in every school in every country. Which is such a nice idea, because the song is plainly encouraging people to find their own truth. The Band are here, so the whole thing has an inspired, effortless feel to it. The fact that there's two versions back to back says a lot about how The Band and Dylan worked together, and about how important they thought this song was. Like A Rolling Stone might be Dylan's masterpiece, but Forever Young is his national anthem."

43 Million Dollar Bash

THE BASEMENT TAPES, 1975

Like Pink's Get The Party Started. Only not worthless.

Chuck Prophet (ex-Green On Red): "Whenever I hear Million Dollar Bash, I always picture Dylan on the balcony of some high-rise Manhattan penthouse, kicking it with Marlon Brando and Lenny Bruce and a gaggle of long-legged socialites, taking it all in and just dreaming of fishing by a stream somewhere. Now here he is in Woodstock with his friends – look at *The Basement Tapes'* cover: what a joker Bob is, how are you gonna play a mandolin with a bow? And they look like the kind of guys you'd want to invite over to your parents' for a barbecue and a softball game.

"This was one of the times, I think, when Dylan knew he was going to have to take an interest in his own music, and seized the moment to just play with his friends. Perhaps he's looking back on all those interchangeable people at the million dollar bash and nursing the motherlode of all hangovers – the '60s."

42 All I Really Want To Do

ANOTHER SIDE OF..., 1964

A cheeky Dylan does his best Jimmy Rodgers – albeit after what sounds like a few tokes..

Dylan had already been cast – as he puts it in Chronicles – as "the high priest of protest". Keen to let some of the air out of his mythos, he opens the transitional *Another Side Of Bob Dylan* with what's ostensibly a love song, although one that is filled with half-rhymed comic wordplay and wrapped in a singing brakeman's yodel. Such is Dylan's magic that fans and critics have variously argued that the tune is among his most heartfelt offerings and a pure piss-take. It's totally fitting then, that by the time he starts snickering during the final chorus, we're not at all sure whether he's laughing with us or at us. (BM)

41 Not Dark Yet

TIME OUT OF MIND, 1997

Hospitalised with heart-threatening histoplasmosis in March '97, Dylan returns flicking the vees at Death.

Andy Gill (Gang Of Four): "I first heard Not Dark Yet about three years ago, on holiday in Sri Lanka, at Christmas. Somebody had the album and I just got obsessed with that track. In some respects, it's not as brilliant lyrically as some earlier songs, but those have an air of pretentiousness to them. Like on *Blonde On Blonde*, you think, is that exactly what Dylan wanted to say? I don't think he needs allusions to intellectual content to convince us he's clever. But the lyrics to Not Dark Yet are really simple. It's exactly what he is: an old man and he's tired. It's Dylan speaking authentically from where he is now, in this time of life, looking at what he's been and seeing where he is at, and expressing it in terms which resonate with many people: "Shadows are falling and I've been here all day/It's too hot to sleep, time is running away"

"I don't think I've ever heard music quite as languorous. It feels very big-old-river, moving very slowly, like the Mississippi when it gets very close to the sea, edging along. It's very Louisiana, hot and sweaty. It's the most incredible atmosphere that you get drawn into. You absolutely sense that the sun is just beyond the horizon, it's not quite dark, but it's just going down, and he's sitting there, hot as fuck, and it's the end of his life. The drums and the bass and the guitar lick is all so very simple, but every time I hear it, I think, how did they get to play that so well? How many times did they rehearse that? It sounds like they played that song 200 times because of the finesse and the relationship between the instruments. And then his voice on the top, which sounds amazing. He's croaking away like he's about to pass out but in the most extraordinary musical way."

40 I'll Keep It With Mine

THE BOOTLEG SERIES VOLUMES 1-3, 1991

Gently ruminative love song favoured here in its scratchy publishing demo form.

Devendra Banhart (San Francisco folkie): "To me, the folk scene right after Bob Dylan was a lot of Bob Dylan impersonators, impersonating someone who was already impersonating someone else. Then, immediately after that, Bob became Bob and did something so completely Bob that no one could imitate him. I got The Witmark Demos bootleg from Currituck Co's Kevin Barker and I love the sound of that version *[from June 1964]* too. It sounds like it was recorded on a hand-held tape recorder. They were recorded not for Dylan to release but for other people to record. I'll Keep It With Mine was written for Nico and like all of Dylan's tunes it's perfect. To go with the song, Kevin also showed me footage of a party where The Byrds are doing keg stands and, over there in the corner, you can see Dylan and Nico making out."

39 Dear Landlord

JOHN WESLEY HARDING, 1967

An open letter to big cheeses everywhere. The message: don't step on my blue suede shoes.

Amid the riddling ballads of 1967's *John Wesley Harding* came this, his first real "sticking it to The Man" song in ages. Like the best blues, it swings nicely while also seeming weighed down with woes both spiritual and economic. Every element here sounds magnificent: the pattering drums, the bubbling bass line, Dylan's own righteous piano chords and suppressed-anger singing (both bearing hints of Ray Charles). So who is this "landlord"? Well, he might be Dylan's own pushy manager, Albert Grossman, possibly the big man upstairs or even, conceivably, a landlord. Whatever, by now his take on authority is less livid than bruised and rueful. (SL)

38 Knockin' On Heaven's Door

PAT GARRETT AND BILLY THE KID, 1973

Peckinpah atmosphere captured in song form as the darkness closes in on a retiring gunslinger.

Rachid Taha (Algerian rai rocker): "It's one of those songs that gets stuck in your head and never comes out. You'll be walking down the street or sitting in a café watching the girls go by and there it is again – damn. I don't know what the verses mean. I was just a teenager when that song came out and didn't speak a word of English, nor did any of my friends, but we could all sing 'Knock knock knockin' on heaven's door'. We didn't know what it meant but we liked the sound of it."

37 Gotta Serve Somebody

SLOW TRAIN COMING, 1979

Bob finds God. They get on.

When Jerry Wexler's co-producer, Barry Beckett, met Dylan at Muscle Shoals he searched keyboard and soul to find three notes bleak enough to announce Gotta Serve Somebody.

That day in May, 1979, from Mark Knopfler to the back-up singers, everybody got Dylan. No matter what they knew of his recent travails, they felt to the marrow his terror and confusion, his needs for musical and moral discipline, and the fervour of new faith with which he recovered equilibrium.

Gotta Serve Somebody grinds. It haunts. It lasts because it's straightforward yet multi-dimensional. It wears a hellfire frown, yet carries some sidelong Dylan laughs down the years. That "You may call me Bobby, you may call me Zimmy" line. Or the comic "You may be workin' in a barbershop/You may know how to cut hair". It's true Dylan, heard above a rumble of thunder from the Old Testament. (PS)

36 Brownsville Girl

KNOCKED OUT LOADED, 1986

Opium reverie where films, desires and reality collide and collude.

An 11-minute epic, Brownsville Girl dominates *Knocked Out Loaded*. Originally titled New Danville Girl, it takes us on a journey full of vivid flashbacks, obsessive references to Gregory Peck movies, racy narrative and evocative imagery. The Brownsville girl is portrayed as a sultry, Hispanic temptress but the suspicion persists she is merely a front in a highly personal parable about the creative process and his own elusive muse. It ends up as a thrilling, magical mystery tour, both lyrically and musically. One of Dylan's parting shots is "I always said 'Hang on to me baby and let's hope that the roof stays on...'" All Dylan fans will identify with that line. (CI)

35 Isis

DESIRE, 1975

Pyramids escapade prompts "Can't live with 'em/Can't shoot 'em" wisdom.

The first song completed for *Desire*, written with Jacques Levy (previous work: Chestnut Mare with Roger McGuinn). He nailed down Dylan's increasingly back-to-narrative songs to graspable linearity. By contrast with the anguished break-up themes of *Blood On The Tracks* the previous year, Isis is playful, and ultimately leads to reconciliation. It's a hair-raising yarn *à la* Bob Dylan's 115th Dream, where the "I" character ditches his new bride, rides off by horse to grave-rob a pyramid, but returns home to rejoin Isis. "What drives me to you is what drives me insane," he concludes – a pleasant change from all-out warfare. (AP)

At the peak of his powers: Dylan backstage at the Town Hall, New York, 1963

34 Blowin' In The Wind

THE FREEWHEELIN' BOB DYLAN, 1963

Dylan adapts a slave-era spiritual originally called No More Auction Block.

Mavis Staples: "Blowin' In The Wind was the first song I heard from Bobby. I fell in love with it. My father *[Pops Staples]* couldn't understand how someone like Bobby could write such heavy songs as such a young man. But it had an effect on a lot of people. When Sam Cooke heard Blowin' In The Wind he said, 'If a young white guy can write a song like that then I got to get my pen in hand.' And that's when he wrote A Change Is Gonna Come.

"I remember my sister and I were walking down the street one evening and saw a beggar on the sidewalk. And this man started singing in the most beautiful voice: 'How many roads must a man walk down...' It stopped us in our tracks, we couldn't speak, it was so glorious. Bobby touches everyone. It doesn't matter if it's a Sam Cooke or some poor man on the street, they all feel him."

33 You're Gonna Make Me Lonesome When You Go

BLOOD ON THE TRACKS, 1975

Shaken awake by a new affair: "Yer gonna make me give myself a good talkin' to."

Madeleine Peyroux (jazz diva): "Bob Dylan is someone I grew up with. I used to sing his songs when busking on the Metro in Paris and I always had a huge aspiration to record something of his one day. I chose You're Gonna Make Me Lonesome... because it's a love song and Dylan's love songs are special because there's often a twist of bitterness. On this one he admits that things are not going to be perfect either now or any time. It's amazing the way Dylan can take something very simple and turn it into something that's very important. I loved the melody too. That was another reason. I think that Dylan often doesn't get enough credit for his melodic strength."

32 Love Minus Zero/ No Limit

BRINGING IT ALL BACK HOME, 1965

One of his sweetest love songs – apart from the brothel, death and Apocalypse references.

"My love she speaks like silence." Tricky, but then she is quite a woman. Her scent swirls through this honeyed river of song, borne along on gentle tumbles and ripples of guitar. Frankly, we're all enamoured... then she's suddenly a raven at the window! What does it all mean? Sigh. (PS)

"Dylan's love songs are special."

MADELEINE PEYROUX

31 Man In The Long Black Coat OH MERCY, 1989

Woman runs off with a man with "a face like a mask". Is that wise?

Daniel Lanois (producer, *Oh Mercy* and *Time Out Of Mind*): "We spent a lot of time getting the ambience right, recording the neighbourhood crickets – the sound of the New Orleans night. It's a song inspired by the mood of the city. Bob came to the recording of *Oh Mercy* with songs fully written but Man In The Long Black Coat was composed in the studio. It was a hot steamy time down there and that's how the song sounds. On *Oh Mercy* Bob is inside the songs but here he's standing outside, observing. It's a fascinating subject, the idea that someone might escape the confines of the ordinary world by a sudden impulsive act. It's a song about a turning point, one moment that might change a life for ever – like running away to join the circus.

"On day one of recording he showed up with a few pieces of paper, no instruments, not much of anything. I gave him a package price. For $150,000 he got everything: musicians, equipment, mixing... the works. We started to get good results right away but Bob was not used to the stripped-down way I wanted to work. There were moments things got more pared-down than he liked. A lot of his best work from the past had been in the presence of a band getting things live off the floor, and the way I was working, overdubbing and stacking tracks up, was not even a consideration for him.

"But what got captured on *Oh Mercy* went beyond the trickery of the toolbox. There were environmental factors. Bob would never let us work in the daytime. It was a night-time record. As I understand it, human beings are satisfied with a different musical tempo after dark. A slow groove will sound correct at midnight but at lunchtime the next day will sound like it needs to be sped up. Bob was in tune with that idea; he knew exactly what kind of mood he wanted to get across."

30 I'll Be Your Baby Tonight JOHN WESLEY HARDING, 1968

Beautiful, easy-rhyming love song in the spirit of Hank.

The shades are drawn, the bottle uncorked and Pete Drake's lilting lap steel provides the flickering shadows in this succinct and deceptively simple tune with a major Grand Ole Opry vibe. Further evidence that Dylan was wilfully out of step in '68, I'll Be Your Baby Tonight might easily have been written and, given the unfussy nature of its recording, even recorded 20 years before. Gone are the twisty, cryptic lyrics of the period with the return of Bob the laidback romanticist and – as if to further confuse the hardcore – "moon/spoon" couplets underlining the song's appreciation of

29 Girl From The North Country

THE FREEWHEELIN' BOB DYLAN, 1963

Scarborough Fair recast "where the winds hit heavy on the borderline".

Paul Buchanan (Scottish melancholics The Blue Nile): "I must have heard it at a time when I dressed like he does on the cover of the *Freewheelin'* album. I wanted my life to be like that cover. There is something of the same romance about the song; a straightforward enough reminiscence of a lost love, without any cynicism or defeatism. I like the mentions of the girl's hair and coat and, I guess, the third person thing works nicely because it's all kept so simple and defenceless."

28 I Want You BLONDE ON BLONDE, 1966

Proof that even Bob Dylan's pop songs are confusing.

Jeremy Vine (respected BBC Radio DJ): "There's a particular experience I associate with the song. I used to do hospital radio when I was 16, at a psychiatric hospital. Occasionally patients would wander up with requests, and this guy hung around for 90 minutes, clearly deep in thought, and just said 'I Want You by Dylan', so I played it, which was the first time I'd heard the song.

"There are two sides to the track the patient could have keyed into: the uplifting effect if you were feeling troubled, or the disturbed lyrics. Lyrically, it's like a gag, a cartoon, a feature film or a colourful painting. It feels like a bucket that's been tipped out. There are so many images, so much going on, from that first line, 'The guilty undertaker sighs/The lonesome organ grinder cries...' It's fabulous. You don't know what these characters are doing. It's like a circus and everyone is jumping around. There's this great combination of confusion and the real purity of Dylan's sentiment.

"It feels to me like the lyrics are showing off to someone he didn't know that well, like someone he spent an evening with and it didn't work out, because there's a sense of sustained unfulfilment. It's not something you write for a wife. The trouble with a lot of his lyrics is that when you start digging, they fall apart, which isn't always bad because they're amazing glass constructions. Here, you're caught between the artifice and the real emotion. He dribbles the ball in a fancy way and then scores with a tap-in! I like the way the lyric doesn't drown in its own complication. But most of all, I love I Want You because it makes me feel happy. The melody is wrapped in tinsel, like turning on all the fairylights, all bouncy and joyous. The chord changes all go to the right place, down and up, and it's beautifully structured. Did it take him five minutes to write or five weeks? I know his answer,

© Barry Feinstein

27 All Along the Watchtower JOHN WESLEY HARDING, 1967

A riddle without an end, waiting for a Hendrix guitar solo?

Terry Callier (folk-jazz shaman): "To write songs about things that are close or painful, you have to say something that everybody will be able to identify with. You can't always take your most personal experiences and do that, but Bob Dylan was good at it. As a matter of fact, he was the one that showed us that your personal experiences, if put in a vibrant enough context, were valuable. Because people hadn't been doing that before: people had been saying 'Yes, I love you, you love me, we will be together, 1, 2, 3.' But you start talking about 'There must be some kind of way out of here, said the Joker to the Thief...' Well! Now we're getting down! We're talking about neuroses, psychoses, and other 'oses! He showed us that if you put these things in the right context, in the right emotional patterns and the right combinations of words, this

Slow Train Coming:
Dylan journeys
from Dublin to
Belfast, 1966.

24 I Shall Be Released
GREATEST HITS VOL 2, 1971

Gospel succour for the trapped and jailed.

Tom Robinson (UK protest punk turned BBC DJ): "Our version *[on TRB, 1978]* was pure pragmatism. Everyone knew it. It was the standard left-wing benefit-for-somebody-who's-in-prison song, with the great advantage that it has the same chord sequence running all the way through, so you can teach it to a scratch band in five minutes flat. We were supporting the Free George Ince *[wrongly charged with murder, 1973]* campaign, so it seemed appropriate.

"Coming out of the *Basement Tapes* sessions, Dylan's version has those other-worldly textures. You also get that sense of him 'walking out of the machinery', as Peter Gabriel sings in Solsbury Hill. I think, having read Chronicles, where for the first time you get his version of that period, he just could not have carried on any more, regardless of the motorcycle accident. There was a madness in the expectation, the pressure, the people breaking into the house and ruining his marriage with Sara.

"The songs from this period use these amazing metaphors for explaining or coping with his situation. So on *John Wesley Harding*, Dear Landlord is for his manager Albert Grossman, and in I Shall Be Released he's talking about being in prison but it's perhaps a prison of other people's expectations.

"What I envy most about Dylan is his lightness of touch. Like rhyming 'language' with 'sandwich' *[on Sign Language, duet with Eric Clapton on the latter's No Reason To Cry, 1976]*. He'll put in an absurd line just to get the song on to the next bit. You get to the essence of the song without getting tied down in the mechanics of the rhyme scheme, which is one reason he's so great to cover. His songs are not arrangement-dependent. Anyone can interpret them."

26 Shelter From The Storm
BLOOD ON THE TRACKS, 1975

...because everyone needs a bosom for a pillow.

Sheryl Crow: "I got into Dylan and The Band at high school in about '76 when all my friends were Boston fans. At first, I didn't like Dylan's voice, then when I began writing my own songs I realised his ability to construct the arc of a melody is perfect.

"I've thought about that perfection of his. It's the intervals that set an artist apart. Usually they're identifiable. Look at Sting or Sam Cooke, or how Chris Martin will go up a sixth on the end of a phrase. But Dylan doesn't have that trademark, he just knows what intervals to pick to grow our emotions. And Shelter From The Storm is an example of how good he is at making a verse melody so circular it becomes the hook and he doesn't need a chorus.

"I read one Dylan interview where he said the perfect song for him would be where every line could be the first line of a new song. And I think there's just so little fat in lyrics like Shelter From The Storm that it really is true."

25 Hurricane
DESIRE, 1976

A slight return to protest with a stinging plea for imprisoned boxer Rubin Carter.

A whirlwind of a song, later dispensed by the Rolling Thunder Revue in a rough-and-tumble manner, Dylan's snarled quatrains predated the advent of poetry slams by decades. It's pure poetic passion delivered via the screaming headlines of a scandal sheet. The punchline hits home hard, Dylan dryly noting, "If you're black, you might as well not show up on the street/'less you wanna draw the heat." Malcolm X couldn't have said it better. (AL)

"At first I didn't like Dylan's voice."
SHERYL CROW

23 A Hard Rain's A-Gonna Fall
THE FREEWHEELIN' BOB DYLAN, 1963

An early masterpiece turns protest singing metaphysical.

Based on the traditional English folk ballad Lord Randall, Hard Rain is constructed as a series of questions and answers about the protagonist's travels through an apocalyptic world of pestilence, famine, war and deceit. Yet despite the horrors he's witnessed, he's "Goin' back out, 'fore the rain starts a-fallin'", to do what he can: even if that's just to write a song, to "tell it and think it and speak it and breathe it/And reflect it from the mountain so all souls can see it". Both Leonard Cohen and Joni Mitchell have said they became songwriters after hearing this: it still retains every ounce of that inspirational power. (AB)

22 The Times They Are A-Changin'

THE TIMES THEY ARE A-CHANGIN', 1964

The forces of history mass at our hero's back. Get outtathaway!

Billy Bragg (Brit protest punk icon): "I locked onto Dylan when I was looking for music that had some kind of meaning. I was about 13 or 14. I swapped my copy of the Jackson 5's *Greatest Hits* with a mate at school for *The Times They Are A-Changin'*. I took it home and listened to it and I really found it inspirational. To go from 'A-B-C, 1-2-3' to that was a seismic sea change in my appreciation of music.

"It started with the picture of Dylan on the cover. He's got his head to one side, like he's asking a question: 'All this is happening in the world. What are you going to do about it?' Every track reflects that — Ballad Of Hollis Brown, The Lonesome Death Of Hattie Carroll, Only A Pawn In Their Game.

"And the title track summed it up. Everything's in there. 'Come mothers and fathers/Throughout the land/And don't criticise/What you can't understand.' God, that was incendiary. There's an incredible starkness to the song. It says: are you part of this, or are you going to sit on your butt and do nothing? And that to me was a clarion call.

"I was in Canada about 10 years ago, watching TV and it was used for an advert for a bank. I was furious. About two or three days later I was doing a gig — a union rally in the centre of Toronto. I went up there and whacked the shit out of it with all the venom that I got from The Clash. The place went mad. So whenever I do it now I'm not gentle with it, I don't think you should be gentle with that song.

"He always has been, and always will be, an outsider. He makes outsider music and that's tough to do. I really respect him for that. For me, The Times They Are A-Changin' remains a really key song in the development of Billy Bragg as we know and love him. Without that... I would still be here, but I'd be doing a very poor impersonation of the early Jackson 5. You don't wanna see that."

Nas: "I first heard The Times They Are A-Changin' in a *[1979 street gang]* movie called The Wanderers, which I saw when I was about 14 years old. The song came at a very important point of the movie, where the characters had been runnin' the streets forever, and had gotten old. It had come full circle with their lives, so they had to make a change.

"The verse that blew me away was 'Come senators, congressmen/Please heed the call/Don't stand in the doorway/Don't block up the hall/For he that gets hurt will be he who has stalled.' The words he's saying are words of awakening, but when you add that to the conviction in his voice, you can hear that this is a man fighting to get the truth out. To make a record like that, you have to genuinely have it in your heart to not just love your music and your cause, but to be a part of it, and that's what he does. You can't fake that record."

21 Visions Of Johanna

BLONDE ON BLONDE, 1966

Put another fifty pee in the meter. It's the ghost of 'lectricity.

Steve Harley ('70s Brit glam rocker): "This sparkles with that dreadful mystery that's Dylan's own. Hearing it for the first time has never left my mind. Suddenly I wasn't a 15-year-old listening to music anymore; I was hearing poetry. 'Lights flicker from the opposite loft/In this room the heat pipes just cough/The country music station plays soft.' Then he says: 'But there's nothing, really nothing to turn off.' You think, What the fuck was that? All the time he was thinking of a lost love. Maybe apocryphal, maybe genuine — he's a poet with licence to create. Every pay-off says there's nothing here. Nothing exists. It's all fantasy. Am I awake? Am I asleep? All I've got is visions of Johanna, which keep me up past dawn. The man can't sleep! He's lovesick. But is he really? Or is this poetry? This isn't Wordsworth or Keats. Dylan is beyond them."

20 Ballad Of A Thin Man

HIGHWAY 61 REVISITED, 1965

Funereal sneer-a-thon vs "one-eyed midgets" (think about it) everywhere.

Al Stewart: " I haven't played it in years but I can still remember the words. It's an unspoken rule that the trade-off for fame and fortune in the music business is that you have to be able to accept criticism, but not every artist subscribes to that, and Bob Dylan quite obviously didn't. With Positively 4th Street around the same time, it was clear Dylan was pissed off about a lot of things — and he was writing like a maniac.

"Musically it's beautiful. I love the skinny sound of the record — it suits the title. When I saw Dylan at the Albert Hall in 1966 he played it, and I think it was the only song that he played on piano. There's no swing in the way Dylan plays it, and that gives it this old-fashioned barrelhouse feel, which works really well with the words. And when the organ comes in on top... that's wonderful."

19 Idiot Wind

BLOOD ON THE TRACKS, 1975

Divorce porn wrapped in a wordy riddle. Lovely!

Of all the songs of love and hate on *Blood On The Tracks*, none is as painfully direct or as inscrutably mystifying as Idiot Wind. On the one hand as blatant a chunk of divorce porn as has been committed to vinyl. On the other a riddle, featuring as many unexplained characters and locations as howls of vengeance and pain. It's hardly news that Dylan uses words as swords and smoke screens to defy interpretation and keep his audience at bay. But on an album considered his most confessional, this elusiveness is so remarkable that many seem simply to have ignored it. When people sing along (and they do) to Idiot Wind, they focus on the man crawling past his loved-one's door, or raging at unnamed betrayals, or picturing her – as the song crescendos in contempt and loathing – dead in a ditch, flies buzzing around her eyes.

As for the swaggering cowboy – an escapee from Lily, Rosemary & The Jack Of Hearts – who sings the opening verse and provides much of the imagery, or the murdered Gray, his millionaire wife, the crucified soldier, the fortune teller, or the priest by the burning building, they remain as mysterious as the tramp in Like A Rolling Stone, and insofar as the impact of the song, of as much individual importance. Because what makes this a great song is its passion – so uncontainable at times it seems to take off on its own, podding verses as it goes – and the authority of Dylan's voice.

Maybe it's the relative frailty of his backing band that makes his singing sound so apocalyptic – the way he spits "sweeeeet lady" and "iiiidiot wind" (before ending with the unexpectedly inclusive "we're idiots, babe") – but apocalyptic it is. Whether Dylan is exorcising personal relationship angst, or just writing a contemporary American love-hate-murder ballad, he sure gorges himself here. (SS)

18 Subterranean Homesick Blues

BRINGING IT ALL BACK HOME, 1965

Songwriting as an amphetamine-fuelled, existentialist car chase.

James Blunt (chart-topping UK pop-rocker): "I must have heard this first when I was about 14 or 15. I didn't have any Bob Dylan records of my own, but another kid at school who played the guitar was heavily into him and he kept playing me this track. I remember thinking how flippant it sounded, lackadaisical in many ways. The sense of movement in the song is so infectious, and to me Subterranean Homesick Blues sums up this sense of moving through life. The guitarist in my band has Subterranean Homesick Blues as the polyphonic ringtone for his phone; someone rang him during a rehearsal and I just thought, 'Shit... how does one even start writing a song like that?'"

17 Every Grain Of Sand

SHOT OF LOVE, 1981

Death and judgement stalk our hero. They're behiiiiind youuuuu!

Sheryl Crow: "This was the first religious song I'd heard which transcended all religions. It asks the universal questions that lead people into exploring God, eternity, mortality. I sang it at Johnny Cash's funeral so it has a special meaning for me. It was my choice, but his family told me how important that song was to Johnny. It's interesting to me to think of Dylan's Christian phase. I'd done the born-again thing at 17 but I became a backslider pretty quick.

"The music ebbs back and forth like a waltz, but the song's great strength is the text: 'Like criminals, they have choked the breath of conscience and good cheer' – it's Dickensian! I've called him before to talk about songwriting and he's been amazing. On *The Globe Sessions* [*1998*] I'd recorded some songs – including Redemption Day which was definitely inspired by A Hard Rain's A-Gonna Fall. But I got stuck and I called him. He told me to get the band together and play all the old R&B tunes we knew and change them a little and something would happen. Then he sent me this unreleased song – Mississippi. A Dylan tune nobody's heard before! I did a Byrds or Pettyish version and hoped I would get near to what he was thinking. Recording Mississippi was the catalyst for me writing three more songs. It's like playing tennis with someone who's better than you – it brings your game up."

16 Masters Of War

THE FREEWHEELIN' BOB DYLAN, 1963

Not in our name spits a Dylan in angry-young-man-full-of-portent mode.

Loudon Wainwright III (cult folk ironist): "Writing protest songs is difficult because they often have a very limited life-span. But when Dylan sings, 'You can hide behind walls/You can hide behind desks/I just want you to know/I can see through your masks', you instantly think of The White House and Downing Street today. He attacks the biggest targets going, and there's nothing polite about it. It's a young man's rage – outrage really – not Where Have All The Flowers Gone? There's no choruses, and the guitar playing is... it's unrelenting. His guitar playing swings and rocks really hard.

"The writing itself is great. He'll take a word like 'world', which from the perspective of someone who writes songs is a very hard word to rhyme. But he rhymes it with 'hurled', and that's a way around the problem, and it's not just a way around the problem, but it's a great couplet too.

"I remember seeing him for the first time at the Newport Folk festival at about the time this song came out. He was just this young guy stood on stage with a guitar, but he had balls, and any young person will admire someone who has balls. Let's hope so anyway."

15 Tangled Up In Blue

THE BOOTLEG SERIES VOL 1-3, 1991

Doomed love, Dante, a titty bar and the death of the '60s dream.

Gaz Coombes (Supergrass): "I prefer the demo versions to the one on *Blood On The Tracks*. They're quite slow, downbeat versions, and that's what I love. They're just acoustic guitar, bass and vocals and are more emotional and contemplative, whereas the *Blood On The Tracks* version is quite bouncy. He changed a lot of lyrics after this version. The demos are written in the third person, then when you hear it on *Blood On The Tracks* he uses 'I', which makes you wonder if it was about him all along. I discovered *Blood On The Tapes* when a MOJO writer told me about it! So thanks for that..."

14 Mr Tambourine Man

BRINGING IT ALL BACK HOME, 1965

You invent an entirely new kind of song and get called "corny". You can't please some legends...

Sir Paul McCartney: "I know it's corny, but I heard him do it at the Albert Hall *[May 9, 1965]*, and was aching for him to do it and knowing Dylan I thought he may not do it. It was the show where the folkies thought he'd sold out. How crap is that? It was fantastic. First half was folky, and then the second half was electric with The Band. But then somebody starts going, 'He's deserted the folk world!' Yeah, no wonder, look at you mate! I was lucky to be there."

Brian Wilson: "My favourite Bob Dylan song is Mr Tambourine Man because my wife and I sing that to our baby boy, Dylan, every day."

13 Highway 61 Revisited

HIGHWAY 61 REVISITED, 1965

The bible, race and World War III played out along America's jugular vein.

Jon King (Gang Of Four): "When I was 11, the boys in the art classes were allowed to play any music they liked, which was *Highway 61 Revisited* and *Blonde On Blonde*. We didn't have a record player at home, and I'd never heard anything like it. What got me was the sound of his voice: suddenly you had someone who put songs together that played with words – I wasn't sure what he was saying, but I knew he was being brilliantly sarcastic and clever, and sneering at the people who were boring, and I loved it. Highway 61 bisects the American North and South, and represents an escape from the tedium of living a constrained, pre-defined life. But in that text, I saw so much. Like the way he plays with the story, and the whole issue of race. He wasn't trying to be obvious, which is too easy. He was being complicated without being necessarily vague. There was this sense that you were involved in a cultural conversation, and Dylan created the conversations to beat all conversations."

12 Love Sick
TIME OUT OF MIND, 1997

Slashing, rumble-type chords lacerate poor old Bob. Darn it, he's in love again.

Marianne Faithfull: "I heard *Time Out Of Mind* as soon as it came out; I'm a 'rush out and buy Bob' person. I love the whole record, but Love Sick is my favourite. Beautiful. Everything. The words, the melody, the passion in the singing. I loved it immediately. For the longest time I thought it was called I'm Sick Of Love, because that's what he sings. But being love sick and being sick of love are two entirely different things. And yet obviously the same to an old romantic like Mr D. And that is such a brilliant writer's thing to do. Love is hard for all of us but it's very, very hard for an artist. He talks about being tired and hearing the clock tick – this is someone with lots to do, lots of work, he's got no time for anything and on top of that there's this love, and he can't do a thing about it. The lyrics are actually very straightforward. Someone else singing it might make them sound sappy, but the way Dylan sings – very intense and strong and not at all detached – it's a statement, and a great one, about love."

11 The Lonesome Death Of Hattie Carroll
THE TIMES THEY ARE A-CHANGIN', 1964

Socialite whips black servant to death. Is sentenced to hell.

Bill Fay ('70s UK Dylan acolyte): "Just before I started writing, in '64, I started playing guitar by practising The Lonesome Death Of Hattie Carroll. I heard it purely by chance in Bangor as a student, we used to listen to Dylan before he'd filtered into the mainstream. He was so powerful melodically. His voice was amazingly mature for such a young man, but with tracks like Hattie Carroll he was saying something with lovely tunes and a great vocal sound. Take away Dylan's persona and they still stood out. Over the years I've realised that his music is about access. Hattie Carroll? It's five chords. Even in '64 I knew four of them. When you first start out, you can play Dylan. His songs are about the people and for the people so it makes sense that they're accessible. Even a recent track like Mississippi, you can climb inside. There are gems scattered throughout."

"Dylan's songs are about and for the people."

BILL FAY

10 Just Like A Woman
BLONDE ON BLONDE, 1966

Baby's got new clothes, but Bob can see right through them. Or at least he claims to.

Jimmy Webb: "This was when I understood how deep Dylan's well really was. It wasn't a folk song, it wasn't protest, it was just a great love song, which had an immediate impact on me. I had just dropped out of college to commit to the life of a songwriter. I was very much in love with a girl who was inspiring a lot of the music I was writing, and this song seemed to cut to the heart of what I was feeling emotionally at the time. All these years later I still marvel at what an absolutely stunning piece of writing it is.

"What a fortuitous nexus of rhyme and purpose is the chorus: 'She takes just like a woman/She makes love just like a woman/Then she aches just like a woman/But she breaks just like a little girl.' As songwriters we live for the moment when words fall together like that. The way everything leads toward that last line is masterful. That would be enough for most writers, but the third verse reveals Dylan's strategy to be much larger. When he says 'Please don't let on that you knew me whe/I was hungry and it was your world,' he steps on-camera and addresses this person directly to deliver one final twist. There's a lifetime of listening in these details and layered subtleties. Any serious student of songwriting will find a complete education in this one composition."

9 Mississippi
LOVE AND THEFT, 2001

Stately vocal carries a warning from history.

Mississippi was recorded for *Time Out Of Mind*, put to one side, and re-cut for *Love And Theft*. Daniel Lanois, Dylan reckoned, had wanted its treatment to be "sexy, sexy and more sexy" – but Dylan felt such ideas did precious little justice to "knifelike lyrics trying to convey majesty and heroism".

If those words suggested some vainglorious conceit, Mississippi is way more complicated. There is majesty in here, but it's bound up with the power and grace of simple honesty: "Got nothing for you, I had nothing before / Don't even have anything for myself any more." Dylan offers no end of defeats and setbacks, at least one sighing apology, and the quiet triumph of merely having made it through.

Yet though you can get lost in the stanzas rooted in the dread that defined *Time Out Of Mind*, there are glimpses of a new beginning. "Stick with me baby, stick with me anyhow," he implores. And note that upward melodic glide, the redemptive sound of that process known as "starting over".

But as that silver lining starts glinting, he ends with totally barren thoughts. He charms his quarry like an old romantic, then slams the door shut: "Well, the emptiness is endless, cold as the clay." Confused? Of course. Straight answers are not Dylan's business. (JH)

8 It's Alright, Ma (I'm Only Bleeding)
BRINGING IT ALL BACK HOME, 1965

And if his thought-dreams could be seen, they'd put his head upon the guillotine...

David Crosby: "When I first heard Dylan in New York I didn't like his singing. I thought, Why doesn't everybody like me more? But then I went to see him perform and I got it... his songs! They were so good and there was one after another after another. Asking for a favourite is like asking a parent, Hey, which is your favourite child? Bob Dylan has a good three dozen flat-out sterling pieces of material that we can safely refer to as classics. But when I first heard It's Alright, Ma it really was such a knockout. 'Darkness at the break of noon/Shadows even the silver spoon' – hey, that's the apocalypse coming, nothing less."

7 It's All Over Now, Baby Blue
BRINGING IT ALL BACK HOME, 1965

Stately vocal carries a warning from history.

Richard Thompson: "Sounds like it's curtains for Baby Blue, which has led some to speculate that it's an updating of the story of Mary, Queen Of Scots; Bob may have heard Mary, Queen Of Scots' Lament in England in winter '62, or maybe he's just a history buff. She was fond of blue stockings – she wore sky-blue hose with an interwoven silver thread when she was beheaded in 1587. The orphan (or soon to be) 'crying like a fire in the sun' might be her son, and the 'empty-handed painter' her secretary-lover David Rizzio. One might also speculate about the presence of the Earl of Bothwell and her husband, Lord Darnley. The action is shifted to Greenwich Village, and is beautifully updated and made immediate. A great song by someone who knows the tradition, innovates and builds on it."

6 It Ain't Me, Babe
ANOTHER SIDE OF..., 1964

She wants Bob. Is she crazy or sumpin?

Tom McRae (folkish Brit singer-songwriter): "This is no gentle let-down to a former lover... it's a health warning. 'Go away from my window and leave at your own chosen speed,' he sings in a lilting voice, when what he actually means is 'I'm an asshole, you better run'.."

Charlie Sexton (Dylan sideman): "In the past when I've seen BD do a show or when I played with him, at times it seems as if there was a circle of light surrounding him regardless of what the lights in the show are doing. Some songs go through changes and various arrangements but this one changed very little. Except there was always something new from Bob vocally, in phrasing, phrasing that could dazzle Miles Davis."

Dylan relaxes
backstage at the
City Hall, Sheffield,
April 1965.

5 Blind Willie McTell

THE BOOTLEG SERIES VOLUMES 1-3, 1991

Out of Dylan's difficult '80s, a gem buried for a decade.

Martin Carthy (UK folk majordomo): "It blows this massive hole through the romantic notion of the South. It's about corruptibility. And it has an amazing emotional impact, which counts for everything. When he sang Hard Rain in The Troubadour in London in 1962 the audience was thunderstruck. They'd never heard anything like it. To take a songwriting idea like you find in Nottamun Town – a 'song of life' in the folk lingo – and develop it like he did in Hard Rain was absolutely awe-inspiring. I was absolutely stunned. And Blind Willie McTell had the same effect on me. It's everything a song should be. It's concise, it's eloquent and it also happens to be a beautiful piece of music. I love the position of the narrator in the song – sitting in a New Orleans hotel room contemplating the whole history of the south, the murder amid the magnolias, but not with anger for a change. It's a... rumination. A great word for a great song."

4 Desolation Row

HIGHWAY 61 REVISITED, 1965

Post-messianic stress leads to despairing 11-minute state-of-the-nation address.

Roy Harper (eccentric folk veteran): "Desolation Row, I thought when I heard it, That's exactly where we're at. It contained all the elements of where civilisation had been for years, but wasn't delivered with the overt sense of humour of his earlier songs. Dylan was no longer the carefree young vibe thief of the freewheelin' age. He was expected to be the next messiah, just as he was becoming more human. There were rumours of hard drugs and self-examination. Like a lot of us, he was floundering.

"The more I thought of it, the more Desolation Row seemed a collection of impressions thrown at a page. It was riveting, desperate. I could identify with that. It called the world to account. The song was a delineation, a final notice of departure. We all know the characters the song describes. The Millais painting of the drowned Ophelia lingers in my mind, dead in the head at 22, living vicariously, peeping into Desolation Row for moments of delicious embarrassment, only to resume her role in some Salvation Army equivalent. Robin Hood, Cinderella, Bette Davis etc, they're all there along with a million inferences about the humdrum of seedy human life, usually set at midnight and beyond, while daytime insurance men check that no one escapes to Desolation Row. And then there's the last verse written by someone on the outside. A token note from someone who's no longer part of the scene, who misses the freedom, but who perhaps couldn't handle the hand-to-mouth abandonment, or perhaps the grime. We never get to find out. And it doesn't matter. It never did. And it never will."

3 Sad Eyed Lady Of The Lowlands

BLONDE ON BLONDE, 1966

Eleven minutes-plus of serpentine psychodrama. It goes on and on and on.

Al Kooper (Dylan sideman, philosopher): "This is what 4am sounds like. We recorded it at that hour – but many tracks have been transported to tape then and none proclaims its birthtime as saliently as this. An amazing song, a brilliant reading, an incandescent author – and when had we heard of a mercury mouth, a magazine husband, warehouse eyes, streetcar visions that you place on the grass, sheet metal memories of Cannery Row, and of course, your Arabian drum? Never before, I believe.

"Using simple chords in new patterns, he wove his tale for over 11 minutes, but I defy you to stop in the middle to answer the phone. It's riveting: that voice and harmonica, the intricacies of musicians who had laboured for the likes of George Jones and Tammy Wynette suddenly challenged to provide musical sets for a play they'd never seen or heard before, and rising to the occasion with bravado."

Robert Wyatt: "For years I promised Alfie [*Wyatt's wife of 30 years, Alfreda Benge*] that I'd cover it for her. I think she knows I'll never do that now but maybe, when Alfie's forgotten all about it, I will. One of the things I like about jazz is that it goes on and on and on. This song has that kind of momentum. It builds and grows, builds and grows, and it's a simple structure. Another thing that's so great about it is the band on it, Al Kooper's on Hammond, and they roll along, beautiful. Alfie read somewhere that (*laughs*) he didn't tell them how long the song was going to be, so they keep thinking they're coming to the ending, surging towards an end, which is brilliant, Miles Davis-like in its wickedness. And then he'll drone away another verse! So they're playing as if... they keep building towards the climax, all the time! I suppose it's like very clever sex, really."

2 Positively 4th Street

GREATEST HITS VOL.1, 1967

Dylan's most shocking put-down: "You'd rather see me paralysed!"

Johnny Echols (Love): "It deals with the duplicity of human beings and the nebulous nature of friendship. It's an incredibly important thing to cling on to in life. I knew that even back in 1965 when this came out. I immediately connected with Dylan's take on humanity and the nature of hypocrisy. He spoke to me. It's a very New York song but it made perfect sense out on the West Coast. After Dylan went over big you could feel the style of music changing everywhere. Previously, songs sort of went from C to A minor to F to G in a prescribed pattern but with Bob coming from folk music, the songs started to follow wherever the vocal melody went. It had a huge effect on everybody."

Like A Rolling Stone

HIGHWAY 61 REVISITED, 1965

The song that kicked-started the counter-culture revolution.

IN MAY 1965 Bob Dylan quit music. Having completed the UK tour recorded in the movie *Don't Look Back* and holidayed in Portugal, he fell ill in London. The nature of his sickness is a mystery, but it brought on a fit of self-evaluation so serious that Dylan concluded it was time to get out — of music and, by extension, the hysteria that was increasingly surrounding him.

Over the previous weeks, news had arrived of snowballing success in the USA. Subterranean Homesick Blues was in the US Top 40, *Bringing It All Back Home* was about to enter the Top 10 and The Byrds were turning heads with their reading of Mr Tambourine Man. Dylan was facing a new kind of celebrity: if *Don't Look Back* finds him burned out, he now had to prepare for much, much worse.

So he decided to leave his guitar behind, fade into the background, and try his hand at poetry or drama. Yet he could not bury the urge to create: upon his return to the States, he soon came up with a verbal splurge that suggested a mind flying towards hyperactivity. "It was 10 pages long," he recalled in 1966. "It wasn't called anything, just a rhythm thing on paper all about my steady hatred directed at some point that was honest. In the end it wasn't hatred, it was telling someone something that they didn't know, telling them they were lucky. Revenge, that's a better word."

"I had never thought of it as a song," he added, "until one day I was at the piano, and on the paper it was singing, 'How does it feel?' in a slow motion pace... it was like swimming in lava. In your eyesight, you see your victim swimming in lava. Hanging by their arms from a birch tree. Skipping, kicking the tree, hitting a nail with your foot. Seeing someone in the pain they were bound to meet up with."

This was Like A Rolling Stone, written over a few days in a rented cabin in Woodstock. Upon its completion, Dylan found his enthusiasm revived, and forgot about quitting music. Here, after all, was the sound of a world way beyond Blowin' In The Wind and The Times They Are A-Changin' — a place that made even the likes of Mr Tambourine Man and It's All Over Now Baby Blue seem rather fusty and square. In time, the song would work its liberating wonders on Dylan's audience — but the first person it set free was the author himself.

"Everything is changed now from before," he said in the autumn of '65. This was after Newport, where he had made his debut electric guitar performance — effectively bidding farewell to the folk scene in the process. "Last spring, I guess I was going to quit singing. I was very drained... playing a lot of songs I didn't want to play. I was singing songs I didn't want to sing. But Like A Rolling Stone changed it all. It was something I myself could dig. It's very tiring having other people tell you how much they dig you if you yourself don't dig you."

Superficially, the song's lyric dealt with an unnamed debutante who had fallen from the heights of wealth and status into a new life as a borderline vagrant — indeed, the lyric is packed with enough bile to suggest that, as far as Dylan was concerned, the song's subject had got her just desserts: "People'd call, say, Beware doll, you're bound to fall/You thought they were all/Kiddin' you... You used to laugh about/Everybody that was hangin' out/Now you don't talk so loud..."

Nonetheless, because of its chorus, the song combined such sentiments with a real sense of sudden freedom: as if life on the street, striking a deal with the "mystery tramp" and pawning one's possessions represented the possibility of a new authentic life. The original proponents of such a vision had been the Beat poets, who had exerted quite an influence on Dylan's development; by 1966, scores of American youths would be joyously pouring towards San Francisco to follow their example and experience the joys of deliberate poverty and drug-assisted mind-expansion. In that sense, Like A Rolling Stone marks the passing of the baton: Dylan shouting out the life-code of Ginsberg, Kerouac et al and awakening a new generation.

The song was put to tape over two days, on July 15 and 16, 1965. Initially, Dylan offered it as a piano-based waltz, which rather compromised the song's devil-may-care abandon. However, soon enough it settled into a fluid 4/4 template and was stretched to six minutes. Dylan already had a reputation for recording his songs at breakneck speed, but this one was the focus of a rare perfectionism: having failed to nail it on the first day, the musicians were called back to work on at least nine further takes.

AS FAR AS its music was concerned, it turned a corner when Al Kooper — who came to the sessions hoping to play guitar — sneaked behind an organ and added the exultant riff that cemented the brilliance of Dylan's chorus. According to Howard Sounes's Dylan biography, Dylan's producer Tom Wilson was initially reluctant to bring up Kooper's part in the mix. Fortunately, Dylan disagreed.

Thus, Like A Rolling Stone was completed — and released little more than a month later. It soon reached the top of the Billboard charts, and made its way to Number 4 in the UK. In its poise, its freewheeling arrangement and its unprecedented length, it opened the gates to a new era: one in

> ## "Everything is changed now from before."
> **DYLAN**

which the fripperies of pop would be superseded by the meld of counter-cultural cool and cerebral depth that made up rock music.

Paul McCartney first heard it on a visit to John Lennon in Weybridge: he later remembered "a song that seemed to go on and on forever – it was just beautiful". To a teenaged Bruce Springsteen, it sounded no less magical: "I knew that I was listening to the toughest voice I had ever heard."

The story of Like A Rolling Stone did not end there. It has been a dependable feature of Dylan's live sets ever since, changing context and meaning as its author's career has swerved in new directions. On the Manchester Free Trade Hall tape released as *Live 1966*, it stands as a statement of defiance, aimed at the Luddite aspect of his audience who resented him going electric. On 1974's *Before The Flood* its impassioned reading stands as proof of Dylan's continued vitality, a quality furthered when he plays it live nowadays: it's a sacred signature tune, a sign of Dylan's unchanged artistic essence.

Thirty-seven years after the release of Like A Rolling Stone, the question of who exactly the song is about continues to bug Dylan specialists. Candidates include Joan Baez, Dylan's '65-era road buddy Bobby Neuwirth, and the gorgeous Andy Warhol associate Edie Sedgwick. But such theories miss one crucial point: given that the song was written when Dylan had settled on leaving his celebrity behind, its abiding spirit – if not the forensic details of its lyric – is unquestionably a reflection of the author himself, a point only underlined by the spine-tingling live readings mentioned above. Whenever he plays it, the audience is party to one of rock music's most compelling presences – a figure who, in 1965, had the unique ability to single-handedly push rock music into completely virgin territory. *John Harris*

Just shading it: Dylan recording at Columbia Studios, New York, 1965.

The Lost Songs

Out-takes, leftovers, alternative versions – Dylan's career is full of them. But which ones are worth hearing? Peter Doggett guides you through Dylan rarities.

SINCE THE BIRTH of the bootleg industry in the late 1960s, Dylan collectors have traded unreleased performances like stockbrokers on heat. In recent years, the bottomless potential of the Never Ending Tour has dominated the underground community. But nothing Dylan has managed since 1988 could rival the excitement that would be sparked by the discovery of a fresh set of '60s or '70s studio out-takes, especially if the material were unavailable elsewhere.

Even after a series of authorised archive explorations, such as *Biograph* and the ongoing *Bootleg Series*, hundreds of Dylan compositions have still escaped an official release. Many of these are fragmentary, unfinished or inconsequential, but dozens deserve a wider circulation...

The Troubadour Songs

Dylan hit Manhattan in 1961 as the reincarnation of Woody Guthrie, "my first and last hero". Besides Guthrie's vocal mannerisms, and a fair percentage of his song catalogue, Dylan borrowed his mentor's full palette of troubadour imagery and created a fictitious past that he peddled to journalists and record company alike.

Long Time Gone from 1962 captured the essence of Dylan's manufactured outsiderdom. "My mind got mixed with ramblin' when I was all so young," he lamented, before noting pertinently: "You can have your youth, it'll rot before your eyes." It was an equally jaded adolescence that he celebrated in the train-hopping tale of **Ballad For A Friend** (alias **Reminiscence Blues**), a January 1962 demo that ended when (like the protagonist of I Dreamed I Saw St Augustine five years later) "I hung my head and stole away".

Whatcha Gonna Do, an irrepressibly perky *Freewheelin'*... out-take, recycled some vintage blues clichés, while **Ain't A-Gonna Grieve** was a thinly disguised rewrite of a traditional spiritual tune. Likewise, **Ramblin' Down Through The World** was a blatant adaptation of a Guthrie original, Ramblin' Round, while Woody might also have recognised the scenario of 1963's **Dusty Old Fairgrounds**. Perhaps Dylan's most perfect evocation of the outlaw spirit,

however, came on January 1964's **Guess I'm Doin' Fine**, which read like a celebration of life beyond the edge, but sounded like the confession of a man who'd rambled once too often.

The Protest Songs

It was the finger-pointing poet of protest that the world first took to its heart, but Dylan's catalogue of early-'60s complaints about racism, militarism and other societal sins wasn't exhausted by the plethora of such tunes on *The Freewheelin' Bob Dylan* and *The Times They Are A-Changin'*. Mainstream audiences never heard **I'd Hate To Be You On That Dreadful Day**, for instance, an apocalyptic comedy that used imagery Dylan would employ for real during his 'born again' period. **The Death Of Emmett Till** and **The Ballad Of Donald White** were both released by Dylan, but only under his alter ego of Blind Boy Grunt, on a barely circulated compilation, so these studies of murder and its consequences might as well have remained unissued.

Maybe the archetypal Dylan protest tune, however, though far from the most convincing, was **Long Ago, Far Away**, a catch-all lament about poverty, lynching, war, slavery and (just for good measure) Christ's crucifixion. Taken to verbal extremes, this inclusive approach could result in a song as crass as **You Bin Hidin' Too Long**, sung only once in April 1963, and useful as a dictionary definition of self-righteousness.

Songs Of Romance

The lifestyles of a hobo and prophet allowed little time for romance, although Dylan's early albums were sprinkled with occasional adventures of the heart. But it was his fourth record, *Another Side Of Bob Dylan*, that signalled a shift in perspective to the interior worlds of the bedroom and the mind.

It Ain't Me Babe was Dylan's definitive statement on the illusions of romance, but he had already anticipated its theme in a verse of **Hero Blues**, taped and then rejected during both the *Freewheelin'*... and *Times*... sessions of 1962-63. When it came to undercutting the conventions of the romantic pop song, however, **Love Is Just A Four-Letter Word** –

gifted to his then-partner Joan Baez in 1964 – swept the field with its mixture of ecstatic, almost religious imagery and verbose naivety. Dylan probably realised the song's faults, as he never recorded it himself.

The Birth Of Surrealism

Having rejected political solutions to the insanity of daily existence, Dylan sought a new language to express his alienation and amusement. He found it in the deranged sensory perceptions of poets such as Rimbaud and Baudelaire, and the exaggerated imagery of Allen Ginsberg. When he combined those literary influences with his own mind expansion, Dylan quickly escaped into a playground of the imagination. There were hints of this approach as early as 1963, when he debuted the freeform boogie-woogie of **Bob Dylan's New Orleans Rag**, a tale of exotic doings on Rampart Street.

He refined the style when he reworked Corrina Corrine into 1964's **Denise** ("are you flying or have you flipped?"). But it was *Bringing It All Back Home* and *Highway 61 Revisited* that honed his surrealism into an artform. Two pre-electric tryouts from these albums, **California** and **You Don't Have To Do That** (listed on the session sheet as Bending Down On My Stomach Looking West), looked clearly ahead to the verbal madness to come – with California bequeathing an entire verse, and its skeletal tune, to Outlaw Blues, cut merely a day later.

1965-66 Out-Takes

After the day of acoustic adjustment that opened the *Bringing It All Back Home* sessions in January 1965, Dylan flicked the switch and went electric. Across the next 14 months, he cut four LPs' worth of astonishing music, plus a clutch of singles and some legendary out-takes – most of which later surfaced on *Biograph* and *The Bootleg Series*.

What remains in the vaults is a mix of teasing fragments and throwaways, mostly detritus alongside the jewelled delights of the official albums. Take **Lunatic Princess Revisited**, for instance, attempted during the session that produced Like A Rolling Stone, which extends to little more than

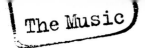

a verse of disconnected images tied to a non-existent melody. Or **Medicine Sunday**, equally lightweight bar a chorus line bequeathed to Temporary Like Achilles. Then there's the extended blues metaphor of **Long Distance Operator**, debuted at late 1965 shows, or the long, gorgeous but ultimately non-revealing instrumental track bootlegged as Number One. None of it matches the fantasy of a lost electric album.

Unfinished Songs

Church With No Upstairs is one of a series of titles rumoured to date from songwriting sessions with The Band's guitarist, Robbie Robertson, between the composing of *Blonde On Blonde* and the fateful bike crash of summer 1966. Journalist Robert Shelton taped them rambling through a semi-improvised tune inspired by a painting by Van Gogh. A majestic stream of unconsciousness, it lent heavily on the structure of Desolation Row, while awaiting a killer hook of any kind. Shelton also recorded fragments of two other songs, possibly titled **If You Want My Love** and **Don't Tell Him**.

Two months later, the camera crew documenting Dylan's 1966 European tour captured another collaboration in Glasgow. One song, copyrighted as **On A Rainy Afternoon**, revealed a melody inspired by Bobby Bland's gorgeous blues ballad, Share Your Love With Me. **What Kind Of Friend Is This** provided fresh lyrics for Koko Taylor's blues tune of almost identical title, while **I Can't Leave Her Behind** was cut tantalisingly short, just at the moment when it threatened to become a Dylan classic.

The Basement Tapes

The *Basement Tapes* sessions of 1967 have passed into mythology as a celebration of Americana. But the impetus for this intensive bout of recording seems to have been a series of urgent requests from Dylan's music publishers, who were desperate for new material after 12 months of silence.

The transition from woodshedding to home recording to publishing demos to bootlegs has been traced many times. Yet the initial batch of *Basement...* tunes circulated by Dylan's publishers didn't come close to exhausting his output from those sessions. Gradually, collectors uncovered songs such as **Get Your Rocks Off**, a slow, sleazy piece of urban blues ignored by Robbie Robertson when he compiled the official LP in 1975. Also neglected was the remarkable **Sign On The Cross**, a strange cross between an Otis Redding ballad and a Hank Williams monologue, which veered back and forth from profound spirituality to comedy. Oddest of all Dylan's creations during this period was **I'm Not There (1956)**, which found him mumbling enigmatically in tongues like an indecipherable prophet.

Only two decades after the fact did other Dylan originals from this period emerge – **All You Have To Do Is Dream**, for instance, a compelling mixture of *Nashville Skyline* country and funk, or the equally unclassifiable **I Can't Make It Alone** and **Gonna Get You Now**. Some titles, such as **Wild Wolf**, remain

With Robbie Robertson (right) and Mickey Jones in Scotland, 1966 – possibly on a rainy afternoon.

a mystery; others, like **I Was Your Teenage Prayer**, were no more sensible than their titles. But *The Basement Tapes* also threw up such oddball offerings as **Bourbon Street**, a duet for drunkard and tipsy tuba; or **Silent Weekend**, a lazy blues tune that could have been written for Charlie Rich.

Harrisongs And Giveaways

On the run from The Beatles after the sessions for their 1968 double album, George Harrison holed up with Dylan and his family for the end of the year. He returned to London with a sheaf of new Dylan compositions, some of which he paraded in front of his uninspired bandmates. The following year, Harrison recorded one Dylan co-write, **I'd Have You Anytime**, and demoed another new Bob tune, the folky **I Don't Want To Do It** – though he didn't release it for another 15 years.

In late spring 1970, Harrison and Dylan collaborated again in New York, jamming through an array of oldies, from Yesterday to Gates Of Eden. Along the way, Dylan improvised two new compositions: the two-verse blues **Telephone Wire** and the mildly satirical **Working On A Guru** – a subject suggested, perhaps, by his English friend's devotion to all things mystic. Neither song justified being revisited at a later date, and neither ever was.

Likewise, there's no evidence that Dylan ever cut his own versions of two co-written songs from this period, **Wanted Man** (with Johnny Cash) and **Champaign, Illinois** (with Carl Perkins). Both exhibited a playful vacation spirit, as if Dylan was luxuriating in the chance to be anyone other than himself.

Pat Garrett Out-Takes

It took persistent lobbying from Kris Kristofferson to persuade cantankerous auteur Sam Peckinpah to cast Dylan in his Western, Pat Garrett And Billy The

Kid, and allow the musician to score the movie. Peckinpah's suspicions of this flaky rock star can't have been assuaged by Dylan's initial musical suggestions. Down in Mexico he cut one complete song, Billy, several instrumentals (such as **Pecos Blues**), plus a lachrymose chant, **Goodbye Holly**. Further sessions in New York yielded the one enduring soundtrack contribution, Knockin' On Heaven's Door, plus several semi-improvised vocal refrains that didn't make the album, including **Rock Me Mama** and **Sweet Amarillo**, but which tapped beautifully into the cowboy ethos that Peckinpah was simultaneously celebrating and undercutting.

Lost In The '70s

After three years of virtual silence, Dylan returned in 1974 with *Planet Waves*. This collaboration with The Band also spawned a long-lost instrumental, **Crosswind Jamboree**, and a revival of **House Of The Rising Sun** from Dylan's debut LP.

With the exception of Up To Me, exposed later on the *Biograph* collection, the sessions for *Blood On The Tracks* concentrated on the songs that were released. But the notebook containing the album's provisional lyrics also included drafts of titles such as **Bell Tower Blues** and **It's Breaking Me Up**, which might exist in demo form somewhere in Dylan's own archive.

The sessions for late 1975's *Desire* were chronicled in Larry Sloman's superb book, On The Road With Bob Dylan. This account remains our only hint of the existence of a song called **Wiretappin'**, although another out-take from this era, **Money Blues**, is in circulation among collectors. *Desire* morphed seamlessly into the doomed celluloid extravaganza that was Renaldo And Clara. To fill out the soundtrack to this four-hour epic, Dylan cut songs such as the lugubrious **Patty's Gone To Laredo**, and the celebratory **Catfish**, neither of which has ever escaped on to a legal record release.

After a two-year pause to consider the claims of debt and divorce, Dylan began work in late 1977 on the project that became *Street Legal*. At this stage, the album was projected to include a tune called **First To Say Goodbye**, although it never seems to have made it as far as the studio. Neither did another bluesy offering from this period, **Legionnaire's Disease**, which was gifted to Billy Cross, the guitarist in Dylan's road band.

The Helena Springs Collaborations

For almost a decade between the late '70s and the late '80s, Dylan employed a succession of female singers in his touring bands. One of them, Carolyn Dennis, eventually became his wife; another, Clydie King, also enjoyed a close personal relationship with Dylan; while a third, Helena Springs, had the privilege of becoming one of his first regular songwriting partners.

Springs joined Dylan in January 1978, during early rehearsals for his world tour, and a month later, in

Australia, he offered to help her complete several songs she had begun to write. At least six, and possibly as many as a dozen, titles emerged from this collaboration, none of which Dylan has ever released. He cut demos of several, however, offering **Coming From The Heart**, **If I Don't Be There By Morning**, **Walk Out In The Rain** and **Stop Now** to Eric Clapton – who duly cut the first three for his *Backless* LP. Stop Now was arguably the most compelling of this quartet, its stop-start blues structure coming closest to Dylan's own style. Another collaboration, **I Must Love You Too Much**, joined **Coming From The Heart** as an occasional cameo in Dylan's late 1978 US tour. But the most enduring of the Dylan/Springs songs was another sweaty slice of urban blues, **You Treat Me Like A Stepchild**, which Dylan both recorded in his Rundown Studios suite and then took out on the road for several months.

A second batch of Dylan/Springs songs was demoed in summer 1979, possibly without Dylan's vocal involvement. They included **More Than Flesh And Blood**, **Tell Me The Truth One Time** and **The Wandering Kind**, though none of these songs ever entered Dylan's own repertoire.

Born-Again Bob

Dylan's conversion to Christianity in 1979 would prompt his most intensive spell of writing since the mid-'60s. Besides the songs that filled the *Slow Train Coming* and *Saved* albums, and the more spiritual contributions to 1981's *Shot Of Love*, Dylan also performed or recorded at least 10 other songs inspired by his new relationship with Christ. They ranged from minor adaptations of traditional gospel material, such as **Blessed Is The Name**, to rewritings of scripture, such as **No Man Righteous (No, Not One)**, an out-take from the *Slow Train Coming* sessions.

Although critics and fans alike were often contemptuous of his new direction, no objective listener could doubt the passionate conviction of Dylan's performances during this era. Nothing proved the point more powerfully than **Ain't Gonna Go To Hell For Anybody** – one of three new songs, alongside **I Will Love Him** and the bluesy funk of **Cover Down, Break Through** – introduced into his repertoire in April 1980. Ain't Gonna Go To Hell For Anybody not only utilised the full dynamics of his live band, but night after night drove Dylan to a feverish pitch of vocal intensity.

Other "born-again" songs, such as **City Of Gold**, **Jesus Is The One** and the only-aired-once **Thief On The Cross** also managed to convey some of the depth of Dylan's spiritual immersion. But one of his greatest songs from this era never made it to the stage, or beyond the rehearsal studio. **Yonder Comes Sin**, which briefly surfaced around September 1980, was a supercharged parade of mankind's iniquity, told with the kind of humour and attention to detail last found on *Desire*. But Dylan clearly had problems with the song, vetoing its inclusion on *The Bootleg Series* a decade later.

'80s Out-Takes

Like most artists of his generation, Dylan foundered as recording technology underwent a revolution in the '80s. The last of his albums to be recorded strictly under the old regime – live band, no overdubbing – was 1981's *Shot Of Love*. Sadly omitted from that album was his reconciliation plea, **Let's Keep It Between Us**, debuted on stage the previous year and later recorded by Bonnie Raitt.

In a 1981 interview, Dylan announced his intention to attempt an entirely instrumental record, which probably explains his decision to cut a series of vocal-less tracks in April 1981, with titles such as **Walkin' On Eggs** and **Straw Hat**. That same month, he also cut tentative versions of more songs that were never aired again, including **Fur Slippers**, **Ah Ah Ah**, **Yes Sir No Sir** and **Magic**. The last of these, built around the guitar intro from Chuck Berry's Brown-Eyed Handsome Man, was a fiery piece of funk that might conceivably have translated into a hit single if he'd ever perfected it.

From the 1983 sessions for *Infidels* onwards, Dylan had to contend with producers and their whims. But no producer could have rescued **Julius And Ethel**, a banal ditty about the Rosenberg atom bomb "spies" of the 1950s. **Who Loves You More**, written a few months later, was no better. Dylan hadn't abandoned his instrumental concept, either, copyrighting pieces such as **Dark Groove** and **Don't Fly Unless It's Safe**. To promote *Infidels*, Dylan played a stadium tour, where he debuted the never-recorded **Enough Is Enough** and rehearsed, but never completed, a haunting tune possibly entitled **Almost Done** (which may describe its state rather than its contents). Live shows and rehearsals also gave a platform to the bluesy **Shake** (1985) and **To Fall In Love With You** (1986).

Between 1984 and the return to form of *Oh Mercy* in 1989, Dylan's studio sessions resulted in a morass of cover versions and re-recordings. With playwright Sam Shepard, he wrote the magnificent **New Danville Girl** for 1985's *Empire Burlesque*, and then chose to abandon it for a year before it emerged rewritten as Brownsville Girl on *Knocked Out Loaded*.

Tight-Lipped In The '90s

After a decade in which Dylan's studio sessions leaked like a drain, some degree of security was imposed on his recording environment in the '90s. With the exception of the unmemorable Traveling Wilburys out-take **Like A Ship**, no unissued Dylan songs have surfaced since 1990. That leaves collectors salivating over the prospect of one day hearing the excess material apparently tackled during the sessions for *Time Out Of Mind* in 1997, such as **Red River Shore** and **No Turning Back**, and collaborations with other artists such as Gene Simmons of Kiss (**Laughing When You Want To Cry**), Danny O'Keefe (**Well Well Well**) and the Was Brothers (**Shirley Temple Doesn't Live Here Anymore**).

Down The Highway

Further highs, lows and more than a few oddities... the rest of the Bob Dylan catalogue assessed. By John Harris & David Sheppard.

Bob Dylan
1962

Welcome aboard. Dylan is little more than 20, freshly arrived in New York, and transparently in thrall to Woody Guthrie. The voice is a little mannered, the guitar playing a mite clumsy – but his talent still shines. Most of the songs (House Of The Rising Sun, She's No Good) are covers; Dylan's own peak with the assuredly touching Song To Woody. Baby, Let Me Follow You Down, charmingly, contains a spoken dedication to one Ric Von Schmidt, who taught Dylan the song.

The Times They Are A-Changin'
1964

The last of the protest albums, featuring the globally familiar title track, Ballad Of Hollis Brown, Only A Pawn In Their Game and Lonesome Death Of Hattie Carroll. Quietly, his split from Suze Rotolo is traced in the 3am melancholia of One Too Many Mornings – the most beguiling thing here. That aside, perhaps a little earnest: the cover photo says it all.

Another Side Of Bob Dylan
1964

Here the earnest, politicking Bob Dylan comes a cropper, and our hero regenerates into an altogether looser, hipper individual. The transition is commemorated in My Back Pages ("I was so much older then, I'm younger than that now"), and also marked by the "I've had a weed" giggliness of All I Really Want To Do. Often overlooked, if not forgotten, but well worth purchasing for the hilarious Motorpsycho Nitemare alone.

Self Portrait
1970

Prompted the most famous album review in history: the Rolling Stone piece that began, "What is this shit?". Fair point, frankly: *Self Portrait* was Dylan's oddball attempt to destroy his own myth, again, stuffed with music that is fascinatingly bad. Features a cover of Paul Simon's The Boxer, cuts from the Isle Of Wight set and a song entitled All The Tired Horses on which female backing vocalists warble equestrian nonsense about horses. Thanks, Bob.

New Morning
1970

The album that encapsulates Dylan's Woodstock period, so much so that its title track mentions roosters, rabbits and a "country mile". Often overlooked, perhaps on account of its cornball sleeve, and yet host to a handful of masterstrokes: Sign On The Window, If Not For You, Time Passes Slowly. One to play when the sun's out.

Pat Garrett & Billy The Kid
1973

Incidental music for the epic cowboy flick (Dylan had a peripheral role as the enigmatic Alias). The music – mostly acoustic rambles based on yearning aural themes – fits the idea of frontier America perfectly. As does Knockin' On Heaven's Door, one of three proper songs here, along with the cleverly titled Billy 4 and Billy 7. Recorded not in the Wild West but Burbank, California.

Man with no name: Dylan as Alias in Sam Peckinpah's 1973 film Pat Garrett And Billy The Kid.

Dylan
1973

Off-cuts, mostly from *Self Portrait*, assembled by a record company smarting from Dylan's temporary departure to the Asylum label. "Guaranteed to net only horselaughs," claimed Rolling Stone. Now deleted – so it's actually quite difficult to own the recording of Dylan doing Joni Mitchell's Big Yellow Taxi, Mr Bojangles or Can't Help Falling In Love. Though that's not necessarily a bad thing.

Planet Waves
1974

The only Bob Dylan album recorded in full with The Band. Not bad at all – pointing, in retrospect, towards the full-blown renaissance confirmed by *Blood On The Tracks* and *Desire*. Proof is provided by Forever Young alone, but there's also On A Night Like This, You Angel You and Never Say Goodbye. Plus Dylan's pretty weird sleeve art. Whether as a joke or not, the sleeve spells Richard Manuel's surname "Manual".

Street Legal
1978

Alleged to mark Dylan's first steps towards apocalyptic christianity: "Eden is burning," goes Changing Of The Guards. But it's rushed, even by Dylan's standards – backing vocalists fluff lines, sax players audibly miss their cue. Also, Dylan's voice is starting to get a little too nasal. That said, it's home to Senor (Tales Of Yankee Power) and Baby, Stop Crying, so not exactly a howler.

Saved
1980

Like *Slow Train Coming*, recorded at Muscle Shoals studios, co-produced by Jerry Wexler, and oozing born-again ferocity (A Satisfied Mind, in fact, suggests Dylan playing a vicar in a black American gospel service). By this time, unfortunately, the devil seems to have regained all the best tunes, though Solid Rock has a certain fiery something. The sleeve painting – God picking out only the "chosen" ones – is rather nauseating.

Infidels
1983

Rather spoiled by Dylan's bizarre decision to dump a clutch of great songs – including (the godlike Blind Willie McTell) – in favour of inferior substitutes. The second instalment of Paul Williams' book *Bob Dylan: Performing Artist* tells you how to use bits of *The Bootleg Series Vol III* to create the *Infidels* that could have been; this album is still no disaster, yet you can't help but feel frustrated.

Empire Burlesque
1985

Mixed by New York techno pioneer Arthur Baker and featuring bass/drums godheads Sly & Robbie. Empire Burlesque begins with the deeply '80s but entertainingly breezy skankabout Tight Connection To My Heart (which was much played by the radio at the time), but fails to scrape even modest heights thereafter, chiefly on account of hideous drum sounds which make Jan Hammer sound like Merle Haggard.

Shot Of Love
1981

The worst Dylan sleeve of all time (apart from *Empire Burlesque*), suggestive of a poor Roy Lichtenstein pastiche. It belies the music contained herein; mostly, a marked improvement on *Saved* – as evidenced by the title track, Heart Of Mine, the R&B stomp-in The Groom's Still Waiting At The Altar and confirmed classic Every Grain Of Sand, talked about in hushed terms by Bono and several thousand other Dylan fans.

Knocked Out Loaded
1986

The malaise continues. Pretty horrid echo-laden production, and gospel-esque female backing vocals (some courtesy of Bob's on-off squeeze Carolyn Dennis), which very rarely help Dylan much. Worse, he gets a choir of kids in to sing on the born-again throwback They Killed Him. All that said, contains the top-hole Brownsville Girl, so all is not lost. The Rolling Stones' Ron Wood also features on the album.

Down In The Groove
1988

Sorry and all that, but this is rubbish. Begins with a karaoke-esque reading of Let's Stick Together – which is gut-bustingly hilarious on account of its awfulness – and proceeds accordingly. The Ugliest Girl In The World manages to sound like the woman of the title; Silvio, still included in the live set, just about suggests a faint glimmer of hope. It was time for a creative rebirth. And guess what happened?

The Traveling Wilburys 1988

As supergroups go, the late-'80s teaming of Dylan, George Harrison, Roy Orbison, Tom Petty and Jeff Lynne was sufficiently super. Lynne always seemed a tad Walter Mitty-ish in such company and his sterile production neuters some good songs on this, the first of the stellar cartel's two albums. Only the Harrison-fronted Handle With Care really transcends – though Dylan's highlight, Tweeter And The Monkey Man, is a laugh-out-loud Bruce Springsteen parody.

Under The Red Sky 1990

In the light of its excellent predecessor, *Oh Mercy*, this is something of a clanger. Produced by the Was Brothers, it features George Harrison, David Crosby (mercifully in post cocaine/gun mode), Al Kooper, Bruce Hornsby, Stevie Ray Vaughan, Jimmy Vaughan and Elton John (among others). None of them can breathe much life into things – although Wiggle Wiggle is endearingly daft. "Wiggle wiggle like a big fat snake," Bob grunts.

Good As I Been To You 1992

And so the unthinkable happens: Dylan gets writer's block. In response, he appeases the folkies, 27 years too late, by recording the first of two acoustic albums of trad folk songs – Blackjack Davey, Arthur McBride, You're Gonna Quit Me. The voice is noticeably shot, but age-old intrigue manages to burn through. Best appreciated in the context of Harry Smith's *Anthology Of American Folk Music*.

World Gone Wrong 1993

A similar set to its predecessor, which may just have the edge. One reason alone is Dylan's fascinating sleevenotes – proving that articulating the majesty and mystery of this music is not the sole preserve of Greil Marcus. Sleeve photographed at a Camden Restaurant; Dylan's text also claims the Never Ending Tour ended in 1991, succeeded by the Money Never Runs Out Tour. Tee hee.

Masked And Anonymous
2003

The movie Masked And Anonymous starred Dylan as a post-apocalyptic troubadour called, toe-curlingly, Jack Fate. The soundtrack, though bizarre, has its moments, teaming Dylan and his hot and bluesy touring band's reworkings of catalogue gems such as Down In The Flood and Cold Irons Bound, alongside other artists' takes on Dylan, ranging from the sublime (Los Lobos' On A Night Like This) to the ridiculous (Articolo Thirty-One's Italian rap version of Like A Rolling Stone).

For the kids: Dylan,
MTV Unplugged,
18 November 1994,
Sony Music Studios,
New York.

The Live Albums

Bob Dylan At Budokan 1979

Pre-conversion, Dylan recruits a huge band and heads for the Far East. After the rough-edged glory of Rolling Thunder, this is smooth to the point of bland-out, and Dylan sounds like a dinosaur enemy of the punks.

Real Live 1984

Oh lord. Dylan recruits a band including ex-Stone Mick Taylor and erstwhile Face Ian McLagan, plays a golden oldies set and manages to sound like the very epitome of aged rock boredom. Proof of just how awful the lion's share of Dylan's '80s were.

Dylan And The Dead 1989

The nadir of Dylan's career, from the cover downwards. The vocals are rotten, but there is frankly no excuse for The Grateful Dead's complete inability to get their heads round the fact that Dylan's songs require a bit of fluidity and grace. "Boom, crash, weegle-deegle," they go.

The 30th Anniversary Concert Celebration 1992

The stars gather at Madison Square Garden to cover Bobtunes. Some (including Booker T And The MG's Gotta Serve Somebody) are good, some are rotten; strangely, the most exciting thing is Ron Wood's

reading of Seven Days. Eventually, Dylan comes on and sings, sounding as if he's injured. Very odd.

MTV Unplugged 1994

A rather perfunctory stroll through old chestnuts (Tombstone Blues, The Times They Are A-Changin') and the odd unexpected tune (Dignity, jettisoned from Oh Mercy, and John Brown). As is usually the case with Unpluggeds, singularly devoid of atmosphere, thanks to the probable presence of Sony's entire New York payroll – who sound like they're having a right old laugh.

The Bootleg Series, Vol 4: Bob Dylan Live 1966 1998

A fact: at any one time, there is at least one High Fidelity-esque conversation taking place somewhere about whether this is The Greatest Rock Album Ever Made. It might be: the fluid, white-hot din on the second CD (Tell Me, Momma, I Don't Believe You) is surely the form at its absolute peak, and as strong an argument for concerted amphetamine use as has ever been voiced.

The Bootleg Series, Vol 5: Live 1975 2002

This document of Dylan's free-spirited 1975 Rolling Thunder tour was a must-have slice of Columbia archaeology for Dylanophiles. Sure, some of the acoustic numbers lack magic, however, on multiple electric guitar reworkings of familiar Zimmerman landmarks, this is often

as wild and transcendent as anything in Dylan's back catalogue.

The Bootleg Series Vol 6: Live 1964 2004

Dylan was on a cusp in 1964, poised equidistant between protest past and folk-rock future. Recorded on Halloween night at New York's Philharmonic Hall, this release captures Dylan the troubadour at his compelling peak, essaying voice, guitar and harmonica versions of staples such as With God On Our Side and The Times They Are A-Changin', crowd-pleasing duets with Joan Baez and dreamy, narcotic flights of fancy, including the then unreleased Mr Tambourine Man.

The Box Sets

Biograph 1985

An ideal introduction for the person who wants quite a lot of Dylan, but not that much. Most of the essentials, sprinkled with unreleased stuff – a thrilling live version of Isis, 1981's superlative Caribbean Wind – and hard-to-find songs such as Can You Please Crawl Out Your Window. Lovely booklet, too, replete with insightful Dylan interview.

The Bootleg Series Vols I-III 1991

At last: Dylan does the decent thing and releases the cream of the illicit stuff that has been flowing out of Camden Market since 1969. Features countless pearls: the original 3/4 Like A Rolling Stone, I'll Keep It With Mine, the originals of Idiot Wind and Tangled Up In Blue. Annotated by the late Dylan expert John Bauldie and really quite good.

Eternal Circle

For 30 years, dedicated Bob fans have communicated through a network of Dylan fanzines and, later, websites dedicated to spreading the message. Peter Doggett investigates.

An unsat
mind: I
Woodstock,

IF IT'S TRUE, as the old Columbia Records ads claimed, that No-one Sings Dylan Like Dylan, then it's equally true that There Are No Fans Like Dylan Fans. The people sometimes known as Bobcats tour the world with their hero, worshipping and even satirising his every move. They exchange rare recordings and fresh interpretations of Visions Of Johanna and Desolation Row; argue about the precise colour of the shirt that Dylan wore at Newport in 1964; and seek out anyone who once stumbled into Dylan's presence 40 years ago for anecdotes and gossip.

Where there are fans, there are fanzines. The first English language Dylan magazine, **Talking Bob Zimmerman Blues,** came out of America in 1974. Strangely, the USA's contribution to Dylan periodicals has been fairly slight, with the likes of **On The Tracks** and **Mr Tambourine Man** failing to match their UK counterparts. Only the now-defunct **Look Back** justified a regular subscription.

By comparison, Britain has produced an array of fine Dylan mags. There was just enough of an organised Dylan community by the end of the '70s for a convention to be held, at which collectors, fans and critics who'd been swapping tapes or theories for years finally met face to face. After that, it was inevitable that the Dylan network would spawn in-house magazines. More often than not, these have co-existed in harmony over the past 25 years but, as is inevitably the case in any human hothouse, there have been episodes of conflict and drama more suited to a soap opera than a fanbase.

However, all sides concur that the single most important figure in the Dylan fanzine world was former MOJO and Q magazine man John Bauldie, who died tragically in a helicopter crash in 1996. In early 1981, Bauldie advertised the imminent arrival of a Dylan magazine, with organisation to match, and waited to gauge the response. It was overwhelming, giving him the impetus to form Wanted Man, and a magazine entitled **The Telegraph**.

The magazine began life in slightly frivolous style, but from the start Bauldie never hid his intention that it should evolve into a journal of scholarship and record. The Telegraph survived an early existential debate about the nature of fandom, and grew from a skinny newsletter into a sizeable colour production filled with exclusive interviews and lengthy critical pieces, often with an academic bias. Bauldie's humour and irrepressibly readable prose ensured that the magazine rarely became pretentious. Since his death, The Bridge has picked up the torch, though without the sheer verve of the original.

Britain's other major Dylan zine is **Isis**, which has undergone a similar transformation down the years. It has never lost sight of its responsibility to chronicle Dylan's work and activities, via both Ian Woodward's long-running Wicked Messenger news pages, and regular coverage of new bootlegs, tapes and underground DVDs. It even carries a highly amusing cartoon strip starring the Sad Dylan Fans. But in recent years it has also became a reservoir of interviews and groundbreaking historical research, as evidenced by a book-length anthology of its finest moments.

Andrew Muir's gloriously idiosyncratic **Homer, The Slut** carved a unique niche in the '90s with a mix of first-person confession and incisive critique. Muir now edits **Judas**, a glossy forum for intelligent writing about Dylan which (alongside Isis) goes some way towards filling the gap left by the demise of The Telegraph. **Freewheelin'** magazine began as a private club, went public in the late '90s, and now exists solely as a website. **Dignity** was another intended successor to The Telegraph's crown which never quite established an identity of its own.

GIVEN DYLAN'S RELUCTANCE to allow photographers into his gigs, and his absolute abhorrence of bootleg recordings, it is remarkable that his official website, **www.bobdylan.com**, should have offered several dozen free downloads over the last seven or eight years. Stranger still, these aren't commonly available studio cuts, but otherwise unobtainable live performances (or field recordings, as they're officially known). It's hard to imagine Dylan himself selecting the material, but someone in his office clearly has an ear for what collectors would want. The result has been authorised access to many of the unusual cover versions that Dylan has performed in recent times, such as his

Bobcats tour the world with their hero, worshipping and even satirising his every move.

heartfelt but at times hysterically funny tribute to George Harrison, in the form of a once-in-a-lifetime rendition of Something. The website also briefly made available one of Dylan's very rare post-'70s performances of Idiot Wind, though at the time of writing that has vanished from the site. Downloads aside, bobdylan.com also handles information about gigs and new releases, plus a wide selection of Dylan lyrics and photos.

Aside from the official Dylan website, the one place that is essential for any interested party is **www.expectingrain.com**. Every day, its compiler lists new links to Dylan-related information and articles that have been made available on the web. By itself, this would easily justify Expecting Rain's existence. But the site also holds the definitive collection of links to other Dylan websites – everything from fanzine sites to academic studies – making this an essential first port of call.

One site that can be reached either directly or via Expecting Rain deserves special mention: Bill Pagel's **Bob Dates** (my.execpc.com/~billp61/dates.html). As its name suggests, it's a clearing-house of information about Dylan's current and recent touring schedule. It's where you'll find up-to-the-minute information about obtaining tickets for forthcoming gigs, plus setlists and reviews of each show, often posted within minutes of Dylan leaving the stage. Its many contributors remain starry-eyed about the quality of Dylan's performances, but its open-to-all format allows any gig-goer to express themselves in front of an audience of Bob's most devoted followers.

"I don't care what people expect of me. Doesn't concern me. I'm doing God's work. That's all I know."

BOB DYLAN

Index

Contributors

Stuart Bailie was Assistant Editor of the New Musical Express between 1993-'96. He wrote the authorised Thin Lizzy biography, The Ballad Of The Thin Man, in 1997. Based in Belfast, he writes for various publications and has presented the BBC Radio Ulster show Across The Line since 1999.

Johnny Black is a long-time MOJO contributor who has written frequently on Bob Dylan. He has had several books published and maintains Rocksource, a massive chronological rock events database.

Clark Collis is Senior Writer at the US music magazine Blender and has written for, among other titles, MOJO, Q, The Guardian and The Daily Telegraph.

Peter Doggett is the author of Are You Ready For The Country and a former editor of Record Collector magazine. He is currently writing a book about revolutionary politics and music in the late '60s.

Ben Edmonds is former Editor of Creem and a long-time contributor to Rolling Stone, among other publications. He is currently MOJO's US correspondent.

Barry Feinstein's photographs have appeared in numerous publications including Time, Newsweek and MOJO. He accompanied Dylan as his tour photographer throughout Europe in 1966 and took the cover picture for The Times They Are A-Changin' and the 2005 Bootleg Series release No Direction Home. He has worked as a stills photographer and cameraman on many major movies and received countless awards.

David Gahr has been photographing musicians since 1959. His work has appeared in countless magazines including MOJO, People and Rolling Stone. He photographed Dylan on countless occasions including his pivotal performance at the 1965 Newport Festival.

Andy Gill is the pop critic of The Independent and has written for a host of music magazines including MOJO, Q and Rolling Stone. His second book, A Simple Twist of Fate: Bob Dylan And The Making Of Blood On The Tracks, was published in 2004.

John Harris writes about music for MOJO, Q, Rolling Stone, The Guardian and The Observer. His first book, The Last Party: Britpop, Blair And The Demise Of English Rock, was published in 2003.

Don Hunstein has taken photographs of some of the biggest names in pop, jazz and classical music, and his work has appeared on over 200 record sleeves, among them Bob Dylan's 1962 debut and The Freewheelin' Bob Dylan.

Richard Jobes is an academic and journalist who has written extensively about music, literature and politics.

Peter Kane is a freelance music journalist who began writing for the UK weekly music paper Sounds and has been a long-time contributor to Q.

Nick Kent began contributing articles and reviews to the British underground press at the age of 19 and was soon writing for the re-vamped New Musical Express. In the '80s he began contributing to The Face, Arena, The Sunday Times and Details, among others, before moving to France, where he works as a scriptwriter and director for French TV and also contributes to various publications including MOJO. A collection of his best work, The Dark Stuff, was published in 1994 to rave reviews.

Daniel Kramer is a photographer and film director, whose Dylan photographs include the cover shots for the Highway 61 Revisited and Bringing It All Back Home albums. His 1967 book, Bob Dylan: A Portrait Of The Artist's Early Years, was the first major Dylan publication.

Steve Lowe is a freelance music writer who has contributed to various publications including Q, MOJO and The Observer.

Jim Marshall photographed Dylan throughout the '60s and also captured some of the most iconic images of the era, taking pictures of Jimi Hendrix, Janis Joplin, Johnny Cash, The Who and The Beatles' last ever concert at San Francisco's Candlestick Park. He is the author of several books and has over 500 album covers to his credit.

Greil Marcus is one of the world's most respected music critics, whose work has been published in, among others, Rolling Stone, Creem, New Musical Express and MOJO. His books include the groundbreaking Lipstick Traces: A Secret History Of The 20th Century and Invisible Republic: Bob Dylan's Basement Tapes.

Charles Shaar Murray is the award-winning author of Crosstown Traffic and Boogie Man, a former Associate Editor of New Musical Express, and a contributor to various publications including The Independent, The Observer and MOJO.

Lucy O'Brien is author of the acclaimed She Bop: The Definitive History Of Women In Rock, Pop & Soul, plus biographies of Dusty Springfield and Annie Lennox. A former writer for New Musical Express, she now contributes to various publications including MOJO and The Guardian, and is working on a biography of Madonna.

Ken Regan accompanied Dylan on his 1975 Rolling Thunder Revue and has worked extensively in the film and music industry. His photographs have appeared in countless publications, including Newsweek, MOJO and Time.

Jerry Schatzberg is a photographer whose subjects have included Jimi Hendrix, Andy Warhol and Bob Dylan, whom he photographed between 1965 and 1966, including the sleeve for Dylan's Blonde On Blonde album. Later an award-winning film-maker, his movies include The Panic In Needle Park, The Seduction Of Joe Tynan and Scarecrow.

David Sheppard combines writing for various publications, including Q, MOJO, Mail On Sunday and the Glasgow Herald, with a musical career as a multi-instrumentalist in left-of-centre combos such as State River Widening and The Wisdom Of Harry. He is also the author of two titles in the Kill Your Idols/Musicmakers biographical series: Leonard Cohen and Elvis Costello.

Phil Sutcliffe has written about music since 1974 for Sounds, Smash Hits, The Face, Northern Echo, Q, MOJO and the Los Angeles Times.

THANKS TO Chris Catchpole, Elisita Balbontin, Brian David Stevens, Patrick Fox, Mike Johnson, J200 courtesy of Gibson Guitars www.gibson.com, William Howell, Phill Kalli, Pete Mauney, Raj Prem Fine Art Photography, Kate Simon, Soho Soundhouse, Ian Whent.